THE CLASSICS
OF **WESTERN**
SPIRITUALITY

THE CLASSICS OF WESTERN SPIRITUALITY
A Library of the Great Spiritual Masters

President and Publisher
Mark-David Janus, CSP

EDITORIAL BOARD

JONATHAN EDWARDS

Spiritual Writings

Selected and Introduced by
Kyle C. Strobel, Adriaan C. Neele,
and Kenneth P. Minkema

Paulist Press
New York / Mahwah, NJ

Caseside image: Jonathan Edwards (detail), by Caffy Whitney, 2012, courtesy of Don Kistler and the Northampton Press

Caseside design by Sharyn Banks
Book design by Lynn Else

Library of Congress Cataloging-in-Publication Data

Names: Edwards, Jonathan, 1703–1758, author. | Strobel, Kyle, 1978– editor.
Title: Jonathan Edwards : spiritual writings / selected and introduced by Kyle C. Strobel, Adriaan C. Neele, and Kenneth P. Minkema.
Description: New York : Paulist Press, 2019. | Series: The classics of Western spirituality | Includes bibliographical references and index.
Identifiers: LCCN 2018000071 (print) | LCCN 2018036144 (ebook) | ISBN 9781587686276 (eBook) | ISBN 9780809106349 (hardcover : alk. paper)
Subjects: LCSH: Congregational churches—Doctrines—History—18th century. | Reformed Church—Doctrines—History—18th century.
Classification: LCC BX7260.E3 (ebook) | LCC BX7260.E3 A25 2019 (print) | DDC 230/.58—dc23
LC record available at https://lccn.loc.gov/2018000071

ISBN 978-0-8091-0634-9 (hardcover)
ISBN 978-1-58768-627-6 (e-book)

Published by Paulist Press
997 Macarthur Boulevard
Mahwah, New Jersey 07430

www.paulistpress.com

Printed and bound in the
United States of America

CONTENTS

Contents

Contents

ABOUT THE CONTRIBUTORS

Kyle C. Strobel is associate professor of spiritual theology and formation at Talbot School of Theology, Biola University, California. He holds a PhD from the University of Aberdeen.

Adriaan C. Neele is director of the doctoral program and professor of historical theology at Puritan Reformed Theological Seminary in Grand Rapids, Michigan. He holds a PhD from the University of Utrecht.

Kenneth P. Minkema is the executive editor of *The Works of Jonathan Edwards* and of the Jonathan Edwards Center & Online Archive at Yale University. He holds a PhD from the University of Connecticut.

All three have published extensively on Jonathan Edwards.

A WORD ABOUT REFERENCES TO EDWARDS'S WRITINGS

Where possible, references to Edwards's writings are to *The Works of Jonathan Edwards* (1957–2008), published by Yale University Press in twenty-six volumes, or to *The Works of Jonathan Edwards Online* (edwards.yale.edu), the digital archive maintained by the Jonathan Edwards Center at Yale University. References to the printed and digital archive of the Edwards *Works* are given as "WJE" or "WJEO" plus the volume and page numbers.

While many of the selections presented below are part of the classic Edwards canon and have been previously published in either the printed or digital series, some are here made available in print for the first time. These include the sermons *The Spiritual Enjoyments and Comforts Believers Have through Christ, The Saints Often Miss Sweet Communion with Christ*, and *True Grace Is Divine*. Yet another sermon, *The Portion of the Righteous*, was printed in an inaccurate version in the nineteenth century and in subsequent reprints, but the excerpt included in this volume is part of a newly edited rendition of the entire sermon from its original manuscript.

Within the edited texts below, the reader will notice words or passages within curly ({ }) or square ([ ]) brackets. Text within curly brackets is supplied where Edwards drew a dash in the manuscript, his way of indicating the insertion of a repeated word or phrase, while text within square brackets indicates editorial interpolations in which Edwards skipped or miswrote a word, or where the manuscript is damaged or illegible.

ACKNOWLEDGMENTS

While most of the texts presented here were edited by members of the Yale edition of *The Works of Jonathan Edwards* (1957–2008), several were edited more recently as part of the Jonathan Edwards Center's Global Sermon Editing Project, an online community-sourcing initiative through which volunteers were trained to edit transcripts of Edwards's sermons. The particular editors who participated in this project are identified in notes in the appropriate spots in individual parts of this volume.

PRELUDE

Locating Jonathan Edwards's Spirituality

Adriaan C. Neele

The spirituality of Jonathan Edwards (1703–58) is rooted, to a great degree, in two streams of medieval piety, but mediated by post-Reformation reformed practical works (*theologia practica*). Medieval piety was formed, in large part, by the schools (*schola*) or university tradition and the monastic tradition of bridal mysticism (*Brautmystik*). Both traditions would resurface together in early modern Protestant theology, the immediate background of the spirituality of Jonathan Edwards.

The university or Scholastic tradition recognized a distinction in speculative and practical theology (*theologia speculativa et practica*). With the rise of interest during the thirteenth century in Aristotle's writings, conceptions of nature and of the extent of theology were created in part by the philosopher's classification of the forms of knowledge, science (*scientia*), and wisdom (*sapientia*).[1] Franciscans such as Alexander of Hales (ca. 1183–1245) and Bonaventure (1221–74) insisted on the affective, practical, and experimental character of theology, excluding it from consideration as *scientia* in the Aristotelian sense of a rational or speculative discipline.[2] St. Thomas Aquinas, on the other hand, not only argued in the *Summa Theologica* (known to Edwards during his studies at Yale College[3]) that "sacred doctrine is a science,"[4] but also raised the question of whether sacred doctrine was a practical science—to which Thomas, reflecting Dominican theology, replied, "It is not a practical

1

but a speculative science."[5] These fairly broad characteristics of theology found their culmination in Duns Scotus's (d. 1308) formulation of theology. Scotus not only resonated with Franciscan theology, integrating more Aristotelian philosophy than previous expositors, but also considered theology as a discipline oriented toward the ultimate goal of humanity in God: in essence, *praxis*—that is to say, a knowledge not known for its own sake but directed to God.[6]

This medieval Scholastic discussion on the character of theology—expository to matters of faith and on the issue of whether theology is theoretical or practical—would resurface in the works of Protestant Scholastic theologians, including but not limited to early modern Reformed theologians who were well known in early eighteenth-century New England. These figures included Johannes Cloppenburg (1592–1652), Johannes Coccejus (1603–69), Johannes Hoornbeek (1617–66), and Johannes à Marck (1656–1731),[7] who all recognized theology as a mixed discipline, both *theoretica* and *practica*. However, they leaned toward the *practica*, while rejecting the anthropological character proposed by the Remonstrants (commonly labeled "Arminians"). However, Edwards's own inquiry about whether theology was speculative or *practica* was inspired, in particular, by the prolegomena of the work of Petrus van Mastricht and Francis Turretin, scholars with whom Edwards was deeply acquainted. Turretin, for example, posed the question explicitly, "Is theology theoretical or practical?," searching not only for an understanding of the essence of theology, but also delving into controversies "of this time," such as the Remonstrants and Socinians[8]—a concern Mastricht shared.[9] Turretin asserted, furthermore, that a theoretical or speculative system was occupied in contemplation alone, with knowledge as its object, contrary to a practical theology, which had operation for its object.[10] Therefore, the Genevan theologian concluded that theology was neither theoretical nor practical, but a mixed discipline, and yet more practical than speculative. The mixed nature of theology appears, Turretin explained, "from its ultimate goal, which is praxis… indeed nothing in theology is theoretical to such a degree and so remote from praxis that it does not bring about the admiration and worship of God; nor is a theory salvific unless it is referred to praxis."[11] In fact, early modern Reformed piety was understood as a realization of the spiritual and ethical implications of the doctrinal foundation laid down during the Reformation, whereby orthodox doctrine and piety converged. In other words, it was an expression of the Protestant Reformation tenet of *sola fide*, a living faith,[12] and a working out of William Ames's (1576–1633) definition of theology, which is a living unto God.[13]

Edwards, then, was the recipient of this Scholastic distinction of theology, and he deployed such distinctions in sermons and treatises. In regard to the former, his assertion of the necessity of the knowledge of divinity corresponded with Aquinas's opening inquiry in the *Summa Theologica* on the necessity of the nature and extent of sacred doctrine.[14] The perceptible Thomistic quality in Edwards's view of theology, however, is modified when we consider his observation that "there are two kinds of knowledge of the things of divinity, viz., *speculative* and *practical*, or in other terms, *natural* and *spiritual*."[15] This observation was not peculiar to the preacher of Northampton, Massachusetts, but placed him in a long-standing trajectory of Scholastic debate about whether theology was a science or wisdom, as well as in a discussion about Scholastic distinctions, present in medieval and Protestant Scholastic systems of theology. Such distinctions were deployed by Edwards for spiritual discernment, as attested in a sermon series of 1738–39, *The Wise and Foolish Virgins* (excerpted below), which was foundational for *A Treatise Concerning Religious Affections* (1746; also excerpted below):

> There is a distinction to be made between a mere *notional understanding*, wherein the mind only beholds things in the exercise of a speculative faculty; and *the sense of the heart*, wherein the mind don't only *speculate* and *behold*, but *relishes* and *feels*....The Apostle seems to make a distinction between mere speculative knowledge of the things of religion, and spiritual knowledge, in calling that "the form of knowledge, and of the truth."[16]

Edwards's attention to affective piety in the union and communion with God in Christ resonated strongly with the monastic tradition of bridal mysticism, perhaps epitomized in Bernard of Clairvaux

(1090–1153). Bernard's *opera* are saturated with the words of Scripture. In the eighty-six sermons on the *Canticle* (*Cantica Canticorum*), for example, there are an estimated six thousand citations of Scripture. The devotional character of Bernard's piety, much like Edwards's, included attention to consolation, admonition, self-examination, and exhortation. Bernard viewed the relationship between the divine Word and the individual soul as a spiritual marriage of the heavenly Bridegroom and the human bride. The sacramental humaneness of his mysticism, with love as its central focus, shaped Christian piety, spirituality, and mysticism—and is captured in Bernard's allegorical interpretation of the *Canticle*. Commenting on the biblical words, Bernard draws an analogy between the suffering and crucified Christ—his feet, hands, and mouth—and the purgative, illuminative, and unitive way. The medieval spiritualist inhaled and exhaled Scripture, whereby the daily monastic routine of the exercises of piety (*exercitione pietatis*) consisted of the reading (*lectio*) and reflecting (*mediatio*) of Scripture, the communion of the saints (*contemplatio in communio*), prayer (*oratio*), nurturing and deepening one's relationship with God. The heart of religious experiential affection was, for Bernard, the love of God and human reciprocal love to God. This love (*caritas*) did not seek itself, but the other. It is love that unites the Trinity.[17] "God is loving, and he loves himself [*ex se toto*], because the whole Trinity loves," Bernard wrote.[18] Love, then, was God *in se*, and a divine gift, and thus the source of one's reciprocal love was the love that God granted (*causa diligendi Deaum, Deus est*),[19] and was the true life of the soul (*vera animæ vita Deus est*).[20] God, therefore, was the efficient and final cause of love, demonstrating the divine gracious character.[21] The church, as God's bride, then, could not merit (*meritum*) love, but Bernard ascribed this to divine grace, asserting, "Whatever you put on the account of merit, will be lost by grace. I do not want merit, whereby grace is displaced. I shiver of everything that comes from myself" (*de meo est*).[22]

Furthermore, for Bernard, this love was granted by God in Christ, though focused more on the humility of the Savior than on the resurrected Christ. Fundamental for the medieval Christian was a practice of piety (*praxis pietatis*), or affective piety centered on the humanity of Christ, his suffering, cross, and death. These Bernardine themes of love, *Brautmystik*, and Christ's humiliation were appropriated by the *Devotia Moderna*, Martin Luther (1483–1546), and John Calvin (1509–64), but resurfaced even more strongly in post-Reformation German or Lutheran Pietism, English Puritanism, and Reformed Orthodoxy—though its Christology, for the latter, was more directed to the work of redemption.[23] On the one hand, the deep acquaintance of Edwards with early modern devotional works of English Puritanism, and the practical theology (*theologia practica*) of the Reformed Orthodoxy, provided an indirect familiarity with medieval piety. On the other hand, Bernardine piety was also enforced by German Pietists. Among these, Edwards read Johann Arndt (1555–1621), a Lutheran theologian who wrote several influential books of mystical and devotional Christianity, including his principal work, *Vom wahres Christentum* (*True Christianity*), which was motivated by medievalists such as Johannes Tauler (ca. 1300–1361) and Thomas à Kempis (ca. 1380–1471), the author of the *Imitation of Christ*, who was particularly appreciative of Bernard's commentary on the *Canticle*. Edwards also read the works and followed the career of August Herman Francke (1663–1727), whose printed conversion narrative and construction of a great evangelical center at Halle in Saxony were internationally known.

In fact, through these mediating works, Edwards was the recipient of the medieval Scholastic tradition that described faith seeking understanding (*fides quaerens intellectum*), and the monastic tradition that was more directed to experiential or affective faith. The traditions were not mutually exclusive, but came together in early modern Protestant theology, and, it can be argued, in the theology of Jonathan Edwards.

What we find in this volume, therefore, is the reception of a catholicity of spirituality arising from Scripture that resonated with various medieval traditions of piety, mediated by early modern Protestant religious practitioners, and appropriated by Edwards in the context of New England's spiritual backslidings and awakenings.

INTRODUCTION

Kyle C. Strobel

The New England divine Jonathan Edwards (1703–58) was a tutor, pastor, theologian, teacher, missionary, and college president throughout his illustrious career. His writings and stature as a thinker has led to his being deemed "America's Greatest Theologian," a somewhat ironic title considering that Edwards died in 1758 as a British colonist and thus was not actually "American." Nonetheless, he has become the icon of early American theology, instigating and fueling the New Divinity, America's first major theological school of thought. While Edwards is often considered one of the great *minds* of the Christian tradition, with a particular focus on his philosophical acumen, he never would have allowed his intellect to be separated from his affect, or his academic rigor to be bifurcated from his spiritual depth.

In this introduction we provide an overview of Edwards's spirituality, followed by a brief description of the sections of this volume. The goal is to provide the framework of Edwards's spiritual vision so that the reader can understand each work as a part of a broader whole. Edwards's spirituality, at once Reformed while also surprisingly similar to the broad scope of the Christian tradition, was driven by his understanding of God and redemption; therefore we must start with his development of God and God's self-giving. Spirituality, what Edwards would have called true religion, experiential religion, or piety, is ultimately focused on God and his self-giving as Son and Spirit. Everything else flowed from this reality. To understand the writings in this volume, therefore, it is necessary to locate them in their broader theological context to unveil the depth of Edwards's spiritual theology. From there we will turn to features of Edwards's spirituality, such as contemplation, spiritual practices, and his under-standing of the texture and experience of the spiritual life. But the order of this development is important. Because Edwards understood spirituality as a feature of God's self-giving, we must engage his work from the "top down"—from God's life in itself to our participation in that life.[1]

GOD'S KNOWLEDGE, AND THE KNOWLEDGE OF GOD

God's life is the infinite actuality of divine blessedness—beatitude known and experienced in the eternal effulgence of the divine Being. When Edwards develops his account of God, his start-ing point is *this* divine blessedness.[2] In his "Discourse on the Trinity," Edwards begins with this assumption: "When we speak of God's hap-piness, the account that we are wont to give of it is that God is infinitely happy in the enjoyment of himself, in perfectly beholding and infinitely loving, and rejoicing in, his own essence and perfec-tions" (WJE 21:113). God's life is perfect happiness, and happiness is understood as a *contemplative* act.[3] The Father, in contemplating himself, generates the divine idea (the Son), and as the Father and Son gaze upon one another love pours forth between them as the spiration of the Spirit. Edwards's account of God's infinite blessed-ness utilizes the beatific vision as the form of God's self-contemplation. Whereas the beatific vision is usually exposited as the goal awaiting the Christian in eternity, Edwards articulates God's life as the primal form of beatific glory. In this sense, the goal of glorification, and God's own life of infinite beatific actuality, are one and the same. To use language that will be important below, we can say that God's life is religious affection in pure act. God's life is fundamental because Edwardsean spirituality entails a participation in God's own beatific glory—it is being caught up in the self-knowing and self-loving of God that define God's eternal life *in se*.

It is important that God's life is not an eternal *speculative* gaze of the Father upon the Son, such that God's life could be understood solely in an intellective register. Rather, God's self-contemplation is always linked, essentially, to the movement of love that defines God as love.[4] Edwards claims that "the Deity becomes all act; the divine essence itself flows out and is as it were breathed forth in love and joy."[5] The overall model Edwards develops—God as religious affection in pure act—assumes three key features of God's life. First, God is personal. Second, God's life is an eternal contemplation or mutual gazing between Father and Son. Third, God's life is not merely intellective, but affective. There is an "infinitely holy and sweet energy" between the Father and Son, which is the Holy Spirit as the love of God (WJE 21:121). This picture of God's life assumes that, as a personal being, God experiences perfection as infinite happiness within himself. This is God's fullness, and this fullness entails a personal gazing and an infinite loving. In Edwards's words, "the fullness of the Godhead is the fullness of his understanding, consisting in his knowledge, and the fullness of his will, consisting in his virtue and happiness. And therefore the external glory of God consists in the communication of these" (WJE 8:528). God's internal glory is his fullness of understanding and will, and this is what God communicates to his creation.

Edwards's description asserts that God's life is the archetype for all true knowledge of God, and, therefore, is the archetype for true religion. This means that the spiritual life is not simply a way of life, although it entails that, but is first and foremost a participation in God's contemplative existence. Because the archetype is God's life of religious affection, true knowledge of God must be affectionate knowledge. Without affection humankind would be left with mere intellection, a kind of detached contemplation of *deity*, but not the intellectual grasp of the God of love:

> There is a distinction to be made between a mere *notional understanding*, wherein the mind only beholds things in the exercise of a speculative faculty; and *the sense of the heart*, wherein the mind don't only *speculate* and *behold*, but *relishes* and *feels*. That sort of knowledge, by which a man has a sensible perception of amiableness and loathsomeness, or of sweetness and nauseousness, is not just the same sort of knowledge with that, by which he knows what a triangle is,

and what a square is. The one is mere speculative knowledge; the other sensible knowledge, in which more than the mere intellect is concerned; the heart is the proper subject of it, or the soul as a being that not only beholds, but has inclination, and is pleased or displeased. (WJE 2:272)

To have speculative knowledge of God, but not affective knowledge, is to fail to truly *see* God; it would be to have simply natural rather than spiritual knowledge of God. This would be a failure to know God as he knows himself: in love. To know God truly requires a knowledge of the heart, and therefore necessitates that one come to see God as beautiful. This means that knowledge of God *is* intellectual, but never solely intellectual. To know God one must see him spiritually through the intellect and respond in love through the will. Two key notions emerge from the preceding. The first concerns Edwards's use of the term *see*. He assumes, as is clear from the quote above, that the soul must behold God. Knowledge of God is more than intellection, but it is not less, and the intellective faculty of the soul allows a person to see spiritually.[6] Second is the notion of beauty in Edwards's account. We develop each of these in turn.

One doesn't have to read Edwards's work for long before realizing how *visual* it is—quite natural for someone who read the works of Isaac Newton so assiduously. Edwards seems to paint with words, calling to mind vibrant images that, for better or worse, are hard to forget. This visual reality is important for understanding faith, since Edwards follows a long tradition of grounding faith in its perfection: the beatific vision. Faith is a kind of seeing for Edwards, taking the Apostle Paul's claim that by faith we "see through a glass darkly" (KJV 1 Cor 13:12). Faith is the pilgrim anticipation of the beatific vision; the sight of faith is not entirely different from seeing beatifically, but it is dark and indirect. Edwards calls the sight of faith a "reflected light," comparing the sight of the sun's light reflected off the moon.[7] Edwards claims, furthermore, that the affectionate knowledge of God's beauty and glory is "of the same nature and kind" with the beatific sight in heaven, "differing only in degree and circumstances: what God gives them here, is a foretaste of heavenly happiness" (WJE 2:133). The "circumstances" of the believer are different compared to the saints in glory: believers are in the fleshly body and in a fallen world, and the "degree" of this light is different because God's self-giving is less in the age of faith. But while the circumstances and degree differ, the believer still perceives the same glory that will be known in full in eternity.

The life of faith is founded upon a vision of God's beauty in Christ. Jesus claimed that he was the image of the invisible God (Col 1:15), the "reflection of God's glory" (Heb 1:3), and that whoever sees him "has seen the Father" (John 14:9).[8] To see God in Christ by faith, therefore, one must behold him as beautiful, and not merely *understand* that he is beautiful. Edwards claims,

> So there is a difference between believing that a person is beautiful, and having a sense of his beauty. The former may be obtained by hearsay, but the latter only by seeing the countenance. There is a wide difference between mere speculative, rational judging anything to be excellent, and having a sense of its sweetness, and beauty. The former rests only in the head, speculation only is concerned in it; but the heart is concerned in the latter. When the heart is sensible of the beauty and amiableness of a thing, it necessarily feels pleasure in the apprehension. (WJE 17:414)

In seeing Christ's beauty, there is a new foundation laid in the heart by the Spirit. Edwards recognizes the difference between his previous experience of "the things of religion" and his experience after he had received the Spirit: "Those former delights, never reached the heart; and did not arise from any sight of the divine excellency of the things of God; or any taste of the soul-satisfying, and life-giving good, there is in them" (WJE 16:795). Afterward, his delights "were totally of another kind; and what I then had no more notion or idea of, than one born blind has of pleasant and beautiful colors" (WJE 16:794). By seeing Christ's beauty, Edwards believes he was caught up in the sight of Christ that defines the blessedness of God. Edwards was now partaking of this blessedness. The communication of "spiritual wisdom and grace" is a communication of God's life, and as such, Edwards would declare, "there is nothing the creature receives that is so much of God, of his nature, *so much a participation of the Deity*: 'tis a kind of emanation of God's beauty, and is related to God as the light is to the sun" (WJE 17:422; emphasis added). To see Christ truly, one must see him as the Father does, from within the Spirit of love—the light that illumines the beauty of God in the face of Jesus Christ and calls forth *affectionate* knowledge from the illumined soul. "When a person is converted," Edwards claims, "then the day dawns and the daystar arises in his heart. There is a beam of divine light let into the soul, but this light always brings love into the heart. The soul the same moment that 'tis filled with spiritual light 'tis also filled with divine love. The heart immediately goes out after God and the Lord Jesus Christ."[9] But this Spirit does not only illumine Christ, the Spirit unites the believer to Christ such that they are one. "We being members of the Son," Edwards proclaims to his people, "are partakers in our measure, of the Father's love to the Son, and complacence in him" (WJE 19:593).

If God's life is defined as religious affection in pure act, and if the creature is called to have an affectionate knowledge of God that is somehow a foretaste of the beatific vision, then salvation must somehow break open God's own affectionate knowledge so that the creature can partake in it. This is exactly what we see in Edwards's account. "They, being in Christ, shall partake of the love of God the Father to Christ. And as the Son knows the Father, so they shall partake with him in his sight of God, as being as it were parts of him."[10] Furthermore, "it is in our partaking of the same Holy Spirit that our communion with God consists....In partaking with the Father and the Son of the Holy Ghost, we possess and enjoy the love and grace of the Father and the Son: for the Holy Ghost is that love and grace."[11] Likewise, "the saints shall enjoy God as partaking with Christ *of his* enjoyment of God."[12] The doctrine of salvation, as a description of God's self-giving in Christ and the Spirit, helps to frame how Edwards understands spirituality as a kind of participation in the life of God.

SALVATION AS PARTICIPATION

Edwards's account of salvation is based on participation in the life of God, such that what is Christ's by nature is offered to his people by grace.[13] This requires a partaking of the divine understanding and will—the divine fullness—in a creaturely and finite way. In the tradition, the image of the sun radiating forth and making the creature luminescent is often utilized to depict this participation. Basil the Great, for instance, states, "Just as when a sunbeam falls on bright and transparent bodies, they themselves become brilliant too."[14] It is in this same vein that Edwards writes, "But the soul of a saint receives light from the Sun of Righteousness, in such a manner, that its nature is changed, and it becomes properly a luminous thing: not only does the sun shine in the saints, but they also become little suns, partaking of the nature of the fountain of their light" (WJE 2:343). This participation continues into eternity: "the soul which only had a little spark of divine love in it in this world shall be, as it were, wholly turned into love; and be like the sun, not having a spot in it, but being wholly a bright, ardent flame" (WJE 8:374–75).

This participation never entails a partaking of the divine *essence*, which would make one God, but is still a participation in the divine nature, as Peter claims in 2 Peter 1:4. Edwards clearly rejects the former for the latter, saying,

> Light and heat may in a special manner be said to be the proper nature of the sun: and yet none will say that everything to which the sun communicates a little of its light and heat has therefore communicated to it the essence of the sun, and is sunned with the sun, or becomes the same being with the sun, or becomes equal to that immense fountain of light and heat. A diamond or crystal that is held forth in the sun's beams may properly be said to have some of the sun's brightness communicated to it; for though it hasn't the same individual brightness with that which is inherent in the sun, and be immensely less in degree, yet it is something of the same nature. (WJE 16:203)

The way one becomes "an ardent flame" is through a participation in the divine light and heat. The Son represents the divine light and the Spirit the divine heat, the knowledge and love of God, respectively. For true spirituality, there cannot be one without the other. For a creature to become light and heat, they must see and love the Son, and in so doing, they must partake in the "Sonship" of the Son.[15] Salvation, therefore, names a relational participation in God's life through a participation in the divine knowing and willing such that one shares by grace what is Christ's by nature. This is why Edwards is able to talk about the believer's fellowship with God as a participation in divine glory and happiness: "The saints are exalted to glorious dignity, even to union and fellowship with God him[self], to be in some respects *divine* in glory and happiness" (WJE 18:241). Glory and happiness are terms that describe God's communicable fullness, such that the saints can be considered divine (with the important qualifier of "in some respects"). He expands this qualification by noting, "yet care is taken that it should not be in themselves, but in a person that is God; and they must be as it were emptied of themselves in order to it" (WJE 18:241–42).

In Edwards's spirituality, the focus of the spiritual life is real participation of the divine persons as they overflow from the eternal life of God to his people. This participation is always relational because God is seen to be persons in the infinite actuality of love and communion, focusing the relational ascent of the believer within the Sonship of the Son to the Father. Edwards states, "The way in which the saints will come to an intimate full enjoyment of the Father is not by the Father's majesty…but by their ascending to him by their union with Christ's person" (WJE 18:375). We will address the ascent motif below, but first it is necessary to focus on the nature of God's self-giving and how that further locates Edwards's understanding of Christian spirituality.

THE END OF CREATION, LOVE, AND THE MOVEMENT OF GOD

If God's life is the foundation and end of all spirituality, the movement of God *to* his creation and *for* his creation helps frame what this spirituality entails. Edwards describes God's self-giving as a willed emanation of himself to the creature, saying,

> Here is both an emanation and remanation. The reful-
> gence shines upon and into the creature, and is reflected
> back to the luminary. The beams of glory come from God,
> and are something of God, and are refunded back again to
> their original. So that the whole is of God, and in God, and
> to God; and God is the beginning, middle, and end in this
> affair. (WJE 8:531)

The movement of God to his creation is an emanation seeking remanation. God shines himself into creation and seeks to have his light
received and illumined back to him. To receive this emanation and
remanate it back entails seeing God's beauty in Christ by the Spirit,
and participating in this beauty so that one becomes beautiful. The
spiritual life of the Christian, therefore, in the Edwardsean idiom, is
beholding beauty for the sake of becoming beautiful.

This movement of God in his self-giving to the creature takes
on a twofold form: one is historical-redemptive and the other is
personal-spiritual. In divine providence, God orders history along
the contours of his emanation and remanation, which Edwards
develops exegetically through the *Merkabah* (Ezek 1:4–28).[16] Rather
than utilizing his meditation on Ezekiel 1 to develop something akin
to the Merkabah mystics, Edwards interprets the Merkabah as unveil-
ing the providential movement of God through his creative act as
cyclical movements of glory *for* glory. Edwards argues that Ezekiel's
vision of wheels within wheels represents how interconnected and
cyclical the movements of providence are, all being ultimately oriented to the largest wheel that makes one grand movement from
God and back to him—emanation and remanation. Edwards's view
of the wheels within the wheels is the template he uses to structure
his understanding of God's providential activity in his book *A History
of the Work of Redemption*.[17] Relatedly, in his posthumously published treatise *The End for Which God Created the World*, Edwards
states,

> The whole universe, including all creatures animate and
> inanimate, in all its actings, proceedings, revolutions,
> and entire series of events, should proceed from a regard

and with a view to *God*, as the supreme and last end of all: that every wheel, both great and small, in all its rotations, should move with a constant invariable regard to him as the ultimate end of all; as perfectly and uniformly as if the whole system were animated and directed by one common soul. (WJE 8:424–25)

This vision of reality not only shows the interconnection between God and his providential activity, but it highlights how Christians are living with their heavenly counterparts. There is an interconnection between this world and the heavenly world, since heaven has now come to live in the heart of believers, and since believers partake in Christ's relation to the Father. The grand wheel of the chariot, in this sense, moves not only earthly history but heavenly history as well along its cyclical trajectory.[18] Furthermore, Edwards claims that the four beasts that pull the chariot are "wisdom, power, goodness, and justice," which are "the four attributes of God that have [to do] with the world, and these only; the rest concerns himself" (WJE 13:191–95). These four attributes are external to God's life *in se*, and they are the four attributes that God desires to exercise in his creation of the world.[19] These beasts pull the chariot of providence and each wheel is bound up in the other, turning all of history along its contours of glory until, at last, the grand wheel comes to rest at the judgment seat of God.[20]

There is emanation and there is remanation; there is God's providential movement in love and glory, and the culmination of that movement as it follows its course back to God. This historical-redemptive scheme of wheels within wheels organizes Edwards's understanding of a God-infused history and helps to fund his contemplation of God in nature. It is from within this God-saturated movement through time that each human creature should come to discover themselves. God's creatures are not left aside because of this grand movement, isolated and small beings too insignificant to mention. Rather, the emanation and remanation of God's providential movements are mirrored within each redeemed life. In the life of affection, the Christian receives the emanation of God's self-giving and remanates it back to him through religious affection; this is the

16

personal-spiritual dimension to God's emanation and remanation. Recalling Edwards's description of the Son as the light and the Spirit as the heat of God's self-revelation, the Christian is one who has "become aflame" with the knowledge and love of God. This points to God's gift of the "religion of heaven": "A glorious work of the Spirit of God has been wrought in [believers'] hearts, renewing their hearts, as it were, by bringing down some of that light, and some of that holy pure flame, which is in the world of love [heaven], and giving it place in them" (WJE 8:387–88). The religion of heaven sets aflame the glorified Christian in love. In the heavenly state, "the soul hereby shall be inflamed with love."[21] The life in heaven is the telos of all spirituality, and therefore the saints and even angels define the movement of Christian faithfulness:

> The saints and angels in heaven, that have religion in its highest perfection, are exceedingly affected with what they behold and contemplate, of God's perfections and works. They are all as a pure heavenly flame of fire, in their love, and in the greatness and strength of their joy and gratitude: their praises are represented, as the voice of many waters, and as the voice of a great thunder. Now the only reason why their affections are so much higher than the holy affections of saints on earth, is, they see the things they are affected by, more according to their truth, and have their affections more conformed to the nature of things. And therefore, if religious affections in men here below, are but of the same nature and kind with theirs, the higher they are, and the nearer they are to theirs in degree, the better; because therein they will be so much the more conformed to truth, as theirs are.[22]

The higher the affections are here, the more they share in common with the affections of eternity. This movement of the affections presupposed an infinite movement of God to give himself to the glorified creature. To portray this, the image of God as a fountain was helpful to highlight the actuality of God's life—God's intrinsic communicativeness—but also pointing to God's propensity to overflow to his creatures. When Edwards's wife Sarah had a spiritual experience, she narrated it using this kind of language:

> I seemed to myself to perceive a glow of divine love come down from the heart of Christ in heaven, into my heart, in a constant stream, like a stream or pencil of sweet light. At the same time, my heart and soul all flowed out in love to Christ; so that there seemed to be a constant flowing and reflowing of heavenly and divine love, from Christ's heart to mine. (see "Narrative of Sarah Pierpont Edwards," below, part 2)

This image of the fountain focuses first and foremost on God's inner life as a fountain of love pouring forth between the Father and the Son in the Holy Spirit. As that love is poured forth to Christ "without measure," it is then poured out to the hearts of God's people. Speaking specifically of heaven, Edwards states, "love flows out from him towards all the inhabitants of heaven. It flows out in the first place necessarily and infinitely towards his only begotten Son, being poured forth without measure, as to an object which is infinite, and so fully adequate to God's love in its fountain" (WJE 8:373). As it is with heaven, so it is with the affectionate life on earth: "As from true divine love flow all Christian affections,…love is the fountain, and the other affections are the streams. The various faculties, principles and affections of the human nature, are as it were many channels from one fountain" (WJE 2:150–51). In the personal-spiritual dimension of God's emanation and remanation, the creature is caught up in God's movement of self-glorification by his work of redemption to make the creature internal to his self-love and self-glorification.

LOVE AND ASCENSION

The notion of emanation and remanation calls to mind the descent and ascent of God as a form of spiritual existence. Ascent and ascension are, of course, central themes in the history of

Christian spirituality. Greg Peters, in his taxonomy of spiritual classics, suggests that two of the three archetypes for spiritual writings are the way of love and the way of ascent (the third being "the threefold way").[23] In Edwards, these two ways are united in one, such that he will say, "The soul which is winged with love shall have no weight tied to the feet to hinder its flight" (WJE 8:379). This ascension follows the contours of Christ's life because it is always an ascension *in Christ*. "Inasmuch as he was a divine person," Edwards explains, "he brought down divinity with him to us, and so as it were he brought God down to men. And then he ascended to God, and inasmuch as he was in the human nature, he carried up humanity with him to God, and so as it were carried man up to God."[24] Christ has sanctified space in the divine life for creatures to have fellowship with God, and this space is simply Christ's person. "We, by being in Christ a divine person, do as it were ascend up to God, through the infinite distance, and have hereby advantage for the full enjoyment of him also" (WJE 19:594). The ascent of the Christian is in the person of Christ, and therefore entails a relational knowing of God—a seeing and knowing the Son in the outpouring love and affection of the Spirit, who binds Christians to his life. To enjoy the Father, therefore, entails a union and communion with Christ in love, such that one can ascend to the Father in the person of the Son. Those that ascend "shall dwell with God, and see God, and enjoy the most high God, who is infinitely above all creatures, even the highest angels," which leads not only to "imperfect degrees" of happiness, but to the "perfection of heavenly glory."[25] This perfection will not be known before death, but at times, Edwards boldly declares,

> God is sometimes pleased to remove the veil, to draw the curtain, and give the saints sweet views. Sometimes, there is as it were a window or gap opened in heaven, and Christ shows himself through the lattice. They have sometimes beams of sweet light breaking forth from above into the soul, and God and the Redeemer sometimes comes to them, and makes friendly visits to them, and manifests himself to them.[26]

This revealing of Christ "through the lattice" is what Sarah Pierpont Edwards seemed to have experienced (an experience Edwards shared). Edwards described her experience by saying that she was "swallowed up with light and love and a sweet solace, rest and joy of soul...more than once continuing for five or six hours together...in that clear and lively view or sense of the infinite beauty and amiableness of Christ's person" (WJE 4:332). While this intensity was not normal, Edwards does believe that Christ unveils himself to encourage his people in their ascent of the divine ladder. Edwards warns his people away from worldly endeavors to secure transcendence, describing temptations to ascend using worldly "rungs," by pointing them to the only ladder that can lead to true happiness. Whereas those who seek worldly things have their hearts set on worldliness, Edwards claims that those on the ladder of ascent have the tendency of their hearts heavenward. For those who are on Jacob's ladder, their "motion is God-ward," ascending to the Father within Christ himself.[27]

To be caught up in the love of God is to ascend within that love to Christ by the Spirit. Edwards understood that this is a difficult reality to express: "As to a definition of divine love, things of this nature are not properly capable of a definition. They are better felt than defined" (WJE 21:173). But as a participation in God's love, the spiritual life is defined by love. In the first sermon in his series on 1 Corinthians 13, Edwards develops the doctrine: "All that virtue which is saving, and distinguishing of true Christians from others, is summed up in Christian or divine love" (WJE 8:131). The nature of the Spirit is love, Edwards explains, and since the Christian is called to partake in the divine nature (2 Pet 1:4), the Christian is called to love. "It is the Spirit which infuses love to God," Edwards avers (WJE 8:132). Love is the foundation of all other virtues, being the "sum of all grace," and "the most essential ingredient in faith and hope" (WJE 8:327). In this sense, Edwards claims in his "Treatise on Grace," "love is the quintessence and soul of all grace, wherein the divinity and holiness of all that belongs to charity does properly and essentially consist." The divinity and holiness of the Christian life are moored in love. Furthermore, in perfection, this love will be free from all mixtures, stripped of these appurtenances and that clothing that it has in the present state, and it shall lose many other of its denominations, especially from the peculiar manner and exercises accommodated to the imperfect circumstances of the present state....All other names will be swallowed up in the name of charity or love. (WJE 21:170)

Love names the reality of being caught up in the Sonship of the Son, so that the people of God share in the love of the Father upon the Son (John 17:26). As the Christian ascends, the virtues become more and more purified by love, so that their nature as love becomes more and more clear. In eternity, they shall simply be the pure fire of love fueled by the God of love who burns in that place as an everlasting flame.

ECSTATIC SPIRITUALITY

The nature of Edwards's understanding of anthropology, based on his articulation of the divine movement of love, means that a proper reception of God's revelation entails an ecstatic movement of the soul. After describing the Spirit's procession as the pure act of love between Father and Son, Edwards claims, "There is an image of this in created beings that approach to perfect action: how frequently do we say that the saints of heaven are all transformed into love, dissolved into joy, become activity itself, changed into mere ecstasy" (WJE 13:260–61). In heaven, likewise, the saints will have "ravishing delights" that "shall rise and increase to all eternity" (WJE 10:429). Early in his life Edwards mused in a notebook on holiness, claiming, "We drink in strange notions of holiness from our childhood, as if it were a melancholy, morose, sour and unpleasant thing; but there is nothing in it but what is sweet and ravishingly lovely." He continues to describe holiness as "a divine beauty" that makes the soul "heavenly and far purer than anything here on earth," and that it brings a "sweet calmness" and a "calm ecstasy" to the soul (WJE 13:163; see "Miscellanies" no. a, below, part 3).

Edwards holds together the notion of religious affection as the "vigorous and sensible exercises of the inclination and will of the soul" (WJE 2:96), with the idea that holiness brings with it a calming nature. Edwards rejects the notion that we must choose between rest and activity, or between contemplation and action. Again, God's life holds the key. God's life is both pure and infinite movement as well as pure and infinite rest. To be ravished by God, therefore, is to partake in God's ravishing rest of love. This ravishment is a transformation *into love itself* that takes place through a sight of God and a participation in his contemplative life (1 John 3:2). The beatific vision ravishes the soul because it is the sight creatures were created for, and because it is a sight of love discovered in love: "the love of so glorious a Being is infinitely valuable, and the discoveries of it are capable of ravishing the soul above all other loves" (WJE 17:67).

Because the beatific vision provides the teleology of faithful Christian living, the ecstatic and ravishing nature of that vision orients the spiritual life. The beatific vision, therefore, is the ultimate end of every spiritual act, whether contemplation or action, because God is the ultimate end of all Christian activity. As we have already seen, God's life and nature are the dominant notions that give shape to Edwards's spirituality. In eternity, this entails overflowing in the fountain that is God's life: "Thus they shall eat and drink abundantly," Edwards proclaims, "and swim in the ocean of love, and be eternally swallowed up in the infinitely bright, and infinitely mild and sweet beams of divine love, eternally receiving that light, eternally full of it, and eternally compassed round with it, and everlastingly reflecting it back again to the fountain of it" (see *Spiritual Appetites Need No Bounds*, below, part 2). This fountain of love at the heart of heaven is the defining feature of the heavenly realm, making it "the world of love" because the God of love pours himself out in that place.

Like a grand symphony, every saint is in harmony with God's own musical life of love. This harmony is possible because of the beatific vision. Or, in other words, this harmony simply *is* the beatific vision. To see God, Edwards claims, entails that one has "an immediate and certain understanding of God's glorious excellency and love" (WJE 17:64). As a revealed sight of God, the beatific vision is a sight of God from within God's sight of the believer. To see God is to see him from *within* his own loving. Seeing God is not catching a random glimpse of God, as if God could be seen and not realize he had been spotted. Rather, the sight creatures have of God is caused by a specific kind of love upon them, illumining them so that they can see him as he is. Furthermore, as an act of love, this vision is *pro me* ("for me"). It is not just any vision of God; it is the vision of God by one who is loved of God.

In the experience of the beatific vision, human creatures are fully activated such that "the soul hereby shall be enflamed with love," and "the soul shall as it were all dissolve in love in the arms of the glorious Son of God, and breathe itself wholly in ecstasies of divine love into his bosom." By sharing in the divine nature and participating in the divine blessedness, the creature is activated in a way that mirrors the reality of God's life of pure actuality. The vision is not passive beholding, in other words, as if the contemplation of God muted the action of the soul, but is an active rest that is a finite mirroring of God's infinite pure act. By being caught up in God's act of love, in the revelation of his beauty and glory, the understanding beholds without hindrance and loves without pride, "adoring at God's feet, and yet embraced in the arms of his love." The soul will be perfectly satisfied in every way because it does not just receive the effects of God, but God himself: "God will communicate and, as it were, *pour forth himself* into the soul" (see *The Portion of the Righteous*, below, part 2).

This reality continues for eternity because God is infinite and cannot be exhausted by the searching eyes of finite beings. The creature continues to embrace and commune with God eternally, where "the heart is drawn nearer and nearer to God, and the union with him becomes more firm and close: and at the same time the creature becomes more and more conformed to God," becoming "nearer and nearer to an identity with that which is in God" (WJE 8:443). This is the end of Edwards's understanding of participation: there is a nearer and nearer identity between God and the creature, but there is never a collapse of identity. The creature does not become less by embracing God so fully, but becomes fully alive in the effulgence of God's overflow. This vision of God, embrace of God, and union with God orient Christian spirituality *in full*. God's life, and the creaturely teleology of seeing God, form all Christian practice along specific contours. One place this plays out in Edwards's spirituality concerns his understanding of action and contemplation, to which we now turn.

ACTION AND CONTEMPLATION

Utilizing Mary and Martha as archetypes, the spiritual tradition often understood action and contemplation as contrasting vocations.[28] Edwards would not follow suit, refusing to bifurcate between action and contemplation because they are united in God's life, and because the spiritual life is a participation in that life. God's life consists in affectionate contemplation that is so fully activated that it is a kind of rest, but not rest without movement, but rest as the fulfillment of movement. Similarly, for the creature, this archetype is mirrored in spiritual maturity through religious affection, which is, as we've seen, ecstatic in nature. In its perfection in the beatific vision, the contemplation of the glorified believer is a movement of love as "pure flame." This language of fire denotes the energy and movement of the person ecstatically longing for God. More explicitly, in that state of perfection, the saints "shall *perpetually* behold God's glory and *perpetually* enjoy his love. But they shall not remain in a state of inactivity, merely receiving from God; but they return to him and shall enjoy him in a way of serving and glorifying him" (WJE 17:259; emphasis added). Returning to God and enjoying him is the affectionate reality of the spiritual life, and that affection is the religious engine of all true service. All creaturely life is driven by affection, and the spiritual life is no different. In its perfection, the spiritual life is a life of ecstasy; the soul is ravished as it gazes upon the God of beauty and experiences his life of love. The life of faith longs for this end, but only knows it in part.

There is, in some sense, an erotic vein to this notion of action and contemplation united in affection. Edwards's affection for God left him longing for God, and he often turned to imagery from the Song of Songs (or Canticles, as Edwards referred to it) to describe this longing, as several selections in this volume show. This orientation led Edwards toward practices of silence, solitude, meditation, and contemplation because it was focused on God's beauty and participation in God's own contemplative life. In this sense, the erotic and the spiritual themes merge together in Edwards's poem about his wife-to-be Sarah when he first saw her as a young girl (see "Apostrophe to Sarah Pierpont," below, part 2). This short work serves as a helpful overview of Edwards's spirituality. In it we get a picture of faithfulness, of a person filled with the sweet delight of God, who is so taken up by this delight that "she hardly cares for anything, except to meditate upon him—that she expects after a while to be received up where he is, to be raised out of the world and caught up into heaven" (WJE 16:789). This ideal Christian longs to dwell with God, "and to be ravished with his love, favor, delight, forever" (WJE 16:790). Sarah represents a person who is unwavering in her commitment to God because she is so captivated by him. His description of her is helpful in this regard: "She is of a wonderful sweetness, calmness and universal benevolence of mind....She will sometimes go about, singing sweetly, from place to [place]; and seems to be always full of joy and pleasure; and no one knows for what. She loves to be alone, and to wander in the fields and on the mountains, and seems to have someone invisible always conversing with her" (WJE 16:790). Edwards's poem to Sarah is more than just a love-struck ode to a future bride, but is his vision of the Christian ideal. It is not surprising that his own narrative of his spiritual experience overlaps well with this description of Sarah's. Each component—from the ravishment of God's love to the desire to be alone contemplating God—serves to highlight Edwards's vision for spirituality. But it would be short-sighted to narrow it to this alone. If we stopped at this point, Edwards would only be a contemplative, and we would miss the ecclesial and missional components to his thought. These are important because Edwards is not articulating spirituality from within a monastery, but from within the church. This does not mute his contemplative spirituality, but it locates it within his broader understanding of ecclesial and familial vocations.

IMMANENT AND PRACTICAL ACTS OF GRACE

This broad picture provides mooring for the spiritual practices Edwards engaged in and commended to others, which he broke down into two kinds: first, what he calls "immanent acts" or immanent exercises of grace; and second, practical acts, or "effective exercises" of grace. Immanent acts of grace are "exercises of grace that remain within the soul, that begin and are terminated there, without any immediate relation to anything to be done outwardly, or to be brought to pass in practice" (WJE 2:422). Edwards's example of an immanent act of grace is contemplation, which he claims does not "directly proceed *to*, or terminate *in* anything beyond the thoughts of the mind." This does not mean that immanent acts of grace do not lead to outward practice; they will, as all exercises of grace do, but they do so "more remotely" (WJE 2:422–23). Immanent acts of grace form the soul; that is their primary teleology. But as they form the soul in love, they help form a person to live faithfully. The goal of these immanent acts of grace is to form and reform the soul around the beauty of God—tuning the soul to sing the song of eternity. This experience of God allows one to rest in him and depend upon him more fully in every moment. Because of this, the focus remains on God rather than on one's experience as such. One of the ways Edwards discerns true religious experience from false is that when a Christian has these experiences, she speaks of God, and not of the experiences themselves. The true saint, Edwards explains,

> has his mind too much captivated and engaged by what he views without himself, to stand at that time to view himself, and his own attainments: it would be a diversion which he could not bear, to take his eye off from the ravishing object of his contemplation, to survey his own experience, and to spend time in thinking with himself, what an high attainment this is. (WJE 2:252–53)

The second grouping of spiritual exercises of grace, the practical or effective exercises, are directly oriented to "outward actions."

Edwards describes these practices by saying, "As when a saint gives a cup of cold water to a disciple, in and from the exercise of the grace of charity; or voluntarily endures persecution, in the way of his duty, immediately from the exercise of a supreme love to Christ. Here is the exertion of grace producing its effect in outward actions" (WJE 2:422–23). In his preaching ministry, Edwards had a lot to say about serving the poor and caring for the disenfranchised. Because contemplation forms the soul in love, the contemplative is formed in affection toward God and neighbor, inclining them to serve and give themselves in love as God has in Christ. Vocationally, Edwards understood these acts as fundamental callings for all Christians. Nonetheless, while neither the contemplative nor active are optional vocations for the evangelical Christian, they are nonetheless ordered from the contemplative to the active: "Our inward acquaintance with God, surely belongs to the head of experimental religion," Edwards avers, prioritizing the inward reality of Christian spirituality, but doing so in a way that does not neglect the active. But Edwards makes this claim from within a discussion of spiritual practice, stating, "Not only does the most important and distinguishing part of Christian experience, lie in spiritual practice; but such is the nature of that sort of exercises of grace, wherein spiritual practice consists, that nothing is so properly called by the name of experimental religion" (WJE 2:452). In this vein, Edwards claims,

> Christian or holy practice is spiritual practice; and that is not the motion of a body, that knows not how, or when, nor wherefore it moves: but spiritual practice in man, is the practice of a spirit and body jointly, or the practice of a spirit, animating, commanding and actuating a body, to which it is united, and over which it has power given it by the Creator. And therefore the main thing in this holy practice, is the holy acts of the mind, directing and governing the motions of the body. And the motions of the body are to be looked upon as belonging to Christian practice, only secondarily, and as they are dependent and consequent on the acts of the soul. (WJE 2:450)

For Edwards, the motions of the body are secondary, not in value, but as they are animated by the governance of the soul. The movement of the heart in affection bears fruit in movements of the body in faithfulness. Edwards does not hesitate to focus on contemplation because he is not worried that immanent acts will somehow lead to antinomianism. Rather, quite the opposite. Contemplation and the immanent exercises of grace on the soul form the soul to live faithfully in the world because they form the soul in love: "Love to God and Christ, divine love, is the foundation of all those other affections that are exercised in Christian zeal" (WJE 22:141).

THE TEXTURE OF EDWARDS'S SPIRITUALITY

Before turning to an overview of this volume, in its broad movement, it is important to pull several threads together and provide a picture of the lived reality of Edwards's spirituality. The spiritual life, as Edwards articulates it, takes on a very specific texture and posture of Christian existence. As already noted, Edwards claims that holiness "appeared to me to be of a sweet, pleasant, charming, serene, calm nature. It seemed to me, it brought an expressible purity, brightness, peacefulness and ravishment to the soul" (WJE 16:796; see "Personal Narrative," below, part 1). The believer in eternity is in a kind of ravished rest, where they are captivated fully by the beauty, glory, and love of God, and yet their soul is at peace. In contrast, Edwards compares the life of sinfulness as a tempestuous ocean. To address how the Christian seeks and obtains the calmness of holiness, we turn to three sections: "Double-Knowledge," "Means of Grace," and "Striving after God."

Double-Knowledge

The notion of "double-knowledge" is that the knowledge of God and the knowledge of self are connected. In Edwards's words, "Of all kinds of knowledge that we can ever obtain, the knowledge of God, and the knowledge of ourselves, are the most important" (WJE

1:133). Edwards believes that the great sin of the heart is spiritual pride, and the only real solution to spiritual pride is humility (see WJE 22:523–35). But humility, to be true humility, entails this double-knowledge. To have humility, one must know who God is and who they are. Because of this, self-examination is fundamental to all spiritual practice, and is something he would often utilize in his personal spiritual discipline and in his sermon applications. Edwards worried that his people, all churchgoing colonists, might be adept at religious practice without true humility, affection, or grace. Self-examination is a way to unveil the truth about one's heart, but self-examination is never an end in itself, as if knowledge of self is enough; the end of self-examination is dependence and a deepening of faith. Therefore, true self-examination always leads to action (WJE 2:195) because true self-examination addresses the driving mechanisms of the heart: "Thus, all of our actions ought to be strictly examined and tried, and not only barely to consider the outward action as it is in itself: but also from what principle our actions do arise from; what internal principle we act and live [by], for actions are either good or bad according to the principle whence they arise" (WJE 10:488; see *The Duty of Self-Examination*, below, part 4).

By focusing so fully on God's self-giving as the gracious act of God, Edwards is able to encourage his people to search the deepest parts of their souls. There is a sense that this is one of the key strengths and emphases in Reformed spirituality. If you are saved by who Christ is and what he did, and not what is in yourself, then you can honestly attend to sin for what it is, without fear or anxiety. For Edwards, he was not afraid to find darkness and wickedness in his heart because he knew this would only fuel his humility and dependence. Therefore, Edwards can encourage his congregation, "you should be very diligent and particular in searching your past life, that you may be sensible what a life you have lived, that you see your way in the valley, and know what you have done; should often be bringing as many particular acts of sin to mind as you can, endeavoring that none may be hid from you, and buried in oblivion."[29] Edwards shows his own experience with this, writing, "I confess that experience teaches me, the need of constantly maintaining of a watchful and jealous eye over my own heart," because he has discovered how easy it has been to be "extremely and totally blinded concerning myself" (WJE 16:677).

Edwards came to discover that sanctification isn't marked by a defeat of sin as much as by a recognition of it. Therefore, the progression of spiritual depth and breadth for Edwards is an ascent into total dependence. This runs against his expectations and experience in his youth, which he reflects upon when he states, "It is affecting to me to think, how ignorant I was, when I was a young Christian, of the bottomless, infinite depths of wickedness, pride, hypocrisy and deceit left in my heart" (WJE 16:803). Edwards's maturity tempered his view of God's work on the soul and gave him a more realistic picture of the experience of Christian spirituality. This is important to remember for this volume, since his early writings, such as his "Resolutions" and his "Diary," reflect some of what Edwards would later claim was the result of "too great a dependence on my own strength; which afterwards proved a great damage to me" (WJE 16:795). This should be taken into consideration when these early works are read. Furthermore, Edwards admits later in his life that when he looks back on his early Christian life he seems like "a far better Christian, for two or three years after my first conversion, than I am now," but is now much more dependent upon God (WJE 16:803). Christian maturity required that Edwards confront the depths of his sin, which meant that he must give himself to self-examination.

Edwards's pastoral care navigated similar terrain, such as when he writes to his daughter, "Retire often from this vain world, and all its bubbles, empty shadows, and vain amusements, and converse with God alone; and seek that divine grace and comfort, the least drop of which is more worth than all the riches, gaiety, pleasures and entertainments of the whole world" (WJE 16:289–90). In a pastoral letter to a young woman, Edwards writes,

> Under special difficulties, or when in great need of or great longings after any particular mercies for your self or others, set apart a day of secret fasting and prayer alone; and let the day be spent not only in petitions for the mercies you desired, but in searching your heart, and looking over

your past life, and confessing your sins before God not as is wont to be done in public prayer, but by a very particular rehearsal before God, of the sins of your past life from your childhood hitherto, before and after conversion, with particular circumstances and aggravations, also very particularly and fully as possible, spreading all the abominations of your heart before him. (WJE 16:94; see "Letter to Deborah Hatheway," below, part 4)

One might object that, since God has forgotten the sins of his people, his people should forget them as well. Edwards demurs. It is precisely because our sins have been forgiven that we should explore them. Furthermore, Edwards recognizes that sins, even past sins, have formed people's souls in deep ways that continue to affect them even now (see "Directions for Judging of Persons' Experiences," below, part 5). By exploring one's sin, Edwards believes, the person will be able to grasp onto God in an ever-deepening embrace.

Means of Grace

In Edwards's context, spiritual practices were known as "means of grace."[30] One typical Puritan delineation of these means of grace was the following: (1) public means, (2) private means, and (3) extraordinary help. In the first category, "public means," three were often suggested: preaching, sacraments, and prayer with thanksgiving and psalms. In the second category, "private means," were listed watchfulness, meditation, the armor of the Christian (Eph 6:11–18), experience, company and family exercise, prayer, and reading. The third group, "extraordinary help," included solemn thanksgiving and fasting.[31] This is the kind of delineation Edwards would have been working with, if not with slight variations. One way that Edwards divided the means of grace was into public, family, and personal means, highlighting the role of the family in his view of spirituality.[32] As *God's Wisdom in His Stated Method of Bestowing Grace* and "Miscellanies" no. 539, included in part 4, illustrate, Edwards's assumed practices were Scripture (heard or read), instructions of parents and ministers, baptism, communion, meditation on

Scripture, Sabbath, family education and order, contemplation of Christian truths, prayer (in its various methods and settings), and the struggle to live ethically (acts of justice, and so forth), as well as fasting, experiencing the beauty of nature, "conferencing," and observing days of thanksgiving, rounded out by self-examination, acts of charity, and reading spiritual books (WJE 18:85–88).

These spiritual practices unveil the rigor that Edwards expected from his people, while the threefold categorization reveals the interconnection between the public and private sectors of spiritual existence. The public means focused on the practices of the church and represented the broadest sphere of spiritual existence, which then narrowed to the more intimate in the spiritual existence of families. Edwards believed the family should be the church in miniature, claiming, "Every Christian family ought to be as it were a little church, consecrated to Christ, and wholly influenced and govern by his rules. And family education and order are some of the chief of the means of grace. If these fail, all other means are like to prove ineffectual" (WJE 25:484). The church and the family provided an overarching rhythm of life that served as the context for the private spiritual life. Far from an isolated endeavor, Edwards's spirituality was ultimately oriented by the ecclesial and familial life of the Christian.

It is important to highlight that the means of grace are not ways to generate virtue or habits per se, but are ways of faithfulness to present oneself to God for his work on the soul (based on the infusion of the Spirit). Edwards uses three biblical stories to explain how this works: Jesus's healing of the disabled man at the pool of Bethesda (John 5), Jesus's turning water into wine (John 2), and Elijah's challenging the prophets of Baal (1 Kings 18). In each of these examples there is something natural: the water in the pool at Bethesda, the water in the pots at the wedding, and the firewood drenched in water by Elijah. In all three situations there is something supernatural that must come about to change the natural into something supernatural: the supernatural healing of the man at Bethesda, the water into wine, and the descent of fire upon Elijah's water-saturated wood. Using Jesus's act of changing water into wine, Edwards explains how hearing a sermon can be a means of grace: "They can be abundant in preaching the Word, which, as it comes only from them, is but water, a dead letter, a sapless, tasteless, spiritless thing; but this is what Christ will bless for the supply [of] his church with wine" (WJE 15:359). The means of grace still entail action and effort, therefore, but they are ultimately ways to give oneself to God. Edwards claims, "Attending and using means of grace is no more than a waiting upon God for his grace…'tis watching at wisdom's gates, and waiting at the posts of her doors"; furthermore, "without means there could be no opportunity for grace to act, there could be no matter for grace to act upon." Therefore, "the soul is supplied with matter for grace to act upon, when God shall be pleased to infuse it" (WJE 18:88, 85). Along these lines, Edwards addresses the natural function that these means provide:

> (1) They supply the mind with notions, or speculative ideas, of the things of religion. (2) They may have an effect upon mere natural reason, in a measure to gain the assent of the judgment. (3) They may have an effect upon the natural principles of heart, to give, in a degree, a sense of the natural good or evil of those things that they have a notion of, and so may accordingly move the heart with fear, etc. (WJE 18:85)

No amount of spiritual practice can grow a person spiritually, but, along the same lines, without the natural "matter" for grace to work on, grace would not be able to grow the person either. Practices are necessary but not sufficient conditions for the spiritual growth of a Christian.

The means of grace are not only broken down into public, family, and private means, they are also ordered. Edwards claims that "the chief of the means of grace is the Word of God: that standing revelation of the *mind* and *will* of God that he gives the world, and it is as it were the sum of all means" (WJE 25:285; emphasis added). It is by this means of grace that all others discover the truth. But the word is not alone: "God uses all manner of means with us; he speaks to us not only by his Word, but by sensible figures and representations of spiritual things," for example, baptism and the Lord's Supper (see *God's Wisdom*, below, part 4). Because knowledge of God is affectionate knowledge, the means of grace are oriented along these lines as well: "such means are to be desired, as have much of a tendency to move the affections," Edwards claims, and have "a tendency deeply to affect the hearts of those who attend these means" (WJE 2:121). Edwards's focus on the Bible as God's word is perhaps *the* central feature of his spirituality. This is not surprising. The divine light of God refracts through the biblical text to captivate the minds and hearts of believers. For Edwards, as for the Reformed in general, the Scripture has different senses, even if those are seen as applications of the "literal meaning" of Scripture.[33] But to properly *hear* God's word, ultimately one must have a "spiritual sense" of the word spoken. This spiritual sense creates a right *taste* for the Scriptures—it improves the spiritual "relish" or appetite of the heart for a proper anticipation to understand and receive God's word—and therefore this sense helps guide the Christian's interpretation (WJE 2:284–85).

Along with the word, Edwards assumes a certain prayerfulness to the means of grace. "Conversation between God and mankind in this world is maintained by God's Word on his part, and prayer on ours" (WJE 23:350), Edwards claims, and "faith in God is expressed in praying to God" (WJE 21:439). The proper response to God's word is prayer, and prayer is the "voice of faith" (WJE 19:787). Every means of grace is oriented to God, and therefore if someone were to use one of these means and wasn't prayerful, the spiritual practice would be disordered. This is true even with prayer itself, which is why Edwards claims, "The *good*, that shall be sought by prayer...is God himself" (WJE 5:315). The means of grace, we could say, are opportunities for communion with God. If, therefore, someone were to enact the means of grace to try to generate virtue, this would be no other than self-help. In Edwards's understanding of spirituality, this is one of the great temptations for the Christian (the *Pharisaic* temptation). By ordering spirituality around a participation in God's life, Edwards's focus is on means of grace for communion with God. Through the means of grace, Christians "present themselves" (Rom 12:1) to God and trust that God will provide the grace necessary for this to be a truly *spiritual* act. This self-presentation is a way to seek the "tune" of heaven, since the Christian life is learning a song Christians will sing for eternity. In Edwards's words,

Before they knew but how to sing praise to God: they were unlearned; they could make no melody in God's ear; they had no skill in divine music; they had not learned the tune, nor could they sound one harmonious note. Their hearts were like an instrument that is unstrung and broken, wholly out of tune. The notes were most jarring and discordant. If they pretended to sing praise to God, it was howling and not singing in God's ears.

But now God has put their hearts in tune. Now there is some inward harmony. Now there is divine harmony that is melodious unto God. (WJE 22:233–34)

As noted above, heaven orients the Christian entirely—their prayer, contemplation, and even the tune of their hearts need to harmonize with that realm. This conception allows Edwards to hold tightly together action and contemplation. One contemplates and takes on the tune of heaven because God is the fountain of love there, and that love orients all properly Christian action in the world. Edwards can push hard on the idea that God has done all for the believer, and yet he can still push the Christian to rigorous spiritual practice. It is to this final notion that we turn now.

Striving after God

One would be forgiven for assuming that Edwards's theocentric focus would automatically undermine any meaningful account of Christian striving. This is often the caricature of Reformed theology, but that is not what one finds in Edwards's spirituality. As we've seen with the means of grace and Edwards's understanding of action and contemplation, the Christian is called to strive, even though that striving is not sufficient for spiritual growth in itself. Even in addressing unbelievers, Edwards will admonish them to give themselves to the "great work of seeking salvation" (WJE 19:384). He does not shy away from focusing on how much effort the Christian life entails, even though he does so from within a theological system that focuses as robustly as possible on God's governance and election. For instance, Edwards states that "there is indeed a great deal of difficulty attending all duties required of those that would obtain heaven" (WJE 19:284), and "that there is a greater probability that they will obtain salvation that seek it earnestly than they that seek it negligently" (WJE 14:344).

For the believer, this striving is not for salvation, but from within salvation. Furthermore, the nature of holiness leads one to desire more and more of it—communion with God satisfies even as it deepens the longing needing to be satisfied. "Nothing short of perfect holiness will satisfy the appetite and craving of their souls," Edwards asserts. "A godly man has a spirit to desire perfect holiness, and to long after it" (WJE 19:684). For the believer, holiness is now an appetite just as much as hunger or thirst. The believer's spiritual thirst is not simply a desire to have a small taste, but to drink deeply of God. Because of this desire, sin of any kind is abhorred. Sin is seen as an aberration—as the defilement of the good—and as such, it is that which cannot satisfy. The spiritually mature "hate all sin in all degrees, and don't only hate it in others, but they hate it mainly and chiefly in themselves" (WJE 19:686). Edwards continues by asserting,

> A godly man is a mortal enemy to his sins. Nothing will satisfy him, but his life is as it were bloodthirsty towards sin. He never will give his lusts any peace as long as they have any room in his heart, and till he has wholly expelled them thence. Nor will he ever give himself any rest, till they are utterly rooted out and destroyed, root and branch. (WJE 19:687–88)

Afraid of hypocrites, Edwards warns his people against a false notion of spirituality that fails to take the commands of the law seriously. He seeks a difficult balance: on the one hand, he prioritizes God's grace, sovereignty, and election; and on the other, he refutes antinomianism and lax spirituality. This leads to a distinctively Reformed kind of ascesis.[34] This included a resolution "to maintain the strictest temperance in eating and drinking," and to practice self-denial (WJE 16:754, 761; see "Resolutions," below, part 1). Edwards writes that self-denial consists in two things:

First, in a man's denying his worldly inclinations, and in forsaking and renouncing all worldly objects and enjoyments; and secondly, in denying his natural self-exaltation, and renouncing his own dignity and glory, and in being emptied of himself; so that he does freely, and from his very heart, as it were renounce himself, and annihilate himself. Thus the Christian doth, in evangelical humiliation. And this latter is the greatest and most difficult part of self-denial: although they always go together, and one never truly is, where the other is not; yet natural men can come much nearer to the former than the latter. Many anchorites and recluses have abandoned (though without any true mortification) the wealth, and pleasures, and common enjoyments of the world, who were far from renouncing their own dignity and righteousness; they never denied themselves for Christ, but only sold one lust to feed another, sold a beastly lust to pamper a devilish one; and so were never the better, but their latter end was worse than their beginning. (WJE 2:316)

Edwards's vision of the Christian life is a rigorous calling to self-denial as an "evangelical humiliation"—a response to grace from grace. Eastern Orthodox theologian Alexis Torrance, reflecting upon this aspect of Edwards's spirituality, notes, "The almost monastic tone of Edwards's language here is striking. There is an unremitting arduousness to the Christian life that Edwards is intent on upholding. But for all its difficulty, he does not consider the pursuit of salvation a disheartening task, so long as it is attached to a complete sense of dependency on 'free and sovereign grace' and 'the righteousness of Christ.'"[35] Edwards was committed to a vision of spirituality that did not contrast God's sovereign governance of his creation with a person's striving after or within salvation. In this sense, Edwards believed that the Christian life was a journey to heaven that would entail affliction and even violent effort to grasp hold of the ways of God while putting to death the deeds and desires of the flesh.

A Twofold Vision

Like all Christian spiritual writers, Edwards seeks to give a robust account of God's grace while not allowing that to undermine the striving and effort of the Christian. This, nonetheless, highlights a tension in Edwards's spirituality, a recurring theme in the history of Christian spirituality, that is often personified by the Mary and Martha archetypes. Edwards's vision of Christian existence rejects the bifurcation so often employed between action and contemplation or grace and striving, but there does appear to be two emphases that don't always seem compatible. Perhaps the best way to articulate this tension is by attending to two of Edwards's key archetypes: Sarah Edwards and David Brainerd. The "Sarah Model" of Edwardsean spirituality is highly contemplative and focuses on the more erotic or affective side of Edwards's ecstatic spirituality.[36] On the other side of the spectrum, we find David Brainerd. Brainerd was a missionary who in great zeal and great struggle eventually died in Edwards's home in 1747. Norman Pettit provides a helpful overview of the texture of Brainerd's life: "He had not at any time led a happy life; he was prone to extreme moods of temperament, the blackest of these brought on by exposure to Indian life. Most frustrating of all, his converts were inclined to die" (WJE 7:2). But while Brainerd's missionary efforts saw little fruit, he became a global phenomenon after Edwards edited and published his diary, making Brainerd a model for missions that continues to this day.

In the case of David Brainerd, Edwards seemed to put forth his activism as a model of spiritual striving while also warning against the nature of his self-reflection. In his appendix to Brainerd's diary, excerpted in part 1, Edwards writes, "How greatly Mr. Brainerd's religion differed from that of some pretenders to the experience of a *clear work* of saving conversion wrought on their hearts; who depending on living on that, settle in a cold, careless, and carnal frame of mind, and in a neglect of thorough, earnest religion, in the stated practice of it" (WJE 7:500). In contrast, Norman Pettit helpfully notes, "Edwards was uneasy with the example that Brainerd had set, and with the psychological problems that even the edited diary reveals. He disliked the excessive introspection in which Brainerd engaged. Morbid introversion, he believed, endangered one's state of mind and disrupted the spiritual life" (WJE 7:19). If we recall, self-examination should lead to a praising of God's grace, but Brainerd seemed predisposed to the opposite. He, in contrast, was often pulled down and overwhelmed by his examination to a degree that Edwards found spiritually unhelpful. Nonetheless, he puts Brainerd forward as an example of striving to enter the rest of Christ, and for "being violent to take the kingdom of heaven" (WJE 7:500).

While it would be unhelpful to consider the examples of Sarah and David in stark opposition, the tension between the two is instructive. Edwards saw in them both a striving and an affective piety, a longing for the kingdom and a resting in God's beauty. But Sarah seemed to lean one way and find a much deeper sort of communion with God, while Brainerd leaned the other and often found despair. Both figures, along with Edwards himself, struggled with "melancholy," a sort of depression that textured all of their spiritual experiences, though Sarah seemed less disposed to despair. The tension felt between the two does, it seems, reveal the temptations inherent in this kind of spirituality. Edwards desires a complete focus on God that should, simultaneously, allow persons to see themselves truly. Edwards talks about being "swallowed up" in God, but the self is never lost; it is ravished and made alive in communion with the divine. But the focus on the self and the weightiness of sin could lead one away from God to get lost in the self. This could easily lead to a different kind of being "swallowed up," this time by a focus on one's sin that appears so vast that one cannot breathe. Notice Edwards's own self-description in his "Personal Narrative":

> My wickedness, as I am in myself, has long appeared to me perfectly ineffable, and infinitely swallowing up all thought and imagination; like an infinite deluge, or infinite mountains over my head. I know not how to express better, what my sins appear to me to be, than by heaping infinite upon infinite, and multiplying infinite by infinite. I go about very often, for this many years, with these expressions in my mind, and in my mouth, "Infinite upon infinite. Infinite upon infinite!" (WJE 16:802)

Whereas Sarah tends toward losing herself in God, Jonathan and David seem to push in the other direction. This is not the idea, of course; the goal is to be captivated by God in such a way that they can see their sin, in all of its depravity, and therefore rejoice all the more in what God has achieved on the cross. If it is difficult to see how this should lead to one wandering around moaning, "Infinite upon infinite," then one must achieve a deeper understanding of Puritan appropriation of teachings about the weight and pervasiveness of personal guilt. But Sarah, David, and Jonathan himself held these tensions together in a piety that was rigorous, affective, and focused entirely on the sovereign God who governs history—for the good or ill of the people he created. God's glory was all-encompassing, and so this formed Edwards's spirituality in a way that created a deep tension between the effusive God of love and the overwhelming reality of sinfulness.

Ultimately, Brainerd became the image of Edwards's spirituality that he presented most fully to the world. Edwards found in Brainerd a fellow sufferer who managed to balance his depressive and overwhelming view of sin, however imperfectly, with being captivated by God's beauty and glory, not resting in spiritual appearances, but in God himself. What Edwards finds in Brainerd specifically is not only a depiction of true religion, therefore, but an enfleshed model of Edwardsean spirituality that could serve as a light in the darkness of the antinomianism, Pharisaism, and lax spirituality of his day. In Edwards's words,

> The foregoing account of Mr. Brainerd's life may afford matter of conviction that there is indeed such a thing as true experimental religion, arising from immediate divine influences, supernaturally enlightening and convincing the mind, and powerfully impressing, quickening, sanctifying, and governing the heart; which religion is indeed an amiable thing, to happy tendency, and of no hurtful consequence to human society; not-withstanding there having been so many pretences and appearances of what is called experimental vital religion, that have proved to be nothing but vain, pernicious enthusiasm. (WJE 7:520)

In all of his brokenness—perhaps *because of* his brokenness—Edwards also finds in Brainerd an example of the true experimental religion that did not give in to the excesses of the revivals, the antinomianism of the heretical groups, or the hypocrisy of "vain religion." What Edwards provided in his theological argumentation, he hoped could be duplicated through Brainerd's diary in a much broader way.

OVERVIEW OF THE VOLUME

The texts we have chosen in this volume serve to reveal the breadth and depth of Edwards's spirituality described in this introduction. We have organized these texts in five parts: (1) General Contours of Edwards's Spirituality; (2) Affections; (3) Beauty; (4) Means of Grace; and (5) The Internal and External Work of Grace. Each part contains an introduction to the constituent texts.

There is a purposeful focus on grace in the ordering of this volume that might not be obvious except for the final two sections. But in Edwards's spirituality, true grace is divine, and therefore the life of affection and beauty is the grace-filled life. Grace is God's self-giving, and therefore the movements of this volume are focused around the Christian's participation in God's life, so that the life of God refracts through the believer into action in the world.

Part One

The General
Contours
of Edwards's
Spirituality

INTRODUCTION
TO PART ONE

To provide an overview of major texts, themes, and practices in Edwards's spirituality, this first part presents selections from several of the well-known, and regrettably few, autobiographical writings in his canon, as well as a previously unpublished sermon by him, his meditation on one of the most famous passages in the Bible, the twenty-third psalm. This part also includes religious profiles by Edwards of several individuals whom he knew. In his descriptions of their religious experiences and practices, we can see indexes of his own piety, the sort of disciplines and qualities that he valued.

The "Diary" and "Resolutions" are, for the most part, products of Edwards's youth, and reveal an earnest soul intent, through introspection, self-monitoring, and asceticism, to achieve deeper spiritual experiences, culminating in regeneration. It is important to point out that in this stringent method, Edwards was emulating the spiritual discipline of the Reformed, Puritan, and Pietist traditions, often called "precisianism," for its constant and close examination of motive and action. Precisianism, in turn, was derived not only from a shared or catholic Christian heritage but was also formative of modern evangelicalism. This practice of piety was part of the *ordo salutis*, the order of salvation, which Puritan preachers portrayed as occurring in stages, from conviction to humiliation to enlightenment. This "morphology" of conversion has been labelled "preparationism" because the discipline called for the soul to prepare itself, through use of the "means of grace"—hearing sermons, reading Scripture and religious literature, partaking of the Lord's Supper, doing charity, engaging in godly conversation, and so forth—for the next stage of spiritual development and growth, and for conversion itself (see the general introduction). And yet, in the process of following the preparationist model and the means of grace, Edwards noticed something different about, or even broader than, his own experience, which set him on a lifelong search into the nature of conversion and the distinction of true from counterfeit marks of grace.

Edwards began the "Diary" and "Resolutions" at about the same time, when, still a student, he was preaching on a supply basis to a small Presbyterian congregation—basically a house church—in New York City. The two documents interact, as shown in Edwards's references to a particular "Resolution" in the "Diary," or vice versa, as if the "Diary" provided the experimental data and the "Resolution" the resulting spiritual or behavioral theorem. Entries run, in a concentrated manner, through the period when he was a tutor at Yale College from 1724 to 1726, then peter out over subsequent years as his pastoral and familial duties increased. In the "Diary" he recorded daily efforts to achieve a holy life and practice, and his reflections on his successes and failures. Out of these reflections arose "Resolutions," a list of desiderata for godly living. That he abandoned the "Diary" and does not mention the "Resolutions" later in life suggests that he came to view those records as the products of an idealistic period; however, they are nonetheless vital, and oft-reprinted, sources for understanding the "personal" Edwards.

The "Personal Narrative," too, has had a robust publication life. Edwards wrote this piece, part retrospective, part summary of personally inspirational and devotional themes, in 1740, in reply to a request from a correspondent. This composition partakes of the genre of spiritual autobiography, which was extremely popular in colonial New England, not least because applicants for full church membership often were required to present to the congregation an account of their experiences. These "relations" were augmented by a body of scribal and printed autobiographical literature. Thus, when Edwards wrote his, he was participating in a tried and true form. His structure and content, however, have been cited as a new mode of self-disclosure, with the use of the affective language that characterized the recent revivals.

By the time Edwards composed his "Personal Narrative," the event for which he and his Northampton, Massachusetts, congregation had become internationally known had come and gone. The Connecticut River Valley Awakening of 1734–35 began in Edwards's church and spread throughout the region. Edwards wrote an account of the revival, which was published in London in 1737 as *A Faithful Narrative of the Surprising Work of God* and soon translated into several languages. The text became a manual of sorts for revivalists on a transatlantic basis. It provided demographics, social history, psychology, and spiritual biography, including the account of the experiences of one of Edwards's parishioners, twenty-one-year-old Abigail Hutchinson. In the tradition of the *ars morienda*, the art of dying, Edwards presented Hutchinson as an exemplar of the departing believer, obtaining assurance of salvation even as she is on her deathbed.

Edwards became adept at presenting individuals as models of evangelical piety in his writings as a way of recommending the spiritual attitudes and practices of pan-Protestant evangelicalism. Later in his career, Edwards presented another exemplar, this time the missionary David Brainerd. Inspired by the ferment of the Great Awakening of the 1740s, Brainerd was expelled from Yale College, but went on to preach to Native Americans in New York, New Jersey, and Pennsylvania. Due to his relentless exertions, he contracted tuberculosis. A friend of the Edwards family, he spent the last weeks at their home and died there (his grave in Northampton's cemetery is a pilgrimage site). Edwards decided to put aside other projects and publish an account of Brainerd's life, drawn from his published journals and his manuscript diaries. The result was a saint's life in the Protestant mode that revealed Brainerd's spiritual struggles and victories and his selfless sacrifice. Edwards's presentation of Brainerd, which has never gone out of print since first published in 1749, became one of the key texts in American foreign and domestic missions. In an appendix to the work, Edwards describes the main features of Brainerd's spirituality that, in many ways, is a thinly veiled synopsis of his own.

Another important aspect of Edwards's inherited spirituality is the teaching that one must be "weaned" from the world, "die daily," in the pursuit of divine things, so that the vicissitudes of life do not aversely affect one. The final selection in this part, *The Spiritual*

Enjoyments and Comforts Believers Have through Christ, has Edwards preaching in 1738 on David's famous words in Psalm 23, about how the Lord like a shepherd led the hunted slayer of Goliath "beside still waters" and out of reach of his pursuer, King Saul. Here, Edwards finds a description of the consolation that believers, in the midst of afflictions and worldly cares, discover in Christ.

"DIARY"

Dec. 18, [1722]. This day made the thirty-fifth Resolution. The reason why I, in the least, question my interest in God's love and favor, is, 1. Because I cannot speak so fully to my experience of that preparatory work, of which divines speak; 2. I do not remember that I experienced regeneration, exactly in those steps, in which divines say it is generally wrought; 3. I do not feel the Christian graces sensibly enough, particularly faith. I fear they are only such hypocritical outside affections, which wicked men may feel, as well as others. They do not seem to be sufficiently inward, full, sincere, entire and hearty. They do not seem so substantial, and so wrought into my very nature, as I could wish. 4. Because I am sometimes guilty of sins of omission and commission. Lately I have doubted whether I do not transgress in evil speaking. This day, resolved, No....

Wednesday, Jan. 2, 1722—23. Dull. I find by experience, that let me make resolutions, and do what I will, with never so many inventions, it is all nothing, and to no purpose at all, without the motions of the Spirit of God: for if the Spirit of God should be as much withdrawn from me always, as for the week past, notwithstanding all I do, I should not grow; but should languish, and miserably fade away. I perceive, if God should withdraw his Spirit a little more, I should not hesitate to break my resolutions, and should soon arrive at my old state. There is no dependence upon myself. Our resolutions may be at the highest one day, and yet, the next day, we may be in a miserable dead condition, not at all like the same person who resolved. It is to no purpose to resolve, except we depend on the grace of God; for if it were not for his mere grace, one might be a very good man one day, and a very wicked one the next. I find also by experience, that there is no guessing out the ends of providence, in particular dispensations towards me—any otherwise than as afflictions come as corrections for sin, and God intends when we meet with them, to desire us to look back on our ways, and see wherein we have done amiss, and lament that particular sin, and all our sins, before him—knowing this, also, that all things shall work together for our good; not knowing in what way, indeed, but trusting in God.

Saturday evening, Jan. 5. A little redeemed from a long dreadful dullness, about reading the Scriptures. This week, have been unhappily low in the weekly account; and what are the reasons of it? abundance of listlessness and sloth; and, if this should continue much longer, I perceive that other sins will begin to discover themselves. It used to appear to me, that I had not much sin remaining; but now, I perceive that there are great remainders of sin. Where may it not bring me to, if God should leave me? Sin is not enough mortified. Without the influences of the Spirit of God, the old serpent would begin to rouse up himself from his frozen state, and would come to life again. Resolved, that I have been negligent in two things: in not striving enough in duty; and in not forcing myself upon religious thoughts.

Sabbath day, Jan. 6, at night. Much concerned about the improvement of precious time. Intend to live in continual mortification, without ceasing, and even to weary myself thereby, as long as I am in this world, and never to expect or desire any worldly ease or pleasure....

Wednesday, Jan. 9, at night. Decayed. I am sometimes apt to think I have a great deal more of holiness than I have. I find now and then that abominable corruption which is directly contrary to what I read of eminent Christians. I do not seem to be half so careful to improve time, to do everything quick, and in as short a time as I possibly can, nor to be perpetually engaged to think about religion, as I was yesterday and the day before, nor indeed as I have been at certain times, perhaps a twelvemonth ago. If my resolutions of that nature, from that time, had always been kept alive and awake, how much better might I have been, than I now am. How deceitful is my heart! I take up a strong resolution, but how soon does it weaken!

Thursday, Jan. 10, about noon. Reviving. 'Tis a great dishonor to Christ, in whom I hope I have an interest, to be uneasy at my worldly state and condition. When I see the prosperity of others, and that all things go easy with them—the world is smooth to them, and they are happy in many respects, and very prosperous, or are advanced to much honor etc.—to grudge and envy them, or be the least uneasy at it; to wish or long for the same prosperity, and that it would ever be so with me. Wherefore concluded always to rejoice in everyone's prosperity, and to expect for myself no happiness of that nature as long as I live; but depend upon afflictions, and betake myself entirely to another happiness.

I think I find myself much more sprightly and healthy, both in body and mind, for my self-denial in eating, drinking, and sleeping.

I think it would be advantageous every morning to consider my business and temptations; and what sins I shall be exposed to that day; and to make a resolution how to improve the day, and to avoid those sins. And so at the beginning of every week, month and year.

I never knew before what was meant by not setting our hearts upon these things. 'Tis not to care about them, to depend upon them, to afflict ourselves much with fears of losing them, nor please ourselves with expectation of obtaining them, or hope of the continuance of them. At night made the 41st Resolution.

Saturday, Jan. 12, in the morning. I have this day solemnly renewed my baptismal covenant and self-dedication, which I renewed when I was received into communion of the church. I have been before God; and have given myself, all that I am and have to God, so that I am not in any respect my own: I can challenge no right in myself, I can challenge no right in this understanding, this will, these affections that are in me; neither have I any right to this body, or any of its members: no right to this tongue, these hands, nor feet; no right to these senses, these eyes, these ears, this smell or taste. I have given myself clear away, and have not retained anything as my own. I have been to God this morning, and told him that I gave myself *wholly* to him. I have given every power to him; so that for the future I will challenge no right in myself, in any respect. I have expressly promised him, and do now promise almighty God, that by his grace I will not. I have this morning told him, that I did take him for my whole portion and felicity, looking on nothing else as any part of my happiness, nor acting as if it were; and his law for the constant rule of my obedience; and would fight with all my might against the world, the flesh, and the devil, to the end of my life. And did believe in Jesus Christ, and receive him as a prince and a Savior; and would adhere to the faith and obedience of the gospel, how hazardous and difficult soever the profession and practice of it may be. That I did receive the blessed Spirit as my teacher, sanctifier, and only comforter; and cherish all his motions to enlighten, purify, confirm, comfort, and assist me. This I have done. And I pray God, for the sake of Christ, to look upon it as a self-dedication; and to receive me now as entirely his own, and deal with me in all respects as such; whether he afflicts me or prospers me, or whatever he pleases to do with me, who am his. Now, henceforth I am not to act in any respect as my own. I shall act as my own, if I ever make use of any of my powers to anything that is not to the glory of God, and don't make the glorifying him my whole and entire business; if I murmur in the least at afflictions; if I grieve at the prosperity of others; if I am anyway uncharitable; if I am angry because of injuries; if I revenge; if I do anything, purely to please myself, or if I avoid anything for the sake of my ease; if I omit anything because it is great self-denial; if I trust to myself: if I take any of the praise of any good that I do, or rather God does by me; or if I am any way proud.

This day made the forty-second and forty-third Resolutions. Whether or no, any other end ought to have any influence at all, on any of my actions or, whether any action ought to be any otherwise, in any respect, than if nothing else but religion had the least influence on my mind. Answer, No. Wherefore, I make the forty-fourth Resolution.

Query: whether any delight, or satisfaction, ought to be allowed, because any other end is obtained, besides a religious one? In the afternoon, I answer, Yes; because, if [we] should never suffer ourselves to rejoice, but because we have obtained a religious end, we should never rejoice at the sight of friends, we should not allow ourselves any pleasure in our food, whereby the animal spirits would be withdrawn, and good digestion hindered. But the query is to be answered thus: we never ought to allow any joy or sorrow, but what helps religion. Wherefore, I make the 45th Resolution.

The reason why I so soon grow lifeless, and unfit for the business I am about, I have found out, is only because I have been used to suffer myself soon to leave off, for the sake of ease, and so, I have got a habit of expecting ease; and therefore, when I think I have exercised myself a good while, I cannot keep myself to it any longer, because I expect to be released, as my due and right. And then, I am deceived, as if I were really tired and weary. Whereas, if I did not expect ease, and was resolved to afflict myself by business, as much as I could, I should continue with as much vigor to my business, without vacation time to rest. Thus, I have found it in reading the Scriptures; and thus, I have found it in prayer; and thus, I believe it to be in getting sermons by heart, and other things.

At night. This week, the weekly account rose higher than ordinary. It is suggested to me, that too constant a mortification, and too vigorous application to religion, may be prejudicial to health. But nevertheless, I will plainly feel it and experience it, before I cease, on this account. It is no matter how much tired and weary I am, if my health is not impaired....

Jan. 15, Tuesday, about two or three of clock. I have been all this day decaying. It seemed yesterday, the day before and Saturday, that I should always retain the same resolution to the same height. But alas! how soon do I decay. O how weak, how infirm, how unable to do anything of myself. What a poor, inconsistent being! What a miserable wretch, without the assistance of God's Spirit. While I stand, I am ready to think I stand by my own strength, and upon my own legs; and I am ready to triumph over my (spiritual) enemies, as if it were I myself that caused them to flee. When alas, I am but a poor infant, upheld by Jesus Christ; who holds me up, and gives me liberty to smile to see my enemies flee, when he drives them before me; and so I laugh, as if I myself did it, when it is only Jesus Christ leads me along, and fights himself against my enemies. And now, the Lord has a little left me; how weak do I find myself. O let it teach me to depend less on myself, to be more humble, and to give more of the praise of my ability to Jesus Christ. The heart of man is deceitful above all things, and desperately wicked, who can know it? [Jer 17:9].

The occasion of my decaying is a little melancholy. My spirits are down, and I am concerned because I fear I lost some friendship the last night. And my spirits being low, my resolutions have lost their strength. I differ today from yesterday, in these things. I do not resolve anything today, half so strongly. I am not so perpetually thinking on and renewing my resolutions as I was then. I am not half so vigorous as I was then; nor am I half so careful to do everything with vigor. Then, I kept continually acting; but now, I do things slowly, and satisfy myself by thinking of religion in the meantime. I am not so careful to go quick from one business to another. I felt humiliation, about sunset. What shall I do frequently, with a good grace, to fall into Christian discourse and conference? At night. The next time I am in such a lifeless frame, I will force myself to go quick from one thing to another, and do those things with vigor, in which vigor would ever be useful. The things, which take off my mind, when bent on religion, are commonly some remarkable change and alteration: journeys, change of place, change of business, change of studies, and change of other circumstances; or something that makes me melancholy; or some sin....

Jan. 20, Sabbath day. At night. The last week I was sunk so low, that I fear it will be a long time 'ere I shall be recovered. I fell exceedingly low in the weekly account. I find my heart so deceitful, that I am almost discouraged from making any more resolutions. Wherein have I been negligent in the week past; and how could I have done better, to help the dreadful, low estate in which I am sunk?...

Feb. 5, Tuesday. At night. I have thought that this being so exceedingly careful, and so particularly anxious, to force myself to think of religion, at all leisure moments, has exceedingly distracted my mind, and made me altogether unfit for that, and everything else. I have thought that this caused the dreadful, low condition I was in on the fifteenth of January. I think I stretched myself further than I could bear, and so broke. For now, it seems to me, though I know not why, that I do not do enough to prepare for another world. I do not seem to press forward, to fight and wrestle, as the apostles used to speak. I do not seem so greatly and constantly to mortify and deny myself, as the mortification of which they speak represents. Therefore, wherein ought I to do more in this way? I answer: I am again grown too careless about eating, drinking and sleeping—not careful enough about evil speaking....

Wednesday, May 22. In the morning. *Memorandum*. To take special care of these following things: evil speaking, fretting, eating, drinking and sleeping, speaking simple verity, joining in prayer, slightiness in secret prayer, listlessness and negligence, and thoughts that cherish sin....

Friday, June 1. Afternoon. I have abundant cause, O my merciful Father, to love thee ardently, and greatly to bless and praise thee, that thou hast heard me in my earnest request, and hast so answered my prayer for mercy to keep from decay and sinking. O, graciously, of thy mere goodness, still continue to pity my misery, by reason of my sinfulness. O my dear Redeemer, I commit myself, together with my prayer and thanksgiving into thine hand....

Saturday morning, June 29. It is best to be careful in prayer, not to put up those petitions of which I do not feel a sincere desire: thereby, my prayer is rendered less sincere, less acceptable to God, and less useful to myself....

Saturday morning, Aug. 10. Transferred my determination of July 23, to the sixty-fourth Resolution, and that of July 26, to the sixty-fifth. About sunset. As a help against that inward shameful hypocrisy, to confess frankly to myself all that which I find in myself, either infirmity or sin; also to confess to God, and open the whole case to him, when it is what concerns religion, and humbly and earnestly implore of him the help that is needed; not in the least to endeavor to smother over what is in my heart, but to bring it all out to God and my conscience. By this means, I may arrive at a greater knowledge of my own heart. When I find difficulty in finding a subject of religious meditation, in vacancies, to pitch at random on what alights to my thoughts, and to go from that to other things which that shall bring into my mind, and follow this progression as a clue, till I come to what I can meditate on with profit and attention, and then to follow that, according to last Thursday's determination.[1]...

Sabbath evening, Sept. 22. To praise God, by singing psalms in prose, and by singing forth the meditations of my heart in prose....

Friday night, Oct. 12. I see there are some things quite contrary to the soundness and perfection of Christianity, in which almost all good men do allow themselves, and where innate corruption has an unrestrained secret vent, which they never take notice of, or think to be no hurt, or cloak under the name of virtue; which things exceedingly darken the brightness, and hide the loveliness, of Christianity. Who can understand his errors? O that I might be kept from secret faults!...

Tuesday forenoon, Nov. 26. 'Tis a most evil and pernicious practice in meditations on afflictions, to sit ruminating on the aggravations of the affliction, and reckoning up the evil, dark circumstances thereof, and dwelling long on the dark side; it doubles and trebles the affliction. And so when speaking of them to others, to make them as bad as we can, and use our eloquence to set forth our own troubles, and are all the while making new trouble, and feeding and pampering the old; whereas the contrary practice would starve our afflictions. If we dwelt on the light side of things in our thoughts, and extenuated them all that possibly we could, when speaking of them, we should think little of them ourselves; and the affliction would really, in a great measure, vanish away....

Friday night, Jan. 3. The time and pains laid out in seeking the world is to be proportioned to the necessity, usefulness, and importance of it, with respect to another world, together with the uncertainty of succeeding, the uncertainty of living, and of retaining; provided that nothing that our duty enjoins, or that is amiable, be omitted, and nothing sinful or unbecoming be done for the sake of it....

"RESOLUTIONS"

Being sensible that I am unable to do anything without God's help, I do humbly entreat him by his grace to enable me to keep these Resolutions, so far as they are agreeable to his will, for Christ's sake.

Remember to read over these Resolutions once a week.

1. Resolved, that I will do whatsoever I think to be most to God's glory, and my own good, profit, and pleasure, in the whole of my duration, without any consideration of the time, whether now, or never so many myriads of ages hence. Resolved to do whatever I

think to be my duty, and most for the good and advantage of mankind in general. Resolved to do this, whatever difficulties I meet with, how many and how great soever.

2. Resolved, to be continually endeavoring to find out some new invention and contrivance to promote the fore-mentioned things.

3. Resolved, if ever I shall fall and grow dull, so as to neglect to keep any part of these Resolutions, to repent of all I can remember, when I come to myself again.

4. Resolved, never to do any manner of thing, whether in soul or body, less or more, but what tends to the glory of God; nor be, nor suffer it, if I can avoid it.

5. Resolved, never to lose one moment of time; but improve it the most profitable way I possibly can.

6. Resolved, to live with all my might, while I do live.

7. Resolved, never to do anything, which I should be afraid to do, if it were the last hour of my life.

8. Resolved, to act, in all respects, both speaking and doing, as if nobody had been so vile as I, and as if I had committed the same sins, or had the same infirmities or failings as others; and that I will let the knowledge of their failings promote nothing but shame in myself, and prove only an occasion of my confessing my own sins and misery to God....

9. Resolved, to think much on all occasions of my own dying, and of the common circumstances which attend death.

10. Resolved, when I feel pain, to think of the pains of martyrdom, and of hell.

11. Resolved, when I think of any theorem in divinity to be solved, immediately to do what I can towards solving it, if circumstances don't hinder.

12. Resolved, if I take delight in it as a gratification of pride, or vanity, or on any such account, immediately to throw it by.

13. Resolved, to be endeavoring to find out fit objects of charity and liberality.

14. Resolved, never to do anything out of revenge.

15. Resolved, never to suffer the least motions of anger to irrational beings.

16. Resolved, never to speak evil of anyone, so that it shall tend to his dishonor, more or less, upon no account except for some real good.

17. Resolved, that I will live so as I shall wish I had done when I come to die.

18. Resolved, to live so at all times, as I think is best in my devout frames, and when I have clearest notions of things of the gospel, and another world.

19. Resolved, never to do anything, which I should be afraid to do, if I expected it would not be above an hour, before I should hear the last trump.

20. Resolved, to maintain the strictest temperance in eating and drinking.

21. Resolved, never to do anything, which if I should see in another, I should count a just occasion to despise him for, or to think any way the more meanly of him.

22. Resolved, to endeavor to obtain for myself as much happiness, in the other world, as I possibly can, with all the power, might, vigor, and vehemence, yea violence, I am capable of, or can bring myself to exert, in any way that can be thought of.

23. Resolved, frequently to take some deliberate action, which seems most unlikely to be done, for the glory of God, and trace it back to the original intention, designs and ends of it; and if I find it not to be for God's glory, to repute it as a breach of the fourth Resolution.

24. Resolved, whenever I do any conspicuously evil action, to trace it back, till I come to the original cause; and then both carefully endeavor to do so no more, and to fight and pray with all my might against the original of it.

25. Resolved, to examine carefully, and constantly, what that one thing in me is, which causes me in the least to doubt of the love of God; and to direct all my forces against it.

26. Resolved, to cast away such things, as I find do abate my assurance.

27. Resolved, never willfully to omit anything, except the omission be for the glory of God; and frequently to examine my omissions.

28. Resolved, to study the Scriptures so steadily, constantly, and frequently, as that I may find, and plainly perceive myself to grow in the knowledge of the same.

29. Resolved, never to count that a prayer, nor to let that pass as a prayer, nor that as a petition of a prayer, which is so made, that I cannot hope that God will answer it; nor that as a confession, which I cannot hope God will accept.

30. Resolved, to strive to my utmost every week to be brought higher in religion, and to a higher exercise of grace, than I was the week before.

31. Resolved, never to say anything at all against anybody, but when it is perfectly agreeable to the highest degree of Christian honor, and of love to mankind, agreeable to the lowest humility, and sense of my own faults and failings, and agreeable to the golden rule; often, when I have said anything against anyone, to bring it to, and try it strictly by the test of this Resolution.

32. Resolved, to be strictly and firmly faithful to my trust, that that in Prov. 20:6, "A faithful man who can find?" may not be partly fulfilled in me.

33. Resolved, always to do what I can towards making, maintaining, establishing and preserving peace, when it can be without over-balancing detriment in other respects. *Dec. 26, 1722.*

34. Resolved, in narrations never to speak anything but the pure and simple verity.

35. Resolved, whenever I so much question whether I have done my duty, as that my quiet and calm is thereby disturbed, to set it down, and also how the question was resolved. *Dec. 18, 1722.*

36. Resolved, never to speak evil of any, except I have some particular good call for it. *Dec. 19, 1722.*

37. Resolved, to inquire every night, as I am going to bed, wherein I have been negligent, what sin I have committed, and wherein I have denied myself: also at the end of every week, month and year. *Dec. 22, and 26, 1722.*

38. Resolved, never to speak anything that is ridiculous, sportive, or matter of laughter on the Lord's day. *Sabbath evening, Dec. 23, 1722.*

39. Resolved, never to do anything that I so much question the lawfulness of, as that I intend, at the same time, to consider and examine afterwards, whether it be lawful or no: except I as much question the lawfulness of the omission.

40. Resolved, to inquire every night, before I go to bed, whether I have acted in the best way I possibly could, with respect to eating and drinking. *Jan. 7, 1723.*

41. Resolved, to ask myself at the end of every day, week, month, and year, wherein I could possibly in any respect have done better. *Jan. 11, 1723.*

42. Resolved, frequently to renew the dedication of myself to God, which was made at my baptism; which I solemnly renewed, when I was received into the communion of the church; and which I have solemnly re-made this twelfth day of January, 1722–23.

43. Resolved, never henceforward, till I die, to act as if I were any way my own, but entirely and altogether God's, agreeable to what is to be found in Saturday, January 12. *Jan. 12, 1723.*

44. Resolved, that no other end but religion, shall have any influence at all on any of my actions; and that no action shall be, in the least circumstance, any otherwise than the religious end will carry it. *Jan. 12, 1723.*

45. Resolved, never to allow any pleasure or grief, joy, or sorrow, nor any affection at all, nor any degree of affection, nor any circumstance relating to it, but what helps religion. *Jan. 12, and 13, 1723.*

46. Resolved, never to allow the least measure of any fretting uneasiness at my father or mother. Resolved, to suffer no effects of it, so much as in the least alteration of speech, or motion of my eye: and to be especially careful of it, with respect to any of our family.

47. Resolved, to endeavor to my utmost to deny whatever is not most agreeable to a good, and universally sweet and benevolent, quiet, peaceable, contented, easy, compassionate, generous, humble, meek, modest, submissive, obliging, diligent and industrious, charitable, even, patient, moderate, forgiving, sincere temper; and to do at all times what such a temper would lead me to. Examine strictly every week, whether I have done so. *Sabbath morning, May 5, 1723.*

48. Resolved, constantly, with the utmost niceness and diligence, and the strictest scrutiny, to be looking into the state of my

soul, that I may know whether I have truly an interest in Christ or no; that when I come to die, I may not have any negligence respecting this to repent of. *May 26, 1723.*

49. Resolved, that this never shall be, if I can help it.

50. Resolved, I will act so as I think I shall judge would have been best, and most prudent, when I come into the future world. *July 5, 1723.*

51. Resolved, that I will act so, in every respect, as I think I shall wish I had done, if I should at last be damned. *July 8, 1723.*

52. I frequently hear persons in old age say how they would live, if they were to live their lives over again: Resolved, that I will live just so as I can think I shall wish I had done, supposing I live to old age. *July 8, 1723.*

53. Resolved, to improve every opportunity, when I am in the best and happiest frame of mind, to cast and venture my soul on the Lord Jesus Christ, to trust and confide in him, and consecrate myself wholly to him; that from this I may have assurance of my safety, knowing that I confide in my Redeemer. *July 8, 1723.*

54. Whenever I hear anything spoken in conversation of any person, if I think it would be praiseworthy in me, Resolved to endeavor to imitate it. *July 8, 1723.*

55. Resolved, to endeavor to my utmost to act as I can think I should do, if I had already seen the happiness of heaven, and hell torments. *July 8, 1723.*

56. Resolved, never to give over, nor in the least to slacken my fight with my corruptions, however unsuccessful I may be.

57. Resolved, when I fear misfortunes and adversities, to examine whether I have done my duty, and resolve to do it; and let it be just as providence orders it, I will as far as I can, be concerned about nothing but my duty and my sin. *June 9,* and *July 13, 1723.*

58. Resolved, not only to refrain from an air of dislike, fretfulness, and anger in conversation, but to exhibit an air of love, cheerfulness, and benignity. *May 27,* and *July 13, 1723.*

59. Resolved, when I am most conscious of provocations to ill nature and anger, that I will strive most to feel and act good-naturedly; yea, at such times, to manifest good nature, though I think that in

other respects it would be disadvantageous, and so as would be imprudent at other times. *May 12, July 11*, and *July 13*.

60. Resolved, whenever my feelings begin to appear in the least out of order, when I am conscious of the least uneasiness within, or the least irregularity without, I will then subject myself to the strictest examination. *July 4,* and *13, 1723*.

61. Resolved, that I will not give way to that listlessness which I find unbends and relaxes my mind from being fully and fixedly set on religion, whatever excuse I may have for it—that what my listlessness inclines me to do, is best to be done, etc. *May 21,* and *July 13, 1723*.

62. Resolved, never to do anything but duty; and then according to Eph. 6:6–8, do it willingly and cheerfully as unto the Lord, and not to man; "knowing that whatever good thing any man doth, the same shall he receive of the Lord." *June 25,* and *July 13, 1723*.

63. On the supposition that there never was to be but one individual in the world, at any one time, who was properly a complete Christian, in all respects of a right stamp, having Christianity always shining in its true luster, and appearing excellent and lovely, from whatever part and under whatever character viewed: Resolved, to act just as I would do, if I strove with all my might to be that one, who should live in my time. *Jan. 14,* and *July 13, 1723*.

64. Resolved, when I find those "groanings which cannot be uttered" [Rom 8:26], of which the apostle speaks, and those "breakings of soul for the longing it hath," of which the Psalmist speaks, Psalm 119:20, that I will promote them to the utmost of my power, and that I will not be weary of earnestly endeavoring to vent my desires, nor of the repetitions of such earnestness. *July 23,* and *August 10, 1723*.

65. Resolved, very much to exercise myself in this all my life long, viz. with the greatest openness I am capable of, to declare my ways to God, and lay open my soul to him: all my sins, temptations, difficulties, sorrows, fears, hopes, desires, and every thing, and every circumstance; according to Dr. Manton's twenty-seventh sermon on the 119th Psalm. *July 26,* and *Aug. 10, 1723*.

66. Resolved, that I will endeavor always to keep a benign aspect, and air of acting and speaking in all places, and in all companies, except it should so happen that duty requires otherwise.

67. Resolved, after afflictions, to inquire, what I am the better for them, what good I have got by them, and what I might have got by them.

68. Resolved, to confess frankly to myself all that which I find in myself, either infirmity or sin; and, if it be what concerns religion, also to confess the whole case to God, and implore needed help. *July 23*, and *August 10, 1723*.

69. Resolved, always to do that, which I shall wish I had done when I see others do it. *Aug. 11, 1723*.

70. Let there be something of benevolence, in all that I speak. *Aug. 17, 1723*.

"PERSONAL NARRATIVE" (1740)

I had a variety of concerns and exercises about my soul from my childhood; but had two more remarkable seasons of awakening, before I met with that change by which I was brought to those new dispositions, and that new sense of things, that I have since had. The first time was when I was a boy, some years before I went to college, at a time of remarkable awakening in my father's congregation. I was then very much affected for many months, and concerned about the things of religion, and my soul's salvation; and was abundant in duties. I used to pray five times a day in secret, and to spend much time in religious talk with other boys; and used to meet with them to pray together. I experienced I know not what kind of delight in religion. My mind was much engaged in it, and had much self-righteous pleasure; and it was my delight to abound in religious duties. I, with some of my schoolmates, joined together, and built a booth in a swamp, in a very secret and retired place, for a place of prayer. And besides, I had particular secret places of my own in the woods, where I used to retire by myself; and used to be from time to time much affected. My affections seemed to be lively and easily moved, and I seemed to be in my element, when engaged in religious duties. And I am ready to think, many are deceived with such affections, and such a kind of delight, as I then had in religion, and mistake it for grace.

But in process of time, my convictions and affections wore off; and I entirely lost all those affections and delights, and left off secret prayer, at least as to any constant performance of it; and returned like a dog to his vomit, and went on in ways of sin.

Indeed, I was at some times very uneasy, especially towards the latter part of the time of my being at college. Till it pleased God, in my last year at college, at a time when I was in the midst of many uneasy thoughts about the state of my soul, to seize me with a pleurisy; in which he brought me nigh to the grave, and shook me over the pit of hell.

But yet, it was not long after my recovery before I fell again into my old ways of sin. But God would not suffer me to go on with any quietness; but I had great and violent inward struggles: till after many conflicts with wicked inclinations, and repeated resolutions, and bonds that I laid myself under by a kind of vows to God, I was brought wholly to break off all former wicked ways, and all ways of known outward sin; and to apply myself to seek my salvation, and practice the duties of religion: but without that kind of affection and delight that I had formerly experienced. My concern now wrought more by inward struggles and conflicts, and self-reflections. I made seeking my salvation the main business of my life. But yet it seems to me, I sought after a miserable manner, which has made me sometimes since to question, whether ever it issued in that which was saving; being ready to doubt, whether such miserable seeking was ever succeeded. But yet I was brought to seek salvation, in a manner that I never was before. I felt a spirit to part with all things in the world, for an interest in Christ. My concern continued and prevailed, with many exercising things and inward struggles; but yet it never seemed to be proper to express my concern that I had, by the name of terror.

From my childhood up, my mind had been wont to be full of objections to the doctrine of God's sovereignty, in choosing whom he would to eternal life, and rejecting whom he pleased; leaving them eternally to perish, and be everlastingly tormented in hell. It used to appear like a horrible doctrine to me. But I remember the time very well, when I seemed to be convinced, and fully satisfied, as to this sovereignty of God, and his justice in thus eternally disposing of men, according to his sovereign pleasure. But never could give an account, how, or by what means, I was thus convinced; not in the least imagining, in the time of it, nor a long time after, that there was any extraordinary influence of God's Spirit in it: but only that now I saw further, and my reason apprehended the justice and reasonableness of it. However, my mind rested in it; and it put an end to all those cavils and objections that had till then abode with me, all the preceding part of my life. And there has been a wonderful alteration in my mind, with respect to the doctrine of God's sovereignty, from that day to this; so that I scarce ever have found so much as the rising of an objection against God's sovereignty, in the most absolute sense, in showing mercy on whom he will show mercy, and hardening and eternally damning whom he will. God's absolute sovereignty, and justice, with respect to salvation and damnation, is what my mind seems to rest assured of, as much as of anything that I see with my eyes; at least it is so at times. But I have oftentimes since that first conviction had quite another kind of sense of God's sovereignty than I had then. I have often since, not only had a conviction, but a *delightful* conviction. The doctrine of God's sovereignty has very often appeared an exceeding pleasant, bright, and sweet doctrine to me; and absolute sovereignty is what I love to ascribe to God. But my first conviction was not with this.

The first that I remember that ever I found anything of that sort of inward, sweet delight in God and divine things, that I have lived much in since, was on reading those words, 1 Timothy 1:17, "Now unto the King eternal, immortal, invisible, the only wise God, be honor and glory forever and ever, Amen." As I read the words, there came into my soul, and was as it were diffused through it, a sense of the glory of the divine being; a new sense, quite different from anything I ever experienced before. Never any words of Scripture seemed to me as these words did. I thought with myself, how excellent a Being that was; and how happy I should be, if I might enjoy that God, and be wrapped up to God in heaven, and be as it were swallowed up in him. I kept saying, and as it were singing over these words of

Scripture to myself; and went to prayer, to pray to God that I might enjoy him; and prayed in a manner quite different from what I used to do; with a new sort of affection. But it never came into my thought that there was anything spiritual, or of a saving nature in this.

From about that time, I began to have a new kind of apprehensions and ideas of Christ, and the work of redemption, and the glorious way of salvation by him. I had an inward, sweet sense of these things, that at times came into my heart; and my soul was led away in pleasant views and contemplations of them. And my mind was greatly engaged to spend my time in reading and meditating on Christ; and the beauty and excellency of his person, and the lovely way of salvation, by free grace in him. I found no books so delightful to me, as those that treated of these subjects. Those words (Song of Solomon 2:1) used to be abundantly with me: "I am the rose of Sharon, the lily of the valleys." The words seemed to me sweetly to represent the loveliness and beauty of Jesus Christ. And the whole Book of Canticles used to be pleasant to me; and I used to be much in reading it, about that time. And found, from time to time, an inward sweetness, that used, as it were, to carry me away in my contemplations; in what I know not how to express otherwise, than by a calm, sweet abstraction of soul from all the concerns of this world; and a kind of vision, or fixed ideas and imaginations, of being alone in the mountains, or some solitary wilderness, far from all mankind, sweetly conversing with Christ, and wrapped and swallowed up in God. The sense I had of divine things would often of a sudden as it were kindle up a sweet burning in my heart; an ardor of my soul, that I know not how to express.

Not long after I first began to experience these things, I gave an account to my father, of some things that had passed in my mind. I was pretty much affected by the discourse we had together. And when the discourse was ended, I walked abroad alone, in a solitary place in my father's pasture, for contemplation. And as I was walking there, and looked up on the sky and clouds; there came into my mind, a sweet sense of the glorious majesty and grace of God, that I know not how to express. I seemed to see them both in a sweet conjunction: majesty and meekness joined together; it was a sweet and gentle and holy majesty; and also a majestic meekness; an awful sweetness; a high, and great and holy gentleness.

After this my sense of divine things gradually increased, and became more and more lively, and had more of that inward sweetness. The appearance of everything was altered: there seemed to be, as it were, a calm, sweet cast, or appearance of divine glory, in almost everything. God's excellency, his wisdom, his purity and love, seemed to appear in everything; in the sun, moon, and stars; in the clouds, and blue sky; in the grass, flowers, trees; in the water, and all nature; which used greatly to fix my mind. I often used to sit and view the moon, for a long time; and so in the daytime, spent much time in viewing the clouds and sky, to behold the sweet glory of God in these things: in the meantime, singing forth with a low voice, my contemplations of the Creator and Redeemer. And scarce anything, among all the works of nature, was so sweet to me as thunder and lightning. Formerly nothing had been so terrible to me. I used to be a person uncommonly terrified with thunder; and it used to strike me with terror, when I saw a thunderstorm rising. But now, on the contrary, it rejoiced me. I felt God at the first appearance of a thunderstorm. And used to take the opportunity at such times to fix myself to view the clouds, and see the lightnings play, and hear the majestic and awful voice of God's thunder, which often times was exceeding entertaining, leading me to sweet contemplations of my great and glorious God. And while I viewed, used to spend my time, as it always seemed natural to me, to sing or chant forth my meditations; to speak my thoughts in soliloquies, and speak with a singing voice.

I felt then a great satisfaction as to my good estate. But that did not content me. I had vehement longings of soul after God and Christ, and after more holiness; wherewith my heart seemed to be full, and ready to break; which often brought to my mind the words of the Psalmist, Psalms 119:28, "My soul breaketh for the longing it hath." I often felt a mourning and lamenting in my heart that I had not turned to God sooner, that I might have had more time to grow in grace. My mind was greatly fixed on divine things; I was almost perpetually in the contemplation of them. Spent most of my time in thinking of divine things, year after year. And used to spend abundance of my time in walking alone in the woods, and solitary places, for meditation, soliloquy, and prayer, and converse with God. And it was always my manner, at such times, to sing forth my contemplations. And was almost constantly in ejaculatory prayer, wherever I was. Prayer seemed to be natural to me; as the breath, by which the inward burnings of my heart had vent.

The delights which I now felt in things of religion were of an exceeding different kind, from those forementioned, that I had when I was a boy. They were totally of another kind; and what I then had no more notion or idea of, than one born blind has of pleasant and beautiful colors. They were of a more inward, pure, soul-animating, and refreshing nature. Those former delights never reached the heart; and did not arise from any sight of the divine excellency of the things of God; or any taste of the soul-satisfying, and life-giving good, there is in them.

My sense of divine things seemed gradually to increase, till I went to preach at New York; which was about a year and a half after they began. While I was there, I felt them, very sensibly, in a much higher degree, than I had done before. My longings after God and holiness, were much increased. Pure and humble, holy and heavenly Christianity, appeared exceeding amiable to me. I felt in me a burning desire to be in everything a complete Christian; and conformed to the blessed image of Christ: and that I might live in all things, according to the pure, sweet, and blessed rules of the gospel. I had an eager thirsting after progress in these things. My longings after it put me upon pursuing and pressing after them. It was my continual strife day and night, and constant inquiry, how I should be more holy, and live more holily, and more becoming a child of God, and disciple of Christ. I sought an increase of grace and holiness, and that I might live an holy life, with vastly more earnestness, than ever I sought grace before I had it. I used to be continually examining myself, and studying and contriving for likely ways and means how I should live holily, with far greater diligence and earnestness, than ever I pursued anything in my life, but with too great a dependence on my own strength, which afterwards proved a great damage to me. My experience had not then taught me, as it has done since, my extreme feebleness and impotence, every manner of way; and the innumerable and bottomless depths of secret corruption and deceit that there was in my heart. However, I went on with my eager pursuit after more holiness and sweet conformity to Christ.

The heaven I desired was a heaven of holiness: to be with God, and to spend my eternity in divine love and holy communion with Christ. My mind was very much taken up with contemplations on heaven, and the enjoyments of those there, and living there in perfect holiness, humility, and love. And it used at that time to appear a great part of the happiness of heaven, that there the saints could express their love to Christ. It appeared to me a great clog and hindrance and burden to me, that what I felt within, I could not express to God, and give vent to, as I desired. The inward ardor of my soul seemed to be hindered and pent up, and could not freely flame out as it would. I used often to think how in heaven, this sweet principle should freely and fully vent and express itself. Heaven appeared to me exceeding delightful as a world of love. It appeared to me that all happiness consisted in living in pure, humble, heavenly, divine love.

I remember the thoughts I used then to have of holiness. I remember I then said sometimes to myself, I do certainly know that I love holiness, such as the gospel prescribes. It appeared to me there was nothing in it but what was ravishingly lovely. It appeared to me to be the highest beauty and amiableness, above all other beauties: that it was a divine beauty, far purer than anything here upon earth; and that everything else, was like mire, filth, and defilement, in comparison of it.

Holiness, as I then wrote down some of my contemplations on it, appeared to me to be of a sweet, pleasant, charming, serene, calm nature. It seemed to me it brought an inexpressible purity, brightness, peacefulness, and ravishment to the soul: and that it made the soul like a field or garden of God, with all manner of pleasant flowers; that is all pleasant, delightful, and undisturbed, enjoying a sweet calm, and the gently vivifying beams of the sun. The soul of a true Christian, as I then wrote my meditations, appeared like such a little white flower, as we see in the spring of the year; low and humble on the ground, opening its bosom, to receive the pleasant beams of the sun's glory; rejoicing as it were, in a calm rapture; diffusing around a sweet fragrancy; standing peacefully and lovingly, in the midst of other flowers round about; all in like manner opening their bosoms, to drink in the light of the sun.

There was no part of creature holiness that I then, and at other times, had so great a sense of the loveliness of, as humility, brokenness of heart, and poverty of spirit; and there was nothing that I had such a spirit to long for. My heart as it were panted after this, to lie low before GOD, and in the dust; that I might be nothing, and that God might be all; that I might become as a little child.

While I was there at New York, I sometimes was much affected with reflections on my past life, considering how late it was, before I began to be truly religious; and how wickedly I had lived till then; and once so as to weep abundantly, and for a considerable time together.

On January 12, 1722/3, I made a solemn dedication of myself to God, and wrote it down; giving up myself, and all that I had to God; to be for the future in no respect my own; to act as one that had no right to himself, in any respect. And solemnly vowed to take God for my whole portion and felicity; looking on nothing else as any part of my happiness, nor acting as if it were; and his law for the constant rule of my obedience; engaging to fight with all my might, against the world, the flesh, and the devil, to the end of my life. But have reason to be infinitely humbled, when I consider, how much I have failed of answering my obligation.

I had then abundance of sweet religious conversation in the family where I lived, with Mr. John Smith, and his pious mother. My heart was knit in affection to those in whom were appearances of true piety; and I could bear the thoughts of no other companions, but such as were holy, and the disciples of the blessed Jesus.

I had great longings for the advancement of Christ's kingdom in the world. My secret prayer used to be in great part taken up in praying for it. If I heard the least hint of anything that happened in any part of the world, that appeared to me, in some respect or other, to have a favorable aspect on the interest of Christ's kingdom, my soul eagerly catched at it; and it would much animate and refresh me. I used to be earnest to read public news-letters, mainly for that end; to see if I could not find some news favorable to the interest of religion in the world.

I very frequently used to retire into a solitary place, on the banks of Hudson's River, at some distance from the city, for contemplation on divine things, and secret converse with God; and had many sweet hours there. Sometimes Mr. Smith and I walked there together, to converse of the things of God; and our conversation used much to turn on the advancement of Christ's kingdom in the world, and the glorious things that God would accomplish for his church in the latter days.

I had then, and at other times, the greatest delight in the Holy Scriptures of any book whatsoever. Oftentimes in reading it, every word seemed to touch my heart. I felt a harmony between something in my heart and those sweet and powerful words. I seemed often to see so much light, exhibited by every sentence, and such a refreshing ravishing food communicated, that I could not get along in reading. Used oftentimes to dwell long on one sentence, to see the wonders contained in it; and yet almost every sentence seemed to be full of wonders.

I came away from New York in the month of April 1723, and had a most bitter parting with Madam Smith and her son. My heart seemed to sink within me, at leaving the family and city, where I had enjoyed so many sweet and pleasant days. I went from New York to Wethersfield by water. As I sailed away, I kept sight of the city as long as I could; and when I was out of sight of it, it would affect me much to look that way, with a kind of melancholy mixed with sweetness. However, that night after this sorrowful parting, I was greatly comforted in God at Westchester, where we went ashore to lodge; and had a pleasant time of it all the voyage to Saybrook. It was sweet to me to think of meeting dear Christians in heaven, where we should never part more. At Saybrook we went ashore to lodge on Saturday, and there kept Sabbath; where I had a sweet and refreshing season, walking alone in the fields.

After I came home to Windsor, remained much in a like frame of my mind as I had been in at New York; but only sometimes felt my heart ready to sink with the thoughts of my friends at New York. And my refuge and support was in contemplations on the heavenly state, as I find in my diary of May 1, 1723. It was my comfort to think of that state, where there is fullness of joy; where reigns heavenly, sweet, calm, and delightful love, without alloy; where there are continually the dearest expressions of this love; where is the enjoyment of the persons loved, without ever parting; where these persons that appear so lovely in this world, will really be inexpressibly more lovely, and full of love to us. And how sweetly will the mutual lovers join together to sing the praises of God and the Lamb! How full will it fill us with joy, to think that this enjoyment, these sweet exercises will never cease or come to an end; but will last to all eternity!

Continued much in the same frame in the general that I had been in at New York, till I went to New Haven, to live there as tutor of the college, having one special season of uncommon sweetness: particularly once at Bolton, in a journey from Boston, walking out alone in the fields. After I went to New Haven, I sunk in religion; my mind being diverted from my eager and violent pursuits after holiness by some affairs that greatly perplexed and distracted my mind.

In September 1725, was taken ill at New Haven; and endeavoring to go home to Windsor, was so ill at the North Village, that I could go no farther; where I lay sick for about a quarter of a year. And in this sickness, God was pleased to visit me again with the sweet influences of his spirit. My mind was greatly engaged there on divine, pleasant contemplations, and longings of soul. I observed that those who watched with me would often be looking out for the morning, and seemed to wish for it. Which brought to my mind those words of the Psalmist, which my soul with sweetness made its own language, "My soul waiteth for the Lord more than they that watch for the morning: I say, more than they that watch for the morning" [Ps 130:6]. And when the light of the morning came, and the beams of the sun came in at the windows, it refreshed my soul from one morning to another. It seemed to me to be some image of the sweet light of God's glory.

I remember, about that time, I used greatly to long for the conversion of some that I was concerned with. It seemed to me I could gladly honor them, and with delight be a servant to them, and lie at their feet, if they were but truly holy.

But sometime after this, I was again greatly diverted in my mind, with some temporal concerns,[2] that exceedingly took up my thoughts, greatly to the wounding of my soul; and went on through

71

various exercises that it would be tedious to relate, that gave me much more experience of my own heart than ever I had before.

Since I came to this town,[3] I have often had sweet complacency in God in views of his glorious perfections, and the excellency of Jesus Christ. God has appeared to me a glorious and lovely being, chiefly on the account of his holiness. The holiness of God has always appeared to me the most lovely of all his attributes. The doctrines of God's absolute sovereignty, and free grace, in showing mercy to whom he would show mercy, and man's absolute dependence on the operations of God's Holy Spirit, have very often appeared to me as sweet and glorious doctrines. These doctrines have been much my delight. God's sovereignty has ever appeared to me as great part of his glory. It has often been sweet to me to go to God, and adore him as a sovereign God, and ask sovereign mercy of him.

I have loved the doctrines of the gospel: they have been to my soul like green pastures. The gospel has seemed to me to be the richest treasure; the treasure that I have most desired, and longed that it might dwell richly in me. The way of salvation by Christ has appeared in a general way glorious and excellent, and most pleasant and beautiful. It has often seemed to me that it would in a great measure spoil heaven, to receive it in any other way. That text has often been affecting and delightful to me, Isaiah 32:2, "A man shall be an hiding place from the wind, and a covert from the tempest," etc.

It has often appeared sweet to me to be united to Christ; to have him for my head, and to be a member of his body; and also to have Christ for my teacher and prophet. I very often think with sweetness and longings and pantings of soul of being a little child, taking hold of Christ, to be led by him through the wilderness of this world. That text, Matthew 18 at the beginning, has often been sweet to me, "Except ye be converted, and become as little children," etc. I love to think of coming to Christ, to receive salvation of him, poor in spirit, and quite empty of self; humbly exalting him alone; cut entirely off from my own root, and to grow into, and out of Christ: to have God in Christ to be all in all; and to live by faith on the Son of God, a life of humble, unfeigned confidence in him. That Scripture has often been sweet to me, Psalms 115:1, "Not unto us, O Lord, not unto us, but unto thy name give glory, for thy mercy, and for thy truth's sake."

And those words of Christ, Luke 10:21, "In that hour Jesus rejoiced in spirit, and said, I thank thee, O Father, Lord of heaven and earth, that thou hast hid these things from the wise and prudent, and hast revealed them unto babes: even so Father, for so it seemed good in thy sight." That sovereignty of God that Christ rejoiced in seemed to me to be worthy to be rejoiced in; and that rejoicing of Christ seemed to me to show the excellency of Christ, and the spirit that he was of.

Sometimes only mentioning a single word causes my heart to burn within me; or only seeing the name of Christ, or the name of some attribute of God. And God has appeared glorious to me, on account of the Trinity. It has made me have exalting thoughts of God, that he subsists in three persons; Father, Son, and Holy Ghost.

The sweetest joys and delights I have experienced have not been those that have arisen from a hope of my own good estate; but in a direct view of the glorious things of the gospel. When I enjoy this sweetness, it seems to carry me above the thoughts of my own safe estate. It seems at such times a loss that I cannot bear, to take off my eye from the glorious, pleasant object I behold without me, to turn my eye in upon myself, and my own good estate.

My heart has been much on the advancement of Christ's kingdom in the world. The histories of the past advancement of Christ's kingdom have been sweet to me. When I have read histories of past ages, the pleasantest thing in all my reading has been to read of the kingdom of Christ being promoted. And when I have expected in my reading to come to any such thing, I have lotted upon it[4] all the way as I read. And my mind has been much entertained and delighted with the Scripture promises and prophecies, of the future glorious advancement of Christ's kingdom on earth. I have sometimes had a sense of the excellent fullness of Christ, and his meetness and suitableness as a savior, whereby he has appeared to me, far above all, the chief of ten thousands. And his blood and atonement has appeared sweet, and his righteousness sweet; which is always accompanied with an ardency of spirit, and inward strugglings and breathings and groanings, that cannot be uttered, to be emptied of myself, and swallowed up in Christ.

Once, as I rid out into the woods for my health, *anno* 1737; and having lit from my horse in a retired place, as my manner commonly has been, to walk for divine contemplation and prayer; I had a view, that for me was extraordinary, of the glory of the Son of God; as mediator between God and man; and his wonderful, great, full, pure and sweet grace and love, and meek and gentle condescension. This grace, that appeared to me so calm and sweet, appeared great above the heavens. The person of Christ appeared ineffably excellent, with an excellency great enough to swallow up all thought and conception. Which continued, as near as I can judge, about an hour; which kept me, the bigger part of the time, in a flood of tears, and weeping aloud. I felt withal, an ardency of soul to be, what I know not otherwise how to express, than to be emptied and annihilated; to lie in the dust, and to be full of Christ alone; to love him with a holy and pure love; to trust in him; to live upon him; to serve and follow him, and to be totally wrapped up in the fullness of Christ; and to be perfectly sanctified and made pure, with a divine and heavenly purity. I have several other times had views very much of the same nature, and that have had the same effects.

I have many times had a sense of the glory of the third person in the Trinity, in his office of Sanctifier; in his holy operations communicating divine light and life to the soul. God in the communications of his Holy Spirit has appeared as an infinite fountain of divine glory and sweetness, being full and sufficient to fill and satisfy the soul, pouring forth itself in sweet communications, like the sun in its glory, sweetly and pleasantly diffusing light and life.

I have sometimes had an affecting sense of the excellency of the word of God, as a word of life; as the light of life; a sweet, excellent, life-giving word, accompanied with a thirsting after that word, that it might dwell richly in my heart.

I have often since I lived in this town[5] had very affecting views of my own sinfulness and vileness; very frequently so as to hold me in a kind of loud weeping, sometimes for a considerable time together, so that I have often been forced to shut myself up. I have had a vastly greater sense of my own wickedness, and the badness of my heart, since my conversion, than ever I had before. It has often appeared to me that if God should mark iniquity against me, I should appear the very worst of all mankind; of all that have been since the beginning of the world to this time; and that I should have by far the lowest place in hell. When others that have come to talk with me about their soul concerns have expressed the sense they have had of their own wickedness, by saying that it seemed to them that they were as bad as the devil himself, I thought their expressions seemed exceeding faint and feeble, to represent my wickedness. I thought I should wonder that they should content themselves with such expressions as these, if I had any reason to imagine, that their sin bore any proportion to mine. It seemed to me I should wonder at myself, if I should express my wickedness in such feeble terms as they did.

My wickedness, as I am in myself, has long appeared to me perfectly ineffable, and infinitely swallowing up all thought and imagination, like an infinite deluge, or infinite mountains over my head. I know not how to express better what my sins appear to me to be, than by heaping infinite upon infinite, and multiplying infinite by infinite. I go about very often, for this many years, with these expressions in my mind, and in my mouth, "Infinite upon infinite. Infinite upon infinite!" When I look into my heart, and take a view of my wickedness, it looks like an abyss infinitely deeper than hell. And it appears to me, that were it not for free grace, exalted and raised up to the infinite height of all the fullness and glory of the great Jehovah, and the arm of his power and grace stretched forth, in all the majesty of his power, and in all the glory of his sovereignty, I should appear sunk down in my sins infinitely below hell itself, far beyond sight of everything, but the piercing eye of God's grace, that can pierce even down to such a depth, and to the bottom of such an abyss.

And yet, I ben't in the least inclined to think, that I have a greater conviction of sin than ordinary. It seems to me, my conviction of sin is exceeding small, and faint. It appears to me enough to amaze me that I have no more sense of my sin. I know certainly that I have very little sense of my sinfulness. That my sins appear to me so great, don't seem to me to be, because I have so much more conviction of sin than other Christians, but because I am so much worse, and have so much more wickedness to be convinced of. When I have had these turns of weeping and crying for my sins, I thought I knew in the time of it, that my repentance was nothing to my sin.

I have greatly longed of late for a broken heart, and to lie low before God. And when I ask for humility of God, I can't bear the thoughts of being no more humble than other Christians. It seems to me that though their degrees of humility may be suitable for them, yet it would be a vile self-exaltation in me, not to be the lowest in humility of all mankind. Others speak of their longing to be humbled to the dust. Though that may be a proper expression for them, I always think for myself, that I ought to be humbled down below hell. 'Tis an expression that it has long been natural for me to use in prayer to God. I ought to lie infinitely low before God.

It is affecting to me to think how ignorant I was, when I was a young Christian, of the bottomless, infinite depths of wickedness, pride, hypocrisy, and deceit left in my heart.

I have vastly a greater sense of my universal, exceeding dependence on God's grace and strength, and mere good pleasure, of late, than I used formerly to have; and have experienced more of an abhorrence of my own righteousness. The thought of any comfort or joy, arising in me, on any consideration, or reflection on my own amiableness, or any of my performances or experiences, or any goodness of heart or life, is nauseous and detestable to me. And yet I am greatly afflicted with a proud and self-righteous spirit, much more sensibly than I used to be formerly. I see that serpent rising and putting forth its head, continually, everywhere, all around me.

Though it seems to me, that in some respects I was a far better Christian, for two or three years after my first conversion, than I am now, and lived in a more constant delight and pleasure; yet of late years, I have had a more full and constant sense of the absolute sovereignty of God, and a delight in that sovereignty; and have had more of a sense of the glory of Christ, as a mediator, as revealed in the gospel. On one Saturday night in particular, had a particular discovery of the excellency of the gospel of Christ, above all other doctrines; so that I could not but say to myself, "This is my chosen light, my chosen doctrine"; and of Christ, "This is my chosen prophet." It appeared to me to be sweet beyond all expression, to follow Christ, and to be taught and enlightened and instructed by him; to learn of him, and live to him.

Another Saturday night, January 1738/9, had such a sense, how sweet and blessed a thing it was, to walk in the way of duty, to do that which was right and meet to be done, and agreeable to the holy mind of God, that it caused me to break forth into a kind of a loud weeping, which held me some time; so that I was forced to shut myself up, and fasten the doors. I could not but as it were cry out, "How happy are they which do that which is right in the sight of God! They are blessed indeed, they are the happy ones!" I had at the same time a very affecting sense, how meet and suitable it was that God should govern the world, and order all things according to his own pleasure; and I rejoiced in it, that God reigned, and that his will was done.

EXCERPT FROM *A FAITHFUL NARRATIVE OF THE SURPRISING WORK OF GOD* (1737)

...But to give a clearer idea of the nature and manner of the operations of God's Spirit, in this wonderful effusion of it, I would give an account of two particular instances. The first is an adult person, a young woman whose name was Abigail Hutchinson. I pitch upon her especially because she is now dead, and so it may be more fit to speak freely of her than of living instances, though I am under far greater disadvantages, on other accounts, to give a full and clear narrative of her experiences, than I might of some others; nor can any account be given but what has been retained in the memories of her near friends, and some others, of what they have heard her express in her lifetime.

She was of a rational understanding family: there could be nothing in her education that tended to enthusiasm, but rather to the contrary extreme. 'Tis in no wise the temper of the family to be ostentatious of experiences, and it was far from being her temper. She was before her conversion, to the observation of her neighbors, of a sober and inoffensive conversation; and was a still, quiet, reserved person. She had long been infirm of body, but her infirmity had never been observed at all to incline her to be notional or fanciful, or to occasion anything of religious melancholy. She was under awakenings scarcely a week, before there seemed to be plain evidence of her being savingly converted.

She was first awakened in the winter season, on Monday, by something she heard her brother say of the necessity of being in good earnest in seeking regenerating grace, together with the news of the conversion of the young woman before mentioned, whose conversion so generally affected most of the young people here. This news wrought much upon her, and stirred up a spirit of envy in her towards this young woman, whom she thought very unworthy of being distinguished from others by such a mercy; but withal it engaged her in a firm resolution to do her utmost to obtain the same blessing; and considering with herself what course she should take, she thought that she had not a sufficient knowledge of the principles of religion to render her capable of conversion; whereupon she resolved thoroughly to search the Scriptures; and accordingly immediately began at the beginning of the Bible, intending to read it through. She continued thus till Thursday: and then there was a sudden alteration, by a great increase of her concern, in an extraordinary sense of her own sinfulness, particularly the sinfulness of her nature and wickedness of her heart, which came upon her (as she expressed it) as a flash of lightning, and struck her into an exceeding terror. Upon which she left off reading the Bible in course as she had begun, and turned to the New Testament, to see if she could not find some relief there for her distressed soul.

Her great terror, she said, was that she had sinned against God. Her distress grew more and more for three days; until (as she said) she saw nothing but blackness of darkness before her, and her very flesh trembled for fear of God's wrath: she wondered and was astonished at herself, that she had been so concerned for her body, and had applied so often to physicians to heal that, and had neglected her soul. Her sinfulness appeared with a very awful aspect to her, especially in three things, viz., her original sin, and her sin in murmuring at God's providence, in the weakness and afflictions she had been under, and in want of duty to parents, though others had looked upon her to excel in dutifulness. On Saturday, she was so earnestly engaged in reading the Bible and other books that she continued in it, searching for something to relieve her, till her eyes were so dim that she could not know the letters. Whilst she was thus engaged in reading, prayer, and other religious exercises, she thought of those words of Christ, wherein he warns us not to be as the heathen, that think they shall be heard for their much speaking [Matt 6:7]; which, she said, led her to see that she had trusted to her own prayers and religious performances, and now she was put to a non-plus, and knew not which way to turn herself, or where to seek relief.

While her mind was in this posture, her heart, she said, seemed to fly to the minister for refuge, hoping that he could give her some relief. She came the same day to her brother, with the countenance of a person in distress, expostulating with him, why he had not told her more of her sinfulness, and earnestly inquiring of him what she should do. She seemed that day to feel in herself an enmity against the Bible, which greatly affrighted her. Her sense of her own exceeding sinfulness continued increasing from Thursday till Monday; and she gave this account of it, that it had been an opinion, which till now she had entertained, that she was not guilty of Adam's sin, nor any way concerned in it, because she was not active in it; but that now she saw she was guilty of that sin, and all over defiled by it; and that the sin which she brought into the world with her was alone sufficient to condemn her.

On the Sabbath day she was so ill that her friends thought it not best that she should go to public worship, of which she seemed very desirous: but when she went to bed on the Sabbath-day night, she took up a resolution that she would the next morning go to the minister, hoping to find some relief there. As she awaked on Monday morning, a little before day, she wondered within herself at the easiness and calmness she felt in her mind, which was of that kind which she never felt before; as she thought of this, such words as these were in her mind: "The words of the Lord are pure words, health to the soul and marrow to the bones." And then these words came to her mind, "The blood of Christ cleanses [us] from all sin" [1 John 1:7]; which were accompanied with a lively sense of the excellency of Christ, and his sufficiency to satisfy for the sins of the whole world. She then thought of that expression, "'tis a pleasant thing for the eyes to behold the sun" [Eccl 11:7], which words then seemed to her to be very applicable to Jesus Christ. By these things her mind was led into such contemplations and views of Christ, as filled her exceeding full of joy. She told her brother in the morning that she had seen (i.e., in realizing views by faith) Christ the last night, and that she had really thought that she had not knowledge enough to be converted; "but," says she, "God can make it quite easy!" On Monday she felt all day a constant sweetness in her soul. She had a repetition of the same discoveries of Christ three mornings together that she had on Monday morning, and much in the same manner at each time, waking a little before day; but brighter and brighter every time.

At the last time on Wednesday morning, while in the enjoyment of a spiritual view of Christ's glory and fulness, her soul was filled with distress for Christless persons, to consider what a miserable condition they were in; and she felt in herself a strong inclination immediately to go forth to warn sinners; and proposed it the next day to her brother to assist her in going from house to house; but her brother restrained her, by telling her of the unsuitableness of such a method. She told one of her sisters that day that she loved all mankind, but especially the people of God. Her sister asked her why she loved all mankind. She replied because God had made them. After this, there happened to come into the shop where she was at work, three persons that were thought to have been lately converted; her seeing them as they stepped in one after another into the door so affected her, and so drew forth her love to them, that it overcame her, and she almost fainted: and when they began to talk of the things of religion, it was more than she could bear; they were obliged to cease on that account. It was a very frequent thing with her to be overcome with a flow of affection to them that she thought godly, in conversation with them, and sometimes only at the sight of them.

She had many extraordinary discoveries of the glory of God and Christ; sometimes, in some particular attributes, and sometimes in many. She gave an account that once, as those four words passed through her mind, *wisdom, justice, goodness,* and *truth,* her soul was filled with a sense of the glory of each of these divine attributes, but especially the last; "truth," said she, "sunk the deepest!" And therefore as these words passed, this was repeated, "Truth, truth!" Her mind was so swallowed up with a sense of the glory of God's truth and other perfections, that she said it seemed as though her life was going, and that she saw it was easy with God to take away her life by discoveries of himself. Soon after this she went to a private religious meeting, and her mind was full of a sense and view of the glory of God all the time; and when the exercise was ended, some asked her concerning what she had experienced, and she began to give them an account; but as she was relating it, it revived such a sense of the same things that her strength failed; and they were obliged to take her and lay her upon the bed. Afterwards she was greatly affected, and rejoiced with these words, "Worthy is the Lamb that was slain" [Rev 5:12].

She had several days together a sweet sense of the excellency and loveliness of Christ in his meekness, which disposed her continually to be repeating over these words, which were sweet to her: "meek and lowly in heart, meek and lowly in heart" [Matt 11:29]. She once expressed herself to one of her sisters to this purpose, that she had continued whole days and whole nights in a constant ravishing view of the glory of God and Christ, having enjoyed as much as her life could bear. Once as her brother was speaking of the dying love of Christ, she told him that she had such a sense of it that the mere mentioning it was ready to overcome her.

Once, when she came to me, she told how that at such and such a time she thought she saw as much of God, and had as much joy and pleasure as was possible in this life, and that yet afterwards God discovered himself yet far more abundantly, and she saw the same things that she had seen before, yet more clearly, and in another, and far more excellent and delightful manner, and was filled with a more exceeding sweetness; she likewise gave me such an account of the sense she once had, from day to day, of the glory of Christ, and of God in his various attributes, that it seemed to me she dwelt for days together in a kind of beatific vision of God; and seemed to have, as I thought, as immediate an intercourse with him as a child with a father: and at the same time, she appeared most remote from any high thought of herself and of her own sufficiency; but was like a little child, and expressed a great desire to be instructed, telling me that she longed very often to come to me for instruction, and wanted to live at my house that I might tell her her duty.

She often expressed a sense of the glory of God appearing in the trees, and growth of the fields, and other works of God's hands. She told her sister that lived near the heart of the town that she once thought it a pleasant thing to live in the middle of the town, but now, says she, "I think it much more pleasant to sit and see the wind blowing the trees, and to behold what God has made." She had sometimes the powerful breathings of the Spirit of God on her soul, while reading the Scripture, and would express a sense that she had of the certain truth and divinity thereof. She sometimes would appear with a pleasant smile on her countenance; and once when her sister took notice of it, and asked why she smiled, she replied, "I am brimful of a sweet feeling within!" She often used to express how good and sweet it was to lie low before God, and the lower (said she) the better; and that it was pleasant to think of lying in the dust all the days of her life, mourning for sin. She was wont to manifest a great sense of her own meanness and dependence. She often expressed an exceeding compassion and pitiful love, which she found in her heart towards persons in a Christless condition; which was sometimes so strong that as she was passing by such in the streets, or those that she feared were such, she would be overcome by the sight of them. She once said that she longed to have the whole world saved; she wanted, as it were, to pull them all to her; she could not bear to have one lost.

She had great longings to die, that she might be with Christ; which increased till she thought she did not know how to be patient to wait till God's time should come. But once when she felt those longings, she thought with herself, "If I long to die, why do I go to physicians?" Whence she concluded that her longings for death were not well regulated. After this she often put it to herself, which she should choose, whether to live or to die, to be sick, or to be well; and she found she could not tell, till at last she found herself disposed to say these words: "I am quite willing to live, and quite willing to die; quite willing to be sick, and quite willing to be well; and quite willing for anything that God will bring upon me! And then," said she, "I felt myself perfectly easy, in a full submission to the will of God." She then lamented much that she had been so eager in her longings for death, as it argued want of such a resignation to God as ought to be. She seemed henceforward to continue in this resigned frame till death.

After this her illness increased upon her; and once after she had before spent the greater part of the night in extreme pain, she waked out of a little sleep with these words in her heart and mouth: "I am willing to suffer for Christ's sake, I am willing to spend and be spent for Christ's sake; I am willing to spend my life, even my very life for Christ's sake!" [cf. 2 Cor 12:15]. And though she had an extraordinary resignation with respect to life or death, yet the thoughts of dying were exceeding sweet to her. At a time when her brother was reading in Job, concerning worms feeding on the dead body [Job 21:26; 24:20], she appeared with a pleasant smile; and being inquired of about it, she said it was sweet to her to think of her being in such circumstances. At another time, when her brother mentioned to her the danger there seemed to be that the illness she then labored under might be an occasion of her death, it filled her with joy that almost overcame her. At another time, when she met a company following a corpse to the grave, she said it was sweet to her to think that they would in a little time follow her in like manner.

Her illness in the latter part of it was seated much in her throat; and swelling inward, filled up the pipe so that she could swallow nothing but what was perfectly liquid, and but very little of that, and with great and long strugglings and stranglings, that which she took in flying out at her nostrils till she at last could swallow nothing at all. She had a raging appetite to food, so that she told her sister, when talking with her about her circumstances, that the worst bit that she threw to her swine would be sweet to her; but yet when she saw that she could not swallow it, she seemed to be as perfectly contented without it, as if she had no appetite to it. Others were greatly moved to see what she underwent, and were filled with admiration at her unexampled patience. At a time when she was striving in vain to get down a little food, something liquid, and was very much spent with it, she looked up on her sister with a smile, saying, "O Sister, this is for my good!" At another time, when her sister was speaking of what she underwent, she told her that she lived an heaven upon earth for all that. She used sometimes to say to her sister, under her extreme sufferings, "It is good to be so!" Her sister once asked her why she said so. "Why," says she, "because God would have it so: It is best that things should be as God would have 'em: it looks best to me." After her confinement, as they were leading her from the bed to the door, she seemed overcome by the sight of things abroad, as shewing forth the glory of the Being that had made them. As she lay on her deathbed, she would often say these words, "God is my friend!" And once looking up on her sister with a smile, said, "O Sister! How good it is! How sweet and comfortable it is to consider, and think of heavenly things!" And [she] used this argument to persuade her sister to be much in such meditations.

She expressed on her deathbed an exceeding longing, both for persons in a natural state, that they might be converted, and for the godly that they might see and know more of God. And when those that looked on themselves as in a Christless state came to see her, she would be greatly moved with compassionate affection. One in particular that seemed to be in great distress about the state of her soul, and had come to see her from time to time, she desired her sister to persuade not to come any more, because the sight of her so wrought on her compassions that it overcame her nature. The same week that she died, when she was in distressing circumstances as to her body, some of the neighbors that came to see her asked if she was willing to die. She replied that she was quite willing either to live or die; she was willing to be in pain; she was willing to be so always as she was then, if that was the will of God. She willed what God willed. They asked her whether she was willing to die that night. She answered, "Yes, if it be God's will." And [she] seemed to speak all with that perfect composure of spirit, and with such a cheerful and pleasant countenance that it filled them with admiration.

She was very weak a considerable time before she died, having pined away with famine and thirst, so that her flesh seemed to be dried upon her bones; and therefore could say but little, and manifested her mind very much by signs. She said she had matter enough to fill up all her time with talk, if she had but strength. A few days before her death, some asked her whether she held her integrity still, whether she was not afraid of death. She answered to this purpose, that she had not the least degree of fear of death. They asked her why she would be so confident. She answered, "If I should say otherwise, I should speak contrary to what I know: there is," says she, "indeed a dark entry, that looks something dark, but on the other side there appears such a bright shining light, that I cannot be afraid!" She said not long before she died that she used to be afraid how she should grapple with death; but, says she, "God has shewed me that he can make it easy in great pain." Several days before she died, she could scarcely say anything but just yes, and no, to questions that were asked her, for she seemed to be dying for three days together; but seemed to continue in an admirable sweet composure of soul, without any interruption, to the last, and died as a person that went to sleep, without any struggling, about noon, on Friday, June 27, 1735.

She had long been infirm, and often had been exercised with great pain; but she died chiefly of famine. It was, doubtless, partly owing to her bodily weakness that her nature was so often overcome, and ready to sink with gracious affection; but yet the truth was, that she had more grace, and greater discoveries of God and Christ, than the present frail state did well consist with. She wanted to be where strong grace might have more liberty, and be without the clog of a weak body; there she longed to be, and there she doubtless now is. She was looked upon amongst us, as a very eminent instance of Christian experience; but this is but a very broken and imperfect account I have given of her; her eminency would much more appear, if her experiences were fully related, as she was wont to express and manifest them, while living. I once read this account to some of her pious neighbors, who were acquainted with her, who said, to this purpose, that the picture fell much short of the life; and particularly that it much failed of duly representing her humility, and that admirable lowliness of heart, that at all times appeared in her. But there are (blessed be God!) many living instances of much the like nature, and in some things no less extraordinary....

EXCERPT FROM *AN ACCOUNT OF THE LIFE OF THE LATE REVEREND MR. DAVID BRAINERD* (1749)

An appendix containing some reflections and obser-
vations on the preceding memoirs of Mr. Brainer d.

...The foregoing account of Mr. Brainerd's life may afford matter of conviction that there is indeed such a thing as true experimental religion, arising from immediate divine influences, supernaturally enlightening and convincing the mind, and powerfully impressing, quickening, sanctifying, and governing the heart; which religion is indeed an amiable thing, of happy tendency, and of no hurtful consequence to human society; notwithstanding there having been so many pretences and appearances of what is called experimental vital religion, that have proved to be nothing but vain, pernicious enthusiasm.

If any insist that Mr. Brainerd's religion was enthusiasm, and nothing but a strange heat and blind fervor of mind, arising from the strong fancies and dreams of a notional, whimsical brain; I would ask if it be so that such things as these are the fruits of enthusiasm, viz., a great degree of honesty and simplicity, sincere and earnest desires and endeavors to know and do whatever is right, and to avoid everything that is wrong; a high degree of love to God, delight in the perfections of his nature, placing the happiness of life in him; not only in contemplating him, but in being active in pleasing and serving him; a firm and undoubting belief in the Messiah as the Savior of the world, the great prophet of God, and King of God's church; together with great love to him, delight and complacence in the way of salvation by him, and longing for the enlargement of his kingdom; earnest desires that God may be glorified and the Messiah's kingdom advanced, whatever instruments are made use of; uncommon resignation to the will of God, and that under vast trials; great and universal benevolence to mankind, reaching all sorts of persons without distinction, manifested in sweetness of speech and behavior, kind treatment, mercy, liberality, and earnest seeking the good of the souls and bodies of men; attended with extraordinary humility, meekness, forgiveness of injuries, and love to enemies; and a great abhorrence of a contrary spirit and practice; not only as appearing in others, but whereinsoever it had appeared in himself; causing the most bitter repentance and brokenness of heart on account of any past instances of such a conduct: a modest, discreet, and decent deportment among superiors, inferiors, and equals; a most diligent improvement of time, and earnest care to lose no part of it; great watchfulness against all sorts of sin, of heart, speech, and action: and this example and these endeavors attended with most happy fruits, and blessed effects on others, in humanizing, civilizing, and wonderfully reforming and transforming some of the most brutish savages, idle, immoral drunkards, murderers, gross idolaters, and wizards; bringing them to permanent sobriety, diligence, devotion, honesty, conscientiousness, and charity: and the foregoing amiable virtues and successful labors all ending at last in a marvelous peace, unmoveable stability, calmness, and resignation, in the sensible approaches of death; with longing for the heavenly state; not only for the honors and circumstantial advantages of it, but above all for the moral perfection and holy and blessed employments of it: and these things in a person indisputably of good understanding and judgment: I say, if all these things are the fruits of enthusiasm, why should not enthusiasm be thought a desirable and excellent thing? For what can true religion, what can the best philosophy, do more? If vapors and whimsy will bring men to the most thorough virtue, to the most benign and fruitful morality; and will maintain it through a course of life (attended with many trials) without affectation or self-exaltation, and with an earnest, constant, bearing testimony against the wildness, the extravagances, the bitter zeal, assuming behavior, and separating spirit of enthusiasts; and will do all this more effectually than anything else has ever done in any plain known instance that can be produced; if it be so, I say, what cause then has the world to prize and pray for this blessed whimsicalness, and these benign sort of vapors?

It would perhaps be a prejudice with some against the whole of Mr. Brainerd's religion, if it had begun in the time of the late religious commotion; being ready to conclude (however unreasonably) that nothing good could take its rise from those times. But it was not so; his conversion was before those times, in a time of general deadness (as has been before observed), and therefore at a season when it was impossible that he should receive a taint from any corrupt notions, examples, or customs that had birth in those times.

And whereas there are many who are not professed opposers of what is called experimental religion, who yet doubt of the reality of it, from the bad lives of some professors; and are ready to determine that there is nothing in all the talk about being "born again" [John 3:3, 1 Pet 1:23], being "emptied of self," "brought to a saving close with Christ," etc., because many that pretend to these things, and are thought by others to have been the subjects of 'em, manifest no abiding alteration in their moral disposition and behavior; are as careless, carnal, covetous, etc., as ever; yea, some much worse than ever: it is to be acknowledged and lamented that this is the case with some; but by the preceding account they may be sensible that it is not so with all. There are some indisputable instances of such a change as the Scripture speaks of; an abiding great change, a "renovation of the spirit of the mind" [Eph 4:23], and a "walking in newness of life" [Rom 6:4]. In the foregoing instance particularly, they may see the abiding influence of such a work of conversion as they have heard of from the word of God; the fruits of such experiences through a course of years; under a great variety of circumstances, many changes of state, place, and company; and may see the blessed issue and event of it in life and death....

THE SPIRITUAL ENJOYMENTS AND COMFORTS BELIEVERS HAVE THROUGH CHRIST ATTENDED WITH QUIETNESS AND REST OF SOUL (1738)[6]

Psalm 23:2
He maketh me to lie down in green pastures:
he leadeth me beside the still waters.

The relation that the Lord Jesus Christ bears to his church is often in Scripture represented by that of a shepherd to his flock, both in the Old Testament and New. So it is in Isaiah 40:11, "He shall feed his flock like a shepherd: he shall gather the lambs with his arm, and carry them in his bosom, and shall gently lead those that are with young." So Ezekiel 34:23, "I will set up one shepherd over them, even my servant David; he shall feed them and he shall be their shepherd." So it is in the fifteenth chapter of Luke, in the parable of the shepherd that had an hundred sheep, one of which went astray, and {he went after that which was lost, until he found it}. So it is in the tenth chapter of John, where Christ tells us he is the good shepherd who lays down his life for the sheep, and that he knows his sheep, and is known of them. And so in many other places that might be mentioned. And so it is in this psalm, wherein the Psalmist triumphs and glories in this, that the Lord is his shepherd.

Probably this psalm was written in the time of David's troubles by Saul's persecution, when he was driven away from among the people of Israel, like a sheep from the flock. [David] was not suffered to dwell in any of their cities, but was forced to wander about in the wilderness and mountains and desert places in an exiled state, like a lost sheep, and hunted about from place to place by Saul, as a poor wandering sheep is pursued by a greedy wolf, that thirsted for its blood. Saul, as he was set over the people of Israel as their king, ought to have been a shepherd to the people, to feed them in "the integrity of his heart, and guide them by the skillfulness of his hands" [Ps 78:72]. And so he should have been as a shepherd to David, as one of his good subjects, but instead of that, he was like a ravenous, wild beast, pursuing of him, and watching for his life.

But yet David in those circumstances, comforts himself in this, that the Lord was his shepherd, to take care of him, and to provide for him. And though he was in a state of banishment, driven into the wilderness, yet Christ would take care that he should not want.

He was hunted about, from mountain to hill, in a barren wilderness. For however the land of Canaan was a very fruitful and pleasant land, yet the deserts that were in the confines of that country were exceeding barren, covered over with dry sand and barren rocks, where there was no green grass, and few green things grow. Yet, though David was hunted in such a wilderness, yet he says God was his shepherd, [who] makes him to lie down in green pastures. Another thing observed of those deserts in the confines of the land of Canaan where David wandered, is that they were exceedingly dry and parched, without any springs or streams of water. Though David wandered like a lost sheep in such a wilderness, yet he says that God, being his shepherd, led him "beside the still waters."

And though David's life, if we behold only what was visible, seemed to be in the utmost danger, as much as the life of a poor wandering sheep in a lonely desert that was watched over by a greedy wolf; yet he triumphs in that, that Christ being his shepherd, he was not only full fed, as in green pastures, but he had safety there from anything that might mischief him, signified by the expression of "lying down in green pastures." Lying down to take rest, denotes the safety that he had under the care of his shepherd, who would certainly protect him from wolves and all his enemies. Hosea 2:18, "I will make them to lie down safely."

And though David, as he was pursued of Saul, seemed, as to what was visible, in a most disrested, disquieted condition, chased about from one desert to another, never suffered to be quiet anywhere, Saul like a wolf pursuing him wherever he came; yet here he speaks of rest and quietness he had under Christ his shepherd, that took care of him. He lay down, as a sheep in a green pasture, to take his quiet rest under the watchful eye of a faithful shepherd. And he was led beside still waters, which were not only plentiful and sufficient to quench his thirst, but calm and not rustled with winds and tempests, nor troubled and muddied with the feet of wild beasts, denoting the peace and quietness that attended those spiritual refreshments that he received from Christ his shepherd; and the purity of those enjoyments, as being unmired delights, not defiled and corrupted, nor spoiled with a mixture of trouble.

False shepherds are said to water their flock with waters that are troubled and fouled. Ezekiel 34:18–19, "Seemeth it a small thing unto you to have eaten up the good pasture, but ye must tread down with your feet the residue of your pastures? and to have drunk of the deep waters, but ye must foul the residue with your feet? And as for my flock, they eat that which ye have trodden with your feet; and they drink that which ye have fouled with your feet." But waters that ben't troubled and fouled with the feet of any, are represented as still waters, and are said "to run like oil." Ezekiel 32:2, "Son of man, take up a lamentation for Pharaoh king of Egypt, and say unto him, Thou art like a young lion of the nations, and thou art as a whale in the seas: and thou camest forth with thy rivers, and troubledst the waters with thy feet, and fouledst their rivers"; [vv.] 13–14, "I will destroy also all the beasts thereof from beside the great waters; neither shall the foot of man trouble them any more, nor the hoofs of beasts trouble them. Then will I make their waters deep, and cause their rivers to run like oil, saith the Lord God."

THE SPIRITUAL ENJOYMENTS AND COMFORTS BELIEVERS HAVE THROUGH CHRIST ARE ATTENDED WITH QUIETNESS AND REST OF SOUL

Doctrine

Two *Propositions*:

I. That those spiritual enjoyments and comforts that believers have, they have in and through Christ. And,

II. That those {spiritual enjoyments and comforts} are attended [with quietness and rest of soul].

Prop. I. {That those spiritual enjoyments and comforts that believers have, they have} in and through Christ. All the pasture that they have, is under their shepherd. He, and he only, is the great "shepherd and bishop of our souls," 1 Peter 2:25.

We are, all of us, naturally as lost sheep. Christ, in coming to save us, came to seek and save that which was lost. We were as sheep, wandering in a dry and parched wilderness, where there is no pasture nor any water to drink. There is no other shepherd that delivers those lost sheep out of this world, and provides for them. He only could do it. No other shepherd but this spiritual David was found strong enough to slay the lion and the bear, and to deliver the lamb out of their paws. He had compassion on them, when no other eye pitied them.

Believers have all their spiritual enjoyments through Christ, as 'tis he that has purchased them for them, by laying down his life for them, John 10:11. No other was found sufficient to stand between them and him. None other was found that had love enough to them when they saw the wolf coming; Christ himself [came] to endure the conflict with him, and expose himself to be torn by him, and go to save the sheep, as vv. 12–13 there following: "But he that is an hireling, and not the shepherd, whose own the sheep are not, seeth the wolf coming, and leaveth the sheep, and fleeth: and the wolf catcheth them, and scattereth the sheep. The hireling fleeth, because he is an hireling, and careth not for the sheep." This shepherd has purchased a good and pleasant land for his flock, and large and fat pastures, and a land flowing with pleasant refreshing waters, at a great price; he has paid a great and invaluable sum for it. No other was rich enough, and had anything precious enough, but he.

Believers have all their spiritual enjoyments through Christ, as he leads and directs them to them by his instructions, by the teachings of his word, and by his example, and by the inward teaching of his Holy Spirit. "He calleth his sheep, and leadeth them out. He goeth before them, and the sheep follow him: for they know his voice," John 10:3–4.

And they have spiritual enjoyments by Christ, as 'tis he that actually bestows them upon them. He not only purchases spiritual food for them, but 'tis he that spreads the table before them, and fills their cup, and gives them their spiritual meat and their drink. As in the fifth verse of the context: "Thou preparest a table before me in the presence of mine enemies: thou anointest mine head with oil; my cup runneth over."

And all their spiritual enjoyments, they have in communion and fellowship with him, or as partaking with him. As children sit with parents, and partake with them at their table; and as the disciples, from time to time, eat and drink with Christ.

Yea, Christ himself is the fountain as well as the author of their spiritual good things. He himself, in his spiritual excellencies, and in his love and favor, is as it were their food: his flesh is their meat, and his blood is their drink. He is the bread of life, which came down from heaven. And he is as it were their spiritual clothing: for they put on Christ, and he is their ornament, and armor and beautiful attire. He himself is as it were the shelter under which his sheep have rest and safety. He is their "hiding place from the wind, and covert from the tempest." And they are protected from the scorching heat of the sun, under the shadow of their great Rock. And 'tis he himself that is as a river of cool and still water in a dry place. Isaiah 32:2, "A man shall be an hiding place from the wind, and a covert from the tempest; as rivers of water in a dry place, as the shadow of a great rock in a weary land."

Prop. II. There is quietness and rest that attends those spiritual enjoyments and comforts that believers have through Christ. And therein, those spiritual comforts and good things that Christ bestows on them, do greatly differ from the enjoyments of the world, in [which] the soul can find no true rest. The souls of natural men, whatever outward enjoyments they have, "are like the troubled sea, when it cannot rest, whose waters cast up mire and dirt," Isaiah 57:20.

There is rest of soul to be had in those spiritual enjoyments that believers have through Christ, on the following accounts:

First. Because those spiritual enjoyments and comforts that are received through Christ are fully suited to the nature of the human soul. They indeed ben't suited to the nature of the soul as corrupt, but yet they are suited to the soul of man as human. They are adapted to the human nature as such, though not to corrupt nature.

The spiritual enjoyments that Christ bestows are suited to the nature of the soul of man, as 'tis a spiritual substance, and of an intelligent, rational nature. They are fitted to the noble faculties of the soul, though not to the lusts of the soul, that are contrary to its noble faculties.

God, who made the human nature, did not make it for the same kind of enjoyments with the brute creatures. As man in his principal part is a spirit, so he made him for those enjoyments that are suited to a spiritual nature. He who is the author of nature adapted the human nature of man to the end of man.

Worldly enjoyments ben't suited to man's nature. They are not fitted to answer the demands of a soul of such faculties, and therefore, let him be possessed of never so many of those things, the soul never will be fully at rest in them. No nature will rest in that which don't suit it. But because the spiritual enjoyments that Christ {possesses} are of such a nature as exactly answer the nature of man, therefore the soul of man rests in them. Having found those, it hath found what it needs; it finds its wants supplied.

Second. There is not only a suitableness of nature and quality, but a fullness in degree, to satisfy the utmost extent of our desire and capacity. Those enjoyments are such as afford that kind of comfort and pleasure that the soul of man needs, and not only [so], but to afford as much of that pleasure as the soul needs or can desire. There is [an] exceeding full fountain of good, a fountain that is inexhaustible, that may be compared to a boundless and bottomless ocean. There is enough purchased. The blessings that are purchased are, in some respects, infinite. That objective happiness that Christ has purchased for holiness is infinite, in that it consists in fellowship with, and the enjoyment of, the Father and of himself. Therefore, the soul that is brought to enjoyment of this fountain, rests satisfied in it, because here is enough; it needs no more, and can desire no more.

Man can't have true rest in temporal enjoyments, for they are not large enough to satisfy him. Ecclesiastes 5:10, "He that desires silver shall not be satisfied with silver; nor he that loveth abundance with increase: this is also vanity."

Because those things are limited, and not only [so], but the comfort and pleasure that is to be had in them, is confined within very strait limits. Here is but little room for the soul, to expatiate and expend itself.

Let there be as much of them as there will, the desires will go beyond 'em. The cravings of the soul of man are proportionable to his capacity, and his capacity is communicate with the extent of his thoughts and understanding. So great an enjoyment as man is capable to know of, and have any understanding of, so great he is capable of enjoying; and therefore his desires won't stop till such an enjoyment be obtained, and therefore the soul will be restless till then. But the spiritual enjoyments that believers have in the fountain of 'em is so great, that men's understanding and thoughts can't stretch themselves beyond it, nor ever can reach its limits, for it has no limits; and therefore, here the soul is at rest.

Third. A third reason why the soul finds rest in {these spiritual enjoyments and comforts} is because those comforts and delights are pure delight, without any polluting taints, or mixture of troubles. Those comforts and delights which natural men enjoy are unhallowed and polluted comforts; and so, though they please the corrupt appetite, yet they pollute the soul and debase it. They render the soul worse and more hateful, which must be a foundation of uneasiness and disquietude: for every nature will be distressed with that which militates against its proper perfection, so as to corrupt it and debase it. And though it may please a corrupt appetite, yet, as it is filthy and unholy, it is contrary to man's higher faculties, his understanding and conscience; which will surely make a war in the soul, and cause things to be in a tumult there. Hence what inward remorse and stings do accompany the sweetest pleasures that wicked men enjoy. They can have no rest, but only by clouding their reason, and stupefying and blinding their own mind.

But the enjoyment and comforts {that believers have through Christ}, being pure and holy comforts, there is rest, {there is} approbation, {there is} applause of reason and conscience. The more the understanding is enlightened, the more it applauds. The greater the light in the conscience, the more free from trouble.

The polluted enjoyments of natural men bring unquietness, as they bring shame before God, and before all wise and good spectators. But {the unpolluted enjoyments of Christ bring quietness}.

Thus the comforts that Christ {provides} are attended with rest of soul, as they are pure comforts in this sense, that they are holy delights.

And besides that, they are pure in this sense, that they bring no mixture of trouble, have no sting in them. The earth affords no pure sweets; the enjoyments of the world are all mixed and polluted; its streams are all troubled and muddy. If the enjoyments of the world bring comfort in one respect, they bring vexation in others, and not only trouble of conscience, but even worldly vexation. But those streams of water that Christ leads his flock by the side of are still, and not troubled waters; they are pure, and not muddy. The river that makes glad the city of God is a pure river of water of life, clear as crystal, having no debased or polluted mixture. Indeed, the ungodly have many troubles in the world, but those are not anything that belongs to those spiritual enjoyments that Christ has purchased, nor do they arise from that foundation. They ben't from Christ, but they are a way to sin and the world. Those spiritual enjoyments, so far as they are obtained, are pure, unmixed enjoyments; they have no sting in them, but are pure sweets, and therefore the soul finds rest in them. The sting and vexation that is in temporal enjoyments always disrests {the soul}; but those spiritual {enjoyments} have no such sting.

Fourth. A fourth reason why the soul finds rest in these spiritual enjoyments that are received through Christ is that they are sure enjoyments. There is no rest to be had in the enjoyments of this world, because of their exceeding uncertainty. There is no sure dependence upon them. The enjoyments of the world are no stable foundation to build any comfort upon, and therefore the building that stands on this foundation won't be at rest, for [it] will be tottering and shaking. Let a man have never so much of the enjoyments of the world, he is certain of nothing one day or hour; and how can a man have any rational, well-grounded rest of soul, in that which is so uncertain?

The fashion of this world passeth away, and all the enjoyments and glory of it, is like the surface of the water in Noah's flood, continually fluctuating and changing. And therefore the soul of man is like Noah's dove, who found no rest in the flood for the sole of her feet.

The instability of worldly enjoyments, tends to make the soul restless in them, three ways, viz.:

1. By fear of being deprived of them. For however sweet any enjoyment is to a man, he can't be at all secure of the enjoyment of it for any future time; so that the more he delights in it, the more is he liable to be disquieted with fear of being deprived of it.

2. By disappointment with respect to hope of future enjoyments. For as men have no security of those worldly enjoyments that they have, so they have no certainty of those that they hope for, and are often disappointed, which tends to disrest and vex the mind.

3. By grief for the loss of past enjoyments. The sweeter any temporal enjoyment has been, and the more pleasure it has afforded while it lasted, the more bitterness will it occasion when lost. And so uncertain and instable are worldly enjoyments that the soul that depends upon [them] is kept continually in a restless, continual fear of future evils; and cutting disappointments of hopes of future good and losses of past enjoyments continually sting and vex the soul, so that all is vanity and vexation of spirit.

But those spiritual {enjoyments and comforts that Christ supplies} are sure enjoyments. That comfort stands on a strong foundation. 'Tis built on Christ, the everlasting Rock. He that has them, need not be afraid of being deprived of them.

They need be afraid of no enemies, for he that defends them is mighty, and stronger than all their enemies. He is "the Lord strong and mighty, the Lord mighty in battle" [Ps 24:8]. He can defend his flock from all beasts of prey. They may lie down in their green pastures safely, and none need to make them afraid. "As the mountains are round about Jerusalem, so the Lord is round about his people from henceforth even for ever" [Ps 125:2]. They dwell in sure, quiet habitations, and sure resting places [Isa 32:18]. He that is in Christ "dwells on high: his place of defense shall be in the munitions of rocks: bread shall be given him; his waters shall be sure" [Isa 33:16]. The name of Christ "is his strong tower. He flees to it and is safe" [Prov 18:10]. He need not be afraid that those spiritual enjoyments that Christ has given shall be lost, for they are made sure by "an everlasting covenant, ordered in all things, and sure," 2 Samuel 23:5. And therefore, their enjoyments are called "the sure mercies of David," Isaiah 55:3. There is no possibility of them being finally lost; the foundation is an everlasting foundation. And when they find the sweetness of them, and are greatly delighted in them, they need not be disrested with fears that they shall at last be deprived of this sweetness, but may rest in God's faithful promises that it shall last to all eternity.

Application

[The] *Use* may be of *Exhortation* to all, to seek those spiritual enjoyments that believers receive through Jesus Christ. If it be so, let us not set our hearts on the enjoyments of this world, in which no rest is to be had for our souls; but let those spiritual enjoyments that we have heard of, be those that we choose, and set our hearts upon, and wholly give up ourselves to the pursuit of.

Let those who, from week to week, and from day to day, neglect Christ, and have their hearts taken up in an eagerness after the world, learn prudently to consult their own happiness by what has now been said. Why will ye spend your time and strength, and sin against God, and wrong your own souls, for that which can't afford you any rest? Hearken to the calls of Christ. Come to him for wine and milk, and eat that which is good, and let your soul delight itself in fatness, and take rest in soul-satisfying enjoyments. Come, and Christ will make an everlasting covenant with you, even the sure mercies of David.

Let those that are disrested in temporal enjoyments, that have met with losses of men and dear friends, or that have met with losses and crosses and disappointments in your outward estate and circumstances, and are involved in trouble and vexation by reason of one temporal calamity or another, come to Christ. Quit your expectations from the things of the world, and betake yourself to Christ as your shepherd, who will give you that which your soul may have rest in. And those that are heavy laden with sin, and are disrested with fears of eternal ruin, those that have long been concerned and exercised with some sense of the unsurety of a natural condition, come to Christ, and he will give you that which you may have rest in, Matthew 11:28.

And let those saints that are disrested with spiritual difficulties, darkness, and temptation, like David in a dry, barren wilderness, hunted about by the enemy of souls, from one mountain to another, and from one desert to another, let such persons be exhorted to come to Christ.

It may be you have been wandering from your shepherd: come to him, and he will make you to lie down in green pastures, and lead you beside still waters. He will give you sweet rest. He will spread a table for you in the {presence of your enemies}; he will make your cup to run over. If you come to Christ, he will bestow all manner of spiritual enjoyments, and you shall have rest of soul in all of them.

As particularly,

First. In Christ you shall have glorious objects for the eyes of your soul to behold, in which you shall find rest. You shall have glorious objects of your understanding and contemplation. The glory of God, and beauty of Christ, shall be the objects of your view. And the way of salvation by Christ will be like a green pasture for your soul to feed on; and the glorious gospel, with its various excellent doctrines and divine truths, shall be as a garden to your soul, set with a variety of pleasant plants, flowers and fruits that are ravishing to the eye. In the pleasure that you will have in beholding those lovely objects, your soul shall have sweet rest. Those objects are such as are suited to the faculty of human understanding, and worthy that it should be employed about them. The beauty and glory that is to be seen is sweet enough; you will never desire to see anything more beautiful.

Here is glory enough for you to employ your understanding about to all eternity, to see more and more without ever your getting beyond it, as to the limits of it. Here your eye may, as it were, rove; here your understanding may expatiate as much as it will, forever, and always find enough to fill it.

Those objects are beautiful, without any impurity or deformity, any spot or stain, to trouble the eye of the soul. Here your eye may dwell forever, and never find any blemish to be disturbed with.

Second. In Christ, you shall evince excellent ornaments in yourself, in the possession of which your soul shall have true quietness. You shall be made partakers of God's own image and likeness. Christ will take away sin and filthiness, and will purify you and sanctify you, and make you partakers of his own so excellent spirit and disposition. He will give the Christian spirit, which is a lovely spirit, a spirit of humility, of divine love, holy fear and reverence, holy trust and confidence; a heavenly spirit, a spirit of meekness, of submission, of patience and obedience; a spirit of brotherly kindness, which things are lovely in the sight of God.

And though none should make a righteousness of those, yet there is just reason that they should rejoice in them, and sweetly rest in them, as the gifts of God. They are holy qualifications, divine ornaments becoming the human nature, and its proper beauty and excellency.

And those that have anything of them shall evince them hereafter in perfection, when Christ shall have perfectly sanctified his church, and presented them to himself without spot, or wrinkle, or any such thing.

There is no rest of soul to be had in those external ornaments that {provide not quietness and rest}; but in such ornaments as these, may be possessed in true quietness and satisfaction.

Third. If you come to Christ, he will enable you to [possess] those holy exercises and fruits that will be attended with true peace and rest. [He will] give those outgoings of heart in love, in exercises of repentance, in fruits, doing good, walking in wisdom's way. You shall find pleasures and peace. In the keeping of God's commands is a great reward [Ps 19:11]: peace of conscience, [a] sense of God's favor and acceptance. Though no righteousness [is to be made of those], yet [there is] rest in 'em, as the gifts of God.

In love to the world, [in the] exercise of lust, [there is] no [peace and rest]. [In the] fruits of sin [there is] no [peace and rest].

Fourth. [If you come to Christ, you will find pleasures and peace] in that relative honor. [You will become] children of God, [and obtain an] interest in Christ's righteousness.

Fifth. [If you come to Christ, you will have] those pleasures of friendship and society, in which you shall find rest, [and] peace with God, having all your sins forgiven, that were a wall of separation between God and you. And you shall have the favor of God, and his fatherly love. And you shall have the sweet pleasures of a life of love to Christ, and friendship with him. He will manifest his love to you, as your friend. And you shall have spiritual society with him, in whom you shall have rest.

There is no true rest for the soul in those earthly friendships. There are innumerable things to disturb the comforts and pleasures of such friendship: [the] blemishes of friends, [the] weakness of love, faults in behavior, changeableness, selfishness, unfaithfulness; impotency and inability. Oftentimes, such friendships are the occasion of some of the greatest vexations of life.

And society with earthly friends has many things to disrest persons in it: disagreement in sentiments, indiscretions and follies. And at last, if the friends are dear, [there comes a] final separation by death.

Sixth. [If you come to Christ, you will have] that good hope of future blessings, in which you shall have rest.

Seventh. [Consider,] that as 'tis all of that glory, in which you shall have perfect and eternal rest, sit down in the kingdom of [God], eat and drink with Christ at his table in his kingdom. The rest in glory is represented by the same metaphor of a shepherd's feeding his flock, that is made use of in the text. As you may see in Revelation [7:17, "For the Lamb which is in the midst of the throne shall feed them, and shall lead them unto living fountains of waters: and God shall wipe away all tears from their eyes."]

[You will be] then perfectly free from all that did disquiet. [You will be free] from labors, rest perfectly satisfied, [and be] never disrested with fears of being deprived.

Part Two

Affections

INTRODUCTION
TO PART TWO

"True religion," Edwards famously wrote in *A Treatise Concerning Religious Affections*, "in great part, consists in holy affections." For him, "affections" involved the whole person, understanding and will, head and heart. The selections in this part illustrate the extent and depth of affectionate religious experience for Edwards.

A Treatise Concerning Religious Affections is a most appropriate place to start, since no consideration of Edwards's spirituality would be complete without something from it. It is a work that at once defends but also critiques revival phenomena, and is in many ways the culmination of Edwards's efforts, begun in youth, to distinguish the signs or marks of true as opposed to false conversion. In the first section of the treatise, he provides key definitions and considers the nature of the affections, including a series of features backed by ample scriptural proofs. Only the first part is presented here; in the subsequent parts, he provided lengthy considerations of series of both what can be called "inconclusive" and "more conclusive" signs of true religious affections.

A major theme in Edwards's preaching is "the pleasantness of religion." This involved much more than correcting misapprehensions that the religious life deprived one of gratification; rather, for Edwards, religion brought the soul to beauty, and thus to ultimate happiness. The sermon *Spiritual Appetites Need No Bounds* is his description of the joy that comes from indulging "gracious appetites." The leitmotif is the river of God's love and grace, a river that never runs out. Edwards uses the sensual language of Canticles—which he interprets, in keeping with a long exegetical tradition, as a love song between Christ and the church—to describe what he calls "the beauty of holiness." This lyrical sermon was composed in 1729 for a sacrament service, that is, when the Lord's Supper was celebrated, and speaks to the sacramental piety that flourished in Edwards's day. The text, with its call to eat and drink plentifully, suits Edwards's goals perfectly, and in his hands the text becomes a resplendent invitation to partake, not only of the elements of the sacrament but of the spiritual union that they represent.

As *Spiritual Appetites* illustrates, for Edwards as for many Puritans and their heirs, the Book of Canticles (or Song of Solomon) was a favorite biblical text because the sensual, even erotic language in which it was couched gave creative spiritual leeway. Yet another sermon by Edwards from Canticles, which extends the theme of "communion," is *The Saints Often Miss Sweet Communion with Christ*. Here, Edwards draws the lesson that "a little self-denial" can lead to "sweet communion" with Christ, but that saints, like the beloved, fail to act. Christ is ready to grant the saints communion with him because he has an exceeding love, a love of complacence, towards them; their souls, taken together as the church, are his spouse, and he invites them to be with him. But there are certain duties incumbent on the saints to achieve this communion. Christ does not need or benefit from these duties, but neither does he expect his spouse to be idle or passive.

The Portion of the Righteous, a sermon from 1735, considers in great detail, and in often effusive language, the "happiness of the saints," especially in the stages of the afterlife from death to after the day of judgment. This treatment of Romans 2:10 is especially distinguished for its description of the beatific (or, as Edwards put it, the "beatifical") vision, constituting Edwards's most complete and extended consideration of the topic. As Edwards asserts here, the happiness of the saints does start in this world. It consists in partaking in the excellency of God by bearing the divine image; in the honor of God by being children of God; and in the peace and pleasure of God by enjoying safety and spiritual riches, and the pleasures and joys of their good estate and of God's love: light, rest, life substance, holiness, and glory. But here the saints experience that happiness only partially. So Edwards turns to the happiness of the saints in death, in a "state of separation," at the resurrection and day of judgment, and after the day of judgment. First, death is "rendered no death to them" because, rather than a paroxysm, it becomes a "translation" to a glorious life. The "consummate state of happiness" comes after judgment, which begins with the saints' entrance into heaven, where they will be perfectly happy in the "whole man." This consummate state is characterized by the nature and degree of happiness: the glory of the place and of the saints' bodies, the beauty of their souls and their delight in one another. Here Edwards, in an aside, affirms that the inhabitants of heaven shall see and know loved ones and friends in a joyous reunion, and together they shall converse with one another and with Christ. Finally, they shall "see" God, that is, they shall participate in the beatific vision: in faculty, in the immediate and perfect nature or act of vision, in the Object (which excites and satisfies love), in the manner (communion with Christ), in the means (the Holy Ghost), and in the effects, which include their souls being enflamed with love and satisfied with pleasures, seeing the miseries of the damned, and fully enjoying the degree of glory that God has given them.

As in part 1, where profiles by Edwards of other individuals were instrumental in showing what he valued in spirituality, so here, we present two selections relating to his wife, Sarah Pierpont Edwards. The two probably first met while Edwards was a student at Yale College during the years 1716 to 1720. Sarah's father was the pastor of the First Church of New Haven, and the Pierpont home was on the other side of the town green from the college. The relationship between the two young people continued, and grew, while Jonathan was pursuing his graduate degree. Sometime during 1723, so family tradition has it, he composed a tribute, written on the flyleaf of a book (now lost), which was apparently for Sarah. Thus, the piece has come down to us as the "Apostrophe to Sarah Pierpont." It is a description of her intense, even ecstatic devotion, showing the appropriation of Quietist figures such as the French Catholics Mme. Jeanne Guyon and Bishop François Fénélon, who emphasized an annihilation of the self before God, and a complete lack of care for the things of the world, as a means of being "swallowed" up in, or achieving union with, the divine. Jonathan and Sarah married in 1727 and went on to have eleven children, but their marriage was, as

Jonathan himself described it, "a spiritual union," based on growth in Christian faith and experience.

During early 1742, the height of the Great Awakening, Sarah went through a period of extreme religious affections that included fainting, trance-like spells. When Jonathan took to writing *Some Thoughts Concerning the Revival*, published in 1743, one in a series of works defending the awakenings, he apparently asked Sarah to describe what had happened to her. He included her account in the treatise but made it gender-neutral. We have her first-person record as well, however, and that is what is presented here. But it is noteworthy that following Jonathan's presentation of the "the person's" relation in the published treatise, anticipating skepticism, he exclaimed, "Now if such things are enthusiasm, and the fruits of a distempered brain, let my brain be evermore possessed of that happy distemper!" Whether as a young student or as a wisened theologian of revival, he was still in awe of, even jealous of, his spouse's spiritual experiences.

EXCERPT FROM *A TREATISE CONCERNING RELIGIOUS AFFECTIONS* (1746)

Part I: Concerning the Nature of the Affections, and Their Importance in Religion

1 Peter 1:8
Whom having not seen, ye love: in whom, though now ye see him not, yet believing, ye rejoice with joy unspeakable, and full of glory

In these words, the Apostle represents the state of the minds of the Christians he wrote to, under the persecutions they were then the subjects of. These persecutions are what he has respect to, in the two preceding verses, when he speaks of the trial of their faith, and of their being in heaviness through manifold temptations.

Such trials are of threefold benefit to true religion: hereby the truth of it is manifested, and it appears to be indeed true religion:

they, above all other things, have a tendency to distinguish between true religion and false, and to cause the difference between them evidently to appear. Hence they are called by the name of trials, in the verse next preceding the text, and in innumerable other places: they try the faith and religion of professors, of what sort it is, as apparent gold is tried in the fire, and manifested, whether it be true gold or no. And the faith of true Christians being thus tried and proved to be true, is "found to praise, and honor, and glory," as in that preceding verse.

And then, these trials are of further benefit to true religion; they not only manifest the truth of it, but they make its genuine beauty and amiableness remarkably to appear. True virtue never appears so lovely as when it is most oppressed; and the divine excellency of real Christianity is never exhibited with such advantage, as when under the greatest trials: then it is that true faith appears much more precious than gold; and upon this account, is found to praise, and honor, and glory.

And again, another benefit that such trials are of to true religion is that they purify and increase it. They not only manifest it to be true, but also tend to refine it, and deliver it from those mixtures of that which is false, which encumber and impede it, that nothing may be left but that which is true. They tend to cause the amiableness of true religion to appear to the best advantage, as was before observed; and not only so, but they tend to increase its beauty, by establishing and confirming it, and making it more lively and vigorous, and purifying it from those things that obscured its luster and glory. As gold that is tried in the fire is purged from its alloy, and all remainders of dross, and comes forth more solid and beautiful; so true faith being tried as gold is tried in the fire, becomes more precious; and thus also is found unto praise, and honor, and glory. The Apostle seems to have respect to each of these benefits, that persecutions are of to true religion, in the verse preceding the text.

And in the text, the Apostle observes how true religion operated in the Christians he wrote to, under their persecutions, whereby these benefits of persecution appeared in them; or what manner of operation of true religion in them it was, whereby their religion, under persecution, was manifested to be *true* religion, and eminently appeared in the genuine beauty and amiableness of true religion, and also appeared to be increased and purified, and so was like to be found unto praise, and honor, and glory, at the appearing of Jesus Christ. And there were two kinds of operation, or exercise of true religion in them, under their sufferings, that the Apostle takes notice of in the text, wherein these benefits appeared.

1. *Love to Christ*; "Whom having not seen, ye love." The world was ready to wonder what strange principle it was that influenced them to expose themselves to so great sufferings, to forsake the things that were seen, and renounce all that was dear and pleasant, which was the object of sense: they seemed to the men of the world about them as though they were beside themselves, and to act as though they hated themselves; there was nothing in their view, that could induce them thus to suffer, and support them under, and carry them through such trials. But although there was nothing that was seen, nothing that the world saw, or that the Christians themselves ever saw with their bodily eyes, that thus influenced and supported 'em; yet they had a supernatural principle of love to something *unseen*; they loved Jesus Christ, for they saw him spiritually, whom the world saw not, and whom they themselves had never seen with bodily eyes.

2. *Joy in Christ*. Though their outward sufferings were very grievous, yet their inward spiritual joys were greater than their sufferings, and these supported them, and enabled them to suffer with cheerfulness.

There are two things which the Apostle takes notice of in the text concerning this joy. (1) The manner in which it rises, the way in which Christ, though unseen, is the foundation of it, viz., by faith; which is the evidence of things not seen; "In whom, though now ye see him not, yet believing, ye rejoice." (2) The nature of this joy; "unspeakable and full of glory." "Unspeakable" in the kind of it; very different from worldly joys, and carnal delights; of a vastly more pure, sublime, and heavenly nature, being something supernatural, and truly divine, and so ineffably excellent; the sublimity, and exquisite sweetness of which, there were no words to set forth. Unspeakable also in degree; it pleasing God to give 'em this holy joy, with a liberal hand, and in large measure, in their state of persecution.

Their joy was "full of glory": although the joy was unspeakable, and no words were sufficient to describe it; yet something might be said of it, and no words more fit to represent its excellency, than these, that it was "full of glory"; or, as it is in the original, "glorified joy." In rejoicing with this joy, their minds were filled, as it were, with a glorious brightness, and their natures exalted and perfected: it was a most worthy, noble rejoicing, that did not corrupt and debase the mind, as many carnal joys do; but did greatly beautify and dignify it: it was a prelibation of the joy of heaven, that raised their minds to a degree of heavenly blessedness: it filled their minds with the light of God's glory, and made 'em themselves to shine with some communication of that glory.

Hence the proposition or doctrine that I would raise from these words is this,

DOCTRINE. *True religion, in great part, consists in holy affections.*

We see that the Apostle, in observing and remarking the operations and exercises of religion, in the Christians he wrote to, wherein their religion appeared to be true and of the right kind, when it had its greatest trial of what sort it was, being tried by persecution as gold is tried in the fire, and when their religion not only proved true, but was most pure, and cleansed from its dross and mixtures of that which was not true, and when religion appeared in them most in its genuine excellency and native beauty, and was found to praise, and honor, and glory; he singles out the religious affections of love and joy, that were then in exercise in them: these are the exercises of religion he takes notice of, wherein their religion did thus appear true and pure, and in its proper glory.

Here I would,

I. Show what is intended by the affections,

II. Observe some things which make it evident, that a great part of true religion lies in the affections.

I. It may be inquired, what the affections of the mind are?

I answer, the affections are no other than the more vigorous and sensible exercises of the inclination and will of the soul.

God has indued the soul with two faculties: one is that by which it is capable of perception and speculation, or by which it discerns and views and judges of things; which is called the understanding. The other faculty is that by which the soul does not merely perceive and view things, but is some way inclined with respect to the things it views or considers; either is inclined to 'em, or is disinclined, and averse from 'em; or is the faculty by which the soul don't behold things, as an indifferent unaffected spectator, but either as liking or disliking, pleased or displeased, approving or rejecting. This faculty is called by various names: it is sometimes called the *inclination*; and, as it has respect to the actions that are determined and governed by it, is called the *will*; and the *mind*, with regard to the exercises of this faculty, is often called the *heart*.

The exercises of this faculty are of two sorts; either those by which the soul is carried out towards the things that are in view, in approving of them, being pleased with them, and inclined to them; or those in which the soul opposes the things that are in view, in disapproving them, and in being displeased with them, averse from them, and rejecting them.

And as the exercises of the inclination and will of the soul are various in their kinds, so they are much more various in their degrees. There are some exercises of pleasedness or displeasedness, inclination or disinclination, wherein the soul is carried but a little beyond a state of perfect indifference. And there are other degrees above this, wherein the approbation or dislike, pleasedness or aversion, are stronger; wherein we may rise higher and higher, till the soul comes to act vigorously and sensibly, and the actings of the soul are with that strength that (through the laws of the union which the Creator has fixed between soul and body) the motion of the blood and animal spirits begins to be sensibly altered; whence oftentimes arises some bodily sensation, especially about the heart and vitals, that are the fountain of the fluids of the body; from whence it comes to pass, that the mind, with regard to the exercises of this faculty, perhaps in all nations and ages, is called the *heart*. And it is to be noted, that they are these more vigorous and sensible exercises of this faculty, that are called the *affections*.

The will, and the affections of the soul, are not two faculties; the affections are not essentially distinct from the will, nor do they differ from the mere actings of the will and inclination of the soul, but only in the liveliness and sensibleness of exercise.

It must be confessed that language is here somewhat imperfect, and the meaning of words in a considerable measure loose and unfixed, and not precisely limited by custom, which governs the use of language. In some sense, the affection of the soul differs nothing at all from the will and inclination, and the will never is in any exercise any further than it is affected; it is not moved out of a state of perfect indifference, any otherwise than as it is affected one way or other, and acts nothing any further. But yet there are many actings of the will and inclination that are not so commonly called affections: in everything we do, wherein we act voluntarily, there is an exercise of the will and inclination, 'tis our inclination that governs us in our actions; but all the actings of the inclination and will, in our common actions of life, are not ordinarily called affections. Yet, what are commonly called affections are not essentially different from them, but only in the degree and manner of exercise. In every act of the will whatsoever, the soul either likes or dislikes, is either inclined or disinclined to what is in view; these are not essentially different from those affections of love and hatred: that liking or inclination of the soul to a thing, if it be in a high degree, and be vigorous and lively, is the very same thing with the affection of love; and that disliking and disinclining, if in a great degree, is the very same with hatred. In every act of the will for, or towards something not present, the soul is in some degree inclined to that thing; and that inclination, if in a considerable degree, is the very same with the affection of desire. And in every degree of the act of the will, wherein the soul approves of something present, there is a degree of pleasedness; and that pleasedness, if it be in a considerable degree, is the very same with the affection of joy or delight. And if the will disapproves of what is present, the soul is in some degree displeased, and if that displeasedness be great, 'tis the very same with the affection of grief or sorrow.

Such seems to be our nature, and such the laws of the union of soul and body, that there never is any case whatsoever, any lively and vigorous exercise of the will or inclination of the soul, without some effect upon the body, in some alteration of the motion of its fluids, and especially of the animal spirits. And on the other hand, from the same laws of the union of soul and body, the constitution of the body, and the motion of its fluids, may promote the exercise of the affections. But yet, it is not the body, but the mind only, that is the proper seat of the affections. The body of man is no more capable of being really the subject of love or hatred, joy or sorrow, fear or hope, than the body of a tree, or than the same body of man is capable of thinking and understanding. As 'tis the soul only that has ideas, so 'tis the soul only that is pleased or displeased with its ideas. As 'tis the soul only that thinks, so 'tis the soul only that loves or hates, rejoices or is grieved at what it thinks of. Nor are these motions of the animal spirits, and fluids of the body, anything properly belonging to the nature of the affections; though they always accompany them, in the present state; but are only effects or concomitants of the affections, that are entirely distinct from the affections themselves, and no way essential to them; so that an unbodied spirit may be as capable of love and hatred, joy or sorrow, hope or fear, or other affections, as one that is united to a body.

The *affections* and *passions* are frequently spoken of as the same; and yet, in the more common use of speech, there is in some respect a difference; and affection is a word that in its ordinary signification, seems to be something more extensive than passion, being used for all vigorous lively actings of the will or inclination; but passion for those that are more sudden, and whose effects on the animal spirits are more violent, and the mind more overpowered, and less in its own command.

As all the exercises of the inclination and will, are either in approving and liking, or disapproving and rejecting; so the affections are of two sorts: they are those by which the soul is carried out to what is in view, cleaving to it, or seeking it; or those by which it is averse from it, and opposes it.

Of the former sort are love, desire, hope, joy, gratitude, complacence. Of the latter kind, are hatred, fear, anger, grief, and such like, which it is needless now to stand particularly to define.

And there are some affections wherein there is a composition of each of the aforementioned kinds of actings of the will; as in the affection of pity, there is something of the former kind, towards the person suffering, and something of the latter, towards what he suffers. And so in zeal, there is in it high approbation of some person or thing, together with vigorous opposition to what is conceived to be contrary to it.

There are other mixed affections that might be also mentioned, but I hasten to the

II. Second thing proposed, which was to observe some things that render it evident, that true religion, in great part, consists in the affections. And here,

1. What has been said of the nature of the affections, makes this evident, and may be sufficient, without adding anything further, to put this matter out of doubt: for who will deny that true religion consists, in a great measure, in vigorous and lively actings of the inclination and will of the soul, or the fervent exercises of the heart.

That religion which God requires, and will accept, does not consist in weak, dull, and lifeless wouldings, raising us but a little above a state of indifference: God, in his word, greatly insists upon it, that we be in good earnest, fervent in spirit, and our hearts vigorously engaged in religion: Romans 12:11, "Be ye fervent in spirit, serving the Lord." Deuteronomy 10:12, "And now Israel, what doth the Lord thy God require of thee, but to fear the Lord thy God, to walk in all his ways, and to love him, and to serve the Lord thy God, with all thy heart, and with all thy soul?" And ch. 6:4–5, "Hear, O Israel; the Lord our God is one Lord; and thou shalt love the Lord thy God, with all thy heart, and with all thy soul, and with all thy might." 'Tis such a fervent, vigorous engagedness of the heart in religion, that is the fruit of a real circumcision of the heart, or true regeneration, and that has the promises of life; Deuteronomy 30:6, "And the Lord thy God will circumcise thine heart, and the heart of thy seed, to love the Lord thy God, with all thy heart, and with all thy soul, that thou mayest live."

If we ben't in good earnest in religion, and our wills and inclinations be not strongly exercised, we are nothing. The things of religion are so great, that there can be no suitableness in the exercises of our hearts, to their nature and importance, unless they be lively and powerful. In nothing is vigor in the actings of our inclinations so requisite as in religion; and in nothing is lukewarmness so odious. True religion is evermore a powerful thing; and the power of it appears, in the first place, in the inward exercises of it in the heart, where is the principal and original seat of it. Hence true religion is called the power of godliness, in distinction from the external appearances of it, that are the form of it, 2 Timothy 3:5, "Having a form of godliness, but denying the power of it." The Spirit of God in those that have sound and solid religion, is a spirit of powerful holy affection; and therefore, God is said to have given them the spirit "of power, and of love, and of a sound mind" (2 Tim 1:7). And such, when they receive the Spirit of God, in his sanctifying and saving influences, are said to be baptized with the Holy Ghost, and with fire; by reason of the power and fervor of those exercises the Spirit of God excites in their hearts, whereby their hearts, when grace is in exercise, may be said to burn within them, as is said of the disciples (Luke 24:32).

The business of religion is, from time to time, compared to those exercises, wherein men are wont to have their hearts and strength greatly exercised and engaged; such as running, wrestling or agonizing for a great prize or crown, and fighting with strong enemies that seek our lives, and warring as those that by violence take a city or kingdom.

And though true grace has various degrees, and there are some that are but babes in Christ, in whom the exercise of the inclination and will towards divine and heavenly things is comparatively weak; yet everyone that has the power of godliness in his heart, has his inclinations and heart exercised towards God and divine things, with such strength and vigor, that these holy exercises do prevail in him above all carnal or natural affections, and are effectual to overcome them: for every true disciple of Christ loves him above father or mother, wife and children, brethren and sisters, houses and lands; yea, than his own life. From hence it follows, that wherever true religion is, there are vigorous exercises of the inclination and will towards divine objects: but by what was said before, the vigorous, lively, and sensible exercises of the will are no other than the affections of the soul.

2. The Author of the human nature has not only given affections to men, but has made very much the spring of men's actions. As the affections do not only necessarily belong to the human nature, but are a very great part of it; so (inasmuch as by regeneration, persons are renewed in the whole man, and sanctified throughout) holy affections do not only necessarily belong to true religion, but are a very great part of that. And as true religion is of a practical nature, and God has so constituted the human nature, that the affections are very much the spring of men's actions, this also shows, that true religion must consist very much in the affections.

Such is man's nature, that he is very inactive, any otherwise than he is influenced by some affection, either love or hatred, desire, hope, fear, or some other. These affections we see to be the springs that set men a-going, in all the affairs of life, and engage them in all their pursuits: these are the things that put men forward, and carry 'em along, in all their worldly business; and especially are men excited and animated by these, in all affairs, wherein they are earnestly engaged, and which they pursue with vigor. We see the world of mankind to be exceedingly busy and active; and the affections of men are the springs of the motion: take away all love and hatred, all hope and fear, all anger, zeal, and affectionate desire, and the world would be, in a great measure, motionless and dead; there would be no such thing as activity amongst mankind, or any earnest pursuit whatsoever. 'Tis affection that engages the covetous man, and him that is greedy of worldly profits, in his pursuits; and it is by the affections that the ambitious man is put forward in his pursuit of worldly glory; and 'tis the affections also that actuate the voluptuous man, in his pursuit of pleasure and sensual delights: the world continues, from age to age, in a continual commotion and agitation, in a pursuit of these things; but take away all affection, and the spring of all this motion would be gone, and the motion itself would cease. And as in worldly things, worldly affections are very much the spring of men's motion and action; so in religious matters, the spring of their actions are very much religious affections: he that has doctrinal knowledge and speculation only, without affection, never is engaged in the business of religion.

3. Nothing is more manifest in fact, than that the things of religion take hold of men's souls, no further than they affect them. There are multitudes that often hear the Word of God, and therein hear of those things that are infinitely great and important, and that most nearly concern them, and all that is heard seems to be wholly ineffectual upon them, and to make no alteration in their disposition or behavior; and the reason is, they are not affected with what they hear. There are many that often hear of the glorious perfections of God, his almighty power, and boundless wisdom, his infinite majesty, and that holiness of God, by which he is of purer eyes than to behold evil, and cannot look on iniquity, and the heavens are not pure in his sight, and of God's infinite goodness and mercy, and hear of the great works of God's wisdom, power, and goodness, wherein there appear the admirable manifestations of these perfections; they hear particularly of the unspeakable love of God and Christ, and of the great things that Christ has done and suffered, and of the great things of another world, of eternal misery, in bearing the fierceness and wrath of almighty God, and of endless blessedness and glory in the presence of God, and the enjoyment of his dear love; they also hear the peremptory commands of God, and his gracious counsels and warnings, and the sweet invitation of the gospel; I say, they often hear these things, and yet remain as they were before, with no sensible alteration on them, either in heart or practice, because they are not affected with what they hear; and ever will be so till they are affected. I am bold to assert that there never was any considerable change wrought in the mind or conversation of any one person, by anything of a religious nature, that ever he read, heard, or saw, that had not his affections moved. Never was a natural man engaged earnestly to seek his salvation; never were any such brought to cry after wisdom, and lift up their voice for understanding, and to wrestle with God in prayer for mercy; and never was one humbled, and brought to the foot of God, from anything that ever he heard or imagined of his own unworthiness and deservings of God's displeasure; nor was ever one induced to fly for refuge unto Christ, while his heart remained unaffected. Nor was there ever a saint awakened out of a cold, lifeless frame, or recovered from a declining state in religion, and brought back from a lamentable departure from God, without having his heart affected. And in a word, there never was anything considerable brought to pass in the heart or life of any man living, by the things of religion, that had not his heart deeply affected by those things.

4. The Holy Scriptures do everywhere place religion very much in the affections: such as fear, hope, love, hatred, desire, joy, sorrow, gratitude, compassion, and zeal.

The Scriptures place much of religion in godly fear; insomuch that 'tis often spoken of as the character of those that are truly religious persons, that they tremble at God's word, that they fear before him, that their flesh trembles for fear of him, and that they are afraid of his judgments, that his excellency makes them afraid, and his dread falls upon them; and the like; and a compellation commonly given the saints in Scripture is fearers of God, or they that fear the Lord. And because the fear of God is a great part of true godliness, hence true godliness in general is very commonly called by the name of the fear of God, as everyone knows, that knows anything of the Bible.

So hope in God and in the promises of his word is often spoken of in the Scripture as a very considerable part of true religion. 'Tis mentioned as one of the three great things of which religion consists (1 Cor 13:13). Hope in the Lord is also frequently mentioned as the character of the saints: Psalm 146:5, "Happy is he that hath the God of Jacob for his help, whose hope is in the Lord his God." Jeremiah 17:7, "Blessed is the man that trusteth in the Lord, whose hope the Lord is." Psalm 31:24, "Be of good courage, and he shall strengthen your heart, all ye that hope in the Lord." And the like in many other places. Religious fear and hope are, once and again, joined together, as jointly constituting the character of the true saints. Psalm 33:18, "Behold the eye of the Lord is upon them that fear him, upon them that hope in his mercy." Psalm 147:11, "The Lord taketh pleasure in them that fear him, in those that hope in his mercy." Hope is so great a part of true religion that the Apostle says we are saved by hope (Romans 8:24). And this is spoken of as the helmet of the Christian soldier: 1 Thessalonians 5:8, "and for an helmet, the hope of salvation"; and the sure and steadfast anchor of the soul, which preserves it from being cast away by the storms of this evil world, Hebrews 6:19. "Which hope we have, as an anchor of the soul, both sure and steadfast, and which entereth into that within the veil." 'Tis spoken of as a great fruit and benefit which true saints receive by Christ's resurrection, 1 Peter 1:3. "Blessed be the God and Father of our Lord Jesus Christ, which according to his abundant mercy, hath begotten us again unto a lively hope, by the resurrection of Jesus Christ from the dead."

The Scriptures place religion very much in the affection of love, in love to God, and the Lord Jesus Christ, and love to the people of God, and to mankind. The texts in which this is manifest, both in the Old Testament, and New, are innumerable. But of this more afterwards.

The contrary affection of hatred also, as having sin for its object, is spoken of in Scripture as no inconsiderable part of true religion. It is spoken of as that by which true religion may be known and distinguished, Proverbs 8:13. "The fear of the Lord is to hate evil." And accordingly the saints are called upon to give evidence of their sincerity by this, Psalm 97:10, "Ye that fear the Lord hate evil." And the Psalmist often mentions it as an evidence of his sincerity, Psalm 101:2–3, "I will walk within my house with a perfect heart; I will set no wicked thing before mine eyes: I hate the work of them that turn aside." Psalm 119:104, "I hate every false way." So v. 128. Again, Psalm 139:21, "Do I not hate them, O Lord, that hate thee?"

So holy desire, exercised in longings, hungerings, and thirstings after God and holiness, is often mentioned in Scripture as an important part of true religion; Isaiah 26:8, "The desire of our soul is to thy name, and to the remembrance of thee." Psalm 27:4, "One thing have I desired of the Lord, and that will I seek after; that I may dwell in the house of the Lord, all the days of my life, to behold the beauty of the Lord, and to inquire in his temple." Psalm 42:1–2, "As the heart panteth after the water-brooks, so panteth my soul after thee, O God; my soul thirsteth for God, for the living God: when shall I come and appear before God?" Psalm 63:1–2, "My soul thirsteth for thee; my flesh longeth for thee, in a dry and thirsty land, where no water is, to see thy power and thy glory, so as I have seen thee in the sanctuary." Psalm 84:1–2, "How amiable are thy tabernacles, O Lord of hosts! My soul longeth, yea, even fainteth, for the courts of the Lord; my heart and my flesh crieth out for the living God." Psalm 119:20, "My soul breaketh for the longing it hath unto thy judgments, at all times." So Psalm 73:25 and 143:6–7 and 130:6, Canticles 3:1–2 and 6:8. Such a holy desire and thirst of soul is mentioned as one of those great things which renders or denotes a man truly blessed, in the beginning of Christ's Sermon on the Mount, Matthew 5:6. "Blessed are they that do hunger and thirst after righteousness, for they shall be filled." And this holy thirst is spoken of as a great thing in the condition of a participation of the blessings of eternal life, Revelation 21:6. "I will give unto him that is athirst, of the fountain of the water of life freely."

The Scriptures speak of holy *joy*, as a great part of true religion. So it is represented in the text. And as an important part of religion, it is often exhorted to, and pressed, with great earnestness; Psalm 37:4, "Delight thyself in the Lord, and he shall give thee the desires of thine heart."

Psalm 97:12, "Rejoice in the Lord, ye righteous." So Psalm 33:1, "Rejoice in the Lord, O ye righteous." Matthew 5:12, "Rejoice, and be exceeding glad." Philippians 3:1, "Finally brethren, rejoice in the Lord." And ch. 4:4, "Rejoice in the Lord alway, and again I say rejoice." 1 Thessalonians 5:16, "Rejoice evermore." Psalms 149:2, "Let Israel rejoice in him that made him; let the children of Zion be joyful in their King." This is mentioned among the principal fruits of the spirit of grace, Galatians 5:22. "The fruit of the spirit is love, joy," etc. The Psalmist mentions his holy joy, as an evidence of his sincerity, Psalm 119:14, "I have rejoiced in the way of thy testimonies, as much as in all riches."

Religious *sorrow, mourning,* and *brokenness of heart,* are also frequently spoken of as a great part of true religion. These things are often mentioned as distinguishing qualities of the true saints, and a great part of their character; Matthew 5:4, "Blessed are they that mourn; for they shall be comforted." Psalm 34:18, "The Lord is nigh unto them that are of a broken heart, and saveth such as be of a contrite spirit." Isaiah 61:1–2, "The Lord hath anointed me...to bind up the broken-hearted...to comfort all that mourn." This godly sorrow and brokenness of heart is often spoken of, not only as a great thing in the distinguishing character of the saints, but that in them, which is peculiarly acceptable and pleasing to God; Psalm 51:17, "The sacrifices of God are a broken spirit; a broken and a contrite heart, O

God, thou wilt not despise." Isaiah 57:15, "Thus saith the high and lofty One that inhabiteth eternity, whose name is Holy: I dwell in the high and holy place, with him also that is of a humble and contrite spirit, to revive the spirit of the humble, and to revive the heart of the contrite ones." Ch. 66:2, "To this man will I look, even to him that is poor, and of a contrite spirit."

Another affection often mentioned, as that in the exercise of which much of true religion appears, is *gratitude*, especially as exercised in thankfulness and praise to God. This being so much spoken of in the Book of Psalms and other parts of the Holy Scriptures, I need not mention particular texts.

Again, the Holy Scriptures do frequently speak of *compassion or mercy* as a very great and essential thing in true religion; insomuch that good men are in Scripture denominated from hence; and a merciful man, and a good man, are equivalent terms in Scripture; Isaiah 57:1, "The righteous perisheth, and no man layeth it to heart; and merciful men are taken away." And the Scripture chooses out this quality as that by which, in a peculiar manner, a righteous man is deciphered; Psalm 37:21, "The righteous showeth mercy, and giveth"; and v. 26, "He is ever merciful, and lendeth." And Proverbs 14:31, "He that honoreth the Lord, hath mercy on the poor." And Colossians 3:12, "Put ye on, as the elect of God, holy and beloved, bowels of mercies," etc. This is one of those great things by which those who are truly blessed are described by our Savior, Matthew 5:7. "Blessed are the merciful, for they shall obtain mercy." And this Christ also speaks of, as one of the weightier matters of the law, Matthew 23:23. "Woe unto you, scribes and Pharisees, hypocrites; for ye pay tithe of mint, and anise, and cummin, and have omitted the weightier matters of the law, judgment, mercy, and faith." To the like purpose is that, Micah 6:8, "He hath showed thee, O man, what is good: and what doth the Lord require of thee, but to do justice, and love mercy, and walk humbly with thy God?" And also that, Hosea 6:6, "For I desired mercy, and not sacrifice." Which seems to have been a text much delighted in by our Savior, by his manner of citing it once and again (Matthew 9:13 and Matthew 12:7).

Zeal is also spoken of as a very essential part of the religion of true saints. 'Tis spoken of as a great thing Christ had in view, in giving himself for our redemption; Titus 2:14, "Who gave himself for us, that he might redeem us from all iniquity, and purify unto himself a peculiar people, zealous of good works." And is spoken of as the great thing wanting in the lukewarm Laodiceans (Revelation 3:15–16, 19).

I have mentioned but a few texts, out of an innumerable multitude, all over the Scripture, which place religion very much in the affections. But what has been observed may be sufficient to show that they who would deny that much of true religion lies in the affections, and maintain the contrary, must throw away what we have been wont to own for our Bible, and get some other rule, by which to judge of the nature of religion.

5. The Scriptures do represent true religion as being summarily comprehended in *love*, the chief of the affections, and fountain of all other affections.

So our blessed Savior represents the matter in answer to the lawyer, who asked him which was the great commandment of the law. Matthew 22:37–40, "Jesus said unto him, Thou shalt love the Lord thy God, with all thy heart, and with all thy soul, and with all thy mind: this is the first, and great commandment; and the second is like unto it, Thou shalt love thy neighbor as thyself. On these two commandments hang all the Law and the Prophets." Which last words signify as much, as that these two commandments comprehend all the duty prescribed, and the religion taught in the Law and the Prophets. And the Apostle Paul does from time to time make the same representation of the matter; as in Romans 13:8, "He that loveth another, hath fulfilled the law." And v. 10: "Love is the fulfilling of the law." And Galatians 5:14, "For all the law is fulfilled in one word, even in this, thou shalt love thy neighbor as thyself." So likewise in 1 Timothy 1:5, "Now the end of the commandment is charity, out of a pure heart," etc. So the same Apostle speaks of love as the greatest thing in religion, and as the vitals, essence, and soul of it; without which, the greatest knowledge and gifts, and the most glaring profession, and everything else which appertains to religion, are vain and worthless; and represents it as the fountain from whence proceeds all that is good, in 1 Corinthians 13 throughout; for that which is there rendered "charity," in the original is αγαπη, the proper English of which is "love."

Now although it be true that the love thus spoken of includes the whole of a sincerely benevolent propensity of the soul, towards God and man; yet it may be considered that it is evident from what has been before observed, that this propensity or inclination of the soul, when in sensible and vigorous exercise, becomes *affection*, and is no other than affectionate love. And surely it is such vigorous and fervent love which Christ speaks of, as the sum of all religion, when he speaks of loving God with all our hearts, with all our souls, and with all our minds, and our neighbor as ourselves, as the sum of all that was taught and prescribed in the Law and the Prophets.

Indeed it cannot be supposed when this affection of love is here, and in other Scriptures, spoken of as the sum of all religion, that hereby is meant the act, exclusive of the habit, or that the exercise of the understanding is excluded, which is implied in all reasonable affection. But it is doubtless true, and evident from these Scriptures, that the essence of all true religion lies in holy love; and that in this divine affection, and an habitual disposition to it, and that light which is the foundation of it, and those things which are the fruits of it, consists the whole of religion.

From hence it clearly and certainly appears that great part of true religion consists in the affections. For love is not only one of the affections, but it is the first and chief of the affections, and the fountain of all the affections. From love arises hatred of those things which are contrary to what we love, or which oppose and thwart us in those things that we delight in: and from the various exercises of love and hatred, according to the circumstances of the objects of these affections, as present or absent, certain or uncertain, probable or improbable, arise all those other affections of desire, hope, fear, joy, grief, gratitude, anger, etc. From a vigorous, affectionate, and fervent love to God will necessarily arise other religious affections: hence will arise an intense hatred and abhorrence of sin, fear of sin, and a dread of God's displeasure, gratitude to God for his goodness, complacence and joy in God when God is graciously and sensibly present, and grief when he is absent, and a joyful hope when a future enjoyment of God is expected, and fervent zeal for the glory of God. And in like manner, from a fervent love to men, will arise all other virtuous affections towards men.

6. The religion of the most eminent saints we have an account of in the Scripture consisted much in holy affections.

I shall take particular notice of three eminent saints, which have expressed the frame and sentiments of their own hearts, and so described their own religion, and the manner of their intercourse with God, in the writings which they have left us, that are a part of the sacred canon.

The first instance I shall take notice of is David, that man after God's own heart; who has given us a lively portraiture of his religion, in the Book of Psalms. Those holy songs of his, he has there left us, are nothing else but the expressions and breathings of devout and holy affections; such as a humble and fervent love to God, admiration of his glorious perfections and wonderful works, earnest desires, thirstings and pantings of soul after God, delight and joy in God, a sweet and melting gratitude to God for his great goodness, an holy exultation and triumph of soul in the favor, sufficiency, and faithfulness of God, his love to, and delight in the saints, the excellent of the earth, his great delight in the word and ordinances of God, his grief for his own and others' sins, and his fervent zeal for God, and against the enemies of God and his church. And these expressions of holy affection, which the Psalms of David are everywhere full of, are the more to our present purpose, because those Psalms are not only the expressions of the religion of so eminent a saint, that God speaks of as so agreeable to his mind; but were also, by the direction of the Holy Ghost, penned for the use of the church of God in its public worship, not only in that age, but in after-ages; as being fitted to express the religion of all saints, in all ages, as well as the religion of the Psalmist. And it is moreover to be observed, that David, in the Book of Psalms, speaks not as a private person, but as the Psalmist of Israel, as the subordinate head of the church of God, and leader in their worship and praises; and in many of the psalms, speaks in the name of Christ, as personating him in these breathings forth of holy affection, and in many other psalms, he speaks in the name of the church.

Another instance I shall observe is the Apostle Paul, who was, in many respects, the chief of all the ministers of the New Testament; being above all others, a chosen vessel unto Christ, to bear his name before the Gentiles, and made the chief instrument of propagating and establishing the Christian church in the world, and of distinctly revealing the glorious mysteries of the gospel, for the instruction of the church in all ages; and (as has not been improbably thought by some) the most eminent servant of Christ that ever lived, received to the highest rewards in the heavenly kingdom of his Master. By what is said of him in the Scripture, he appears to have been a person that was full of affection. And 'tis very manifest, that the religion he expresses in his epistles consisted very much in holy affections. It appears by all his expressions of himself that he was, in the course of his life, inflamed, actuated, and entirely swallowed up, by a most ardent love to his glorious Lord, esteeming all things as loss, for the excellency of the knowledge of him, and esteeming them but dung that he might win him. He represents himself, as overpowered by this holy affection, and as it were compelled by it to go forward in his service, through all difficulties and sufferings (2 Cor 5:14–15). And his epistles are full of expressions of an overflowing affection towards the people of Christ: he speaks of his dear love to them, 2 Corinthians 12:19, Philippians 4:1, 2 Timothy 1:2. Of his abundant love, 2 Corinthians 2:4. And of his affectionate and tender love, as of a nurse towards her children, 1 Thessalonians 2:7–8. "But we were gentle among you; even as a nurse cherisheth her children; so being affectionately desirous of you, we were willing to have imparted unto you, not the gospel of God only, but also our own souls, because ye were dear unto us." So also he speaks of his bowels of love (Philippians 1:8, Philemon 1:12 and 20). So he speaks of his earnest care for others, 2 Corinthians 8:16, and of his bowels of pity or mercy towards them, Philippians 2:1, and of his concern for others, even to anguish of heart, 2 Corinthians 2:4. "For out of much affliction, and anguish of heart, I wrote unto you, with many tears; not that ye should be grieved; but that ye might know the love which I have more abundantly unto you." He speaks of the great conflict of his soul for them (Colossians 2:1). He speaks of great and continual grief that he had in his heart from compassion to the Jews (Romans 9:2). He speaks of his mouth's being opened, and his heart enlarged towards Christians, 2 Corinthians 6:11. "O ye Corinthians, our mouth is open unto you, our heart is enlarged!" He often speaks of his affectionate and longing desires (1 Thessalonians 2:8, Romans 1:11, Philippians 1:8 and ch. 4:1, 2 Timothy 1:4). The same Apostle is very often, in his epistles, expressing the affection of joy (2 Corinthians 1:12, and ch. 7:7 and v. 9 and 16; Philippians 1:4, and ch. 2:1–2, and ch. 3:3; Colossians 1:24; 1 Thessalonians 3:9). He speaks of his rejoicing with great joy (Philippians 4:10, Philemon 1:7), of his joying and rejoicing (Philippians 2:1, 2:7), and of his rejoicing exceedingly (2 Corinthians 7:13). And of his being filled with comfort, and being exceeding joyful (2 Corinthians 7:4). He speaks of himself as always rejoicing (2 Corinthians 6:10). So he speaks of the triumphs of his soul (2 Corinthians 2:14). And of his glorying in tribulation (2 Thessalonians 1:4 and Romans 5:3). He also expresses the affection of hope; in Philippians 1:20, he speaks of his earnest expectation, and his hope. He likewise expresses an affection of godly jealousy (2 Corinthians 11:2–3). And it appears by his whole history, after his conversion, in the Acts, and also by all his epistles, and the accounts he gives of himself there, that the affection of zeal, as having the cause of his Master, and the interest and prosperity of his church, for its object, was mighty in him, continually inflaming his heart, strongly engaging to those great and constant labors he went through, in instructing, exhorting, warning, and reproving others, travailing in birth with them; conflicting with those powerful and innumerable enemies who continually opposed him, wrestling with principalities and powers, not fighting as one who beats the air, running the race set before him, continually pressing forward through all manner of difficulties and sufferings; so that others thought him quite beside himself. And how full he was of affection does further appear by his being so full of tears: in 2 Corinthians 2:4 he speaks of his many tears, and so Acts 20:19. And of his tears that he shed continually, night and day, v. 31.

Now if anyone can consider these accounts given in the Scripture of this great apostle, and which he gives of himself, and yet not see that his religion consisted much in affection, must have a strange faculty of managing his eyes, to shut out the light which shines most full in his face.

The other instance I shall mention is of the apostle John, that beloved disciple, who was the nearest and dearest to his Master of any of the Twelve, and was by him admitted to the greatest privileges of any of them: being not only one of the three who were admitted to be present with him in the mount at his transfiguration, and at the raising of Jairus's daughter, and whom he took with him when he was in his agony, and one of the three spoken of by the Apostle Paul, as the three main pillars of the Christian church; but was favored above all, in being admitted to lean on his Master's bosom, at his Last Supper, and in being chosen by Christ as the disciple to whom he would reveal his wonderful dispensations towards his church, to the end of time; as we have an account in the Book of Revelation: and to shut up the canon of the New Testament, and of the whole Scripture; being preserved much longer than all the rest of the apostles, to set all things in order in the Christian church, after their death.

It is evident by all his writings (as is generally observed by divines), that he was a person remarkably full of affection: his addresses to those whom he wrote to, being inexpressibly tender and pathetical, breathing nothing but the most fervent love, as though he were all made up of sweet and holy affection. The proofs of which can't be given without disadvantage, unless we should transcribe his whole writings.

7. He whom God sent into the world, to be the light of the world, and head of the whole church, and the perfect example of true religion and virtue, for the imitation of all, the shepherd whom the whole flock should follow wherever he goes, even the Lord Jesus Christ, was a person who was remarkably of a tender and affectionate heart; and his virtue was expressed very much in the exercise of holy affections. He was the greatest instance of ardency, vigor, and strength of love, to both God and man, that ever was. It was these affections which got the victory, in that mighty struggle and conflict of his affections, in his agonies, when he prayed more earnestly, and offered strong crying and tears, and wrestled in tears and in blood. Such was the power of the exercises of his holy love, that they were stronger than death, and in that great struggle, overcame those strong exercises of the natural affections of fear and grief, when he was sore amazed, and his soul was exceeding sorrowful, even unto death. And he also appeared to be full of affection in the course of his life. We read of his great zeal, fulfilling that in the sixty-ninth Psalm: "The

zeal of thine house hath eaten me up" (John 2:17). We read of his grief for the sins of men, Mark 3:5. "He looked round about on them with anger, being grieved for the hardness of their hearts." And his breaking forth in tears and exclamations, from the consideration of the sin and misery of ungodly men, and on the sight of the city of Jerusalem, which was full of such inhabitants, Luke 19:41–42. "And when he was come near, he beheld the city, and wept over it, saying, If thou hadst known, even thou at least in this thy day, the things which belong unto thy peace! but now they are hid from thine eyes." With ch. 13:34, "O Jerusalem, Jerusalem, which killeth the prophets, and stonest them that are sent unto thee, how often would I have gathered thy children together, as a hen doth gather her brood under her wings, and ye would not!" We read of Christ's earnest desire, Luke 22:15. "With desire have I desired to eat this passover with you, before I suffer." We often read of the affection of pity or compassion in Christ (Matthew 15:32 and 18:34, Luke 7:13), and of his being moved with compassion (Matthew 9:36 and 14:14 and Mark 6:34). And how tender did his heart appear to be, on occasion of Mary's and Martha's mourning for their brother, and coming to him with their complaints and tears; their tears soon drew tears from his eyes: he was affected with their grief, and wept with them, though he knew their sorrow should so soon be turned into joy, by their brother's being raised from the dead; see John 11. And how ineffably affectionate was that last and dying discourse which Jesus had with his eleven disciples the evening before he was crucified, when he told them he was going away, and foretold them the great difficulties and sufferings they should meet with in the world, when he was gone; and comforted and counseled 'em, as his dear little children, and bequeathed to them his Holy Spirit, and therein his peace, and his comfort and joy, as it were in his last will and testament, in the thirteenth, fourteenth, fifteenth, and sixteenth chapters of John; and concluded the whole with that affectionate intercessory prayer for them, and his whole church, in John 17. Of all the discourses ever penned, or uttered by the mouth of any man, this seems to be the most affectionate, and affecting.

8. The religion of heaven consists very much in *affection*.

There is doubtless true religion in heaven, and true religion in its utmost purity and perfection. But according to the Scripture representation of the heavenly state, the religion of heaven consists chiefly in holy and mighty love and joy, and the expression of these in most fervent and exalted praises. So that the religion of the saints in heaven consists in the same things with that religion of the saints on earth, which is spoken of in our text, viz., love, and joy unspeakable, and full of glory. Now it would be very foolish to pretend that because the saints in heaven be not united to flesh and blood, and have no animal fluids to be moved (through the laws of union of soul and body), with those great emotions of their soul, that therefore their exceeding love and joy are no affections. We are not speaking of the affections of the body, but of the affections of the soul, the chief of which are love and joy. When these are in the soul, whether that be in the body or out of it, the soul is affected and moved. And when they are in the soul, in that strength in which they are in the saints in heaven, the soul is mightily affected and moved, or, which is the same thing, has great affections. 'Tis true, we don't experimentally know what love and joy are in a soul out of a body, or in a glorified body; i.e., we have not had experience of love and joy in a soul in these circumstances; but the saints on earth do know what divine love and joy in the soul are, and they know what love and joy are of the same kind, with the love and joy which are in heaven, in separate souls there. The love and joy of the saints on earth is the beginning and dawning of the light, life, and blessedness of heaven, and is like their love and joy there; or rather, the same in nature, though not the same with it, or like to it, in degree and circumstances. This is evident by many Scriptures, as Proverbs 4:18; John 4:14 and ch. 6:40, 47, 50–51, 54, 58; 1 John 3:15; 1 Corinthians 13:8–12. 'Tis unreasonable therefore to suppose that the love and joy of the saints in heaven not only differ in degree and circumstances from the holy love and joy of the saints on earth, but is so entirely different in nature, that they are no affections; and merely because they have no blood and animal spirits to be set in motion by them, which motion of the blood and animal spirits is not of the essence of these affections, in men on the earth, but the effect of them; although by their reaction they may make some circumstantial difference in the sensation of the mind. There is a sensation of the mind which loves and rejoices, that is antecedent to any effects on the fluids of the body; and this sensation of the mind therefore don't depend on these motions in the body, and so may be in the soul without the body. And wherever there are the exercises of love and joy, there is that sensation of the mind, whether it be in the body, or out; and that inward sensation, or kind of spiritual sense, or feeling, and motion of the soul, is what is called affection; the soul when it thus feels (if I may so say), and is thus moved, is said to be affected, and especially when this inward sensation and motion, are to a very high degree, as they are in the saints in heaven. If we can learn anything of the state of heaven from the Scripture, the love and joy that the saints have there, is exceeding great and vigorous; impressing the heart with the strongest and most lively sensation, of inexpressible sweetness, mightily moving, animating, and engaging them, making them like to a flame of fire. And if such love and joy be not affections, then the word *affection* is of no use in language. Will any say that the saints in heaven, in beholding the face of their Father, and the glory of their Redeemer, and contemplating his wonderful works, and particularly his laying down his life for them, have their hearts nothing moved and affected, by all which they behold or consider?

Hence therefore the religion of heaven, consisting chiefly in holy love and joy, consists very much in affection: and therefore undoubtedly, true religion consists very much in affection. The way to learn the true nature of anything is to go where that thing is to be found in its purity and perfection. If we would know the nature of true gold, we must view it, not in the ore, but when it is refined. If we would learn what true religion is, we must go where there is true religion, and nothing but true religion, and in its highest perfection, without any defect or mixture. All who are truly religious are not of this world, they are strangers here, and belong to heaven; they are born from above, heaven is their native country, and the nature which they receive by this heavenly birth is an heavenly nature, they receive an anointing from above; that principle of true religion which is in them is a communication of the religion of heaven; their grace is the dawn of glory; and God fits them for that world by conforming them to it.

9. This appears from the nature and design of the ordinances and duties which God hath appointed, as means and expressions of true religion.

To instance in the duty of prayer: 'tis manifest, we are not appointed, in this duty, to declare God's perfections, his majesty, holiness, goodness, and all-sufficiency, and our own meanness, emptiness, dependence, and unworthiness, and our wants and desires, to inform God of these things, or to incline his heart, and prevail with him to be willing to show us mercy; but suitably to affect our own hearts with the things we express, and so to prepare us to receive the blessings we ask. And such gestures, and manner of external behavior in the worship of God, which custom has made to be significations of humility and reverence, can be of no further use than as they have some tendency to affect our own hearts, or the hearts of others.

And the duty of singing praises to God seems to be appointed wholly to excite and express religious affections. No other reason can be assigned why we should express ourselves to God in verse, rather than in prose, and do it with music, but only that such is our nature and frame, that these things have a tendency to move our affections.

The same thing appears in the nature and design of the sacraments, which God hath appointed. God, considering our frame, hath not only appointed that we should be told of the great things of the gospel, and of the redemption of Christ, and instructed in them by his word; but also that they should be, as it were, exhibited to our view, in sensible representations, in the sacraments, the more to affect us with them.

And the impressing divine things on the hearts and affections of men is evidently one great and main end for which God has ordained that his word delivered in the Holy Scriptures should be opened, applied, and set home upon men, in preaching. And therefore it don't answer the aim which God had in this institution merely for men to have good commentaries and expositions on the Scripture, and other good books of divinity; because, although these may tend, as well as preaching, to give men a good doctrinal or speculative understanding of the things of the Word of God, yet they have not an equal tendency to impress them on men's hearts and affections. God hath appointed a particular and lively application of his word, to men, in the preaching of it, as a fit means to affect sinners, with the importance of the things of religion, and their own misery, and necessity of a remedy, and the glory and sufficiency of a remedy provided; and to stir up the pure minds of the saints, and quicken their affections, by often bringing the great things of religion to their remembrance, and setting them before them in their proper colors, though they know them, and have been fully instructed in them already (2 Pet 1:12–13). And particularly, to promote those two affections in them which are spoken of in the text, love and joy: Christ "gave some, apostles, and some, prophets; and some, evangelists; and some, pastors and teachers, that the body of Christ might be edified in love" (Ephesians 4:11–12, 16). The Apostle, in instructing and counseling Timothy, concerning the work of the ministry, informs him that the great end of that word which a minister is to preach, is *love or charity* (1 Timothy 1:3–5). And another affection which God has appointed preaching as a means to promote in the saints is *joy*; and therefore ministers are called helpers of their joy (2 Corinthians 1:24).

10. 'Tis an evidence that true religion, or holiness of heart, lies very much in the affection of the heart, that the Scriptures place the sin of the heart very much in hardness of heart. Thus the Scriptures do everywhere. It was hardness of heart which excited grief and displeasure in Christ towards the Jews, Mark 3:5. "He looked round about on them with anger, being grieved for the hardness of their hearts." It is from men's having such a heart as this, that they treasure up wrath for themselves. Romans 2:5, "After thy hardness and impenitent heart, treasurest up unto thy self wrath, against the day of wrath, and revelation of the righteous judgment of God." The reason given why the house of Israel would not obey God was that they were hardhearted. Ezekiel 3:7, "But the house of Israel will not hearken unto thee; for they will not hearken unto me: for all the house of Israel are impudent and hard-hearted." The wickedness of that perverse rebellious generation in the wilderness is ascribed to the hardness of their hearts; Psalm 95:7–10, "Today, if ye will hear my voice, harden not your heart, as in the provocation, and as in the day of temptation in the wilderness; when your fathers tempted me, proved me, and saw my work: forty years long was I grieved with this generation, and said it is a people that do err in their heart," etc. This is spoken of as to what prevented Zedekiah's turning to the Lord, 2 Chronicles 36:13. "He stiffened his neck, and hardened his heart, from turning to the Lord God of Israel." This principle is spoken of as that from whence men are without the fear of God, and depart from God's ways. Isaiah 63:17, "O Lord, why has thou made us to err from thy ways, and hardened our heart from thy fear?" And men's rejecting Christ, and opposing Christianity, is laid to this principle; Acts 19:9, "But when divers were hardened, and believed not, but spake evil of that way before the multitude"; God's leaving men to the power of the sin and corruption of the heart is often expressed by God's hardening their hearts; Romans 9:18. "Therefore hath he mercy on whom he will have mercy, and whom he will he hardeneth." John 12:40, "He hath blinded their mind, and hardened their hearts." And the Apostle seems to speak of an evil heart, that departs from the living God, and a hard heart, as the same thing, Hebrews 3:8. "Harden not your heart, as in the provocation," etc. Verses 12–13, "Take heed brethren, lest there be in any of you an evil heart of unbelief in departing from the living God; but exhort one another daily, while it is called Today; lest any of you be hardened through the deceitfulness of sin." And that great work of God in conversion, which consists in delivering a person from the power of sin, and mortifying corruption, is expressed, once and again, by God's taking away the heart of stone, and giving an heart of flesh (Ezekiel 11:19 and ch. 36:26).

Now by a hard heart is plainly meant an unaffected heart, or a heart not easy to be moved with virtuous affections, like a stone, insensible, stupid, unmoved, and hard to be impressed. Hence the hard heart is called a stony heart, and is opposed to an heart of flesh, that has feeling, and is sensibly touched and moved. We read in Scripture of a hard heart, and a tender heart: and doubtless we are to understand these, as contrary the one to the other. But what is a tender heart, but a heart which is easily impressed by what ought to affect it? God commends Josiah, because his heart was tender; and 'tis evident by those things which are mentioned as expressions and evidences of this tenderness of heart, that by his heart being tender is meant, his heart being easily moved with religious and pious affection; 2 Kings 22:19, "Because thine heart was tender, and thou hast humbled thyself before the Lord, when thou heardst what I spake against this place, and against the inhabitants thereof, that they should become a desolation, and a curse, and hast rent thy clothes, and hast wept before me; I also have heard thee, saith the Lord." And this is one thing wherein it is necessary we should become as little children, in order to our entering into the kingdom of God, even that we should have our hearts tender, and easily affected and moved in spiritual and divine things, as little children have in other things.

'Tis very plain in some places, in the texts themselves, that by hardness of heart is meant a heart void of affection. So to signify the ostrich's being without natural affection to her young, it is said, Job 39:16, "She hardeneth her heart against her young ones, as though they were not hers." So a person having a heart unaffected in time of danger, is expressed by his hardening his heart, Proverbs 28:14. "Happy is the man that feareth alway; but he that hardeneth his heart shall fall into mischief."

Now therefore since it is so plain that by a hard heart, in Scripture, is meant a heart destitute of pious affections, and since also the Scriptures do so frequently place the sin and corruption of the heart in hardness of heart; it is evident that the grace and holiness of the heart, on the contrary, must, in a great measure, consist in its having pious affections, and being easily susceptive of such affection. Divines are generally agreed that sin radically and fundamentally consists in what is negative, or privative, having its root and foundation in a privation or want of holiness. And therefore undoubtedly, if it be so that sin does very much consist in hardness of heart, and so in the want of pious affections of heart, holiness does consist very much in those pious affections.

I am far from supposing that all affections do show a tender heart: hatred, anger, vainglory, and other selfish and self-exalting affections may greatly prevail in the hardest heart. But yet it is evident that hardness of heart, and tenderness of heart, are expressions that relate to the affections of the heart, and denote the heart's being susceptible of, or shut up against, certain affections, of which I shall have occasion to speak more afterwards.

Upon the whole, I think it clearly and abundantly evident that true religion lies very much in the affections. Not that I think these arguments prove that religion in the hearts of the truly godly is ever in exact proportion to the degree of affection, and present emotion of the mind. For undoubtedly, there is much affection in the true saints which is not spiritual: their religious affections are often mixed; all is not from grace, but much from nature. And though the affections have not their seat in the body, yet the constitution of the body may very much contribute to the present emotion of the mind. And the degree of religion is rather to be judged of by the fixedness and strength of the habit that is exercised in affection, whereby holy affection is habitual, than by the degree of the present exercise: and the strength of that habit is not always in proportion to outward effects and manifestations, or inward effects, in the hurry and vehemence, and sudden changes of the course of the thoughts of the mind. But yet it is evident that religion consists so much in affection, as that without holy affection there is no true religion: and no light in the understanding is good, which don't produce holy affection in the heart; no habit or principle in the heart is good, which has no such exercise; and no external fruit is good, which don't proceed from such exercises.

Having thus considered the evidence of the proposition laid down, I proceed to some inferences.

1. We may hence learn how great their error is, who are for discarding all religious affections, as having nothing solid or substantial in them.

There seems to be too much of a disposition this way, prevailing in this land at this time. Because many who, in the late extraordinary season, appeared to have great religious affections did not manifest a right temper of mind, and run into many errors, in the time of their affection, and the heat of their zeal; and because the high affections of many seem to be so soon come to nothing, and some who seemed to be mightily raised and swallowed with joy and zeal, for a while, seem to have returned like the dog to his vomit: hence religious affections in general are grown out of credit, with great numbers, as though true religion did not at all consist in them. Thus we easily and naturally run from one extreme to another. A little while ago we were in the other extreme; there was a prevalent disposition to look upon all high religious affections as eminent exercises of true grace, without much inquiring into the nature and source of those affections, and the manner in which they arose: if persons did but appear to be indeed very much moved and raised, so as to be full of religious talk, and express themselves with great warmth and earnestness, and to be "filled," or to be "very full," as the phrases were; it was too much the manner, without further examination, to conclude such persons were full of the Spirit of God, and had eminent experience of his gracious influences. This was the extreme which was prevailing three or four years ago. But of late, instead of esteeming and admiring all religious affections, without distinction, it is a thing much more prevalent to reject and to discard all without distinction. Herein appears the subtlety of Satan. While he saw that affections were much in vogue, knowing the greater part of the land were not versed in such things, and had not had much experience of great religious affections, to enable them to judge well of 'em, and distinguish between true and false; then he knew he could best play his game, by sowing tares amongst the wheat, and mingling false affections with the works of God's Spirit: he knew this to be a likely way to delude and eternally ruin many souls, and greatly to wound religion in the saints, and entangle them in a dreadful wilderness, and by and by, to bring all religion into disrepute. But now, when the ill consequences of these false affections appear, and 'tis become very apparent, that some of those emotions which made a glaring show, and were by many greatly admired, were in reality nothing; the devil sees it to be for his interest to go another way to work, and to endeavor to his utmost to propagate and establish a persuasion, that all affections and sensible emotions of the mind, in things of religion, are nothing at all to be regarded, but are rather to be avoided, and carefully guarded against, as things of a pernicious tendency. This he knows is the way to bring all religion to a mere lifeless formality, and effectually shut out the power of godliness, and every thing which is spiritual, and to have all true Christianity turned out of doors. For although to true religion, there must indeed be something else besides affection; yet true religion consists so much in the affections, that there can be no true religion without them. He who has no religious affection is in a state of spiritual death, and is wholly destitute of the powerful, quickening, saving influences of the Spirit of God upon his heart. As there is no true religion where there is nothing else but affection; so there is no true religion where there is no religious affection. As on the one hand, there must be light in the understanding, as well as an affected fervent heart, where there is heat without light, there can be nothing divine or heavenly in that heart; so on the other hand, where there is a kind of light without heat, a head stored with notions and speculations, with a cold and unaffected heart, there can be nothing divine in that light, that knowledge is no true spiritual knowledge of divine things. If the great things of religion are rightly understood, they will affect the heart. The reason why men are not affected by such infinitely great, important, glorious, and wonderful things, as they often hear and read of in the word of God, is undoubtedly because they are blind; if they were not so, it would be impossible, and utterly inconsistent with human nature, that their hearts should be otherwise, than strongly impressed, and greatly moved by such things.

This manner of slighting all religious affections is the way exceedingly to harden the hearts of men, and to encourage 'em in their stupidity and senselessness, and to keep 'em in a state of spiritual death as long as they live, and bring 'em at last to death eternal. The prevailing prejudice against religious affections at this day, in the land, is apparently of awful effect, to harden the hearts of sinners, and damp the graces of many of the saints, and stund[1] the life and power of religion, and preclude the effect of ordinances, and hold us down in a state of dullness and apathy, and undoubtedly causes many persons greatly to offend God, in entertaining mean and low thoughts of the extraordinary work he has lately wrought in this land.

And for persons to despise and cry down all religious affections is the way to shut all religion out of their own hearts, and to make thorough work in ruining their souls.

They who condemn high affections in others are certainly not likely to have high affections themselves. And let it be considered that they who have but little religious affection have certainly but little religion. And they who condemn others for their religious affections, and have none themselves, have no religion.

There are false affections, and there are true. A man's having much affection don't prove that he has any true religion; but if he has no affection, it proves that he has no true religion. The right way is not to reject all affections, nor to approve all; but to distinguish between affections, approving some, and rejecting others; separating between the wheat and the chaff, the gold and the dross, the precious and the vile.

2. If it be so, that true religion lies much in the affections, hence we may infer that such means are to be desired as have much of a tendency to move the affections. Such books, and such a way of preaching the word, and administration of ordinances, and such a way of worshiping God in prayer, and singing praises, is much to be desired, as has a tendency deeply to affect the hearts of those who attend these means.

Such a kind of means, would formerly have been highly approved of and applauded by the generality of the people of the land, as the most excellent and profitable, and having the greatest tendency to promote the ends of the means of grace. But the prevailing taste seems of late strangely to be altered: that pathetical manner of praying and preaching which would formerly have been admired and extolled, and that for this reason, because it had such a tendency to move the affections, now, in great multitudes, immediately excites disgust, and moves no other affections, than those of displeasure and contempt.

Perhaps, formerly the generality (at least of the common people) were in the extreme of looking too much to an affectionate address, in public performances; but now, a very great part of the people seem to have gone far into a contrary extreme. Indeed there may be such means, as may have a great tendency to stir up the passions of weak and ignorant persons, and yet have no great tendency to benefit their souls. For though they may have a tendency to excite affections, they may have little or none to excite gracious affections, or any affections tending to grace. But undoubtedly, if the things of religion, in the means used, are treated according to their nature, and exhibited truly, so as tends to convey just apprehensions, and a right judgment of them; the more they have a tendency to move the affections, the better.

3. If true religion lies much in the affections, hence we may learn what great cause we have to be ashamed and confounded before God, that we are no more affected with the great things of religion. It appears from what has been said, that this arises from our having so little true religion.

God has given to mankind affections, for the same purpose which he has given all the faculties and principles of the human soul for, viz., that they might be subservient to man's chief end, and the great business for which God has created him, that is the business of religion. And yet how common is it among mankind that their affections are much more exercised and engaged in other matters, than in religion! In things which concern men's worldly interest, their outward delights, their honor and reputation, and their natural relations, they have their desires eager, their appetites vehement, their love warm and affectionate, their zeal ardent; in these things their hearts are tender and sensible, easily moved, deeply impressed, much concerned, very sensibly affected, and greatly engaged; much depressed with grief at worldly losses, and highly raised with joy at worldly successes and prosperity. But how insensible and unmoved are most men, about the great things of another world! How dull are their affections! How heavy and hard their hearts in these matters! Here their love is cold, their desires languid, their zeal low, and their gratitude small. How they can sit and hear of the infinite height and depth and length and breadth of the love of God in Christ Jesus, of his giving his infinitely dear Son, to be offered up a sacrifice for the sins of men, and of the unparalleled love of the innocent, holy, and tender Lamb of God, manifested in his dying agonies, his bloody sweat, his loud and bitter cries, and bleeding heart, and all this for enemies, to redeem them from deserved, eternal burnings, and to bring to unspeakable and everlasting joy and glory; and yet be cold, and heavy, insensible, and regardless! Where are the exercises of our affections proper, if not here? What is it that does more require them? And what can be a fit occasion of their lively and vigorous exercise, if not such an one as this? Can anything be set in our view, greater and more important? Anything more wonderful and surprising? Or more nearly concerning our interest? Can we suppose the wise Creator implanted such principles in the human nature as the affections to be of use to us, and to be exercised on certain proper occasions, but to lie still on such an occasion as this? Can any Christian, who believes the truth of these things, entertain such thoughts?

If we ought ever to exercise our affections at all, and if the Creator hadn't unwisely constituted the human nature, in making these principles a part of it, when they are vain and useless; then they ought to be exercised about those objects which are most worthy of them. But is there anything which Christians can find in heaven or earth, so worthy to be the objects of their admiration and love, their earnest and longing desires, their hope, and their rejoicing, and their fervent zeal, as those things that are held forth to us in the gospel of Jesus Christ? In which, not only are things declared most worthy to affect us, but they are exhibited in the most affecting manner. The glory and beauty of the blessed Jehovah, which is most worthy in itself, to be the object of our admiration and love, is there exhibited in the most affecting manner that can be conceived of, as it appears shining in all its luster, in the face of an incarnate, infinitely loving, meek, compassionate, dying Redeemer. All the virtues of the Lamb of God, his humility, patience, meekness, submission, obedience, love, and compassion, are exhibited to our view, in a manner the most tending to move our affections, of any that can be imagined; as they all had their greatest trial, and their highest exercise, and so their brightest manifestation, when he was in the most affecting circumstances; even when he was under his last sufferings, those unutterable and unparalleled sufferings, he endured, from his tender love and pity to us. There also, the hateful nature of our sins is manifested in the most affecting manner possible; as we see the dreadful effects of them, in what our Redeemer, who undertook to answer for us, suffered for them. And there we have the most affecting manifestations of God's hatred of sin, and his wrath and justice in punishing it; as we see his justice in the strictness and inflexibleness of it, and his wrath in its terribleness, in so dreadfully punishing our sins, in One who was infinitely dear to him, and loving to us. So has God disposed things, in the affair of our redemption, and in his glorious dispensations, revealed to us in the gospel, as though everything were purposely contrived in such a manner, as to have the greatest, possible tendency to reach our hearts in the most tender part, and move our affections most sensibly and strongly. How great cause have we therefore to be humbled to the dust, that we are no more affected!

ఴ

SPIRITUAL APPETITES NEED NO BOUNDS (1729)

Canticles 5:1
Eat, O friends; drink, yea, drink abundantly, O beloved.

Christ, in [the] latter part of the foregoing chapter, had compared his spouse, the church, to a garden of pleasant fruits and the sweetest spices, beginning with the twelfth verse: "A garden enclosed is my sister, my spouse; a spring shut up, a fountain sealed. Thy plants are an orchard of pomegranates, with pleasant fruits; camphire, with spikenard, spikenard and saffron; calamus and cinnamon, with all trees of frankincense; myrrh and aloes, with all the chief spices: a fountain of gardens, a well of living waters, and streams from Lebanon." In the last verse, we have the church praying that the wind should blow upon her garden, that the spices thereof might flow out, or that they might put forth themselves and grow and be brought to perfection, and might send forth their fragrancy, that her garden might be prepared for the reception and entertainment of her spouse. By which we are to understand no other than that the Holy Spirit would come and breathe his gracious influences upon the heart of the spouse, to cause her graces to flow and to be in a vigorous exercise, that it might be the more fitted for Christ's presence and enjoyment. And then we have the spouse inviting of Christ to come into his garden and eat his pleasant fruits; that is, to come into her heart and accept of her faith and love and gracious exercises, and give the tokens of his acceptance of the same.

In this verse, we have Christ answering this invitation. "I am come into my garden, my sister, my spouse: I have gathered my myrrh with my spice; I have eaten my honeycomb with my honey; I have drunk my wine with my milk."

And then, in the words of our text, he reciprocates [the] invitation. As the church invited Christ to feed on the graces of her heart, he accepts of that and invites her to feast on his love and grace: "Eat, O friends; drink, yea, drink abundantly, O beloved." Agreeable to that in Revelation 3:20, "If any man hear my voice, and opens the door, I will come in to him, and will sup with him, and he with me."

In the words we may observe,

1. Who this invitation is directed [to]: the friends and the spouse of Christ, which are the same; the church, which is his beloved, is made up of believers that are his friends. John 15:15, "I call you not servants; for the servant knoweth not what his lord doeth: but I have called you friends; for all things that I have heard of my Father I have made known unto you."

2. What they are invited to: to eat and drink, to partake of his spiritual benefits and delights, and satisfy their spiritual appetites.

3. In what manner he would have them to eat and drink: that is, abundantly. "Drink; yea, drink abundantly." It is in the Hebrew, "Drink; yea, be drunken, O beloved." Christ would not have his people to lay any restraint upon themselves at this spiritual feast. There are no rules of temperance that take place here. And therefore the doctrine is:

Doctrine

Persons need not and ought not to set any bounds to their spiritual and gracious appetites.

Man, when he was first created, was made with two different kinds of appetites: with natural or animal appetites, and with holy and spiritual appetites. The former were given only to be as servants unto the latter, and so were to be in subjection to them. They were given to be restrained and kept within their proper bounds and limits by the superior and spiritual appetites, and then they did their proper work. But if by any means they exceeded those bounds, they necessarily suppressed those spiritual appetites.

By the fall, the spiritual appetite was lost, and so the animal [appetites] were left sole masters, and having no superior principle to restrain them. In regeneration, the spiritual appetites is again in some measure restored, and the sensual appetite is again restrained and kept within bounds by it. And it is our duty, with all possible care, watchfulness, and resolution, to restrain them and to see that they don't go beyond their due bounds.

And this is one main part of the work that a Christian has to do in this militant state: to mortify carnal affections, to subdue his animal appetite, to crucify the flesh with the affections and lusts, to keep under the body and bring it {into subjection}.

Herein chiefly consists the difficulty of a Christian's work. The animal appetites are very strong and impatient of any restraint. It is a bearing the cross daily and like cutting off of a right hand; and it looks with a frightful countenance to carnal men, and is what makes many afraid indeed to embrace Christianity and a holy life.

However, there is something else in Christianity besides self-denial or restraining our inclination. There is a crown as well as a cross. And though we are so strictly required to restrain and keep within bounds our animal inclinations, yet God don't desire we should set any bounds to spiritual and gracious inclinations, which are the most excellent.

He that is truly born again, as he has an animal appetite to meat and drink, so he hungers and thirsts after righteousness. 'Tis his meat and his drink to do the will of his Father which is in heaven. He thirsts for God, for the living God, and sometimes his heart pants after God as the hart panteth after the water brooks [Ps 42:1]. He has an appetite to Jesus Christ, who is the bread which came down from heaven. His soul lives upon Christ as his spiritual meat and drink.

He has an appetite to the word of [God] as to the food of his soul: for he lives not by bread alone, but by every word which proceedeth out of the mouth of God [Matt 4:4]. He as a newborn babe desires the sincere milk of the word, that he may grow thereby [1 Pet 2:2]. He has not only a desire from a rational consideration of the need and benefit of it, but 'tis a desire immediately flowing from his nature, like the natural appetite.

As the covetous man desires earthly riches, so the regenerated person desires spiritual riches. He esteems grace in his soul as the best riches; he looks upon wisdom as better than gold and silver, and he is ambitious of the honor which is of God, to be a child of God and an heir of glory. And as the sensualist eagerly pursues sensual delights, he longs for those pleasures that are spiritual: the pleasure of seeing the glory of Christ, and enjoying his love and having communion with him; the pleasure and joys of the Holy Ghost that consist in the sweet and powerful exercise of grace, of faith and love, submission, thankfulness, charity, and brotherly kindness. And with respect to those appetites self-denial has nothing to do, but here [they] may give themselves an unbounded liberty.

Here we shall,

I. Just show what is meant by not [setting any bounds to your spiritual and gracious appetites].

II. Insist on the two propositions contained in the Doctrine.

[I.] By not setting any bounds to those gracious appetites, these two things are intended:

First. The not restraining of those appetites with respect to their degree or exercise. Men cannot exceed in the degree of those appetites. There is no such thing as any inordinateness in holy affections; there is no such thing as excess in longings after the discoveries of the beauty of Christ Jesus, or greater degrees of holiness, or the enjoyment of communion with God. Men may be as covetous as they please (if I may so speak) after spiritual riches, as eager as they please to heap up treasure in heaven, as ambitious as they please of spiritual and eternal honor and glory, and as voluptuous as they please with respect to spiritual pleasure.

Persons neither need nor ought to keep those inclinations and desires from increasing to any degree whatsoever, and there cannot be a too frequent or too powerful exercise of them.

A person can neither have too strongly energated a principle and habit of such inclinations, nor be in a frame wherein they are too much under their prevailing exercise.

Second. By not setting any bounds to those appetites, is meant the not laying any restraint upon ourselves with respect to gratifying of them. Persons may indulge them as much as they please; they may give themselves their full swing. They may not only allow a very eager thirst and enlarged desire, but they may drink their fill; there is no excess. They may and ought to seek all the spiritual wealth they can obtain. They may to their utmost indulge their hungerings after righteousness, and after the word of God, and after all spiritual pleasures. They may indulge those appetites as much as they will in their thoughts and meditations and in their practice. They may drink, yea, swim in the rivers of spiritual pleasure.

[II. We shall insist on the two Propositions contained in the Doctrine.]

First Prop. Persons need not lay any restraints upon those appetites. And that for these reasons:

1. There is nothing in the nature of those appetites that forbids their being exercised or indulged to any degree. The sensitive appetites have something in their own nature that requires their being restrained by certain rules and kept in certain bounds. They are of such a nature, that if a lease be given them, they become odious and abominable, and they debase the nature of man. They darken and blind the understanding, and hinder those exercises of the rational nature as are becoming of the station God has set us in, and drive on to those actions that are not consistent with the proper excellency and dignity of human nature. The unrestrained indulging [of] those appetites is in itself many ways contrary to reason.

But [it] is not so with respect to spiritual and gracious appetites. They are not, to whatsoever degree they are, any way unlovely or unreasonable. They were not intended to be governed and restrained by any superior and more excellent principle as animal appetites were, and therefore they cannot be inordinate. It is not [in] any degree of them, or of the gratification of them, contrary to the rational nature, because to the greater degree they are and the more they are gratified, the more doth the man act according to reason and justice.

2. God hath set no bounds by any prohibition. God hath set bounds and limits with respect to animal appetites, hath fenced up the way by his holy and dreadful commandments; he hath told us how far, in what manner and in what circumstances they may be allowed and indulged and how they may not, upon pain of his holy displeasure. But here God hath left the way open; he leaves us

without any manner of restraint. A wide and boundless world of spiritual pleasure and blessedness is before us.

3. Our own interest will lay no restraint [upon] us here. An unrestrained indulgence of the sensual appetite is in itself many ways contrary to our own interest: a living in such a way will naturally lead to ruin. Sensual lust, or inordinate bodily appetites—which are the same thing—are a spring of woe and misery in whatsoever soul they reside, and especially in whatsoever soul they bear rule: they bring the greatest confusion into the soul, and therefore destroy the peace of it; they are contrary to reason, and therefore reason will be fighting against them, which will cause war and tumult in the soul; they bring guilt upon the mind, which is inconsistent with the tranquility of the mind, and naturally produces horror and misery.

And they also many ways destroy one's outward peace and comfort. A sensual life involves men in many kinds of misery and sorrow in this world.

But it is not so with respect to the indulgence of spiritual appetites. If one is never so craving of spiritual enjoyments, and takes never so full a swing in spiritual delights and pleasures, they are not contrary to any superior interest, nor ordinarily to any inferior interest; but on the contrary, those appetites are the true spring of the soul's peace and happiness, and the stronger they are and the more indulged, so much the greater is that soul's happiness. And the inferior interests, the interests of the outward man, they are ordinarily promoted thereby: for length of days are in their right hand, and in their left hand are riches and honor [Prov 3:16].

There is no disapprobation of reason or judgment or remorse of conscience that ensues the fully and freely enjoying those pleasures, but are of the conscience most highly approved; and they leave no sting behind them, but a sweet relish upon the mind, a peace and serenity that is ineffable.

Second Prop. Persons ought not to lay any restraint or to set any bounds to their spiritual appetites. It is perhaps a case that can hardly happen, that any person should voluntarily and intentionally restrain their spiritual appetites. But they ought not to suffer them to be restrained by the prevalency of contrary inclinations; they ought not to suffer them to be kept down by worldly cares and pleasures.

Neither ought persons to rest in any past or present degree of gracious appetite or enjoyment of the objects of it, but to their utmost to be increasing the same, to be endeavoring by all possible ways to inflame their desires and to obtain more spiritual pleasures.

So that is not only what we may do and that we need not be afraid to do, but what God hath commanded and what it is our duty to do. For which we shall give these three reasons:

1. These gracious and holy inclinations and appetites are the true and the highest perfection of our nature. The animal appetites are good in their place, because they subserve to that in man which is more excellent; but their goodness don't consist in their being subservient to themselves. But that which is the highest excellency and perfection of nature is good, as [it is] subservient to itself; it can't be in too high a degree. A man surely cannot be the more imperfect for having a great deal of that which is the highest perfection of his nature. He can't have too much of that which is his true excellency, unless he can be too excellent.

'Tis by those holy inclinations that men are like God and have his image, and it is their duty to conform themselves to their utmost to God's holy nature.

2. 'Tis in those enjoyments that are the objects of those spiritual appetites, wherein consists the happiness that man was made for. God has given every man a necessary desire after happiness; he unavoidably seeks it. It is impossible he should do otherwise, and 'tis in the satisfying of those gracious appetites wherein consists the happiness God designed him [for]; and therefore men, as they ought to seek this happiness, ought to indulge those appetites to obtain as much of those spiritual satisfactions as lies in their power.

As God designed man for this happiness, he intended those appetites should be satisfied. He has promised that such hungerings and thirstings should be filled. Men therefore ought to endeavor that they obtain the satisfying of them, as they ought to do what belongs to them to do in order to their being the way to obtain the promises.

3. Let those appetites be never so strong and vigorous, yet they will not be equal to the merit of their objects. When men's appetites are violent towards earthly enjoyments, they are beyond the dessert of their objects. Those things are not worth the so eager desires of a rational creature. Temporal pleasures ben't worthy, that the soul of man should be wholly possessed and governed by desires after them.

But 'tis not so with respect to spiritual enjoyments. They are of so exalted and excellent a nature that it is impossible that our desires after them should exceed their desert; yea, they cannot be equal to it. Our hungerings and thirstings after God and Jesus Christ and after holiness can't be too great for the value of the things, for they are things of infinite value.

And in this world, we all fall shamefully short: our appetites, our desires [are] miserably cold and languid in comparison of what they deserve of us. We ought therefore to our utmost to promote and increase them.

Application

[*Use*] I [of] *Inference*. Hence we learn the unreasonableness of carnal men's prejudice against religion, as though it were a thing that abridged men of all the pleasure of life. Although it limits man with respect to one sort of pleasures, viz., those that are of the more base and inferior, those that are common to the beasts, yet it lays no restraint upon [him] with respect to those pleasures that are the best and sweetest, and are most able to delight and satisfy the soul. Those delights that are agreeable to the rational nature and worthy of such a creature as man, and that don't debase but exalt and perfect him, and that are also of the most exquisite sweetness, we are allowed and directed to indulge ourselves in to our utmost.

Religion is not a sour thing that is contrived for nothing but to cross our inclinations and to cut us short of the delights of life. No, it is quite of another nature: it abridges us of no pleasures, but only such as of their own nature (however pleasing for the present) do lay a foundation for woe and misery. They are in their own nature a poison, that though sweet in the mouth, do really as it were destroy the constitution of the soul. Proverbs 23:32, "At last it will bite like a serpent, and sting like an adder." But as for those delights that better the soul and have a tendency to the future, as well as the present well-being of it, they are allowed fully and are promoted by religion; yea, true religion is the only source from whence they flow.

How much happier therefore is the man that chooses a holy and a spiritual religious life, than he that chooses a carnal, sensual life. Sensual men may be ready to think they should be happy men if there were nothing to restrain their enjoyment of their [appetites], if they might at all time satisfy their appetites, and have their full swing at their pleasures with impunity and without any danger of any succeeding inconvenience. But if it were so, they would be but miserable men in comparison of the godly man who enjoys the pleasures of acquaintance with the glorious God and his Son Jesus Christ, and a communion of the holy and blessed Spirit of God and Christ, and a true peace of conscience and inward testimonies of the favor and acceptance of God and [Christ], and have liberty without restraint to indulge themselves in the enjoyment of those pleasures. "Wisdom's ways are ways of pleasantness, and all her paths are peace," Proverbs 3:17.

Indeed, the spiritual appetites in this world are but low, and the advantages for indulging of them are also comparatively but small; but how great will be the happiness of the saints in heaven, where those appetites will be raised to a most vigorous and perfect exercise, and shall be under all possible advantages for the satisfying of them. They shall be surrounded with those things that are the objects of them; they shall be in God's presence and in the presence of the Lamb, and shall behold his glory and have the Holy Spirit in abundant measures poured forth into their souls, etc.

Use II is to *Exhort* you to the utmost to promote and indulge spiritual and gracious appetites. It is to repeat and apply to you that invitation of Christ that we have in the text: "Eat, O friends; drink, yea, drink abundantly." We, in Christ's stead, entreat you that are the followers of Christ thus to do. By all means, endeavor to raise and to obtain satisfaction for holy inclinations; delight yourselves in the Lord.

One would think you should not need urging to indulge your appetites and to enjoy your pleasures. Carnal men, by all the arguments that can be used, can scarcely be restrained from indulging their carnal appetites. 'Tis a shame that the saints should need a great many arguments to move them to promote their spiritual appetites.

Be exhorted particularly to promote a thirsting desire after Jesus Christ and after that glorious feast of spiritual good things that is provided in him. Delight yourselves in him. Rejoice in him with joy unspeakable and full of glory.

First Direction. Endeavor to increase spiritual appetites by meditating on spiritual objects. We are to restrain lustful appetites all that we can by casting away and avoiding thoughts and meditations upon their objects. We ben't allowed by any means to give a lease to our thoughts concerning those things, because that tends to increase lustful desires after them. But 'tis our duty to be much in meditation on the objects of spiritual desire: we should often be thinking upon the glory and grace of God, the excellency and wonderful love of Christ, the beauty of holiness.

Second Dir. Endeavor to promote spiritual appetites by laying yourself in the way of allurement. We are to avoid being in the way of temptation with respect to our carnal appetites. Job made a covenant with his eyes [Job 31:1]. But we ought to take all opportunities to lay ourselves in the way of enticement with respect to our gracious inclinations. Thus you should be often with God in prayer, and then you will be in the way of having your heart drawn forth to him. We ought to be frequent in reading and constant in hearing the word. And particularly to this end, we ought carefully and with the utmost seriousness and consideration attend the sacrament of the Lord's Supper: this was appointed for this end, to draw forth the longings of our souls towards Jesus Christ. Here are the glorious objects of spiritual desire by visible signs represented to our view. We have Christ evidently set forth crucified {in this sacrament}. Here we have that spiritual meat and drink represented and offered to excite our hunger and thirst; here we have all that spiritual feast represented which God has provided for poor souls; and here we may hope in some measure to have our longing souls satisfied in this world by the gracious communications of the Spirit of God.

Third Dir. Watch the first beginnings of the exercise of these inclinations, and promote them. We are to watch the first beginnings of lustful inclinations, to suppress [them], but here we are to do the contrary: whenever we feel these desires and longings, we should endeavor to forwards [them] by meditation and prayer. We should express our longings to God; they will increase by being expressed. We should be earnest in our prayers for the things we long for. The Apostle speaks of groanings in prayer that cannot be uttered, Romans 8:26.

Fourth Dir. Live in the practice of these inclinations. If you long after God and Jesus Christ, then often go to God and Christ and converse with them. If you long to be near to God, then draw near to him. If you hunger and thirst after righteousness, then take great care to live in the practice of righteousness, to live a more holy and heavenly life. If you long to be more like Christ, then act like him, walk as he walked. This is the way to have your holy inclinations increased, and hereby they will in some measure be satisfied.

THE SAINTS OFTEN MISS SWEET COMMUNION WITH CHRIST FOR WANT OF A LITTLE SELF-DENIAL (1737)[2]

Canticles 5:3–6
I have put off my coat; how shall I put it on? I have washed my feet;
how shall I defile them. My beloved put in his hand by the hole of
the door, and my bowels were moved for him. I rose up to open to
my beloved; and my hands dropped with myrrh, and my fingers
with sweet smelling myrrh, upon the handles of the lock. I opened to
my beloved; but my beloved had withdrawn himself, and was gone:
my soul failed when he spake: I sought him, but I could not find
him; I called him, but he gave me no answer.

The spouse of Christ here gives an account of what passed, with respect to her, on occasion of a special call that she had from her beloved. She gives an account of the call in the foregoing verse, where she begins with giving an account of the frame she was in when this call was made: "I sleep, but my heart waketh," i.e., though her heart was awaked, though she had a principle within her of true religion that in itself was a lively, vigorous, active principle, a principle of grace that was forward to duty, yet she, by reason of the prevalency of the carnal part, was in a dull and sleepy frame, indolent and indisposed to duty.

The expression, "I sleep, but my heart waketh," seems to be of the same import with that which Christ uses with respect to his disciples, when he saw them in a very dull time. Matthew 26:41, "The spirit is willing, but the flesh is weak."

And then the spouse gives an account how, while she was in this frame, Christ her beloved knocked at her door, and called her: "it is the voice of my beloved that knocketh, saying, Open to me, my sister, my love, my dove, my undefiled: for my head is filled with dew, and my locks with the drops of the night." Christ calls her to arise and open to him, to let him in; that was the duty he required of her, and the end was that he might come in and enjoy her company, and she his, that they might sweetly converse together. It was not a stranger that called and knocked, but her own beloved: "'tis the voice of my beloved." He calls her in a very winning manner, with the most endearing expressions and appellations: "Open to me," says he, "my love, my dove, my undefiled." And he knocks and calls in a most importunate manner: "my head," says he, "is filled with the dew, and my locks with the drops of the night."

His thus knocking at the door of his spouse, is represented as being in the night. Her beloved sought entertainment of her, and shelter from the dews and cold damps of the night.

In the text, we have an account of what followed with respect to the spouse who is thus called, and at whose door Christ thus knocks. In which may be observed several things:

1. She is slow in answering his call and opening the door to him, as he requested. She did not do as might have been well expected—arise, and open to him immediately, receiving him with the greatest alacrity and joy—but she is dull about, and delays and excuses herself.

2. For what reason she is thus backward to hearken to Christ's call, viz., her loathness a little to deny herself: "I have put off my coat; how shall I put it on? I have washed my feet; how shall I defile them?" She was in a dull, sleepy frame; it was contrary to her to rise out of her drowse and shake off sweet sleep, and therefore she finds out excuses: she makes an excuse of that, that she shall defile her feet if she rises and lets him in.

3. We may observe how, after her delays and excuses, she was made willing to comply with the request of her beloved: he "put in his hand by the hole of the door," and her "bowels were moved for him."

When her beloved had called, and told her how his head {was filled with dew}, in vain, he further manifested his desire of entrance by putting in his hand "by the hole of the door." Her seeing this moved her; she says, her bowels were moved for him. It wrought on her affections, and made her sensible of her own ingratitude in being so backward to open to him; it roused, and made her delay no longer. This seems to be signified by it, viz., that when the spouse of Christ was not prevailed upon by Christ's outward call, the call of his word, he then quickened her by his own immediate hand, drawing forth her heart by the motions of his spirit, and thereby did as it were put in his hand through the door of her heart.

The "voice of the beloved" probably signifies the external call of Christ, but the hand of Christ signifies inward efficacy. Though Christ's voice did not move her, yet his hand prevailed. While her beloved called to her, she only heard him; but when he put in his hand, then she saw something of him: she saw his hand. Though having Christ only won't prevail on the heart, yet when the soul comes to see something of Christ, that will have effect.

4. Upon this, she rises to open to Christ: "I rose to open to my beloved." Then, after Christ's hand had been put in, she was willing to obey his commands; so that we may observe, that she did not utterly refuse to comply with Christ's call. The manner of saints and natural men is different in this respect. A natural man utterly refuses to open to Christ, though Christ continues calling from time to time. On the other hand, a saint may at first be backward and slow, through a loathness to deny himself, and thereby greatly sin; but yet, they are

commonly wont, when they have considered the matter at length, to comply and yield to their duty. 'Tis not their manner absolutely to refuse obedience to known commands of Christ.

The spouse says of herself, that her "hands dropped with myrrh, and my fingers with sweet-smelling myrrh, upon the handles of the lock": i.e., she opened the door with flowing of sweet affection to Christ. Her heart began to be moved when she first saw him put in his hand through the hole of the door, but that her gracious affection to him, and desires after him, prevailed more and more; and when she opened the door, she did it willingly, as with ardent desires after Christ.

5. We may observe how she was disappointed when she came to open the door: "But my beloved had withdrawn himself, and was gone." She opened with earnest expectation of meeting her beloved there at the door; her hands were perfumed as it were with sweet-smelling myrrh, to prepare them to take hold of him and embrace him, as soon as ever the door was open. Her heart was full of eager desires and expectations of the happy meeting she should there have with him. But behold, when she had opened the door, he was not there, but had withdrawn himself. If she had arose and opened to him when he first called, she might have met with him then. But, as she says, her "soul failed when he spake": i.e., when he first called, her heart failed her; she did not find it in her heart then to arise and open to him, and now she suffers for it. Now she is risen and has opened, he is not there. And she says she "sought him, but I could not find him; I called him, but he gave me no answer." Her backwardness to deny herself in her sleepy, sluggish frame, when he first called her, lost her the benefit of sweet communion with her beloved; and not only so, but cost her a great deal of difficulty: for after this, when she went out about the city to try to find him, "The watchmen that went about the city found me, they smote me, they wounded me; the keepers of the walls took away my veil from me." And she was "sick of love": i.e., she was sick, and had her heart sunk with her disappointment of that opportunity of communion with him that she had met with, and so earnestly desired.

Doctrine

'Tis a frequent thing, that the saints miss of sweet communion with Christ, for want of a little self-denial.

I would endeavor to clear up this Doctrine, by speaking to the following Propositions:

I. That Christ stands ready to grant his saints sweet communion with himself.

II. There are duties incumbent on them, or things that they ought to do, that so they may be in the way of communion with Christ.

III. There is a backwardness in the saints to the doing of those things, especially at sometimes and in some instances, so they can[not] be done without self-denial.

IV. Christ is especially wont at such times, as when the saints deny themselves, to grant them sweet communion with himself.

V. That self-denial, through the want of which they miss of {communion with Christ}, is but small.

Proposition I. Christ stands ready to grant his saints sweet communion with him.

Did he not manifest himself ready to have communion with the spouse, in the verse preceding the text? When he came to her door in the night and knocked, saying, "Open to me, my sister, my love, my dove, my undefiled," don't these sweet, endearing appellations manifest a readiness? He was ready, though the spouse was backward. He failed not of willingness on his part, though the spouse, in her dull and sleepy frame, was full of her trivial excuses.

Christ hath an exceeding transcendent love to his saints; he loved them from all eternity; his delights were with them before the foundation of the world, as he says, Proverbs 8:31. He delighted in them as they existed in his foreknowledge. And certainly then, he will not be backward to have communion with them when they come into being, and after they are savingly brought home to himself, and have his image put upon their souls.

Christ loves the saints with a love of complacence; he rejoices over them, he delights in those holy graces and those lovely ornaments that he has put upon them; his heart is as it were ravished with the spiritual beauty that he has given them, and he is delighted in their love to him. As in the ninth and tenth verses of the chapter preceding the text: "Thou hast ravished my heart, my sister, my spouse; thou hast ravished my heart with one of thine eyes, with one chain of thy neck. How fair is thy love, my sister, my spouse! how much better is thy love than wine! and the smell of thine ointments than all spices!"

The souls of the saints are the spouse of Jesus Christ, as they are represented throughout this book of Solomon's Song. Such is his delight in her, that he compares her to "the lily among thorns" [Cant 2:2], and to "a garden enclosed, a spring shut up, a fountain sealed," "a fountain of gardens, a well of living waters, and streams from Lebanon" [Cant 4:12, 15]. He compares her graces to pleasant fruits, and the sweetest and most fragrant spices. He compares her beauty to the light of the morning, to the fairness of the moon and brightness of the sun, ch. 6:10. Such a complacence certainly implies a delight that Christ has in communion with his saints.

Christ manifests his readiness to grant the saints communion with himself, by his often inviting them to it in this book. As in the second chapter, vv. 10, etc.: "My beloved spake, and said unto me, Rise up, my love, my fair one, and come away"; and again, fourth chapter, v. 8: "Come with me from Lebanon, my spouse, with me from Lebanon: look from the top of Amana, from the top of Shenir and Hermon, from the lions' dens, from the mountains of the leopards"; and [the] fifth chapter, v. 1: "Eat, O friends; drink, yea, drink abundantly, O beloved"; and so in the text: "Open to me, my sister, my love, my dove, my undefiled." And with what delight does Christ speak of his intended communion with his spouse. Ch. 7:6–8, "How fair and how pleasant art thou, O love, for delights! This thy stature is like to a palm tree, and thy breasts to clusters of grapes. I said, I will go up to the palm tree, I will take hold of the boughs thereof"; i.e., "I will go and have communion with my spouse."

Christ's love to his saints far exceeds their love to him. He loved them first, and his love is the foundation and as it were the fountain of theirs.

His love to them is such that it made him willing to die for them; and shall not he, that was ready to shed his blood and to suffer the cruel and accursed death of the cross for them, be ready to grant them communion with him? Yea, he died for that end, to make way that they might have communion with him; and since he so readily did that, surely he will be ready, when it is done, to attain his own end in it.

Christ never manifests any backwardness to hold communion with his people, but is ever more ready for it, and acts as one that delights in it. When they are ready for it, he never is backward on his part.

Prop. II. There are duties incumbent on the saints as things that they ought to do, that they may be in the way of communion with Christ. There is nothing required of the saints to make 'em worthy of such a privilege, nothing by which they can merit it. Christ stands ready to grant it to them without. He doesn't need any money or price of theirs to purchase.

But yet, Christ deals with the saints as reasonable, active creatures, and 'tis a mercy to them that he does. And therefore, 'tis expected that they should not be wholly idle and merely passive in this matter, but that they should be actively concerned in what appertains to their coming to this great privilege of communion with himself. 'Tis an honor that Christ puts upon them, that he orders it that it should be so, that there should be an intercourse maintained between him and them, wherein they should be active. And indeed, it belongs to the notions of the communion and converse of two active beings, that they should be mutually active.

Though there be nothing incumbent on the saints, whereby they may merit the privilege of communion with Christ, yet there are things incumbent on them in order to their being prepared for it, and also in order to our voluntary admitting and receiving Christ to communion, whereby we may as it were open the door to receive Christ into our fellowship and communion: for Christ never forces himself upon any against their will.

And if 'tis required of us that we should be willing to receive Christ and to have fellowship, 'tis doubtless required that this willingness be some way expressed in our actions.

Here, it may be *Inquired*, What things are they, that are incumbent on the saints, as they would be in the way to enjoy communion with Christ.

Answer. In general, to yield to Christ and hearken to his calls. All that is required of us, in order to communion with Christ, may indeed be resolved into a voluntary, active admitting and receiving communion with him. Christ is first in seeking communion with us before ever the saints seek or desire communion with him; he is always first, and calls and leads, and all that they have to do is to yield and to follow.

The end of all his calls to us, is our happiness in him. He don't call us to come to him, or to admit him to come to us, that he may be made happy by us: for he stands in no need of us, nor have we anything to bestow upon him to make him happy. But he calls that he may make us happy in him, and in his communion. To this end, he calls us to open to him, and receive him; he calls us to yield ourselves to him, and to follow him.

But more particularly,

1. He calls them away from the pollution of the world, and from communion with other lovers. Indeed, they have their hearts called away from those things in their conversion; they are cleansed in a measure, and have their love to other lovers mortified, but not perfectly purged out of their hearts; but they are still liable to pollute themselves, and to leave Christ for a time, and in a great degree to go after other lovers again, whereby they deprive themselves of communion with Christ.

When they pollute themselves with sensual defilements, thereby they do as it were drive Christ far from them. Never any had much sweet communion with Christ, while they remained in a sensual frame.

No wonder that Christ don't delight to converse with a soul, when defiling itself with that abomination which his soul hates. The King of glory calls his saints to wash and purify themselves from their filthiness, and to put off their filthy rags, that they may be fit to converse with him. So he calls to his church, Isaiah 52:1–2, "Awake, awake; put on thy strength, O Zion; put on thy beautiful garments, O Jerusalem, the holy city: for henceforth there shall no more come into thee the uncircumcised and the unclean. Shake thyself from the dust; arise, and sit down, O Jerusalem: loose thyself from the bands of thy neck, O captive daughter of Zion." There are other lovers that are soliciting the saints, and sometimes do in a great measure prevail, such as worldly profit and worldly advancement, and the objects of their sensual appetites; but Christ calls them away from those, that they may have communion. Christ won't tolerate a rival, he don't come to us to seek a share in our hearts together with other lovers, but that we would forsake all for his sake. He won't converse with us as long as others are entertained, but when we cast off all others for him, then may we expect that he will grant us communion with himself. When Christ's spouse is most undefiled, least polluted with the defilements of the world, and least polluted by other lovers, then will Christ be most ready to have communion with her. Thus we see in the text, when Christ calls his spouse to communion with him, he gives her the character of "undefiled": "my sister, my love, my dove, my undefiled."

2. Christ calls his saints to admit him as the object of their meditations. The believer, by fixing his meditations on Christ, turns the eye of his soul towards him, and fixes it on him, which is necessary in order to communion with him; for how shall we have communion or converse with a person that we don't see, and that our mind is not fixed upon? How should our souls be entertained with communion with Christ, and yet be taken up with other objects?

Therefore, if we would have sensible communion with Christ, 'tis necessary that we should fix our meditations on him. This Christ calls us to, to that end.

'Tis the duty of every Christian to make Christ the daily subject of his meditations. Christ should be the chief object of a believer's contemplations, as he is the most worthy and glorious object. This we are called to by Christ, and that, because we are apt to forget Christ and to be unmindful of him. This is part of what is intended, Canticles 8:6, "Set me as a seal upon thine heart, as a seal upon thine arm: for love is strong as death," and "jealousy is cruel as the grave."

And especially at some times are the saints called to fix their meditations on Christ. Persons should have set times every day wherein they should do this, and it should be especially done on sabbath days. And oftentimes, there are particular calls to it by our particular circumstances, and God's providential dealings with us.

3. Christ calls his saints to wait upon him in the use of the means of his appointment, in a diligent reading and hearing of his word, and keeping his holy Sabbaths, and attending on his ordinances. These are as it were his gates, and the posts of his doors; these are his chambers, where he is wont to meet with his spouse, and to grant her communion with him. Those are "the shepherds' tents" spoken of in the first chapter of Solomon's Song, vv. 7–8. The spouse desires her beloved to tell where he feeds, and where he made his flock to rest at noon, that she might come to him there and enjoy his company and communion. He tells her, "If thou know not, O thou fairest among women, go thy way forth by the footsteps of the flock, and feed thy kids beside the shepherds' tents."

4. He calls them to follow him and walk with him. If we would enjoy communion with Christ, we must follow him where he goes; we must follow his example. We must cleave to him in every case, and not desert him because of the cross that lies in the way. We must cleave to him in every duty that he requires of us. We must follow Christ in our behavior, alone and in secret. We must follow Christ in all our conduct towards men. We must follow him whether in a private or public station, and in our behavior in our families, and among our neighbors, and towards all men. We are called to walk with Christ and cleave to him through the whole of our course through the world.

We are called to follow him in the exercise of those great works that he hath set us an example of: his meekness and humility, his patience, his self-denial, his contempt of the world and his forgiveness, and his wonderful love and charity. Matthew 11:28–29, "Come unto me, all ye that labor and are heavy laden, and I will give you rest. Take my yoke upon you, and learn of me; for I am meek and lowly in heart: and ye shall find rest unto your souls." John 13:15, "For I have given you an example, that ye should do as I have done to you."

I come now to the [third thing proposed]:

Prop. III. There is a backwardness to these things, especially in some cases, so that self-denial is necessary in order to the doing of them.

There are such remains of corruption in the heart of the best, that the thorough complying with the call of Christ in these things is attended with a great deal of difficulty. If it be easy to comply in some cases, yet not in others; there are some duties required that are very difficult, very cross to those principles and inclinations that are naturally predominant in men, and that have great power and strength in the godly. And especially have they a backwardness to them at some times. No godly person is always in a like frame; that duty which is easy to him at one time is very difficult at another. It seems to be no self-denial to do it when the heart is in a spiritual and lively frame, and yet is very cross and contrary in a dull and carnal frame.

So that a thorough yielding to Christ in those his calls, and opening the door to him in them, all can't be done without denying ourselves. When the saints get into ill frames, so as to follow after other lovers and to defile themselves in the pollutions of the world, there is a backwardness to forsake those things. Though Christ calls to it by the preaching of the word otherwise, there is a backwardness to comply with the call, a disposition in the saints to excuse themselves. There is a principle in the heart that loves those pollutions and those rivals of Jesus Christ. When they have insensibly fallen into a way of indulging any lust, and are called to break it off, there is a backwardness to it; there is a loathness to forego the sinful pleasure that has been entertained, and has got footing in the heart; there is a backwardness to cross the sensual appetite, and to keep under the body. And there is oftentimes a great deal of difficulty in fixing the heart in meditations on Jesus Christ. 'Tis work that seems cross to the clination of the heart; the mind seems not to be disposed to it, but flies off from it. And 'tis contrary to the sluggish frame that the soul is in, to take any great matter of pains to fix the thoughts. There is oftentimes a great deal of backwardness to a diligent and attentive use of all the means that Christ has appointed, in order to communion with him: sometimes there is backwardness when Christ calls to prayer, or when he calls to reading the Holy Scriptures, and a dullness of heart on Sabbath days, and in the time of public duties of worship, a backwardness to any diligent attention to them.

So oftentimes there is a backwardness in the saints to follow Christ and cleave to him. It is cross to their present temporal interest, or cross to some sinful inclination; cross to covetousness, or cross to pride, or to slothfulness.

There is a disposition to neglect some duties that are required of 'em, and to find out some excuses or other. There is a backwardness to put [on] the coat when it is put off, and a pretense of unwillingness to defile the feet after they have been washed....

EXCERPT FROM *THE PORTION OF THE RIGHTEOUS* (1735)

...(5) The saints in heaven shall see and converse with Christ.

[1. They] shall see Christ in a twofold sense:

a. They shall see him as appearing in his glorified human nature with their bodily eyes, which will be a most glorious sight. The loveliness of Christ as thus appearing will be a most ravishing thing to them. For though the bodies of the saints shall appear with an exceeding beauty and glory, yet the body of Christ will without doubt immensely surpass it, as much as the brightness of the sun does that of the stars. The glorified body of Christ will be the masterpiece of all God's workmanship in the whole corporeal world. There shall be in his glorious countenance the manifestation of his glorious spiritual perfection, his majesty, his holiness, his surpassing grace and love and meekness. The eye will never be cloyed or glutted in beholding this glorious sight.

When Christ was transfigured in the mount, Peter was for making three tabernacles [Matt 17:4].

Job has respect to this sight of Christ and comforted himself in the thoughts of it, when he says, Job 19:25–27, "For I know that my Redeemer liveth, and that he shall stand at the latter day upon the earth: and though after my skin worms destroy this body, yet in my flesh shall I see God:

whom I shall see for myself, and mine eyes shall behold, and not another; though my reins be consumed within me."

This will be the most glorious sight that the saints will ever see with their bodily eyes, the most glorious sight that ever has been seen or will be seen by any bodily eyes. There will be far more happiness and pleasure redounding to the beholders from this sight than any other. Yea, the eyes of the resurrection body will be given chiefly to behold this sight.

b. They shall see him with the eye of the soul. 'Tis said, they "shall see him as he is," 1 John 3:2; and they "shall know even as Christ is known," 1 Corinthians 13:12. [They shall have] understanding of Christ as mediator, how he has undertaken from all eternity; [they] shall [have an] understanding [of] the eternal covenant of redemption between the Father and the Son; see the love Christ has had to them before the foundation of the world. [They shall] probably understand the mystery of his incarnation, {shall} know and understand the gloriousness of the way of salvation by Christ, which things the angels desire to look into. {They shall have} full understanding of the infinite wisdom of God in contriving the work of salvation.

[They shall] understand that, "what is the height, and depth, and breadth, and length of the love of Christ" to sinners in dying for 'em, [in] undergoing [for 'em].

Now the heart is dull in the consideration of such things. How often [has this been] heard of, with but little affection; how often dull in seeing them set forth in the Lord's Supper, and was cold and lifeless, and had sometimes very little sense of it. But now it shall not be so: now the consideration of the wonderful wisdom of God and the love of Christ in the work of redemption will appear as it is; now there will constantly, without any interruption, be a most lively and full sense of it, without any deadness or coldness. Everything in the work of redemption will now appear in its true glory; the understanding shall wonderfully be opened; it shall be perpetually like the clear hemisphere with the sun in the meridian, and there shall never come even one cloud to darken the mind. And now the saints shall see fully how the excellencies and loveliness of Christ appears in all that he did and suffered. They will now see the loveliness of those excellencies that appeared in Christ's human nature when on earth, his wonderful meekness and his humility, his patience and suffering, his perfect obedience to the Father. And now shall they also see the beauty that appears in Christ's human nature in its glorified state, wherein the excellencies of it appear without a veil.

And then the saints shall see the excellencies of the divine nature of Christ. They shall behold clearly and immediately his divine majesty, and his divine and infinite holiness and grace and love. They shall see Christ as the perfect image of God, an image wherein all the glory of the divine nature is fully expressed; they shall behold him as the brightness of his Father's glory, "and the express image of his person" [Heb 1:3]. Now they will behold that bright and perfect image of God that the Father beheld, and was infinitely happy in beholding from all eternity. But this sight of the glory of Christ in his divine nature belongs to that beatifical vision of which I would speak more particularly hereafter,[3] and therefore there is no need of my insisting any further on it here.

2. They shall converse with Christ; shall not only see this glorious person as at a distance, but they shall be admitted to converse with him. Their sight of his glory and loveliness will fill them with the most exalted exercises of love, which love will cause them to desire conversation, and they shall be admitted to it to the full of their desires. And that at all times they shall dwell with Christ, that they may satisfy their souls with conversing with Christ.

Here are two things may be noted of this conversation with Christ that the saints shall be admitted to in heaven:

a. It shall be most free and intimate. They shall enjoy Christ this way as full as they please; there shall be nothing to forbid them, or hinder or deter them. They shall converse with Christ with the greatest freedom, and shall have no restraint laid upon them; they shall have their full swing at their enjoyment of Christ this way.

Though Christ is so great a person, and in so exalted a state in heaven, being exalted there by God's right hand to the Lord of heaven and earth; yet he will notwithstanding treat them as brethren, and then shall converse with them as friends. So will Christ honor them and advance them. Though Christ is so great a king, Christ will also make them kings, that they may be fit to converse with so glorious a King. Revelation 1:6, "And hath made us kings and priests."

Christ when on earth treated his disciples with great familiarity and freedom. He treated 'em as friends, as he says, John 15:15, "I call you not servants; [for the servant knoweth not what his lord doeth: but I have called you friends]." So in heaven he will not keep them at a greater distance, but admit them nearer, because [they] shall be more fit to be near, [more fit for] union and conversation more intimate. O! how happy will it render them to have so great and glorious and honorable a person treating them with such grace and condescension.

Though they shall see the awful majesty of it, that will not make them afraid, because they will see his love and grace, and condescension and meekness, equal to his majesty. And these [will] draw and invite them to the most intimate conversation. {The} sight of majesty [will] only serve to heighten the pleasure and surprise.

b. This conversation shall be with the greatest endearments and inconceivable manifestations of love. This is evident by those figurative expressions of the church's being the spouse of Christ, being married to Christ and become the Lamb's wife, [to whom Christ] will manifest his love; [he will] unbosom himself to his saints; he will open the intimate and eternal fountain of his love to them, open [the] fountain of his dying love, and will as it were pour forth that fountain into their hearts, which will fill their souls. Then will Christ give his spouse all his love. This love will be as a pure river of water of life, a river of pleasure constantly flowing into the souls of the saints, that shall be in them as rivers of living water; a river that shall be in them, and that they shall be in drinking of and swimming in. And they shall also in their conversing with Christ manifest their love to him; their hearts shall also flow out in a stream, or ascend in a flame of love to Christ continually, a rapturous, transporting love.

The soul shall as it were all dissolve in love in the arms of the glorious Son of God, and breathe itself wholly in ecstasies of divine love into his bosom.

In the most humble and adoring, and yet in the most free and intimate manner.

Those things are what we can say a little of now, and what sometimes, when God helps us, we can conceive a little of: but 'tis but little at the most.

(6) The saints in heaven shall see God. {They shall} not only see that glorious city, and the saints there, and the glorified body of Christ; but they shall see God himself. This is promised to the saints, Matthew 5:8, 1 Corinthians 13:2.

This is that which is called by divines "the beatifical vision," because this is that which the blessedness of the saints in glory does chiefly consist in. This is the highest part of their blessedness; now we are come to the fountain, the infinite fountain of all blessedness. The sight of Christ {glorified}, which has already been spoken of, is not here to be excluded because he is a divine person. The sight of him in his divine nature therefore belongs to the beatifical vision. This vision of God is the heaven of heavens, and therefore I would speak to it a little particularly. And,

1. I would consider the faculty that is the immediate subject of this vision.

2. The nature of the act of vision, or seeing God.

3. The object. And,

4. The manner. And,

167

5. Means.

6. Effects.

And,

1. As to the faculty that is the subject of this sight. 'Tis no sight of anything with the bodily eyes, but 'tis an intellectual view. The beatifical vision of Jesus is not a sight with the eyes of the body, but with the eye of the soul. There is no such thing as seeing God properly with the bodily, because he is a spirit; one of his attributes is that he is invisible. 1 Timothy 1:17, "the King eternal, immortal, invisible." Colossians 1:15, "who is the image of the invisible God." Hebrews 11:27, "as seeing him who is invisible."

This highest blessedness of the soul don't enter in at the door of the bodily senses. This would be to make the blessedness of the soul dependent on the body, or the happiness of men's superior part to be dependent on the inferior. The beatifical vision of God is not any sight with the bodily eyes, because the separate souls of the saints, and the angels which are mere spirits and never were united to bodies, have this view. Matthew 18:10, "their angels do always behold the face of my Father which is in heaven."

'Tis not in beholding any form or visible representation, or shape or color, or shining light that the highest happiness of the soul consists; but 'tis in seeing God, who is a spirit, spiritually, with the eye of the soul.

We have no reason to think that there is any such thing as God's manifesting himself by any natural glorious appearance that is the symbol of his presence in heaven, any otherwise than by the glorified body of Christ.

God was wont under the Old Testament oftentimes to manifest himself by an outward glory, and sometimes in an outward shape or form of a man. But when God manifested himself thus, it was by Christ; it was the second person of the Trinity that was wont thus to appear to men in an outward glory and human shape. John 1:18, "No man hath seen God at any time, the only begotten Son."

But since Christ has actually assumed an human body, there is no need of his assuming any aerial form or shape any more. He is now become visible to the bodily eyes in a more perfect manner, by his having a real body.

The saints that shall see Christ in heaven in his glorified body do much more properly see Christ than if they only saw an assumed shape, or some outward glorious appearance, or the symbol of his presence. For now that which they see is not only a glorious appearance by which Christ is represented, but 'tis real Christ; 'tis his own body. The seeing God or the glorified body of Christ is the most perfect way of seeing God with the bodily eyes that can be: for in seeing a real body that one of the persons of the Trinity has assumed to be his body, and that he dwells in forever as his own, in which the divine majesty and excellency appears as much as 'tis possible for it to appear in outward form or shape, the saints do actually see a divine person with bodily eyes, and in the same manner as we see one another.

But when God showed himself under outward appearances and symbols of his presence only, that was not so proper a sight of a divine person; and it was a mean, imperfect way of God's manifesting himself, suitable to the more imperfect state of the church under the old testament. But now Christ does really subsist in a glorified body, those outward symbols and appearances are done away, as being needless and imperfect. This more imperfect way therefore is altogether needless in heaven, seeing Christ there appears in a glorified body.

This seems to have been an end of God's assuming an human body, viz., that the saints might see God with bodily eyes; that they may see him not only in the understanding, but in all ways of seeing that the human nature is capable of; that we might see God, a divine person, as we see one another. And there is no need of God the Father's manifesting himself in a distinct glorious form, for he that sees the Son sees the Father, as Christ has said, John 14:9; and that, because he "is the image of the invisible God," Colossians 1:15. He is the express and perfect image of the Father, Hebrews 1:3.

But if there be any outward symbol by which God the Father represents himself in heaven, a seeing that is not the beatifical vision: for this is a far more imperfect way of seeing God, than a seeing him with the eye of the soul; the soul is capable of apprehending God in a thousand times more perfect and glorious manner than the eye of the body is. The soul has in itself those powers whereby 'tis sufficiently capable of apprehending spiritual objects, without looking through the windows of the outward senses. The soul is capable of seeing God more immediately and more certainly, and more fully and gloriously, than the eye of the body is.

Having thus considered the faculty [that is the immediate subject of this vision], I proceed,

2. To consider the act of vision. And,

a. This shall be an immediate sight. It will be no apprehension of God's excellency, by arguing of it from his works; neither will it be such a spiritual sight of God as the saints have in this world, seeing of him in his word, or making use of ordinances, which is called a seeing "through a glass, darkly: but then" they shall see him "face to face," 1 Corinthians 13:12. [They] shall not only see the glory of God as being reflected from other things, but they shall see him as we see the sun by his own light in a clear hemisphere; it will be an intuitive view of God that they will have.

What knowledge the saints have of God in this world is like the twilight that is before sun-rising: 'tis not the direct light of the sun, but the light of the sun reflected, and 'tis comparatively a dim light. But hereafter, the saints shall enjoy the perfect day: they shall see God as we immediately behold the sun after it is risen above the horizon, and no cloud or vapor in the heavens to hinder its light.

b. It shall be, according to man's capacity, a perfect sight. It shall not be a comprehensive sight, because 'tis impossible that a finite mind should comprehend God; but yet it shall be

170

perfect in its kind. It shall be perfectly certain, without any doubt or possibility of doubt. There shall be such a view of God in his Being, and in his power and wisdom and holiness, and goodness and love and all-sufficiency, that shall be attended with an intuitive certainty, without any mixture of unbelief, a much greater certainty than any sight with the bodily eyes.

And then it shall be perfectly clear, without any manner of darkness. Now, how much darkness is there mingled with that spiritual sight that the saints have of God's glory in this world; how imperfect is the sight. But then there shall be no obscurity, nothing to cloud the understanding or to hinder the clearness of the view. God shall be hid with no veil, neither shall there be any veil in the heavens. And this sight shall be most enlarged: they shall see vastly more of the glory of God than any of the saints do in this world. The souls of the saints shall be like the angels in extensiveness of understanding.

I proceed now,

3. To consider this vision with respect to its object. And what is to be said on this head, may be comprehended in these two things, viz.,

[a.] That they shall see everything in God that tends to excite and enflame love; and,

b. Everything in him that gratifies love.

a. They shall see everything in God that tends to excite and inflame love, i.e., everything that is lovely {in God that} tends to exalt their esteem and admiration, tends to win and endear the heart. [They shall] behold the infinite excellency and glory of God; shall have a blessed-making sight of his glorious majesty, of his infinite holiness; shall see as those angels do, of whom we read in Isaiah 6:3, that, standing before the throne, cry "Holy, holy, holy, is the Lord of hosts."

[They shall] behold the infinite grace and goodness of God then, that that glorious fountain and ocean be opened fully to their view. Then shall they behold of all [God's] excellency and loveliness. They shall have a clear sight of his immense glory and excellency.

b. They shall see everything in God that gratifies love. They shall see in him all that love desires. Love desires the love of the beloved. So the saints in glory shall see God's transcendent love to them; God will make ineffable manifestations of his love to them. They shall see as much love in God towards them as they desire; they neither will nor can crave any more. This very manifestation that God will make of himself, that will cause the beatifical vision, will be an act of love in God; it will be from the exceeding love of God to them that he will give them this vision, which will add an immense sweetness to it. When they see God so glorious, and at the same [time] see how greatly this God loves them, what delight that [shall] cause in the soul. Love desires union: they shall therefore see this glorious God united to them, and see themselves united to him; they shall see that he is their Father, and that they are his children. They shall see God gloriously present with them: God with them, and God in them, and they in God. Love desires the possessions of its object: therefore they shall see God as their own God; when they behold this transcendent, glorious God, they shall see [him] as their own. When they shall see that glorious power and wisdom of God, they shall see it as altogether engaged for them. When they shall see the beauty of God's holiness, they shall see it as their own, for them to enjoy forever. When they see the boundless ocean of God's goodness and grace, they shall see it to be all theirs.

I come now,

4. To consider the manner in which they shall see and enjoy God: and that is as having communion with Christ therein. The saints shall enjoy God as partaking with Christ of his enjoyment of God: for they are united to him, and are glorified and made happy in the enjoyment of God as his members. As the members of the body do partake of the life and health of the head, so the saints in glory shall be happy as partaking of the blessedness of the Son of God. They, being in Christ, shall partake of the love of God the Father to Christ. And as the Son knows the Father, so they shall partake with him in his sight of God, as being as it were parts of him. As he is in the bosom of the Father, so are they in the bosom of the Father. As he has immense joy in the love of the Father, so have they, every one of them in their measure, the same joy in the love of the Father.

Herein they shall enjoy God in a more exalted and excellent manner than man would have done if he had never fallen. For doubtless that happiness that Christ himself partakes of in his Father's bosom is transcendently sweet and excellent. And how happy therefore are they that are admitted to partake of that pure stream of delight with him.

5. The means by which God shall grant this vision of himself: which is the Holy Ghost. As 'tis by the Holy Ghost that a spiritual sight of God is given in this world, so 'tis the same Holy Spirit by which a beatifical vision is given of God in heaven. The saints in heaven are as dependent on God for all their holiness and all their light as the saints on earth; all is from God by his Holy Spirit, as it is here. They shall have this beatifical vision of God, because they will be full of God, filled with the Holy Spirit of God. The Holy Ghost is the pure river of water of life that proceeds from the throne of God and the Lamb, spoken of in the twenty-second chapter of Revelation, first verse.

6. The effects of the vision: and they are that the soul hereby shall be enflamed with love, and satisfied with pleasure.

a. It shall be enflamed with love. The soul shall not be an inactive spectator, but shall be most active, shall be in the most ardent exercise of love towards the object seen. The soul shall be as it were all eye to behold, and yet all act to love, all a flame of love. The soul shall be as full of love as it shall be of light, and of both it shall be as full as it can hold. The understanding will be in its most perfect act in beholding, and the will will be in its most perfect act in loving. This love will be perfectly such as it ought to be; it shall be perfectly humble. Then the soul shall be in its place at all times, adoring at God's feet, and yet embraced in the arms of his love.

This love shall excite them to praise. And therefore singing praises and hallelujahs shall be what they shall unweariedly be employed in.

b. This sight of God shall satisfy the soul with pleasure. So great will the joy be, that the soul will desire no greater; it shall be full of grace as the large desires of the soul can stretch themselves to. So sweet shall it be, that the soul will desire nothing sweeter. So pure and excellent will it be, that the soul will desire nothing better. Psalm 17:15, "As for me, I shall behold thy face in righteousness: I shall be satisfied, when I awake, with thy likeness." When the soul beholds the glory and love for God, it shall be as it were at the same time filled with the glory and love of God. It shall receive satisfying pleasures, for it shall receive God; God will communicate and as it were pour forth himself into the soul. And with what inexpressible sweetness and complacency will the soul open itself to be thus filled, as the heavens open before the sun to be filled with his light and pleasant influences.

[2.] Having thus considered wherein the eternal happiness of the saints consists, I proceed next to consider some circumstances of it:

(1) 'Tis what will add sweetness to the happiness of heaven, that 'tis all the fruit of free grace and the dying love of Christ. The saints in this world are of that spirit, that they choose the way of salvation by free and sovereign grace, and

salvation in this way seems better and sweeter by far than if they could have it by their own works. Much more will this exceedingly heighten the sweetness of their happiness when they are in heaven, when their love and their humility will be perfect. When they consider their own unworthiness, what vile creatures they were when they came into the world—which then they will be abundantly more sensible of than they are now—and consider what exceeding glory God has advanced them to, what a sweet admiration will it beget in them of free grace.

And what a sweetness will it add, to think that all this glorious blessedness that they are in possession [of], is not of themselves, but is the fruit of the love of that glorious person which they shall then see in his glory, the fruit of his dying love, that it was bought by his precious blood. How will it add to {their admiration}, to consider what great and extreme sufferings Christ underwent to purchase this for them.

It adds greatly to the value of a gift, if it be that which we received of a dear friend as a token of his love: it is more highly prized. But how greatly then will heaven be the more prized by the saints, when they consider it as the fruit of the love of a person so glorious and excellent, and one that is so exceedingly beloved by them, and that 'tis the fruit of so great love, even love that appeared in shedding his own precious blood to purchase this blessedness for them.

(2) It will give them the greater sense of their own blessedness, to see the misery that the damned are in, and consider how exceeding different their own state is from theirs. The saints shall see the misery of the wicked: they shall see their state at the day of judgment; they shall see them at the left hand with devils, shall hear the sentence pronounced, and see it executed. And it looks as if the misery of the wicked would in some respect be in the view of the saints in glory. Such a supposition is both rational and scriptural: 'tis rational, for the misery of the damned is for the glory of God's justice, and doubtless God's justice shall be glorified in the sight of those that are in heaven. 'Tis also scriptural: thus we

read, Revelation 14:10, that {the damned} "shall be tormented in the presence of the holy angels, and in the presence of the Lamb"; i.e., {in the sight} of the whole heavenly assembly. Thus also the smoke of Babylon, or of the Antichristian church, is said to "ascend up forever and ever" in sight of {the heavenly assembly}. So 'tis said of the saints in an happy state, sixty-sixth [chapter] of Isaiah, last verse: "And they shall go forth, and look on the carcasses of the men that have transgressed against God: for their worm shall not die, neither shall their fire be quenched."

This shall greatly heighten the sense of their own happy state. When they consider how exceeding different their own state is, when they consider how differently God has dealt with themselves from what he has done with them; when they see how dreadful their misery is, and consider that this is the misery they are delivered from and must have unavoidably suffered had not God graciously redeemed them; when they consider that they deserved this misery as well as those that suffer it, but Christ has of his sovereign grace redeemed: this will give 'em exalted thoughts of free grace, and cause them exceedingly to admire it, and will greatly heighten their exercises of love to him who has been so gracious to them, and consequently will heighten their joy in his love.

As the damned's seeing the happiness of the saints in heaven will aggravate their misery, so the saints in heaven seeing the misery of the damned in hell, will give them a greater sense of their own happiness.

(3) There are different degrees of happiness and glory in heaven. As there [are] degrees among the angels—there are thrones, dominions, principalities, and powers—so there are degrees amongst the saints. In heaven are many mansions, and of different degrees of dignity. The glory of the saints above will be in some proportion to their eminency in holiness and good works here. Christ will reward all according to their works. He that gained ten pounds was made ruler over ten cities, and he {that gained} five pounds {was made ruler over five cities}, Luke 19:17[-19]. 2 Corinthians 9:6, "He that

sows sparingly shall reap sparingly; and he that sows bountifully [shall reap also bountifully]."

And the Apostle Paul tells us that as "one star differs [from another star in glory]," 1 Corinthians 15:41, [so there are different degrees of happiness in heaven].

Christ tells us that he that does so much as give "a cup of cold water to a disciple in the name of a disciple, he shall in no wise lose his reward" [Matt 10:42].

But this could not be true if a person should have no greater reward for doing many good works, than if he did but few. And this will be no damp to the happiness of those that have lower degrees of happiness and glory, that there are others advanced in glory above them: for all shall be perfectly happy; every one shall be perfectly satisfied; every vessel that is cast into this ocean of happiness is full, though there are some vessels are larger, and will hold more than others. And there shall be no such thing as envy in heaven, but perfect love shall reign through the whole society. Those that are not so high in glory as others won't envy those that are higher, but they will have so great, strong and pure a love to them, that they will rejoice in their superior happiness; their love to them will be such, that they will rejoice that they are happier than they. So that instead of being a damp to their own happiness, it will add to it: they will see it to be fit, that they that han't been most eminent in works of righteousness should be highest exalted in glory, and they will rejoice in having that done, that is fittest to be done. They won't desire it should be otherwise, but will incline that it would be so. There will be a perfect harmony in that society. Those that are most happy will also be most holy. All will be both perfectly holy and perfectly happy, but yet there will be different degrees of both holiness and happiness, according to the measure of each one's capacity. And therefore, those that are lower in glory will have the greatest love to those that are highest in happiness, because they will see most of the image of God in them; and having the greatest love to them, they will rejoice to see them most happy and highest in glory. And so on the other hand, those that are highest in glory, as they will be the most lovely, so they will be fullest of love. As they will excel in happiness, so they will proportionably excel in benevolence and love to others, and will have more love to God and to the saints than those that are lower in holiness and happiness.

And besides, those that will excel in glory, will also excel in humility. Here in this world, those that are above others are the objects of envy, because that others conceive of them as being lifted up with it. But in heaven it will not be so, but those saints in heaven that excel in happiness, so they will in holiness and consequently in humility. The saints in heaven are more humble than the saints on earth, and still the higher we go among them, the greater humility is there. The highest orders of saints, those that know most of God, see most of the distance between God and them, and consequently are comparatively least in their own eyes, and so are most humble.

The exaltation of some in heaven above the rest, will be so far from diminishing anything of the perfect happiness and joy of the rest that are inferior, that they will be the happier for it. Such be the union that there will be in that society, that they will be partakers of each other's happiness. Then will that be fulfilled in its perfection that is spoken in 1 Corinthians 12:26, if "one of the members be honored, all the members rejoice with it."

(4) This happiness of the saints shall never have any interruption. There will nothing ever come in to be any alloy to it. There never will come any cloud to obscure that light, never will be anything to cool that love; the rivers of pleasure won't fail; the glory and love of God and Christ will forever be the same. And the manifestations of it will have no interruption, and no sin or corruption shall never enter there, no temptation to disturb the blessedness; the divine love in the saints shall never cool. There shall be no inconstancy in any of them. The faculties of the saints shall never flag with height and intenseness of exercise, and they will never be cloyed; their relish of these delights will forever be kept up to its

height. Their glorious society shall not grow weary of their hallelujahs; their glorious exercises, though they are so active and vigorous in them, will be performed with perfect ease. The saints shall not be weary of loving and praising and serving, as the sun is not weary of shining.

(5) And to shut up this whole description: there never shall be any end to this glory and blessedness, and therefore 'tis so often called "eternal life" and "everlasting life." We are told that at the day of judgment, when the wicked "shall go away into everlasting punishment," the righteous go away "into life eternal," Matthew 25:46. The pleasures that are at God's right hand are said to be forevermore, Psalm 16:11. And that this is not merely for a long duration, but an absolute eternity, is evident by that, that [Christ] has said that those that believe on him shall not die, John 6:50. Therefore, Revelation 22:5, in the description of New Jerusalem, [it is said,] "and we shall reign forever and ever."

The eternity of this blessedness shall crown all. If the saints knew that there was to be an end to their happiness, though at never so great a distance, yet it would be a great damp to their joy. So much the greater the happiness is, so much the more uncomfortable would the thoughts of an end be; and so much the more joyful will it be to think that there will be no end. The saints will surely know that there will be no end of this their happiness. There will be no more danger of their happiness coming to an end, than there will be that the Being of God will come to end. As God is eternal, so their happiness is eternal. As long as the fountain lasts, they need not fear but they shall be supplied.

"APOSTROPHE TO SARAH PIERPONT"

They say there is a young lady in [New Haven] who is beloved of that almighty Being, who made and rules the world, and that there are certain seasons in which this great Being, in some way or other invisible, comes to her and fills her mind with exceeding sweet delight, and that she hardly cares for anything, except to meditate on him—that she expects after a while to be received up where he is, to be raised out of the world and caught up into heaven; being assured that he loves her too well to let her remain at a distance from him always. There she is to dwell with him, and to be ravished with his love, favor, and delight forever. Therefore, if you present all the world before her, with the richest of its treasures, she disregards it and cares not for it, and is unmindful of any pain or affliction. She has a strange sweetness in her mind, and sweetness of temper, uncommon purity in her affections; is most just and praiseworthy in all her actions; and you could not persuade her to do anything thought wrong or sinful, if you would give her all the world, lest she should offend this great Being. She is of a wonderful sweetness, calmness, and universal benevolence of mind; especially after those times in which this great God has manifested himself to her mind. She will sometimes go about, singing sweetly, from place to [place]; and seems to be always full of joy and pleasure; and no one knows for what. She loves to be alone, and to wander in the fields and on the mountains, and seems to have someone invisible always conversing with her.

"THE NARRATIVE OF SARAH PIERPONT EDWARDS"⁴

On Tuesday night, Jan. 19, 1742,...I felt very uneasy and unhappy, at my being so low in grace. I thought I very much needed help from God, and found a spirit of earnestness to seek help of him, that I might have more holiness. When I had for a time been earnestly wrestling with God for it, I felt within myself great quietness of spirit, unusual submission to God, and willingness to wait upon him, with respect to the time and manner in which he should help me, and wished that he should take his own time, and his own way, to do it.

The next morning, I found a degree of uneasiness in my mind, at Mr. Edwards's suggesting, that he thought I had failed in some measure in point of prudence, in some conversation I had with Mr. Williams of Hadley,[5] the day before. I found that it seemed to bereave me of the quietness and calm of my mind, in any respect not to have the good opinion of my husband. This I much disliked in myself, as arguing a want of a sufficient rest in God, and felt a disposition to fight against it, and look to God for his help, that I might have a more full and entire rest in him, independent of all other things. I continued in this frame, from early in the morning until about ten o'clock, at which time the Rev. Mr. Reynolds[6] went to prayer in the family.

I had before this so entirely given myself up to God, and resigned up everything into his hands, that I had, for a long time, felt myself quite alone in the world; so that the peace and calm of my mind, and my rest in God, as my only and all sufficient happiness, seemed sensibly above the reach of disturbance from any thing but these two: first. My own good name and fair reputation among men, and especially the esteem and just treatment of the people of this town; secondly. And more especially, the esteem, and love and kind treatment of my husband. At times, indeed, I had seemed to be considerably elevated above the influence of even these things; yet I had not found my calm, and peace and rest in God so sensibly, fully and constantly, above the reach of disturbance from them, until now.

While Mr. Reynolds was at prayer in the family this morning, I felt an earnest desire that, in calling on God, he should say, *Father*, or that he should address the Almighty under that appellation: on which the thought turned in my mind—Why can I say, *Father*?—Can I now at this time, with the confidence of a child, and without the least misgiving of heart, call God my Father? This brought to my mind, two lines of Mr. Erskine's Sonnet:

I see him lay his vengeance by,
And smile in Jesus' face.[7]

I was thus deeply sensible, that my sins did loudly call for vengeance; but I then by faith saw God "lay his vengeance by, and smile in Jesus' face." It appeared to be real and certain that he did so. I had not the least doubt, that he then sweetly smiled upon me, with the look of forgiveness and love, having laid aside all his displeasure towards me, for Jesus's sake; which made me feel very weak, and somewhat faint.

In consequence of this, I felt a strong desire to be alone with God, to go to him, without having any one to interrupt the silent and soft communion, which I earnestly desired between God and my own soul; and accordingly withdrew to my chamber. It should have been mentioned that, before I retired, while Mr. Reynolds was praying, these words, in Romans 8:34, came into my mind: "Who is he that condemneth; it is Christ that died, yea rather that is risen again, who is even at the right hand of God, who also maketh intercession for us"; as well as the following words, "Who shall separate us from the love of Christ," etc.; which occasioned great sweetness and delight in my soul. But when I was alone, the words came to mind with far greater power and sweetness; upon which I took the Bible, and read the words to the end of the chapter, when they were impressed on my heart with vastly greater power and sweetness still. They appeared to me with undoubted certainty as the words of God, and as words which God did pronounce concerning me. I had no more doubt of it than I had of my being. I seemed as it were to hear the great God proclaiming thus to the world concerning me: "Who shall lay anything to thy charge," etc.; and had it strongly impressed on me how impossible it was for anything in heaven or earth, in this world or the future, ever to separate me from the love of God which was in Christ Jesus. I cannot find language to express how *certain* this appeared— the everlasting mountains and hills were but shadows to it. My safety, and happiness, and eternal enjoyment of God's immutable love, seemed as durable and unchangeable as God himself. Melted and overcome by the sweetness of this assurance, I fell into a great flow of tears, and could not forbear weeping aloud. It appeared certain to me that God was my Father, and Christ my Lord and Savior, that he was mine and I his. Under a delightful sense of the immediate presence and love of God, these words seemed to come over and over in my mind, "My God, my all; my God, my all." The presence of God was so near, and so real, that I seemed scarcely conscious of any things else. God the Father, and the Lord Jesus Christ, seemed as distinct persons, both manifesting their inconceivable loveliness, and mildness, and gentleness, and their great and immutable love to me. I seemed to be taken under the care and charge of my God and Savior, in an inexpressibly endearing manner; and Christ appeared to me as a mighty Savior, under the character of the Lion of the Tribe of Judah, taking my heart, with all its corruptions, under his care, and putting it at his feet. In all things which concerned me, I felt myself safe under the protection of the Father and the Savior, who appeared with supreme kindness to keep a record of everything that I did, and of everything that was done to me, purely for my good.

The peace and happiness which I hereupon felt, was altogether inexpressible. It seemed to be that which came from heaven, to be eternal and unchangeable. I seemed to be lifted above earth and hell, out of the reach of everything here below, so that I could look on all the rage and enmity of men or devils, with a kind of holy indifference, and an undisturbed tranquility. At the same time, I felt compassion and love for all mankind, and a deep abasement of soul, under a sense of my own unworthiness. I thought of the ministers who were in the house, and felt willing to undergo any labor and self-denial, if they would but come to the help of the Lord. I also felt myself more perfectly weaned from all things here below than ever before. The whole world, with all its enjoyments, and all its troubles, seemed to be nothing: my God was my all, my only portion. No possible suffering appeared to be worth regarding: all persecutions and torments were a mere nothing. I seemed to dwell on high, and the place of defense to be the munition of rocks.

After some time, the two evils mentioned above, as those which I should have been least able to bear, came to my mind—the ill treatment of the town, and the ill will of my husband; but now I was carried exceedingly above even such things as these, and I could feel that, if I were exposed to them both, they would seem comparatively nothing. There was then a deep snow on the ground, and I could think of being driven from my home into the cold and snow, of being chased from the town with the utmost contempt and malice, and of being left to perish with the cold, as cast out by all the world, with perfect calmness and serenity. It appeared to me that it would not move me, or in the least disturb the inexpressible happiness and peace of my soul. My mind seemed as much above all such things as the sun is above the earth.

I continued in a very sweet and lively sense of divine things, day and night, sleeping and waking, until Saturday, Jan. 23. On Saturday morning, I had a most solemn and deep impression on my mind of the eye of God as fixed upon me, to observe what improvement I made of those spiritual communications I had received from him; as well as of the respect shown Mr. Edwards, who had then been sent for to preach at Leicester. I was sensible that I was sinful enough to bestow it on my pride, or on my sloth, which seemed exceedingly dreadful to me. At night, my soul seemed to be filled with an inexpressibly sweet and pure love to God, and to the children of God; with a refreshing consolation and solace of soul, which made me willing to lie on the earth, at the feet of the servants of God, to declare his gracious dealings with me, and breathe forth before them my love, and gratitude and praise.

The next day, which was the Sabbath [Jan. 24, 1742], I enjoyed a sweet and lively and assured sense of God's infinite grace, and favor and love to me, in taking me out of the depths of hell, and exalting me to the heavenly glory, and the dignity of a royal priesthood.

On Monday night [Jan. 25, 1742], Mr. Edwards being gone that day to Leicester, I heard that Mr. Buell was coming to this town, and from what I had heard of him, and of his success, I had strong hopes that there would be great effects from his labors here. At the same time, I had a deep and affecting impression that the eye of God was ever upon my heart, and that it greatly concerned me to watch my heart, and see to it that I was perfectly resigned to God, with respect to the instruments he should make use of to revive religion in this town, and be entirely willing, if it was God's pleasure, that he should make use of Mr. Buell; and also that other Christians should appear to excel me in Christian experience, and in the benefit they should derive from ministers. I was conscious that it would be exceedingly provoking to God if I should not be thus resigned, and earnestly endeavored to watch my heart, that no feelings of a contrary nature might arise; and was enabled, as I thought, to exercise full resignation, and acquiescence in God's pleasure, as to these things. I was sensible what great cause I had to bless God, for the use he had made of Mr. Edwards hitherto; but thought, if he never blessed his labors any more, and should greatly bless the labors of other ministers, I could entirely acquiesce in his will. It appeared to me meet and proper that God should employ babes and sucklings to advance his kingdom. When I thought of these things, it was my instinctive feeling to say, "Amen, Lord Jesus! Amen, Lord Jesus!" This seemed to be the sweet and instinctive language of my soul.

On Tuesday [Jan. 26, 1742], I remained in a sweet and lively exercise of this resignation, and love to and rest in God, seeming to be in my heart from day to day, far above the reach of everything here below. On Tuesday night, especially the latter part of it, I felt a great earnestness of soul and engagedness in seeking God for the town, that religion might now revive, and that God would bless Mr. Buell to that end. God seemed to be very near to me while I was thus striving with him for these things, and I had a strong hope that what I sought of him would be granted. There seemed naturally and unavoidably to arise in my mind an assurance, that now God would do great things for Northampton.

On Wednesday morning [Jan. 27, 1742], I heard that Mr. Buell arrived the night before at Mr. Phelps's, and that there seemed to be great tokens and effects of the presence of God there, which greatly encouraged and rejoiced me. About an hour and a half after, Mr. Buell came to our house, I sat still in entire resignedness to God, and willingness that God should bless his labors here as much as he pleased; though it were to the enlivening of every saint, and to the conversion of every sinner, in the town. These feelings continued afterwards, when I saw his great success; as I never felt the least rising of heart to the contrary, but my submission was even and uniform, without interruption or disturbance. I rejoiced when I saw the honor which God put upon him, and the respect paid him by the people, and the greater success attending his preaching, than had followed the preaching of Mr. Edwards immediately before he went to Leicester. I found rest and rejoicing in it, and the sweet language of my soul continually was, "Amen, Lord Jesus! Amen, Lord Jesus!"

At three o'clock in the afternoon, a lecture was preached by Mr. Buell. In the latter part of the sermon, one or two appeared much moved, and after the blessing, when the people were going out, several others. To my mind there was the clearest evidence that God was present in the congregation, on the work of redeeming love; and in the clear view of this, I was all at once filled with such intense admiration of the wonderful condescension and grace of God, in returning again to Northampton, as overwhelmed my soul, and immediately took away my bodily strength. This was accompanied with an earnest longing that those of us, who were the children of God, might now arise and strive. It appeared to me that the angels in heaven sung praises, for such wonderful, free and sovereign grace, and my heart was lifted up in adoration and praise. I continued to have clear views of the future world, of eternal happiness and misery, and my heart full of love to the souls of men. On seeing some that I found were in a natural condition, I felt a most tender compassion for them; but especially was I, while I remained in the meeting-house, from time to time overcome, and my strength taken away, by the sight of one and another, whom I regarded as the children of God, and who I had heard were lively and animated in religion. We remained in the meeting-house about three hours, after the public exercises were over. During most of the time, my bodily strength was overcome; and the joy and thankfulness, which were excited in my mind, as I contemplated the great goodness of God, led me to converse with those who were near me, in a very earnest manner.

When I came home, I found Mr. Buell, Mr. Christophers, Mr. Hopkins, Mrs. Eleanor Dwight, the wife of Mr. Joseph Allen, and Mr. Job Strong,[8] at the house. Seeing and conversing with them on the divine goodness renewed my former feelings, and filled me with an intense desire that we might all arise, and, with an active, flowing, and fervent heart give glory to God. The intenseness of my feelings again took away my bodily strength. The words of one of Dr. Watts's Hosannas powerfully affected me; and, in the course of the conversation, I uttered them, as the real language of my heart, with great earnestness and emotion.

> Hosanna to King David's Son,
> Who reigns on a superior throne, etc.[9]

And while I was uttering the words, my mind was so deeply impressed with the love of Christ, and a sense of his immediate presence, that I could with difficulty refrain from rising from my seat, and leaping for joy. I continued to enjoy this intense, and lively and refreshing sense of divine things, accompanied with strong emotions, for nearly an hour; after which I experienced a delightful calm, and peace and rest in God, until I retired for the night; and during the night, both waking and sleeping, I had joyful views of divine things, and a complacential rest of soul in God.

I awoke in the morning of Thursday, Jan. 28th, in the same happy frame of mind, and engaged in the duties of my family with a sweet consciousness, that God was present with me, and with earnest longings of soul for the continuance, and increase, of the blessed fruits of the Holy Spirit in the town. About nine o'clock, these desires became so exceedingly intense, when I saw numbers of the people coming into the house, with an appearance of deep interest in religion, that my bodily strength was much weakened, and it was with difficulty that I could pursue my ordinary avocations. About eleven o'clock, as I accidentally went into the room where Mr. Buell was conversing with some of the people, I heard him say, "O that we, who are the children of God, should be cold and lifeless in religion!" and I felt such a sense of the deep ingratitude manifested by the children of God, in such coldness and deadness, that my strength was immediately taken away, and I sunk down on the spot. Those who were near raised me, and placed me in a chair; and, from the fullness of my heart, I expressed to them, in a very earnest manner, the deep sense I had of the wonderful grace of Christ towards me, of the assurance I had of his having saved me from hell, of my happiness running parallel with eternity, of the duty of giving up all to God, and of the peace and joy inspired by an entire dependence on his mercy and grace. Mr. Buell then read a melting hymn of Dr. Watts,[10] concerning the loveliness of Christ, the enjoyments and employments of heaven, and the Christian's earnest desire of heavenly things; and the truth and reality of the things mentioned in the hymn made so strong an impression on my mind, and my soul was drawn so powerfully towards Christ and heaven, that I leaped unconsciously from my chair. I seemed to be drawn upwards, soul and body, from the earth towards heaven; and it appeared to me that I must naturally and necessarily ascend thither. These feelings continued while the hymn was reading, and during the prayer of Mr. Christophers which followed. After the prayer, Mr. Buell read two other hymns, on the glories of heaven, which moved me so exceedingly, and drew me so strongly heavenwards, that it seemed as it were to draw my body upwards, and I felt as if I must necessarily ascend thither. At length my strength failed me, and I sunk down; when they took me up and laid me on the bed, where I lay for a considerable time, faint with joy, whole contemplating the glories of the heavenly world. After I had lain a while, I felt more perfectly subdued and weaned from the world, and more fully resigned to God, than I had ever been conscious of before. I felt an entire indifference to the opinions, and representations and conduct of mankind respecting me; and a perfect willingness, that God should employ some other instrument than Mr. Edwards, in advancing the work of grace in Northampton. I was entirely swallowed up in God, as my only portion, and his honor and glory was the object of my supreme desire and delight. At the same time, I felt a far greater love to the children of God, than ever before. I seemed to love them as my own soul; and when I saw them, my heart went out towards them, with an inexpressible endearedness and sweetness. I beheld them by faith in their risen and glorified state, with spiritual bodies re-fashioned after the image of Christ's glorified body, and arrayed in the beauty of heaven. The time when they would be so appeared very near, and by faith it seemed as if it were present. This was accompanied with a ravishing sense of the unspeakable joys of the upper world. They appeared to my mind in all their reality and certainty, and as it were in actual and distinct vision; so plain and evident were they to the eye of my faith, I seemed to regard them as begun. These anticipations were renewed over and over, while I lay on the bed, from twelve o'clock till four, being too much exhausted by emotions of joy to rise and sit up; and during most of the time, my feelings prompted me to converse very earnestly, with one and another of the pious women, who were present, on those spiritual and heavenly objects, of which I had so deep an impression. A little while before I arose, Mr. Buell and the people went to meeting.

I continued in a sweet and lively sense of divine things, until I retired to rest. That night, which was Thursday night, Jan. 28, was the sweetest night I ever had in my life. I never before, for so long a time together, enjoyed so much of the light and rest and sweetness of heaven in my soul, but without the least agitation of body during the whole time. The great part of the night I lay awake, sometimes asleep, and sometimes between sleeping and waking. But all night I continued in a constant, clear, and lively sense of the heavenly sweetness of Christ's excellent and transcendent love, of his nearness to me, and of my dearness to him, with an inexpressibly sweet calmness of soul in an entire rest in him. I seemed to myself to perceive a glow of divine love come down from the heart of Christ in heaven, into my heart, in a constant stream, like a stream or pencil of sweet light. At the same time, my heart and soul all flowed out in love to Christ; so that there seemed to be a constant flowing and reflowing of heavenly and divine love, from Christ's heart to mine; and I appeared to myself to float or swim, in these bright, sweet beams of the love of Christ, like the motes swimming in the beams of the sun, or the streams of his light which come in at the window. My soul remained in a kind of heavenly elysium. So far as I am capable of making a comparison, I think that what I felt each minute, during the continuance of the whole time, was worth more than all the outward comfort and pleasure which I had enjoyed in my whole life put together. It was a pure delight, which fed and satisfied the soul. It was pleasure, without the least sting, or any interruption. It was a sweetness, which my soul was lost in. It seemed to be all that my feeble frame could sustain, of that fulness of joy, which is felt by those, who behold the face of Christ, and share his love in the heavenly world. There was but little difference, whether I was asleep or awake, so deep was the impression made on my soul; but if there was any difference, the sweetness was greatest and most uninterrupted, while I was asleep.

As I awoke early the next morning, which was Friday [Jan. 29, 1742], I was led to think of Mr. Williams of Hadley preaching that day in the town, as had been appointed; and to examine my heart, whether I was willing that he, who was a neighboring minister, should be extraordinarily blessed, and made a greater instrument of good in the town, than Mr. Edwards; and was enabled to say, with respect to that matter, "Amen, Lord Jesus!" and to be entirely willing, if God pleased, that he should be the instrument of converting every soul in the town. My soul acquiesced fully in the will of God, as to the instrument, if his work of renewing grace did but go on.

This lively sense of the beauty and excellency of divine things continued during the morning, accompanied with peculiar sweetness and delight. To my own imagination, my soul seemed to be gone out of me to God and Christ in heaven, and to have very little relation to my body. God and Christ were so present to me, and so near me, that I seemed removed from myself. The spiritual beauty of the Father and the Savior seemed to engross my whole mind; and it was the instinctive feeling of my heart, "Thou art; and there is none beside thee." I never felt such an entire emptiness of self-love, or any regard to any private, selfish interest of my own. It seemed to me that I had entirely done with myself. I felt that the opinions of the world concerning me were nothing, and that I had no more to do with any outward interest of my own, than with that of a person whom I never saw. The glory of God seemed to be all, and in all, and to swallow up every wish and desire of my heart.

Mr. Sheldon[11] came into the house about ten o'clock, and said to me as he came in, "The Sun of righteousness arose on my soul this morning, before day"; upon which I said to him in reply, "That Sun has not set upon my soul all this night; I have dwelt on high in the heavenly mansions; the light of divine love has surrounded me; my soul has been lost in God, and has almost left the body." This conversation only served to give me a still livelier sense of the reality and excellence of divine things, and that to such a degree as again to take away my strength, and occasion great agitation of body. So strong were my feelings, I could not refrain from conversing with those around me, in a very earnest manner, for about a quarter of an hour, on the infinite riches of divine love in the work of salvation; when, my strength entirely failing, my flesh grew very cold, and they carried me and set me by the fire. As I sat there, I had a most affecting sense of the mighty power of Christ which had been exerted in what he had done for my soul, and in sustaining and keeping down the native corruptions of my heart, and of the glorious and wonderful grace of God in causing the ark to return to Northampton. So intense were my feelings, when speaking of these things, that I could not forbear rising up and leaping with joy and exultation. I felt at the same time an exceedingly strong and tender affection for the children of God, and realized, in a manner exceedingly sweet and ravishing, the meaning of Christ's prayer, in John 17:21, "That they all may be one, as thou Father art in me, and I in thee, that they also may be one in us." This union appeared to me an inconceivable, excellent, and sweet oneness; and at the same time I felt that oneness in my soul, with the children of God who were present. Mr. Christophers then read the hymn out of the *Penitential Cries*, beginning with,

> My soul doth magnify the Lord,
> My spirit doth rejoice.

The whole hymn was deeply affecting to my feelings; but when these words were read,

> My sighs at length are turn'd to songs,
> The Comforter is come,[12]

so conscious was I of the joyful presence of the Holy Spirit, I could scarcely refrain from leaping with transports of joy. This happy frame of mind continued until two o'clock, when Mr. Williams came in, and we soon went to meeting. He preached on the subject of the assurance of faith. The whole sermon was affecting to me, but especially when he came to show the way in which assurance was obtained, and to point out its happy fruits. When I heard him say, that "those, who have assurance, have a foretaste of heavenly glory," I knew the truth of it from what I then felt: I knew that I then tasted the clusters of the heavenly Canaan: my soul was filled and overwhelmed with light, and love, and joy in the Holy Ghost, and seemed just ready to go away from the body. I could scarcely refrain from expressing my joy aloud, in the midst of the service. I had in the meantime an overwhelming sense of the glory of God, as the Great Eternal All, and of the happiness of having my own will entirely subdued to his will. I knew that the foretaste of glory which I then had in my soul, came from him, that I certainly should go to him, and should, as it were, drop into the Divine Being, and be swallowed up in God.

After meeting was done, the congregation waited while Mr. Buell went home, to prepare to give them a lecture. It was almost dark before he came, and, in the meantime, I conversed in a very earnest and joyful manner with those who were with me in the pew. My mind dwelt on the thought that the Lord God Omnipotent reigneth, and it appeared to me that he was going to set up a reign of love on the earth, and that heaven and earth were, as it were, coming together; which so exceedingly moved me that I could not forbear expressing aloud, to those near me, my exultation of soul. This subsided into a heavenly calm, and a rest of soul in God, which was even sweeter than what preceded it. Afterwards, Mr. Buell came and preached; and the same happy frame of mind continued during the evening, and night, and the next day. In the forenoon, I was thinking of the manner in which the children of God had been treated in the world—particularly of their being shut up in prison—and the folly of such attempts to make them miserable seemed to surprise me. It appeared astonishing, that men should think, by this means, to injure those who had such a kingdom within them. Towards night, being informed that Mrs. P—— had expressed her fears lest I should die before Mr. Edwards's return, and he should think the people had killed his wife; I told those who were present that I chose to die in the way that was most agreeable to God's will, and that I should be willing to die in darkness and horror, if it was most for the glory of God.

In the evening, I read those chapters in John, which contain Christ's dying discourse with his disciples, and his prayer with them. After I had done reading, and was in my retirement, a little before bedtime, thinking on what I had read, my soul was so filled with love to Christ, and love to his people, that I fainted under the intenseness of the feeling. I felt, while reading, a delightful acquiescence in the petition to the Father—"I pray not that thou shouldst take them out of the world, but that thou shouldst keep them from the evil." Though it seemed to me infinitely better to die to go to Christ, yet I felt an entire willingness to continue in this world so long as God pleased, to do and suffer what he would have me.

After retiring to rest and sleeping a little while, I awoke and had a very lively consciousness of God's being near me. I had an idea of a shining way, or path of light, between heaven and my soul, somewhat as on Thursday night, except that God seemed nearer to me, and as it were close by, and the way seemed more open, and the communication more immediate and more free. I lay awake most of the night, with a constant delightful sense of God's great love and infinite condescension, and with a continual view of God as *near*, and as *my God*. My soul remained, as on Thursday night, in a kind of heavenly elysium. Whether waking or sleeping, there was no interruption, throughout the night, to the views of my soul, to its heavenly light, and divine, inexpressible sweetness. It was without any agitation or motion of the body. I was led to reflect on God's mercy to me, in giving me, for many years, a willingness to die; and after that, for more than two years past, in making me willing to live, that I might do and suffer whatever he called me to here; whereas, before that, I often used to feel impatient at the thought of living. This then appeared to me, as it had often done before, what gave me much the greatest sense of thankfulness to God. I also thought how God had graciously given me, for a great while, an entire resignation to his will, with respect to the kind and manner of death that I should die; having been made willing to die on the rack, or at the stake, or any other tormenting death, and, if it were God's will, to die in darkness; and how I had that day been made very sensible and fully willing, if it was God's pleasure and for his glory, to die in horror. But now it occurred to me that when I had thus been made willing to live, and to be kept on this dark abode, I used to think of living no longer than to the ordinary age of man. Upon this I was led to ask myself, whether I was not willing to be kept out of heaven even longer; and my whole heart seemed immediately to reply, "Yes, a thousand years, if it be God's will, and for his honor and glory"; and then my heart, in the language of resignation, went further, and with great alacrity and sweetness, to answer as it were over and over again, "Yes, and live a thousand years in horror, if it be most for the glory of God: yea, I am willing to live a thousand year an hell upon earth, if it be most for the honor of God." But then I considered with myself what this would be, to live a hell upon earth for so long a time; and I thought of the torment of my body being so great, awful, and overwhelming, that none could bear to live in the country where the spectacle was seen, and of the torment and horror of my mind being vastly greater than the torment of my body; and it seemed to me that I found a perfect willingness, and sweet quietness and alacrity of soul, in consenting that it should be so, if it were most for the glory of God; so that there was no hesitation, doubt, or darkness in my mind, attending the thoughts of it, but my resignation seemed to be clear, like a light that shone through my soul. I continued saying, "Amen, Lord Jesus! Amen, Lord Jesus! Glorify thyself in me, in my body and my soul," with a calm and sweetness of soul, which banished all reluctance. The glory of God seemed to overcome me and swallow me up, and every conceivable suffering, and everything that was terrible to my nature, seemed to shrink to nothing before it. This resignation continued in its clearness and brightness the rest of the night, and all the next day, and the night following, and on Monday in the forenoon, without interruption or abatement. All this while, whenever I thought of it, the language of my soul was, with the greatest fullness and alacrity, "Amen, Lord Jesus! Amen, Lord Jesus!" In the afternoon of Monday, it was not quite so perceptible and lively, but my mind remained so much in a similar frame, for more than a week, that I could never think of it without an inexpressible sweetness in my soul.

After I had felt this resignation on Saturday night, for some time as I lay in bed, I felt such a disposition to rejoice in God, that I wished to have the world join me in praising him; and was ready to wonder how the world of mankind could lie and sleep, when there was such a God to praise, and rejoice in, and could scarcely forbear calling out to those who were asleep in the house, to arise, and rejoice, and praise God. When I arose in the morning of the Sabbath [Jan. 31, 1742], I felt a love to all mankind, wholly peculiar in its strength and sweetness, far beyond all that I had ever felt before. The power of that love seemed to be inexpressible. I thought, if I were surrounded by enemies, who were venting their malice and cruelty upon me, in tormenting me, it would still be impossible that I should cherish any feelings towards them but those of love, and pity and ardent desires for their happiness. At the same time I thought, if I were cast off by my nearest and dearest friends, and if the feelings and conduct of my husband were to be changed from tenderness and affection to extreme hatred and cruelty, and that every day I could so rest in God, that it would not touch my heart, or diminish my happiness. I could still go on with alacrity in the performance of every act of duty, and my happiness remain undiminished and entire.[13]

I never before felt so far from a disposition to judge and censure others, with respect to the state of their hearts, their sincerity, or their attainments in holiness, as I did that morning. To do this seemed abhorrent to every feeling of my heart. I realized also, in an unusual and very lively manner, how great a part of Christianity lies in the performance of our social and relative duties to one another. The same lively and joyful sense of spiritual and divine things continued throughout the day—a sweet love to God and all mankind, and such an entire rest of soul in God, that it seemed as if nothing that could be said of me, or done to me, could touch my heart, or disturb my enjoyment. The road between heaven and my soul seemed open and wide all the day long; and the consciousness I had of the reality and excellence of heavenly things was so clear, and the affections they excited so intense, that it overcame my strength, and kept my body weak and faint, the great part of the day, so that I could not stand or go without help. The night also was comforting and refreshing.

This delightful frame of mind was continued on Monday [Feb. 1, 1742]. About noon, one of the neighbors, who was conversing with me, expressed himself thus, "One smile from Christ is worth a thousand million pounds," and the words affected me exceedingly, and in a manner which I cannot express. I had a strong sense of the infinite worth of Christ's approbation and love, and at the same time of the grossness of the comparison; and it only astonished me that any one could compare a smile of Christ to any earthly treasure. Towards night, I had a deep sense of the awful greatness of God, and felt with what humility and reverence we ought to behave ourselves before him. Just then, Mr. W—— came in, and spoke with a somewhat light, smiling air, of the flourishing state of religion in the town, which I could scarcely bear to see. It seemed to me that we ought greatly to revere the presence of God, and to behave ourselves with the utmost solemnity and humility, when so great and holy a God was so remarkably present, and to rejoice before him with trembling.

In the evening, these words, in the *Penitential Cries*—"THE COMFORTER IS COME!"—were accompanied to my soul with such conscious certainty, and such intense joy, that immediately it took away my strength, and I was falling to the floor, when some of those who were near me caught me and held me up. And when I repeated the words to the bystanders, the strength of my feelings was increased. The name—"THE COMFORTER"—seemed to denote that the Holy Spirit was the only and infinite Fountain of comfort and joy, and this seemed real and certain to my mind. These words—"THE COMFORTER"—seemed as it were immensely great, enough to fill heaven and earth.

On Tuesday [Feb. 2, 1742] after dinner, Mr. Buell, as he sat at table, began to discourse about the glories of the upper world, which greatly affected me, so as to take away my strength. The views and feelings of the preceding evening, respecting the Great Comforter, were renewed in the most lively and joyful manner; so that my limbs grew cold, and I continued to a considerable degree overcome for about an hour, earnestly expressing to those around me my deep and joyful sense of the presence and divine excellence of the Comforter, and of the glories of heaven.

It was either on Tuesday, or Wednesday, that Mr. W—— came to the house, and informed what account Mr. Lyman,[14] who was just then come from Leicester, on his way from Boston, gave of Mr. Edwards's success in making peace and promoting religion at Leicester. The intelligence inspired me with such an admiring sense of the great goodness of God, in using Mr. Edwards as the instrument of doing good, and promoting the work of salvation, that it immediately overcame me, and took away my strength, so that I could no longer stand on my feet. On Wednesday night [Feb. 3, 1742], Mr. Clark, coming in with Mr. Buell and some of the people, asked me how I felt. I told him that I did not feel at all times alike, but this I thought I could say, that I had given up all to God, and there is nothing like it, nothing like giving up all to him, esteeming all to be his, and resigning all at his call. I told him that many a time within a twelvemonth, I had asked myself when I lay down, how I should feel, if our house and all our property in it should be burnt up, and we should that night be turned out naked; whether I could cheerfully resign all to God; and whether I so saw that all was his, that I could fully consent to his will, in being deprived of it, and that I found, so far as I could judge, an entire resignation to his will, and felt that, if he should thus strip me of every thing, I had nothing to say, but should, I thought, have an entire calm and rest in God, for it was his own, and not mine. After this, Mr. Phelps gave us an account of his own feelings, during a journey from which he had just returned; and then Mr. Pomeroy[15] broke forth in the language of joy, and thankfulness and praise, and continued speaking to us nearly an hour, leading us all the time to rejoice in the visible presence of God, and to adore his infinite goodness and condescension. He concluded by saying, "I would say more, if I could; but words were not made to express these things." This reminded me of the words of Mrs. Rowe:

> More I would speak, but all my words are faint:
> Celestial Love, what eloquence can paint?
> No more, by mortal words, can be expressed;
> But vast Eternity shall tell the rest.[16]

and my former impressions of heavenly and divine things were renewed with so much power, and life and joy, that my strength all failed me, and I remained for some time faint and exhausted. After the people had retired, I had a still more lively and joyful sense of the goodness and all-sufficiency of God, of the pleasure of loving him, and of being alive and active in his service, so that, I could not sit still, but walked the room for some time, in a kind of transport. The contemplation was so refreshing and delightful, so much like a heavenly feast within the soul, that I felt an absolute indifference as to any external circumstances; and, according to my best remembrance, this enlivening of my spirit continued so, that I slept but little that night.

The next day, being Thursday [Feb. 4, 1742], between ten and eleven o'clock, and a room full of people being collected, I heard two persons give a minute account of the enlivening and joyful influences of the Holy Spirit on their own hearts. It was sweet to me, to see others before me in their divine attainments, and to follow after them to heaven. I thought I should rejoice to follow the negro servants in the town to heaven. While I was thus listening, the consideration of the blessed appearances there were of God's being there with us, affected me so powerfully, that the joy and transport of the preceding night were again renewed. After this, they sang an hymn, which greatly moved me, especially the latter part of it, which speaks of the ungratefulness of not having the praises of Christ always on our tongues. Those last words of the hymn seemed to fasten on my mind, and as I repeated them over, I felt such intense love to Christ, and so much delight in praising him, that I could hardly forbear leaping from my chair, and singing aloud for joy and exultation. I continued thus extraordinarily moved until about one o'clock, when the people went away.

Part Three

Beauty

⌁

INTRODUCTION
TO PART THREE

As mentioned in the general introduction to this volume, Edwards was rather unique among theologians in the central place he gave to the concept of beauty, describing God (and Christ) and life in God aesthetically. One of the earliest places he does this in his writings is in the very first entry of his "Miscellanies," Edwards's major repository of entries on theological and philosophical topics, which amounts to over 1,400 entries in nine manuscript volumes. He begins this considerable collection with entry no. a, titled "Of Holiness," which seeks to describe, psalm-like, the beauty of holiness, both in the Godhead and in the saint. It is to this entry that Edwards referred in his "Personal Narrative" after reviewing his private writings, such was the foundational importance of the concept to him.

Another formative concept for Edwards was typology. Indeed, it was a central exegetical as well as spiritual discipline for him. In his expanded typology, which found adumbration and fulfillment in inventive ways between the biblical testaments as well as in human experience and in nature, Edwards again broke the boundaries of his Reformed tradition, but in the process anticipated the sacralization of nature that would occur over the next several centuries. He not only kept a separate notebook of over two hundred entries called "Images of Divine Things," but also a smaller assemblage of "Types," containing hermeneutical statements and Scripture proofs for his views. Entries from the latter are presented here, in which Edwards eloquently proclaims, against anticipated skeptics, his conviction that "the whole universe" is "full of images of divine things, as full as a language is of words."

The three subsequent selections all are variations on the theme of the beauty or "sweetness" of Christ, arguably Edwards's favorite subject for meditation and one that elicited from him some of his most elegant and earnest prose. First come two sermons. *The Sweet Harmony of Christ* describes the mutual love of Christ and the soul, and the *Application on Love to Christ* is "one of the more remarkable meditations on the nature of holy love to issue from the pen of Jonathan Edwards" (WJE 10:605). Then comes the letter to Lady Mary Pepperrell, which seeks to assuage her grief over the loss of a child by holding out to her a portrait of the Christ who wipes away all tears.

Finally, the contemplation of heaven formed an important element in Edwards's spirituality. Surely one of his most sustained and revealing descriptions of the afterlife for glorified saints is "Heaven Is a World of Love," the concluding sermon of his series on 1 Corinthians 13, later published as *Charity and Its Fruits*. In the portion of the sermon given here, Edwards lays out the "cause and fountain" of love in heaven, namely, the God of love; the "objects" of that love, who shall be perfectly happy; the "subjects," in which love reaches in ever heart; and the "principle" of love, both in nature and in degree.

"MISCELLANIES" NO. A, "OF HOLINESS"

[a.] Holiness is a most beautiful and lovely thing. We drink in strange notions of holiness from our childhood, as if it were a melancholy, morose, sour, and unpleasant thing; but there is nothing in it but what is sweet and ravishingly lovely. 'Tis the highest beauty and amiableness, vastly above all other beauties. 'Tis a divine beauty, makes the soul heavenly and far purer than anything here on earth; this world is like mire and filth and defilement to that soul which is sanctified. 'Tis of a sweet, pleasant, charming, lovely, amiable, delightful, serene, calm, and still nature. 'Tis almost too high a beauty for any creatures to be adorned with; it makes the soul a little, sweet, and delightful image of the blessed Jehovah.

Oh, how may angels stand, with pleased, delighted, and charmed eyes, and look, with smiles of pleasure upon their lips, upon that soul that is holy; how may they hover over such a soul, to delight to behold such loveliness! How is it above all the heathen virtues, of a more light, bright, and pure nature, more serene and calm, more peaceful and delightsome! What a sweet calmness, what a calm ecstasy, doth it bring to the soul! How doth it make the soul love itself; how doth it make the pure invisible world love it; yea, how doth God love it and delight in it; how do even the whole creation, the sun, the fields, and trees love a humble holiness; how doth all the world congratulate, embrace, and sing to a sanctified soul!

Oh, of what a sweet, humble nature is holiness! How peaceful and, loving all things but sin, of how refined and exalted a nature is it! How doth it clear change the soul and make it more excellent than other beings! How is it possible that such a divine thing should be on earth? It makes the soul like a delightful field or garden planted by God, with all manner of pleasant flowers growing in the order in which nature has planted them, that is all pleasant and delightful, undisturbed, free from all the noise of man and beast, enjoying a sweet calm and the bright, calm, and gently vivifying beams of the sun forevermore: where the sun is Jesus Christ; the blessed beams and calm breeze, the Holy Spirit; the sweet and delightful flowers, and the pleasant shrill music of the little birds, are the Christian graces. Or like the little white flower: pure, unspotted, and undefined, low and humble, pleasing and harmless; receiving the beams, the pleasant beams of the serene sun, gently moved and a little shaken by a sweet breeze, rejoicing as it were in a calm rapture, diffusing around [a] most delightful fragrancy, standing most peacefully and lovingly in the midst of the other like flowers round about. How calm and serene is the heaven overhead! How free is the world from noise and disturbance! How, if one were but holy enough, would they of themselves [and] as it were naturally ascend from the earth in delight, to enjoy God as Enoch did!

EXCERPTS FROM "TYPES" NOTEBOOK

Types are a certain sort of language, as it were, in which God is wont to speak to us. And there is, as it were, a certain idiom in that language which is to be learned the same that the idiom of any language is, viz., by good acquaintance with the language, either by being naturally trained up in it, learning it by education (but that is not the way in which corrupt mankind learned divine language), or by much use and acquaintance together with a good taste or judgment, by comparing one thing with another and having our senses as it were exercised to discern it (which is the way that adult persons must come to speak any language, and in its true idiom, that is not their native tongue).

Great care should be used, and we should endeavor to be well and thoroughly acquainted, or we shall never understand [or] have a right notion of the idiom of the language. If we go to interpret divine types without this, we shall be just like one that pretends to speak any language that hassn't thoroughly learnt it. We shall use many barbarous expressions that fail entirely of the proper beauty of the language, that are very harsh in the ears of those that are well versed in the language.

God han't expressly explained all the types of Scriptures, but has done so much as is sufficient to teach us the language....

I expect by very ridicule and contempt to be called a man of a very fruitful brain and copious fancy, but they are welcome to it. I am not ashamed to own that I believe that the whole universe, heaven and earth, air and seas, and the divine constitution and history of the Holy Scriptures, be full of images of divine things, as full as a language is of words; and that the multitude of those things that I have mentioned are but a very small part of what is really intended to be signified and typified by these things; but that there is room for persons to be learning more and more of this language and seeing more of that which is declared in it to the end of the world without discovering all.

⁑

THE SWEET HARMONY OF CHRIST (1735)[1]

John 10:4
He goeth before them, and the sheep follow him....

Doctrine

There is a sweet harmony between Christ and the soul of a true Christian.

The harmony that there is consists in three things:

I. A harmony of mutual respect.

II. A harmony of conformity and likeness.

III. {A harmony} of suitableness.

I. There is between Christ and the soul of a true Christian a sweet harmony of mutual respect. This consists,

First. In mutual election or choice. Christ and the true Christian do choose each other: true believers are those that are Christ's chosen ones. Revelation 17:14, "They that are with him are called and chosen." John 15:16, "I have chosen you, and ordained you, that ye should go and bring forth fruit." So likewise is Jesus Christ the object of their choice: he is their chosen one.

A true Christian is one that Christ has chosen before others. He has chosen [some], passing by others, rejecting multitudes, thousands and millions, passing by many of the princes and great ones of the earth. John 15:19, "I have chosen you out of the world."

So is Christ chosen by the true Christian before all earthly things, yea, all created objects. His soul chooses Christ in comparison of them, rejecting and neglecting all other things. This is with him the "pearl of great price," of such exceeding value in his esteem that for the sake of it, he sells all that he has and buys it.

Christ has chosen believers to be a peculiar people to himself, to be his portion and special treasure. And so have they chosen

Christ [to] be their portion and peculiar treasure. He is their chosen happiness. This is the treasure hid in the field, which a true Christian finds, and goes and sells all that he has, and buys that field. True Christians are Christ's chosen disciples. He is their chosen Redeemer and Lord. They choose him above all others to be their Savior, above their own righteousness or any fleshly arm.

Christ hath chosen the soul of the believer to be his spouse and spiritual bride. The soul of the believer mutually chooses Christ to be his best and nearest friend, and of free choice and inclination gives up itself to be espoused unto Christ.

That is the language of Christ to the souls of true Christians. Canticles 1:8 (and also 5:9 and 6:1), "O thou fairest among women." And that is the language of the believer's soul concerning Christ. Psalm 45:2, "Thou art fairer than the sons of men." And Canticles 5:10, "My beloved is the chiefest among ten thousand."

Second. In mutual love. The heart of Christ and the true Christian are united in love: "I love them that love me." Christ is first in love to them, for Christ has loved them with an everlasting love. But when they are converted, their souls are brought into a harmonious agreement with Christ in this respect. Christ hath loved the true Christian with a transcendent love, with a love that in its height, and depth, and breadth passeth knowledge. And they mutually love him with a supreme love, with a love whereby they set him above all (Matthew 10:37). Christ hath loved them with a dying love; and so it is the spirit and temper of a Christian to be ready to lay down his life for Christ, if his honor and glory should call for it.

Christ hath a great esteem and value for his true disciples. They are his jewels, and they are precious in his sight. "Since thou wast precious in mine eyes, thou hast been honorable." So is Christ highly prized by the true Christian. To them that believe, he is precious (1 Pet 2:7); and they are of the same spirit with the Apostle, who says that all things were accounted as loss.

Christ is altogether lovely in the eyes of a Christian. There is nothing in Christ, no attribute or qualification, but that he is lovely to him on the account of it. Not only his goodness and grace, but his justice and sovereignty is lovely to the Christian. Canticles 5:16, "He is altogether lovely." So also the Christian may be said to be wholly lovely in the eyes of Christ; for though there be much remaining deformity, yet 'tis as it were hidden from the eyes of Christ, that he sees it not. He doth not behold iniquity in Jacob, nor see [perverseness in Israel] (Numbers 23:21). And therefore Christ says to his church, Canticles 4:7, "Behold, thou art all fair, my love; there is no spot in thee."

Christ loves the true Christian with a love of benevolence from love to him. He seeks and promises his deliverance from eternal misery and from all evil, and his enjoyment of a most exceeding and eternal glory and happiness. Such is Christ's love to the Christian that nothing is esteemed too good, too great an happiness or honor to be bestowed, or too much to do or to suffer to procure it. The Christian is in his nature of the same spirit and disposition towards Christ. His love to Christ causes him earnestly to define his honor and glory, and to seek that more than all his temporal interests, profits, or pleasures.

Such is Christ's love to a true Christian that he is jealous for his good and welfare, and nothing will soever provoke him than to see any injure him. Matthew 18:6, "If any offend one of these little ones." And such is the spirit of a Christian towards Christ [that] he is jealous for his glory. He has a spirit of zeal for the glory of his Redeemer, and nothing will more grieve and offend him than to see him dishonored and his interest suffering. Christ and the soul of the true Christian have a mutual complacence in each other, and hath delight in the believer. Isaiah 62:5, "As the bridegroom rejoiceth [over the bride, so shall thy God rejoice over thee]." Christ is exceedingly well-pleased and takes sweet delight in the graces and virtues of the Christian, in that beauty and loveliness which he hath put upon him. Canticles 4:9, "Thou hast ravished my heart."

The believer has also a complacence in Christ: he has complacence in the person of Christ, and hath complacence in his offices. He approves of him as a Redeemer. His soul acquiesces in the way of salvation by him, as a sweet, and excellent, and suitable way: it loves the way of true grace by Christ and by his righteousness, and is well-pleased in it, that Christ should have all the glory of his salvation. He takes full contentment in Christ as a Savior. Having found Christ, he desires no other; having found the fountain, he sits down by it; having found Christ, his hungry and thirsty soul is satisfied in him. His burdened soul is eased in him; his fearful soul is confident; his weary soul is at rest. Canticles 2:3, "I sat down under his shadow with great delight." So hath Christ rest and contentment in believers. He says of Zion, i.e., the church, "This is my rest forever: here will I dwell; for I have desired it" (Psalm 132:14).

Christ and the true Christian have desires after each other. Cant. 7:10, "I am my beloved's, and his desire is towards me." And the desire of the Christian's soul is after Christ. Canticles 3:1–2, "By night on my bed I sought him whom my soul loveth: I sought him, but I found him not. I will rise now, and go about the city in the streets and broad ways. I will seek him whom my soul loveth." The true Christian has an admiration of Jesus Christ; he admires his excellencies. Isaiah 63:1, "Who is this that cometh from Edom, with died garments from Bozrah? this that is glorious in his apparel, travelling in the greatness of his strength?" And so Christ is represented as admiring the excellency and beauty of the church. Canticles 6:10, "Who is she that looketh forth as the morning, fair as the moon, clear as the sun, and terrible as an army with banners?"

Christ and the believer do glory in each other. The believer glories in Christ. Canticles 5:16, "This is my beloved, and this is my friend." Canticles 6:3, "I am [my] beloved's, and my beloved is mine." Christ glories in his people: he looks on them as his armor and his crown. Isaiah 62:3, "Thou shalt also be a crown of glory in the hand of the Lord, and a royal diadem in the hand of thy God." Zechariah 9:16, "And they shall be as the stones of a crown."

Third. There is between Christ and the soul of a true Christian a mutual compliance and acceptance. Christ offers himself to man as his lord, redeemer, and portion. The believer with his whole soul closes with the offer and joyfully embraces it.

And the believer comes to Christ to give up himself, soul and body, to him. And though it be but a poor offer, yet Christ readily accepts of it. He that comes to him, he will "in no wise cast out" [John 6:37].

Christ becomes a suitor to the souls of [believers]. He earnestly and importunately seeks their love. Revelation 3:20, "Behold, I stand at the door, and knock." The believer yields to his suit: he opens the door, and willingly complies with [it], when he seeks [it] of them.

And on the other hand, the believer is a supplicant unto Jesus; and Christ accepts their suit to him, and hears their prayer, and grants their requests. Matthew 21:22, "And all things whatsoever ye shall ask in prayer, believing, ye shall receive." John 14:13–14, "And whatsoever ye shall ask in my name, I will do it, that the Father may be glorified in the Son. If ye shall ask anything in my name, I will do it."

The believer accepts of all Christ's offers, all the benefits that he has purchased, and offers in the gospel. And Christ accepts whatsoever the believer sincerely offers to him: he accepts his love, and this thankfulness, and the graces that he exercises towards him, as Christ well accepted of Mary, when she anointed him with her box of precious [ointment], though others found fault with her [Matt 26:6–13]. Christ accepts of whatsoever they do for him in sincerity, though it be but the giving of a cup of cold water (Matthew 10:42). Christ accepts of all the sincere requests of believers, and will do according to them. So the believer complies with whatsoever Christ requires, submits to his commands, is willing that Christ should have all that glory and respect that he receives. All his commands are agreeable and acceptable. He accounts Christ's yoke easy, and his burden light, and his commands not grievous. Ye esteem the ways of his commands "ways of pleasantness."

Thus I have shown how there is sweet harmony of the first kind, viz., mutual respect between Christ and the soul of a true Christian.

II. There is a sweet harmony of likeness or conformity between Christ and true Christians.

First. Christ hath made himself like to them. He hath conformed himself to them in nature: he took upon him the human nature that he might be conformed in nature to his elect people. Though he was God, yet he became man, that he might be as they are. "The Word was made flesh, and dwelt amongst us," as one of us. Though he was "in the form of God, and thought it not robbery to be equal with God," yet he "took on him the form of a servant," that he might be conformed to us.

And not only so, but that he might conform himself to his people, he became subject to affliction and temptation as they; lived in the same evil world as they do; was subject to the changes and vicissitudes of time as they are; dwelt in a like frail body with them; took the human nature in its weak, broken state to be like them, and took it with those disadvantages that are the fruits of sin; was subject to hunger, and thirst, and weariness, pain, and death as they are; and liable to the afflicting, trying influences of evil spirits as they are, to be conformed to them. Hebrews 4:15, "He was in all points tempted like as we are." And ch. 2, v. 14, "Forasmuch then as the children are partakers of flesh and blood, he also himself likewise takes part of the same"; vv. 16–17, "For verily he took not on him the nature of angels; but he took on him the seed of Abraham. Wherefore in all things it behoved [him] to be made like unto his brethren."

Second. Believers are conformed or made like unto Christ. Christ was conformed to believers in all that was sinless, and believers are conformed to Christ in all that is holy. As they are naturally, there is the greatest deformity between them and Christ. But when they become true Christians, they put on the new man, and are renewed in knowledge, after the image of him that created them. And "beholding as in a glass the glory of the Lord, they are changed into the same image from glory to glory" (2 Cor 3:18). They are of a like spirit and temper with him, and follow his example; they are made partakers of his holiness; they are conformed to Christ in a filial spirit and temper towards God the Father; they are conformed to him in his obedience to the Father. As Christ did whatsoever the Father commanded, so the believer's obedience is universal: he has respect to all God's commands. The believer is conformed to Christ in his contempt of the world, and in meekness and loveliness of heart. As Christ was wonderful meek and lovely, so meekness and humbleness of mind is the temper of the true Christian.

They are conformed to Christ in love and charity. As Christ was a marvelous instance of love and condescension, pity and mercy, so are the people elect of Christ wont to put on "bowels of mercies, kindness, humbleness of mind, meekness, longsuffering, forbearing one another, forgiving one another" (Colossians 3:12–13). They are conformed to the Lamb of God in a patient, lamblike disposition under sufferings, and also in a disposition to labor and deny themselves doing good. Especially are they conformed to Christ's temper and behavior towards them as Christ loved them, so they love one another; as Christ infinitely condescended for them to pity and help them, and deny himself for them, so they are of a condescending spirit and practice; as Christ forgave them, so they are of a forgiving spirit; as Christ has been infinitely rich in his bounty and grace to them, so the true Christian is of a liberal, bountiful, charitable disposition; looks not only on his own things, but also on the things of others. But I proceed, to the

III. *[Third]* thing wherein the harmony between Christ and the soul of the true Christian consists, which is suitableness. And here I would take notice of a threefold harmony of this kind: first, a suitableness of temper and behavior to each other's nature and state; second, a suitableness of temper and behavior to the relation they stand in to each other; and, third, a suitableness of temper and behavior to each other's temper and behavior.

First. There is between Christ and true Christians a suitableness of temper and behavior to each other's nature and state. The temper and behavior of Christ towards them is suitable to their state and nature. They are in themselves poor, little, mean creatures; and Christ, answerably to this, is a person of infinite goodness and condescension. They are in themselves so exceeding sinful and unworthy, infinitely undeserving and ill-deserving; and [Christ] is one that is infinitely rich in free and sovereign grace.

They are in themselves miserable and helpless; and Christ is one of infinite mercy and compassion.

They are in themselves exceeding weak, and continually exposed to all manner of mischief; [and] Christ is full of gracious care and tenderness towards them, and maintains a gracious watch continually for their protection. They are in themselves empty, needy creatures; and Christ is richly communicative.

So the temper and behavior of the true Christian towards Christ is answerable to his nature and state. Christ is in the divine nature: he is the eternal and infinitely glorious Son of God. And answerably hereto, the Christian hath a humble, adoring respect to Christ, pays him divine honor, and exalts him above all. And he also is [in] the human nature, and so is become his brother. Answerably hereto, the Christian hath boldness of access, and has his heart knit to Christ, as a true friend and intimate companion.

Second. There is a suitableness of temper and behavior to the relation they stand in to each other. Christ is the Christian's Lord and King. And agreeably to this relation, the Christian has a spirit of submission to Christ, and resignation to his will, and of obedience to his command. And on the other hand, the heart of Christ is full of clemency and grace towards the Christian, as becomes a lord towards a subject.

Christ is the Christian's head. He is the head of all spirit, life, and gracious influence and communication; and suitably hereto, Christ is free, rich, and unfailing in communicativeness towards the Christian. And on the other hand, there is a spirit of union and dependence in that Christian towards Christ.

Christ is the Savior of the Christian; and suitably hereto, he is merciful and faithful in his work and office. And on the other hand, the Christian hath a spirit of trust and confident reliance on Jesus Christ. Christ is the teacher {of the Christian}; in him [is] the spirit of a disciple. {The Christian} sits at [his] feet. {To the Christian} Christ is the light {of the world}. The soul opens itself to receive this light. Christ is Intercessor: [salvation] comes in his name.

Christ is the friend of [the] Christian, and the one admitted to a state of friendship with him. The soul of the Christian is brought and united to Christ as his spouse. And answerably to this relation, there is a spirit to delight in each other's presence, and communion, and conversation; and [they] are wont freely to open their hearts, and reveal themselves to each other, and dwell with each other. John 14:21, "And I will love him, and manifest myself to him"; v. 23, "And we will come unto him, and make our abode with him."

The Christian has a disposition suitable to this relation under all its difficulties to resort to Christ, to go there for counsel, and pity, and help. And Christ is ready to offer it to him as he needs [it]. John 14:18, "I will not leave you comfortless: I will come unto you."

Third. There is a suitableness of temper and behavior to each other's temper and behavior. In Christ is infinite grace towards them; and suitably hereto is thankfulness and praise towards him.

In him is tenderness and faithfulness; in them is trust and confidence.

The love of Christ to the Christian exceeds the love of all others. He loves them more than any other friend; and suitably to this, the Christians love Christ, Christ above all. But I would now proceed to a brief

Application

[*Use*] I. What we have heard under this Doctrine may well lead us to admire the marvelous grace of Jesus Christ to man. That he should enter into such an union and commerce with such a creature as man is how greatly has Christ herein condescended, and how highly is man hereby honored and exalted. Why should the eternal Son of God, who is infinitely above us, and above any need of us, stoop to be in such a manner concerned with us to establish such an intimate union, such a sweet consent and harmony, such a dear, mutual respect, such a wonderful conformity, an answerableness between him and us?

All is owing to Christ. 'Tis from him [and] begins with him. 'Tis not owing to us; for we are naturally in a state [of] estrangement and great alienation, and should forever have so remained, if we had been let alone. And we did not deserve that Christ should thus deal with us, and should enter into such a sweet, and excellent, and happy union with us; for we are his enemies.

How wonderful was it that the grace of Christ should so triumph over our enmity, especially considering after what manner this is brought about. Christ was not only first in seeking of it, but to make way for it. Though he was in the form of God, [he] became man, and laid down his life. Why should Christ make so much of us, who cannot be profitable to him, who can add nothing to his happiness and glory? What does Christ get by us poor, vile worms, that he should thus lay out himself for an union with us?

[*Use*] II. Hence we may learn the nature of true and sincere Christian piety. This shows the nature and genius of Christianity, what that is wherein it most essentially consists. It don't consist chiefly in any certain profession, or set of principles or tenets; or in any outward form of worship, or an attendance in such or such religious observances; or in outwardly moral behavior; but in such an internal, spiritual harmony between Christ and the soul, as that which has been spoken of.

In that consists the essence of Christianity. He that has this is a Christian; and he that is without it is not worthy of the name, whatever his knowledge, or profession, or orthodoxy, or outward strictness be.

By this, Christianity is most essentially distinguished from all things. By this, 'tis distinguished from the morality of the heathen. And by this, 'tis distinguished [from] the superstition and will-worship of many that are called Christians. And by this, 'tis distinguished from the fair, outward show, or the false affection and zeal of hypocrites. By this, may all pretended descriptions of Christian piety, and precepts to it, and pretenses of it be tried.

The end of the doctrines and precepts of Christianity is to bring about this sweet harmony between the soul and Jesus Christ. And this is the nature and tendency of them. Whatever doctrines or rules of any profession tend to the contrary, they are to be rejected. And whatever pretenses any make to piety, if their prevailing temper be found contrary to this, they are like to be rejected and acknowledged by Christ as his; for his sheep know his voice and follow him.

This Doctrine shows us the excellent and lovely nature of true Christianity. For how exalted is such a harmony between Christ and the soul, as has been spoken of: how does it ennoble and exalt the soul of man, and how excellent does it render his state.

[Use] III. We may particularly hence learn the nature of that great Christian grace of faith in Jesus Christ. The grace of faith is often spoken of in Scripture as that by which especially the union between Christ and the soul is made. And therefore 'tis called in Scripture a coming to Christ, and a receiving Christ. 'Tis a coming to Christ as being drawn to him; 'tis the opposite to disallowing and rejecting of Christ (1 Peter 2:7).

And therefore saving, justifying faith in Christ don't consist merely in the assent of the understanding, nor only in the consent of the will; but 'tis the harmonizing of the whole soul with Jesus Christ, as he is revealed and held forth in the gospel.

'Tis the soul's embracing the revelation of Jesus Christ as its Savior. 'Tis the whole soul's entirely adhering to him and acquiescing in him, according and symphonizing with the revelation and offer of Christ as its Savior. There is an entire yielding to it, and closing with it; adhering to it with the belief, with the inclination and affection; admitting and receiving it with entire credit and respect as true, and worthy, and excellent.

Faith is no other than that harmony in the soul towards Christ that has been spoken of in its most direct act. And it may be defined [as] the soul's entirely uniting and closing with Christ for his Savior, acquiescing in his reality and goodness as a Savior, as the gospel reveals him. And hence it is that by faith that we are justified, not as commending us to God by its excellency as a qualification in us, but as uniting us to Christ. The foundation of persons' acceptance with God, is their union with Christ, or that relation to him, whatsoever that is, by which in Scripture we are said to be in Christ. And faith is that by which we are thus united; for it is the active unition [and] closing with Christ as a Savior.

[*Use*] IV. By this Doctrine we may examine and try ourselves, whether or no we are true Christians. Is there such a sweet harmony subsisting between Christ and our souls? We need not inquire whether or no there be nothing else but harmony; for there is a great deal of discord remaining in the hearts of the best in the world.

And we need not conclude that we are not true Christians, if we can't speak to every particular that has been mentioned herein; for though there be an harmony in all these respects in every Christian, yet it may be very imperfect, and in some instances greatly obscured by indwelling sin. But let us inquire whether or no such a harmony between Christ and the soul appears sweet and delightful to us. Have we a sense of the excellency of it, so as to cause longing desires often? Does a life of such harmony with Christ appear to be the most excellent and happy life? Have we a sense in our hearts of the sweetness of it, and that such a life is far better than all the enjoyments of this world? Can we find it in our hearts to prefer it, prize it vastly above all the profits, and grandeur, and pleasures of the world, if we might have our free choice?

And can we in the general, though not in every particular, and though very imperfect in every particular, find such a spirit towards Christ as has been described? Have we such a spirit to choose, to love, to long after Christ, and to acquiesce in him, and rejoice to cleave to him? How did we find in the hearing of it? Have we felt such a temper of mind? Or are those things what we are wholly strangers to? Is this a sapless, dull story to us, and what is remote from our experience? Or do our hearts in many instances echo to what has been said; so that we can have good grounds to think that such a harmony is begun in our souls, though it be very imperfect?

[Use] V, and last, may be of *Exhortation*, earnestly to seek after such an harmony between Christ and our souls. For motive, consider,

First. How miserable are those that have not attained it. There is no agreement between Christ and you; but on the contrary is a "stone of stumbling and rock of offense." You are strangers to all that has been: "You are without Christ, being aliens from the commonwealth of Israel."

Second. And how beautiful and lovely is a Christian so far as this harmony prevails in his soul. What can render a creature more amiable than to be thus affected, related, and conformed to the Son of God, who is the brightness of the Father's glory, and "the express image of his person." Well may it be said, "The righteous is more excellent than his neighbor."

Third. This shows us also how happy a person a true Christian is, what happy circumstance he is in, and what an happy life must he needs live, so far as he is in the exercise and sense of this sweet harmony between Christ and him. Without doubt this is a sweeter pleasure than all that earth can afford. It need not be difficult to us to believe that this gives peace, that passes all understanding; and that herein is to be had joy, that is unspeakable and full of glory.

Fourth. How inconceivably happy will the true Christian be hereafter, when he shall dwell with Christ, between whom and his soul there is such an harmony. As Christ and the believer are now spiritually so united as we have heard, so Christ will have them to be where he is, forever to dwell with him and partake with him in his glory. And then this union will be perfected, and there shall be nothing remaining to disturb, to interrupt, or allay the harmony; but the mutual respect and love shall be gloriously exalted. The conformity and suitableness shall be perfected, and the same shall be immutably continued, and the sweetness and delight hence arising shall be uninterrupted and everlasting.

FRAGMENT: *APPLICATION ON LOVE TO CHRIST*[2] (1723)

James 1:12
Blessed is the man that endureth temptation; for when he is tried, he shall receive the crown of life, which the Lord hath promised to them that love him.

The Doctrine was,
That those who love Christ shall receive of him a crown of life.

You have heard the Explication of this Doctrine in the forenoon, wherein we have told you who those are that love Christ and briefly described the crown that they shall receive: it is that eternal life, joy, beauty, and glory with which they shall be crowned in the other world. We showed that they should receive this crown, first, as a crown of victory; and second, as a royal crown wherewith they shall be crowned as kings, and here showed what was to be their kingdom, what their royal robes, what their kingly palace, their glorious throne, their honor, their kingly riches, and their royal dainties upon which they are to feast forever. We are now come to make some application of these things to our practice and improvement in Christianity.

Application

[I.] The first *Use* is of *Instruction* or *Inference*.

First. Hence we may learn: if those that love Christ are to receive a crown of life at the hands of Christ, what a dishonorable thing is it for a true Christian to concern himself much about worldly honor and greatness; what a dishonor is it to Jesus Christ, who has promised you this glorious crown that you might despise worldly honors, as if you were not contented with what he has promised, as if the honor of a celestial crown from the hands of Christ were not enough without worldly honor too.

How do you dishonor yourselves by it! Christ has honored you by making [a gift] more excellent than any earthly thing. He has given you grace in your souls, which is heavenly riches, the least grain of which is more worth than mountains of gold and silver. He has honored you by giving of you a right to a crown, not of gold and gems, but of celestial and everlasting glory, and you hope that he will honor you much more yet by actually placing this crown upon your heads and giving to you his own kingdom: placing you upon his own throne, adorning of you with robes of glory, giving you the heavens of heaven as your kingly palace, and himself as your riches, and his eternal love as your royal dainties. And will you now go and dishonor yourself so much as to thirst for silver and gold, or to seek after poor worldly greatness? Will [you] so dishonor your crown that is laid up for you? Will you so much undervalue it as to admit these childish things into your hearts with it; will you do your own crown so much dishonor as to make it so near equal to these things in your affections? Will you regard that honor that Christ is to give you in heaven so little as to seek the honor of men?

Will you who have an immortal crown, in heart thirst for earthly glory? Will you who are to shine with Christ as the sun, follow after poor earthly pomp and show? Will you who have heavenly riches, hug and embrace dirt and dung? Will you who are to be made kings and priests unto God the Father, leave your heavenly kingdom for the baubles of children? You thereby dishonor yourself more than one of the emperors of Rome [Domitian] did, who, although he ruled over the greatest empire in the whole world, yet used to retire constantly by himself, an hour or two every day, to catch flies.

Therefore make not yourself so mean. Leave the thirsting after temporal honor to men of this world who have nothing else; let them take these things and welcome! A thirst after these things is unworthy of you. Remember what a crown you have laid up for [you]; remember what a glorious inheritance you are heir of. When you are actually possessed of your heavenly kingdom, are actually crowned with glory, you will see how despicable these things are.

Let the men of this world know that you value your crown more than that comes to, to desire their foolish, fading glories. Don't dishonor religion, but honor it by letting the world know that you account all other things as loss and dung in comparison of it. If Christians did so, Christianity would not be a thing so much despised in the world. If Christians did but manifest to all that they did merely scorn and despise and trample upon worldly honors, in comparison of that crown of glory which they were to receive, religion would not be so much fled into corners.

One great thing why it is despised is because the religious themselves hide it, and dare not be so bold as to bring it out before the world and do it open honor before the sun; but they imprudently and dishonorably pursue after worldly greatness too, and show that they are not fully contented with their celestial crown, and this makes other men have a mean opinion of religion when they see the professors of religion value it no more.

Wherefore, follow the example of your Redeemer and Head, Jesus Christ, who although he knew himself to be the Son of God, yet despised all sublunary honors and greatness, for he knew them to be unworthy of him who was to be glorified with celestial glory after his resurrection. He scorned all the fine show of kings and princes because he knew how despicable it was in comparison of the glory that awaited him: "He for the joy that was set before him endured the cross, despising the shame, and is now set down on the right hand of the throne of God" [Heb 12:2].

Second. Hence learn how little reason have those that love Christ to regard reproaches. Seeing they are to be crowned hereafter by Jesus Christ with a crown of immortal honor and glory, consider that although you are reproached by wicked men, that hereafter you will be honored as kings; and what are the reproaches, the greatest reproaches that ever despised saint met with, when compared with that glorious crown that is laid up for you? For what is the despite and scorn of wicked men? 'Tis only the scorn of those that are not worthy of the name of men. 'Tis the scorn of those that God scorns, and that he will scorn forever and will be looked upon by him and all intelligent beings as more hateful and despicable than a toad. And what need you, who are to be crowned as kings in Christ's heavenly kingdom, regard the scorn of such? There are none that are truly excellent and worthy to be regarded that will despise you for your holiness, but will greatly respect [and] honor you. [You] need not care who despises you as long as God doth not despise, as long as Christ loves you, which will be as long as he himself has a being. If all the world should hate you, how sweetly and with how much pleasure might you retire into the arms of your dear Savior and solace yourself in his spiritual kisses and embraces, knowing that, let who will hate you, Christ loves you and will honor and crown you with glory before all the world.

But [let] all the world hate you and do their worst despite unto you, you have this to solace yourself: that he that made the world and governs it, he who has made those same persons that scorn you and who has their bodies and souls, their life and breath continually in his hands, he loves you and has given himself to you.

When you have once got your crown of glory on your heads, and are placed by Christ on his throne, and shine forthwith in robes of light, and sit down in his eternal royal banquet of love, you shall suffer no more reproaches forever. You will then be advanced too high to be reached by the spite of men or devils. They shall then gnaw their tongues when they see the unspeakable honor and happiness to which you, whom they formerly reproached, are exalted, and into what misery and eternal disgrace they are cast.

Fear not the expressions of their scorn and hatred; for they, except they repent and mourn for it, shall see with their own eyes you sitting with Jesus Christ, arrayed in kingly robes at the last day, judging of them, and shall see you reigning with him forevermore.

Your reproaches cannot be greater than the reproaches of Christ were, but what glory is he advanced to! He is risen from the dead, he is ascended far above all heavens, he has triumphed over his enemies, he has the keys of hell and death, and breaks his enemies with a rod of iron and dashes in pieces as a potter's vessel; in like manner you shall rise from the dead too. Christ is the firstfruits and you shall follow. You shall triumph one day over your enemies, too; you shall ascend into heaven, too, and shall be made partakers of Christ's glory.

Third. How little reason have those that love Christ to fear death, since thereby they go to receive their crown of life. And it is this passage to their kingdom, just on this side the heavenly Mount Zion, the city of the living God to which you are traveling, there is a valley: it is the valley of death which, as soon as ever you are passed, you immediately ascend this glorious mountain and enter the gate of the city from whence you may look down with pleasure on this shady vale.

This valley is a dreadful, terribly dark valley for the wicked, and it lets them down to a darker pit of misery; but it is so near the hill of Zion, that bright place, that it is made light unto believers. They may pass through it with joy because as soon as ever they are got through it, they are got through all their miseries and immediately receive their crown, immediately are conducted to their throne.

Wherefore fear not, you souls that love Christ, to pass through this valley because it is dark, because there are many frightful appearances in it; for they are shadows and nothing else, and are not able to hurt you. Look through the shade, keep your eye fixed on that heavenly light that is beyond it, and you will not see the darkness that is in it.

We shall, in the

[II.] Second place, improve this Doctrine by way of *Exhortation*. If all those that love Christ are to receive a crown of life at his hands, what more natural improvement follows from it than to exhort and persuade all to love to Christ? We have endeavored to describe the glory of this crown unto you as far as that which is so glorious may fall under our scanty conceptions, and surely here is motive enough to persuade anyone to strive after love to Christ, if such a glorious and never-fading [crown] shall be bestowed on the lovers of him. But we shall offer some other motives to persuade all to this duty:

First. The first and greatest motive is the loveliness of Christ. As all the loveliness that is to be seen in heaven and earth is only the reflection of the rays of his lovely glory, so there is scarce anything that is glorious, sweet, beautiful, and amiable, but what is used to set the beauty of Christ. What is more glorious to look upon among bodies that we behold than the sun, that bright orb that enlightens heaven and earth with its rays? Christ is called the Sun of Righteousness, and he is a sun to whom our sun in the heavens is as darkness; he is called the Bright and the Morning Star; so for his innocency, his sweet condescension, love, and mercy, he is called a Lamb, although he is the Lion of the Tribe of Judah.

He is called the Rose of Sharon and the Lily of the Valley. Sharon, being a delightful and pleasant land, bore the sweetest roses, and the lily of the valley excelling all other lilies for beauty, sweetness, and excellent salutary virtue. He is represented thus to flowers because they are pleasant to behold, beautiful to the eye, and pleasing to the smell. He is compared to a rose and lily because they are the chief of flowers for beauty and sweetness; he is compared to the rose of Sharon and lily of the valley because they are the chief and most excellent of all roses and lilies.

What kind of rose and lily is the Son of God, the blessed Jesus; how wonderful and astonishing that God the Son should compare himself to a rose and lily! What kind of rose and lily is here; how sweet, how beautiful, how fragrant! Here is too great a beauty, too divine a loveliness and heavenly fragrancy to belong to any creature. Certainly this lovely rose and lily has divine perfections. Here is all the loveliness in the universe contained in this rose; yea, here are the beauties and glories of Jehovah himself in this lily: this flower is certainly no creature, but the Creator. Here, O believers, O lovers of Christ, is a rose for you, to be ravished with the fragrancy of it, for your eyes to be delighted with the infinite beauty of, for you to be delighted to all eternity in the enjoyment of. This rose and lily is the brightness of God's glory and the express image of his person, which is so amiable and fragrant that it is the eternal and infinite delight of the Father himself.

This infinitely beautiful rose, this spotless and fragrant lily, was once despised with the loathsome spittle of wicked men, and was torn and rent by their rage, and it was for you, O believers, the vials of God's wrath against your sins were poured out upon it.

Here is a sweet bundle of myrrh for you to lie in your bosom forever. He is as the apple tree among the trees of the wood; you may sit down under his shadow with great delight and his fruit will be sweet to your taste.

Second. Consider for motive the excellent effects of love to Christ. It makes the soul to be of an excellent disposition it is of a transforming nature; if brings on the soul some of the loveliness of the person beloved, and exceedingly to soften and sweeten the mind and to make it meek, humble and charitable, and full of brotherly love. Love to Christ, if it be ardent and lively, transforms the soul very much into love, and destroys envy and malice of every kind, and softens and sweetens every action.

It makes the soul in love with religion and holiness, and sweetens obedience and mortification. Earthly and temporal love makes men glad of an opportunity to labor and spend themselves for the person beloved; they love to deny themselves for them; it takes away the force of pain and turns it into pleasure. So much more doth heavenly love, or love to Christ, make all that they do for Christ pleasant and easy; although they spend and are spent for him, it extracts honey from repentance and mortification.

Of such an excellent nature and tendency is love to Christ. It makes as great a difference in the soul as there is upon the face of the earth in the dead of winter when there are nothing but clouds, cold storms, rain, hail, and snow, and in the spring or summer when all things look green and pleasant. Before the soul hated everything that is truly excellent and loved all that is abominable, but now the soul is transformed, is lovely itself, and it is in love with everything else that is truly so. And it not only makes duty easy, and repentance and mortification pleasant, but it sweetens troubles and crosses themselves because the Christian knows that they are ordered to him by the person whom he dearly loves, and who dearly loves him. How easily can we bear things that come from those we love! These are the excellent effects, and this is the usefulness of love to Christ.

Third. Consider the pleasantness of a life of love to Christ. A life of love, if it be from rational principles, is the most pleasant life in the world. Hatred, malice, and revenge are the greatest disturbers of the pleasures of the mind, and fill it with uneasiness; but in the soul where rational love reigns, there is always pleasure and delight, for love is the principle of all sorrow.

But especially must a life of love to Christ be very pleasant, above all other kinds of living. Because as Christ is of all things most excellent, so is the love of him a more excellent kind of love than any other, and the more excellent and refined the love is, the greater and purer is the pleasure of it.

There is no love so reasonable as love to Christ. Some love those things that are not truly lovely, love from false grounds; yea, some love those things that are above all things hateful. Now from such a love as this can arise no true pleasure, inasmuch as it is without a reason or foundation and at last will end in bitterness. But the love of Christ is the love of that which is truly above all things excellent and lovely, and therefore the pleasures that result from it must be solid, real, substantial, and never-fading.

If any godly man's life is unpleasant to him, it must be only because his love to Christ is but small and not vigorous and active enough, because it lies dormant and is not frequently put into exercise; for it [is] utterly impossible but that those [who] live in the lively exercise of love to him should have those sweet meditations, as to make his life far from unpleasant.

Those that have a vehement love to any person can with pleasure spend their time in thinking of that person and of his perfections and actions. So with what great delight may [those] that love Christ with an active love spend their thoughts upon his glories; with what pleasure may they meditate upon those infinite perfections that he is possessed of, and which make him lovely in their eyes. How must it please them to find out continually new beauties and glories which they saw not before, for the excellencies of Christ are infinite and we may make new discoveries to all eternity, and yet not have discovered all. How doth it fill the soul with a kind of rapture when it has discovered something more of excellency in him who is the object of his highest love.

If men have a dear love to any of their fellow creatures, they desire to see them yet more excellent; they delight to see them attain to new perfections. But now those that are the dear lovers of Christ, they have the pleasure of thinking that he has all possible excellency already: there is no room for desiring that he should be yet more excellent, because there is no excellency or beauty, nor any degree of excellency that they can possibly think of, but what he possesses already, so that they have no new beauties to desire for Christ, but only new beauties to discover in him. Now what a pleasure must it raise in those that love Christ to think that he is so perfectly amiable.

This is a peculiar delight that is raised from no other love but love to Christ.

With what pleasure may he think of the perfections of his divine nature: of his immense greatness, of his eternity, power, and wisdom, etc. With what delight may he think him he loves with his whole heart and soul is God as well as man, is so great that all the nations of the world are to him as the drop of the bucket and small dust of the balance; so powerful that he weighs the mountains in scales and the hills in a balance, and takes up the isles as a very little thing; so wise that he charges his angels with folly; so holy that the heavens are unclean in his sight. With what pleasure may he think that the object of his highest love has made the world by his power and wisdom, that the sun, moon, and stars are the work of his fingers, and he rules all.

How sweet will the thoughts of the perfections of his human nature raise when he thinks of his innocency, condescension, humility, meekness, patience, and charity, the sight of which made the woman so to cry out: "Blessed is the womb that bare thee, and the paps which thou hast sucked," Luke 11:27.

With what joy may the lovers of Christ think and meditate of what he has done for them. When men dearly love any person, with what joy do they catch at kindnesses and expressions of love from them; with what pleasure will they think it over again. So with what inexpressible joy may those that love Christ think of his bowing the heavens and coming down in the form of a servant; of his lying in a manger, of his suffering the reproach of men, of his agony and bloody sweat, of his dying on the cross for their sakes. How pleasing must it be to read over the history of all those wonderful [things] that their well-beloved has done for them while on earth, as it is recorded in the Scriptures, and to think that Christ has done all this for him: that he was born for his sake and lived for his sake, sweat blood for his sake and died for his sake. This must needs beget an uncommon delight.

With what pleasure may the Christian's soul think on Christ in his exalted state. We love to see those whom we truly love highly honored and exalted; so those that ardently love Christ may sweetly spend their time in meditating on Christ triumphing over his enemies, of his glorious ascending to heaven, of his being made head over all things to the church, of his being crowned with a crown of great glory, of his coming to judge the world at the conflagration.

The love of Christ is far more pleasant than any other love upon these following accounts:

1. Christ is far more amiable than any other object in the world.

2. No other love is of so pure, heavenly, and divine a nature as the love of Christ is; and therefore, no other love can raise such a divine and heavenly and exalted pleasure.

3. All that love Christ are certain that they are loved again. Herein is the pleasure of love: to be loved again. If love be not mutual, it is a torment and not a pleasure; but he that knows he loves Christ, knows Christ loves him with a [love] far higher and dearer.

4. There is nothing can deprive those that love Christ either of present communion with, or future enjoyment of, the person loved. Now it is not so in other kinds of love, but they are full of perplexities for fear of being deprived of enjoyment. There are a thousand accidents which may spoil all, and death certainly will separate them; but Christ will be enjoyed to all eternity, and all the world can't hinder it. Christ will receive them into his closest embrace, and in his arms shall they rest forevermore in spite of all the world.

5. The union between Christ and those that love him is more close, and the communion more intimate, than between any other lovers. The believers have the pleasure to think that he whom they love has also loved them so well as to receive [them] so near to himself as to make [them] his bone and his flesh. The believer is joined to Christ and is become one with him. How must this be to those who love him in truth! Love naturally desires a close and inseparable union and intimate communion, but there is no such near or intimate conversation between any other lovers, as between Christ and the Christian.

6. There is no other love so advantageous as love to Christ, and therefore none so pleasant. Love is sweet when the ones loving each other enjoy one another in prosperous circumstances. Now Christ is already crowned with glory, and he will crown those that love him with glory too, so that they shall each other eternally [be] in the greatest glory. So that upon these reasons and many others that might

be mentioned, the love of Christ is far the most delightful love in the world.

And in short, to sum up the whole, the love of Christ has a tendency to fill the soul with an inexpressible sweetness. It sweetens every thought and makes every meditation pleasant; it brings a divine calm upon the mind, and spreads a heavenly fragrancy like Mary's box of ointment. It bedews the soul with the dew of heaven, begets a bright sunshine, and diffuses the beginnings of glory and happiness in embryo. All the world smiles upon such a soul as loves Christ: the sun, moon and stars, fields and trees, do seem to salute him. Such a mind is like a little heaven upon earth.

LETTER TO LADY MARY PEPPERRELL (1751)

[Stockbridge, November 28, 1751]

Madam,

When I the last spring was at your house in Kittery [Massachusetts, later Maine], among other instances of your kind and condescending treatment of me was this, that when I had some discourse with Sir William concerning the Indian affair and Stockbridge, and he generously offered me any assistance in the business of my mission here that his acquaintance and correspondence in London gave him advantage for, and to propose my writing to him on our affairs, you were pleased on this occasion to invite me to write to you at the same time. If I should neglect to do as you then proposed, I should not [only] neglect doing a Christian duty to you, but fail of doing myself a great honor. But as I know from the small acquaintance I had with you that a letter of compliments would not be agreeable to a lady of your disposition, especially under your present melancholy circumstances; so the writing of such a letter is very far from my intention or inclination.

When I saw the evidences of your deep sorrow under the awful frowns of heaven in the (then late) death of your only son, it made an impression on my mind that turned my disposition to quite other things than flattery and ceremony. When you mentioned my writing to you, I soon determined what should be the subject of my letter. It was that which appeared to me to be the most proper subject of contemplation for one in your circumstances, and the subject which above all others appeared to me to be a proper and sufficient source of consolation to one under your heavy affliction: and this was the Lord Jesus Christ— with regard especially to two things, viz., his amiableness and love, or his infinite worthiness, and that we should love him and take him for our only portion, rest, hope, and joy; the other, his great and unparalleled love to us. And I have been of the same mind ever since, being determined, if God favored me with opportunity to write to Your Ladyship, these things should be the subject of my letter.

I will now, therefore, begin with the former of these. Let us think, dear Madam, a little of the loveliness of our blessed Redeemer and his worthiness, that our whole soul should be swallowed up with love to him and delight in him, and that we should salve our hearts in him, rest in him, have sweet complacence and satisfaction of soul in his excellency and beauty, whatever else we are deprived of. The Scripture assures us abundantly of his proper divinity, so that we consider him that came into the world in our nature and died for us, as truly possessed of all the fullness of that infinite glory of the Godhead, his infinite greatness and majesty, his infinite wisdom, his infinitely perfect holiness and purity, righteousness, and goodness. He is called "the brightness of God's glory and the express image of his person." He is that image and exhibition of the infinite beauty of the [Deity], in the viewing of which God the Father had all his infinite happiness from eternity. The eternal and immutable happiness of the Deity himself is represented in Scripture as a kind of social happiness; 'tis the society of the persons of the Trinity. Proverbs 8:30, "Then was I by him as one brought up with him: and I was daily his delight, rejoicing always before him." This glorious person, in the perpetual and eternal view of whose beauty God the Father is infinitely happy, has God sent into the world to be the light of the world, that by him the beauty of the Deity might shine forth in the brightest and fullest manner to the children of men. And infinite wisdom has contrived that we should behold the glory of the Deity in the face of Jesus Christ to the greatest advantage and in such a manner as should be most adapted to the capacity of poor feeble worms, and so as should tend most to engage and invite our attention, to encourage and allure our hearts and give us the most full and perfect acquiescence and delight. For Christ by his incarnation having come down as it were from his infinite height above us, having become one of us, our kinsman and brother, and his glory shining to us through his human nature, the manifestation is marvelously qualified to suit the nature of the human sight; the effulgence of his glory is attempered to our sight. He is indeed a person of infinite majesty to fill our souls with the greatest reverence and adoration. But there is nothing in it that needs to terrify us. For his infinite majesty is joined with as it were infinite meekness, sweet condescension, and humility. So that in the whole there is nothing terrifying or forbidding. There may be the utmost possible reverence and abasement and at the same time our hearts be drawn most sweetly and powerfully to the most free access, the most intimate embrace. When we view his greatness and majesty, we are kept from fear and flight by the view of his gentleness and humility. And when we view his marvelous love and abasement and are encouraged and comforted with that, we are kept from an indecent familiarity by the view of his infinite majesty. And by all together we are filled with most reverential love, humble boldness and familiarity, delightful adoration, and sweet surprise. The glory of Christ is properly, and in the highest sense, divine. He shines in all the brightness of glory that is the Deity, who is light, a luminary infinitely bright. Such is the exceeding brightness of this Sun of Righteousness, that the brightness of the natural sun is as darkness in comparison of it, yea, black as sackcloth of hair. And, therefore, when he shall appear in his glory, the brightness of the sun shall disappear as the brightness of the little stars do when the sun rises (Isaiah 24:23, Matthew 24:29, Revelation 6:12). But although his light is so bright and his beams go forth with infinite strength, yet as they proceed from Christ in the character of the Lamb of God and shine through his meek and lowly humanity, they are infinitely gentle and mild, not dazzling and painful to our feeble eyes, but vivifying and healing, like smooth ointment or a gentle eye salve. Thus the Sun of Righteousness arises on them that fear God's name with healing in his wings, i.e., in his beams (Malachi 4:2). It is like the light of the morning, as a morning without clouds; as the dew on the grass, under whose influence the souls of his people are as the tender grass, springing out of the earth by clear shining after rain. Thus are the beams of his beauty and brightness fitted for the support [of] the healing and reviving of the afflicted. He heals the broken in spirit and bindeth up their wounds. He comes down on the spirits of his people that are as it were cut down by the scythe of adversity— like the rain on the mown grass, and as the showers that water the earth (Psalm 72:6).

But especially are the beams of Christ's glory infinitely softened and sweetened by that other thing which I proposed to consider, viz., his love, his unparalleled, dying love. And here many things are to be considered: one is that the glory of Christ's person very much consists in that infinite goodness and grace, which has so marvelous a manifestation in his love to us. The apostle John tells us that God is light (1 John 1:5) and that he is love (1 John 4:8, 16), and his light is an infinitely sweet light because it is the light of love and especially appears so in the person of our Redeemer, who was infinitely the most wonderful instance of love that ever was. All the perfections of the Deity have their brightest manifestation in the work of redemption, vastly more than in the work of creation. In other works we see God's back parts, but here shines the glory of his face (2 Corinthians 3:18). Yea, in this work are opened the infinite treasures of God's heart (Ephesians 3:8–10). This work is a work of love to us and a work that Christ is the author of. His loveliness and his love have both their greatest and most affecting manifestation in those sufferings he endured for us at his death. Therein above all appeared his holiness, his hatred of sin, and his love to God in that when he desired to save sinners, rather than that a suitable testimony should not be borne against it, he would submit that strict justice should take place in its condemnation and punishment in his own soul's being poured out unto death (Romans 8:3). And such was his regard to God's honor that, rather than the desired happiness of himself should injure it, he would give up himself a sacrifice for sin. Thus, in the same act he appears in the greatest conceivable manifestation of his infinite hatred of sin and also infinite grace and love to sinners. His holiness appeared like a fire burning with infinite vehemence against sin, at the same time that his love to sinners appeared like a sweet flame burning with an infinite fervency of benevolence. 'Tis the glory and beauty of his love to us filthy sinners, that 'tis an infinitely pure love and it tends to the peculiar sweetness and endearment of his infinite holiness; that it has its greatest manifestation in such an act of love to us. All the virtues of Christ, both divine and human, have their greatest manifestation in that marvelous act of his love, his offering up himself a sacrifice for us under those extreme sufferings. Herein especially appears his infinite wisdom. Herein he hath abounded towards us in the riches of his grace in all wisdom and prudence (Ephesians 1:8). Herein appears most his strict justice. Herein, above all other things, appeared the humility of his human nature in being willing to descend so low for us. In his behavior under those last sufferings, above all other things, appeared his obedience to God, his submission to his disposing will, his patience. Herein appeared his meekness when he was [taken] as a lamb to the slaughter and opened not his mouth, but only in prayer that God would forgive his crucifiers. And what an affecting and endearing [thing] is the manifestation of his excellency and amiableness when it chiefly shines forth in such an act of love to us.

The love of Christ another way tends to sweeten and endear all his virtues and excellencies, viz., as his love has brought him into such a relation to us as our friend, our elder brother, our Lord, our head and spiritual husband, our Redeemer, and hath brought us into so strict an union with him that our souls are his beloved bride. Yea, we are the members of his body, his flesh and his bone (Ephesians 5:30).

Now, Madam, let us consider what suitable provision God has made for our consolation under all our afflictions in giving us a Redeemer of such glory and such love, especially when it is considered what were the ends of that great manifestation of his beauty and love in his death. He suffered that we might be delivered. His soul was exceeding sorrowful even unto death, to take away the sting of sorrow and that we might have everlasting consolation. He was oppressed and afflicted that we might be supported. He was overwhelmed in the darkness of death and of hell, that we might have the light of life. He was cast into the furnace of God's wrath, that we might swim in the rivers of pleasure. His heart was overwhelmed in a flood of sorrow and anguish, that our hearts might be filled and overwhelmed with a flood of eternal joy.

And now let it be considered what circumstances our Redeemer now is in. He was dead but is alive, and he lives forevermore. Death may deprive of dear friends, but it can't deprive us of this, our best friend. And we have this friend, this mighty Redeemer, to go to under all affliction, who is not one that can't be touched with the feeling of our afflictions, he having suffered far greater sorrows than we have ever done. And if we are vitally united to him, the union can never be broken; it will remain when we die and when heaven and earth are dissolved. Therefore, in this we may be confident, we need not fear though the earth be removed. In him we may triumph with everlasting joy; now when storms and tempests arise we may have resort to him who is an hiding place from the wind and a covert from the tempest. When we are thirsty, we may come to him who is as rivers of waters in a dry place. When we are weary, we may go to him who is as the shadow of a great rock in a weary land.

Having found him who is as the apple tree among the trees of the wood, we may sit under his shadow with great delight and his fruit may be sweet to our taste. Christ told his disciples that in the world [they] should have trouble, but says he, "In me ye shall have peace." If we are united to him, our souls will be like a tree planted by a river that never dieth. He will be their light in darkness and their morning star that is a bright harbinger of day. And in a little [while], he will arise on our souls as the sun in full glory. And our sun shall no more go down, and there shall be no interposing cloud, no veil on his face or on our hearts, but the Lord shall be our everlasting light and our Redeemer, our glory.

That this glorious Redeemer would manifest his glory and love to you, and apply the little that has been said of these things to your consolation in all your affliction, and abundantly reward your generous favors [to] me when I was at Kittery, is the fervent [prayer] of, Madam, Your Ladyship's most obliged and affectionate friend,

> And most humble servant,
> *Jonathan Edwards*

EXCERPT FROM *CHARITY AND ITS FRUITS* (1738) SERMON FIFTEEN: "HEAVEN IS A WORLD OF LOVE"

1 Corinthians13:8–10
Charity never faileth; but whether there be prophecies, they shall fail; whether there be tongues, they shall cease; whether there be knowledge, it shall vanish away. For we know in part, and we prophesy in part. But when that which is perfect is come, then that which is in part shall be done away.

I have already insisted on the first of these verses singly from the doctrine that the great fruit of the Spirit in which the Holy Ghost shall not only for a season but everlastingly be communicated to the church of Christ is divine love. I would now take a view of this verse together with the two following verses in order to a further instruction. And to that end, I would observe two things in these verses. First, something, which will hereafter be, which will show the great worth and excellence of charity: viz., that charity shall remain when other fruits of the Spirit have failed. And second, in what state of the church this will come to pass, viz., in its perfect state, when that which is in part shall be done away.

There is a twofold imperfect, and so a twofold perfect state of the Christian church. The Christian church in its beginning, in its first age before it was thoroughly established in the world, and settled in its New Testament state, and before the canon of the Scripture was completed, was in an imperfect state, a kind of a state of childhood in comparison with what it will be in the elder and latter ages of the church, when it will be in a state of manhood, or a perfect state in comparison with what it was in the first ages. Again, the church of Christ, as long as it remains in its militant state, and to the end of time is in an imperfect state, a state of childhood, and as the Apostle says in the eleventh verse, thinks and speaks as a child, in comparison with what it will be in the heavenly state, when it comes to a state of manhood and perfection, and to the measure of the stature of the fullness of Christ.

And so there is a twofold failing of those other gifts of the Spirit here mentioned. One is at the end of the first and infant age of the Christian church when the canon of Scripture is complete; and so there are none of them remaining in the church in its later ages, when it shall put away childish things and be in a state of manhood before the end of the world, when the Spirit of God shall be most gloriously poured out and manifested in that love and charity, which is its greatest and everlasting fruit. And again, all common fruits of the Spirit cease at the end of the militant state of the church with respect to particular persons at death, and with respect to the whole church at the end of the world. But charity remains in heaven. There the Spirit shall be poured forth in perfect love into every heart.

The Apostle seems to have respect to both these, but especially the latter. For though the glorious state of the church in its latter age be perfect in comparison with its former state, yet its state in heaven is that state of the church to which the things which the Apostle here says are most applicable, when he says, "when that which is perfect is come, that which is in part shall be done away." "Now we see through a glass darkly; but then face to face; now I know in part; but then shall I know, even as also I am known."

Doctrine

Heaven is a world of love.

The Apostle in the text speaks of a state of the church which is perfect, and therefore a state in which the Holy Spirit shall more perfectly and abundantly be given to the church than it now is. But the way in which it shall be given, when it is so abundantly poured forth, will be in that great fruit of the Spirit, holy and divine love in the hearts of all the blessed inhabitants of that world. So that the heavenly state of the church is a state which is distinguished from its earthly state, as it is that state which God has designed especially for such a communication of his Holy Spirit, and in which it shall be given perfectly; whereas in the present state of the church, it is given with such great imperfection; and also a state in which this shall be, as it were, the only gift or fruit of the Spirit, as being the most perfect and glorious, and which being brought to perfection renders others, which God was wont to communicate to his church on earth, needless.

That we may the better see how heaven is a world of love, I would take the following method in considering this subject:

I. I would consider the great cause and fountain of love which is there.

II. I would consider heaven with regard to the objects of love which it contains.

III. I would consider the love which is there with regard to the subject.

IV. I would consider the principle, or the love itself, which there is in heaven.

V. I would consider the excellent circumstances in which love is there enjoyed and expressed.

VI. The happy effect and fruits of all this.

I. And here the place with respect to the cause and fountain of love which is there. What I shall say may be comprised in this proposition; viz., that the God of love dwells in heaven. Heaven is the palace, or presence-chamber, of the Supreme Being who is both the cause and source of all holy love. God, indeed, with respect to his essence is everywhere. He fills heaven and earth. But yet he is said on some accounts more especially to be in some places rather than others. He was said of old to dwell in the land of Israel above all other lands, and in Jerusalem above all other cities in that land, and in the temple above all other houses in that city, and in the holy of holies above all other apartments in that temple, and on the mercy seat over the ark above all other places in the holy of holies. But heaven is his dwelling place above all other places in the universe.

Those places in which he was said to dwell of old were all but types of this. Heaven is a part of the creation which God has built for this end, to be the place of his glorious presence. And it is his abode forever. Here he will dwell and gloriously manifest himself to eternity. And this renders heaven a world of love; for God is the fountain of love, as the sun is the fountain of light. And therefore the glorious presence of God in heaven fills heaven with love, as the sun placed in the midst of the hemisphere in a clear day fills the world with light. The Apostle tells us that God is love, 1 John 4:8. And therefore seeing he is an infinite Being, it follows that he is an infinite fountain of love. Seeing he is an all-sufficient Being, it follows that he is a full and overflowing and an inexhaustible fountain of love. Seeing he is an unchangeable and eternal Being, he is an unchangeable and eternal source of love. There even in heaven dwells that God from whom every stream of holy love, yea, every drop that is or ever was proceeds.

There dwells God the Father, and so the Son, who are united in infinitely dear and incomprehensible mutual love. There dwells God the Father, who is the Father of mercies, and so the Father of love, who so loved the world that he gave his only begotten Son, that whosoever believeth in him should not perish, but have everlasting life [John 3:16]. There dwells Jesus Christ, the Lamb of God, the Prince of peace and love, who so loved the world that he shed his blood, and poured out his soul unto death for it. There dwells the Mediator, by whom all God's love is expressed to the saints, by whom the fruits of it have been purchased, and through whom they are communicated, and through whom love is imparted to the hearts of all the church. There Christ dwells in both his natures, his human and divine, sitting with the Father in the same throne. There is the Holy Spirit, the spirit of divine love, in whom the very essence of God, as it were, all flows out or is breathed forth in love, and by whose immediate influences all holy love is shed abroad in the hearts of all the church [cf. Rom 5:5]. There in heaven this fountain of love, this eternal three in one, is set open without any obstacle to hinder access to it. There this glorious God is manifested and shines forth in full glory, in beams of love; there the fountain overflows in streams and rivers of love and delight, enough for all to drink at, and to swim in, yea, so as to overflow the world as it were with a deluge of love. I proceed now,

II. To consider heaven with regard to the objects of love which it contains. And under this head I would observe three things:

First. There are none but lovely objects in heaven. There is no odious or polluted person or thing to be seen there. There is nothing wicked and unholy. Revelation 21:27, "And there shall in no wise enter into it anything that defileth, neither whatsoever worketh abomination, or maketh a lie." There is nothing which is deformed either in natural or moral deformity. Everything which is to be beheld there is amiable. The God, who dwells and gloriously manifests himself there, is infinitely lovely. There is to be seen a glorious heavenly Father, a glorious Redeemer; there is to be felt and possessed a glorious Sanctifier. All the persons who belong to that blessed society are lovely. The Father of the family is so, and so are all his children. The Head of the body is so, and so are all the members.

Concerning the angels, there are none who are unlovely. There are no evil angels suffered to infest heaven as they do this world. They are not suffered to come near, but are kept at a distance with a great gulf between them. In the church of saints there are no unlovely persons; there are no false professors, none who pretend to be saints, who are persons of an unchristian, hateful spirit and behavior, as is often the case in this world. There is no one object there to give offense, or at any time to give any occasion for any passion or motion of hatred; but every object shall draw forth love.

Second. Not only shall all objects there be lovely, but each shall be perfectly lovely. There are many things in this world which in general are lovely, but yet are not perfectly free from that which is the contrary. Many men are amiable and worthy to be loved, but yet they are not without those things which are very disagreeable. But it is not so in heaven. There shall be no pollution or deformity of any kind seen in any one person or thing. Everyone is perfectly pure, all over lovely; everything shall be perfectly pleasant. That world is perfectly bright without darkness, perfectly clear without spot. There shall be none appearing with any defects, either natural or moral. There is nothing seen there which is sinful, nothing weak or foolish. Nothing shall appear to which nature is averse, nothing which shall offend the most delicate eye. There shall be no string out of tune to cause any jar in the harmony of that world, no unpleasant note to cause any discord.

That God who so fully manifests himself there is perfect with an absolute and infinite perfection. That Son of God who is the brightness of his Father's glory appears there in his glory, without that veil of outward meanness in which he appeared in this world, as a root out of dry ground destitute of outward glory. There the Holy Spirit shall be poured forth with perfect sweetness, as a pure river of water of life, clear as crystal, Revelation 22 at the beginning; a river whose waters are without any manner of pollution. And every member of that glorious society shall be without blemish of sin or imprudence or any kind of failure. The whole church shall then be presented to Christ as a bride clothed in fine linen, clean and white, without spot or wrinkle. Ephesians 5:25–27, "Christ loved the church, and gave himself for it, that he might sanctify and cleanse it with the washing of water by the word. That he might present it to himself a glorious church, not having spot, or wrinkle, or any such thing, but that it should be holy and without blemish." In that world, wherever the inhabitants turn their eyes they shall see nothing but beauty and glory. In the most stately cities on earth, however magnificent the buildings are, yet the streets are filthy and defiled, being made to be trodden under foot. But the very street of this heavenly city is represented as being as pure gold, like unto transparent glass, Revelation 21:21. That it should be like pure gold only does not sufficiently represent the purity of them; but they are also like the transparent glass or crystal.

Third. There are those objects upon which the saints have set their hearts and loved above all others while in this world. There they will find those things which appeared lovely to them while they dwelt on earth far beyond all they could see here, the things which captivated their souls, and drew them away from the most dear and pleasant of earthly objects. There they find those things which were their delight, upon which they used often to meditate, and with the sweet contemplation of which they used to entertain their minds. There they find the things which they chose for their portion, and which were so dear to them, that for the sake of them they were ready to undergo the severest sufferings, or to forsake father and mother, and wife, and children, and lands [Matt 19:29, Mark 10:29–30]. There they shall dwell with that God whom they have loved with all their hearts, and with all their souls, and with all their minds. There they are brought to be with their beloved Savior. There they have such company as they have loved and longed for, and with which by faith they were conversant even while they dwelt on earth.

Thus having considered the objects of love in heaven, I come now,

III. To consider the love which is there with regard to the subjects of it, or the hearts in which it is. And with respect to this I would observe that love resides and reigns in every heart there. The heart of God is the original seat or subject of it. Divine love is in him not as a subject which receives from another, but as its original seat, where it is of itself. Love is in God as light is in the sun, which does not shine by a reflected light as the moon and planets do, but by his own light, and as the fountain of light. And love flows out from him towards all the inhabitants of heaven. It flows out in the first place [necessarily] and infinitely towards his only begotten Son, being poured forth without measure, as to an object which is infinite, and so fully adequate to God's love in its fountain. Infinite love is infinitely exercised towards him. The fountain does not only send forth large streams towards this object as it does to every other, but the very fountain itself wholly and altogether goes out towards him. And the Son of God is not only the infinite object of love, but he is also an infinite subject of it. He is not only the infinite object of the Father's love, but he also infinitely loves the Father. The infinite essential love of God is, as it were, an infinite and eternal mutual holy energy between the Father and the Son, a pure, holy act whereby the Deity becomes nothing but an infinite and unchangeable act of love, which proceeds from both the Father and the Son. Thus divine love has its seat in the Deity as it is exercised within the Deity, or in God towards himself.

But it does not remain in such exercises only, but it flows out in innumerable streams towards all the created inhabitants of heaven; he loves all the angels and saints there. The love of God flows out towards Christ the Head, and through him to all his members, in whom they were beloved before the foundation of the world, and in whom his love was expressed towards them in time by his death and sufferings, and in their conversion and the great things God has done for them in this world, and is now fully manifested to them in heaven. And the saints and angels are secondarily the subjects of holy love, not as in whom love is as in an original seat, as light is in the sun which shines by its own light, but as it is in the planets which shine by reflecting the light of the sun. And this light is reflected in the first place and chiefly back to the sun itself. As God has given the saints and angels love, so their love is chiefly exercised towards God, the fountain of it, as is most reasonable. They all love God with a supreme love. There is no enemy of God in heaven, but all love him as his children. They all are united with one mind to breathe forth their whole souls in love to their eternal Father, and to Jesus Christ, their common Head. Christ loves all his saints in heaven. His love flows out to his whole church there, and to every individual member of it; and they all with one heart and one soul, without any schism in the body, love their common Redeemer. Every heart is wedded to this spiritual husband. All rejoice in him, the angels concurring. And the angels and saints all love one another. All that glorious society are sincerely united. There is no secret or open enemy among them; not one heart but is full of love, nor one person who is not beloved. As they are all lovely, so all see each other's loveliness with answerable delight and complacence. Everyone there loves every other inhabitant of heaven whom he sees, and so he is mutually beloved by everyone.

Thus having spoken of the fountain and subject of this love, I proceed,

IV. To say something of the principle, or the love itself, which fills the heavenly world. And of this I would take notice, first, of the nature, and second, the degree of it.

First. As to its nature. It is altogether holy and divine. Most of the love which there is in this world is of an unhallowed nature. But in heaven, the love which has place there is not carnal, but spiritual; not proceeding from corrupt principles, not from selfish motives, and to mean and vile purposes; but there love is a pure flame. The saints there love God for his own sake, and each other for God's sake, for the sake of that relation which they bear to God, and that image of God which is upon them.

Second. With respect to the degree of their love, it is perfect. The love which is in the heart of God is perfect, with an absolute, infinite and divine perfection. The love of the angels and saints to God and Christ is perfect in its kind, or with such a perfection as is proper to their nature, perfect with a sinless perfection, and perfect in that it is commensurate with the capacities of their natures. So it is said in the text, when that which is perfect is come, that which is in part shall be done away. Their love shall be without any remains of a contrary principle. Having no pride or selfishness to interrupt or hinder its exercises, their hearts shall be full of love. That which was in the heart as but a grain of mustard seed in this world shall there be as a great tree. The soul which only had a little spark of divine love in it in this world shall be, as it were, wholly turned into love; and be like the sun, not having a spot in it, but being wholly a bright, ardent flame. There shall be no remaining enmity, distaste, coldness and deadness of heart towards God and Christ; not the least remainder of any principle of envy to be exercised towards any angels or saints who are superior in glory, no contempt or slight towards any who are inferior.

Those who have a lower station in glory than others suffer no diminution of their own happiness by seeing others above them in glory. On the contrary they rejoice in it. All that whole society rejoice in each other's happiness; for the love of benevolence is perfect in them. Everyone has not only a sincere but a perfect good will to every other. Sincere and strong love is greatly gratified and delighted in the prosperity of the beloved. And if the love be perfect, the greater the prosperity of the beloved is, the more is the lover pleased and delighted. For the prosperity of the beloved is, as it were, the food of love; and therefore the greater that prosperity is, the more richly is love feasted. The love of benevolence is delighted in beholding the prosperity of another, as the love of complacence is delighted in viewing the beauty of another. So that the superior prosperity of those who are higher in glory is so far from being any damp to the happiness of saints of lower degree that it is an addition to it, or a part of it. There is undoubtedly an inconceivably pure, sweet, and fervent love between the saints in glory; and their love is in proportion to the perfection and amiableness of the objects beloved. And therefore it must necessarily cause delight in them when they see others' happiness and glory to be in proportion to their amiableness, and so in proportion to their love of them. Those who are highest in glory are those who are highest in holiness, and therefore are those who are most beloved by all the saints. For they love those most who are most holy, and so they will all rejoice in it that they are most happy. And it will be a damp to none of the saints to see them who have higher degrees of holiness and likeness to God to be more loved than themselves; for all shall have as much love as they desire, and as great manifestations of love as they can bear; all shall be fully satisfied.

And when there is perfect satisfaction, there is no room for envy. And they will have no temptation to envy those who are above them in glory from their superiors being lifted up with pride. We are apt to conceive that those who are more holy, and more happy than others in heaven, will be elated and lifted up in their spirit above others. Whereas their being above them in holiness implies their being superior to them in humility; for their superior humility is part of their superior holiness. Though all are perfectly free from pride, yet as some will have greater degrees of divine knowledge than others, will have larger capacities to see more of the divine perfections, so they will see more of their own comparative littleness and nothingness, and therefore will be lowest abased in humility. And besides, the inferior in glory will have no temptation to envy those who are higher. For those who are highest will not only be more beloved by the lower saints for their higher holiness, but they will also have more of a spirit of love to others. They will love those who are below them more than other saints of less capacity. They who are in highest degrees of glory will be of largest capacity, and so of greatest knowledge, and will see most of God's loveliness, and consequently will have love to God and love to saints most abounding in their hearts. So that those who are lower in glory will not envy those who are above them. They will be most beloved of those who are highest in glory, and the superior in glory will be so far from slighting those who are inferior, that they will have more abundant love to them, greater degrees of love in proportion to their superior knowledge and happiness; the higher in glory, the more like Christ in this respect. So that they will love them more than those who are their equals. And what puts it beyond doubt that seeing the superior happiness of others will be no damp to their happiness is this, that the superior happiness which they have consists in their greater humility, and their greater love to them, and to God and Christ, whom they will look upon as themselves. Such a sweet and perfect harmony will there be in the heavenly society, and perfect love reigning in every heart towards everyone without control, and without alloy, or any interruption. And no envy, or malice, or revenge, or contempt, or selfishness shall enter there, but shall be kept as far off as earth and hell are from heaven. I come now,

V. To consider some of the excellent circumstances in which love shall be expressed and enjoyed in heaven. As particularly,

First. Love there always meets with answerable returns of love. Love is always mutual, and the returns are always in due proportion.

Love always seeks this. In proportion as any person is beloved, in that proportion his love is desired and prized. And in heaven this inclination or desire of love will never fail of being satisfied. No one person there will ever be grieved that he is slighted by those whom he loves, or that he has not answerable returns. As the saints will love God with an inconceivable ardor of heart, and to the utmost of their capacity; so they will know that he has loved them from eternity, and that he still loves them, and will love them to eternity. And God will then gloriously manifest himself to them, and they shall know that all that happiness and glory of which they are possessed is the fruit of his love. With the same ardor will the saints love the Lord Jesus Christ. And their love shall be accepted, and they shall know that he has loved them with a dying love. They shall then be more sensible than they are now what great love it manifested in Christ, that he should lay down his life for them. Then Christ will open to their view the great fountain of love in his heart far beyond what they ever before saw. Hereby the saints' love to God and Christ is mutual, Proverbs 8:17, "I love them, that love me"; though the love of God to the saints cannot properly be called returns of love, because he loved them first. But the sight of God's love will fill the saints the more with joy and admiration.

The love of the saints to one another will always be mutual and answerable, though we cannot suppose that everyone will in all respects be equally beloved. As some of the saints are more beloved of God than others on earth, as the angel told Daniel he was a man greatly beloved [Dan 9:23], and John is called the beloved disciple [John 19:26], so doubtless those who have been most eminent, and are highest in glory, are most beloved of Christ; and doubtless those saints who are most beloved of Christ and nearest to him in glory are most beloved of all the saints. So we may conclude such saints as the Apostle Paul and Apostle John are more beloved by the saints in heaven than other saints of lower rank. They are more beloved by lower saints themselves than those of equal rank. But then there are answerable returns of love. As such are more beloved by other saints, so they have more love to other saints. The heart of Christ, the Head of the society, is fullest of love. He loves all the saints far more than any of them love each other. But the nearer any saint is to him, the more is he like him in this respect, the fuller his heart is of love.

Second. The joy of heavenly love shall never be damped or interrupted by jealousy. Heavenly lovers will have no doubt of the love of each other. They shall have no fear that their professions and testimonies of love are hypocritical; they shall be perfectly satisfied of the sincerity and strength of each other's love, as much as if there were a window in all their breasts, that they could see each other's hearts. There shall be no such thing as flattery or dissimulation in heaven, but there perfect sincerity shall reign through all. Everyone will be perfectly sincere, having really all that love which they profess. All their expressions of love shall come from the bottom of their hearts. The saints shall know that God loves them, and they shall not doubt of the greatness of his love; and they shall have no doubt of the love of all their fellow heavenly inhabitants. And they shall not be jealous of the constancy of each other's love. They shall have no suspicion that their former love is abated, that they have withdrawn their love in any degree from them for the sake of any rival, or by reason of any thing in themselves which they suspect is disagreeable to them, or anything they have done which is disrelished, or through the inconstancy of their hearts. Nor will they in the least be afraid that their love towards them will ever be abated. There shall be no such thing as inconstancy and unfaithfulness in heaven to molest and disturb the friendship of that blessed society. The saints shall have no fear that the love of God will ever abate towards them, or that Christ will not continue always to love them with the same immutable tenderness. And they shall have no jealousy one of another, for they shall know that by divine grace the love of all the saints is also unchangeable.

Third. They shall have nothing within themselves to clog them in the exercises and expressions of love. In this world they find much to hinder them. They have a great deal of dullness and heaviness. They carry about with them a heavy moulded body, a lump of flesh and blood which is not fitted to be an organ for a soul inflamed with high exercises of divine love, but is found a great clog to the soul, so that they cannot express their love to God as they would. They cannot be so active and lively in it as they desire. Fain would they fly, but they are held down, as with a dead weight at their feet. Fain would they be active as a flame of fire, but they find themselves, as it were, hampered or chained down, that they cannot do as their love inclines them. Love disposes them to praise, but their tongues are not obedient; they want words to express the ardor of their souls, and cannot order their speech by reason of darkness, Job 37:19. And oftentimes for want of expressions they are forced to content themselves with groans that cannot be uttered, Romans 8:26. But in heaven they shall have no such hindrance. They will have no dullness or unwieldiness, no corruption of heart to fight against divine love and hinder suitable expressions, no clog of a heavy lump of clay, or an unfit organ for an inward heavenly flame. They shall have no difficulty in expressing all their love. Their souls, which are like a flame of fire with love, shall not be like a fire pent up but shall be perfectly at liberty. The soul which is winged with love shall have no weight tied to the feet to hinder its flight. There shall be no want of strength or activity, nor any want of words to praise the object of their love. They shall find nothing to hinder them in praising or seeing God, just as their love inclines. Love naturally desires to express itself; and in heaven the love of the saints shall be at liberty to express itself as it desires, either towards God or one another.

Fourth. In heaven love will be expressed with perfect decency and wisdom. Many in this world who are sincere in their hearts, and have indeed a principle of true love to God and their neighbor, yet have not discretion to guide them in the manner and circumstances of expressing it. Their speeches are good, but not suitably adapted to the time, or discreetly ordered in the circumstances of them. There are found in them those indiscretions which greatly obscure the loveliness of grace in the eyes of others who behold them. But in heaven the amiableness of their love shall not be obscured by any such means. There shall be no indecent or indiscreet actions or speeches, no selfish fondness, no needless officiousness, no such thing as affections clouding and darkening reason, or going before reason. But wisdom and discretion shall be as perfect in them as love, and every expression of love in them shall be ordered with the most amiable and perfect decency in all the circumstances of it.

Fifth. There shall be nothing external to keep them at a distance or hinder the most perfect enjoyment of each other's love. There shall be no separation wall to keep them asunder. They shall not be hindered from the full and constant enjoyment of each other's love by distance of habitation, for they shall be together as one family in their heavenly Father's house. There shall be no want of full acquaintance to hinder the greatest possible intimacy; much less shall there be any misunderstanding between them, or wrong construction of things which are said or done; no disunion through difference of tempers and manners, or through different circumstances, or various opinions, or various interests or alliances; for they shall all be united in the same interest, and all alike allied or related to the same God, and the same Savior, and all employed in the same business, serving and glorifying the same God.

Sixth. They shall all be united together in a very near relation. Love seeks a near relation to the object beloved. And in heaven all shall be nearly related. They shall be nearly allied to God, the supreme object of their love; for they shall all be his children. And all shall be nearly related to Christ; for he shall be the Head of the whole society, and husband of the whole church of saints. All together shall constitute his spouse, and they shall be related one to another as brethren. It will all be one society, yea, one family. Ephesians 2:19, "Ye are fellow citizens with the saints, and of the household of God."

Seventh. All shall *have propriety* one in another. Love seeks to have the beloved its own, and divine love rejoices in saying, "My beloved is mine, and I am his," as Canticles 2:16. And in heaven all shall not only be related one to another, but they shall be each other's. The saints shall be God's. He brings them hence to him in glory, as that part of the creation which he has chosen for his peculiar treasure. And on the other hand God shall be theirs. He made over himself to them in an everlasting covenant in this world, and now they shall be in full possession of him as their portion. And so the saints shall be Christ's, for he has bought them with a price, and he shall be *theirs*; for he who gave himself *for* them, will have given himself *to* them. Christ and the saints will have given themselves, the one to the other. And as God and Christ shall be the saints', so the angels shall be "their angels," Matthew 18:10. And the saints shall be one another's.

The Apostle in 2 Corinthians 8:5 speaks of saints in those days as first giving themselves to the Lord, and then to one another by the will of God. But this is done much more perfectly in heaven.

Eighth. They shall enjoy each other's love in perfect and undisturbed prosperity. What oftentimes diminishes the pleasure and sweetness of earthly friendship is that though they live in love, yet they live in poverty, and meet with great difficulties and sore afflictions whereby they are grieved for themselves, and for one another. For love and friendship in such cases, though in some respects lightens each other's burdens, yet in other respects adds to persons' afflictions, because it makes them sharers in others' afflictions. So that they have not only their afflictions to bear, but also those of their afflicted friends. But there shall be no adversity in heaven to give occasion for a pitiful grief of spirit, or to molest those heavenly friends in the enjoyment of each other's friendship. But they shall enjoy one another's love in the greatest prosperity, in glorious riches, having the possession of all things. Revelation 21:7, "He that overcometh shall inherit all things; and I will be his God, and he shall be my son." And in the highest honor rejoicing together in an heavenly kingdom, sitting together on thrones, and all wearing crowns of life. Revelation 5:10, "Hath made us kings and priests." Christ and his disciples, who in this world were together in affliction, and manifested love and friendship to each other under great and sore sufferings, are now in heaven enjoying each other's love in immortal glory, all sorrow and sighing being fled away. Christ and the saints both were acquainted with sorrow and grief in this world, though Christ had the greatest share. But in another world they sit together in heavenly places. Ephesians 2:6, "Hath raised us up together, and made us sit together in heavenly places in Christ Jesus." And so all the saints enjoy each other's love in glory and prosperity in comparison with which the wealth and honor of the greatest earthly princes is sordid beggary. So that as they love one another, they have not only their own but each other's prosperity to rejoice in, and are by love made partakers of each other's glory. Such is every saint's love to other saints that it, as it were, makes that glory, which he sees other saints enjoy, his own. He so rejoices in it that they enjoy such glory, that it is in some respects to him as if he, himself, enjoyed it.

Ninth. All things in that world shall conspire to promote their love, and give advantage for mutual enjoyment. There shall be none there to tempt them to hatred, no busy adversary to make misrepresentations or create misunderstandings. Everyone and everything there shall conspire to promote love, and promote the enjoyment of each other's love. Heaven itself, the place of habitation, is a garden of pleasures, a heavenly paradise fitted in all respects for an abode of heavenly lovers, a place where they may have sweet society and perfect enjoyment of each other's love. All things there, doubtless, remarkably show forth the beauty and loveliness of God and Christ, and have a luster of divine love upon them. The very light which shines in and fills that world is the light of love. It is beams of love; for it is the shining of the glory of the Lamb of God, that most wonderful influence of lamblike meekness and love which fills the heavenly Jerusalem with light. Revelation 22:5, "And there shall be no night there; and they need no candle, neither light of the sun; for the Lord God giveth them light." The glory which is about him who reigns in heaven is compared to the beautiful sight of the rainbow for its pleasantness and sweetness, Revelation 4:3. The same which is used as a fit token of God's love and grace manifested in his covenant, Genesis 9:12–15:

> And God said, This is the token of the covenant which I make between me and you and every living creature that is with you, for perpetual generations; I do set my bow in the cloud, and it shall be for a token of a covenant between me and the earth. And it shall come to pass, when I bring a cloud over the earth, that the bow shall be seen in the cloud. And I will remember my covenant, which is between me and you, and every living creature of all flesh; and the waters shall no more become a flood to destroy all flesh.

The light of the New Jerusalem, which is the light of God's glory, is said to be like a jasper stone. Revelation 21:11, "Having the glory of God; and her light was like unto a stone most precious, even like a jasper stone, clear as crystal." The jasper is a precious stone of a beautiful pleasant color.

Tenth. And lastly. They shall know that they shall forever be continued in the perfect enjoyment of each other's love. They shall know that God and Christ will be forever, and that their love will be continued and be fully manifested forever, and that all their beloved fellow saints shall live forever in glory with the same love in their hearts. And they shall know that they themselves shall ever live to love God, and love the saints, and enjoy their love. They shall be in no fear of any end of this happiness, nor shall they be in any fear or danger of any abatement of it through a weariness of the exercises and expressions of love, or cloyed with the enjoyment of it, or the beloved objects becoming old or decayed, or stale or tasteless. All things shall flourish there in an eternal youth. Age will not diminish anyone's beauty or vigor, and there love shall flourish in everyone's breast, as a living spring perpetually springing, or as a flame which never decays. And the holy pleasure shall be as a river which ever runs, and is always clear and full. The paradise of love shall always be continued as in a perpetual spring. There shall be no autumn or winter; every plant there shall be in perpetual bloom with the same undecaying pleasantness and fragrancy, always springing forth, always blossoming, and always bearing fruit. Psalms 1:3, "His leaf shall not wither." Revelation 22:2, "In the midst of the street of it, and on either side of the river, was there the tree of life, which bare twelve manner of fruits, and yielded her fruit every month."

Thus having taken notice of many of the blessed circumstances with which love in heaven is expressed and enjoyed, I proceed now

VI. And lastly, to speak of the blessed fruits of this love, exercised and enjoyed in these circumstances. And I shall mention only two at this time.

First. The most excellent and perfect behavior of the inhabitants of heaven towards God and one another. Divine love is the sum of all good principles, and therefore is the fountain whence proceed all amiable actions. As this love will be perfect to the perfect exclusion of all sin consisting in enmity against God and fellow creatures, so the fruit of it will be a perfect behavior. Their life in heaven shall be without the least sinful failure or error. They shall never turn aside to the right hand or left in the least degree from the way of holiness. Every action shall be perfect in all its circumstances. Every part of their behavior shall be holy and divine in matter and form and end. We know not particularly how the saints in heaven shall be employed; but in general we know they are employed in praising and serving God. Revelation 22:3, "And there shall be no more curse; but the throne of God and of the Lamb shall be in it; and his servants shall serve him." And this they do perfectly, being influenced by such a love as has been described. And we have reason to think that they are employed so as in some way to be subservient to each other's happiness under God; because they are represented in Scripture as united together as one society, which can be for no other purpose but mutual subserviency. And they are thus mutually subservient by a most excellent and perfectly amiable behavior, one towards another, as a fruit of their perfect love one to another.

Second. The other fruit of this love in heaven exercised in such circumstances is perfect tranquility and joy. Holy, humble and divine love is a principle of wonderful power to give ineffable quietness and tranquility to the soul. It banishes all disturbance, it sweetly composes and brings rest, it makes all things appear calm and sweet. In that soul where divine love reigns, and is in lively exercise, nothing can raise a storm. Those are principles contrary to love which make this world so much like a tempestuous sea. It is selfishness, and revenge, and envy, and such things which keep this world in a constant tumult, and make it a scene of confusion and uproar, where no quiet rest is to be enjoyed, unless it be in renouncing the world, and looking to another world. But what rest is there in that world which the God of love and peace fills with his glorious presence, where the Lamb of God lives and reigns, and fills that world with the pleasant beams of his love; where is nothing to give any offense, no object to be seen but what has perfect sweetness and amiableness; where the saints shall find and enjoy all which they love, and so be perfectly satisfied; where there is no enemy and no enmity in any heart, but perfect love in all to everyone; where there is a perfect harmony between the higher and the lower ranks of inhabitants of that world, none envying another, but everyone resting and rejoicing in the happiness of every other. All their love is holy, humble, and perfectly Christian, without the least impurity or carnality; where love is always mutual, where the love of the beloved is answerable to the love of the lovers; where there is no hypocrisy or dissembling, but perfect simplicity and sincerity; where is no treachery, unfaithfulness, or inconstancy, nor any such thing as jealousy. And no clog or hindrance to the exercises and expressions of love, nor imprudence or indecency in the manner of expressing love, no instance of folly or indiscretion in any word or deed; where there is no separation wall, no misunderstanding or strangeness, but full acquaintance and perfect intimacy in all; no division through different opinions or interests, where all that glorious loving society shall be most nearly and divinely related, and all shall be one another's, having given themselves one to another. And all shall enjoy one another in perfect prosperity, riches, and honor, without any sickness, pain, or persecution, or any enemy to molest them, any talebearer, or busybody to create jealousies and misunderstandings.

And all this in a garden of love, the paradise of God, where everything has a cast of holy love, and everything conspires to promote and stir up love, and nothing to interrupt its exercises; where everything is fitted by an all-wise God for the enjoyment of love under the greatest advantages. And all this shall be without any fading of the beauty of the objects beloved, or any decaying of love in the lover, and any satiety in the faculty which enjoys love. O! what tranquility may we conclude there is in such a world as this! Who can express the sweetness of this peace? What a calm is this, what a heaven of rest is here to arrive at after persons have gone through a world of storms and tempests, a world of pride, and selfishness, and envy, and malice, and scorn, and contempt, and contention and war? What a Canaan of rest, a land flowing with milk and honey to come to after one has gone through a great and terrible wilderness, full of spiteful and poisonous serpents, where no rest could be found? What joy may we conclude springs up in the hearts of the saints after they have passed their wearisome pilgrimage to be brought to such a paradise? Here is joy unspeakable indeed; here is humble, holy, divine joy in its perfection. Love is a sweet principle, especially divine love. It is a spring of sweetness. But here the spring shall become a river, and an ocean. All shall stand about the God of glory, the fountain of love, as it were opening their bosoms to be filled with those effusions of love which are poured forth from thence, as the flowers on the earth in a pleasant spring day open their bosoms to the sun to be filled with his warmth and light, and to flourish in beauty and fragrancy by his rays. Every saint is as a flower in the garden of God, and holy love is the fragrancy and sweet odor which they all send forth, and with which they fill that paradise. Every saint there is as a note in a concert of music which sweetly harmonizes with every other note, and all together employed wholly in praising God and the Lamb; and so all helping one another to their utmost to express their love of the whole society to the glorious Father and Head of it, and [to pour back] love into the fountain of love, whence they are supplied and filled with love and with glory. And thus they will live and thus they will reign in love, and in that godlike joy which is the blessed fruit of it, such as eye hath not seen, nor ear heard, nor hath ever entered into the heart of any in this world to conceive [cf. 1 Cor 2:9]. And thus they will live and reign forever and ever.

Part Four

Means of Grace

INTRODUCTION
TO PART FOUR

Edwards was the inheritor of spiritual disciplines that were characteristic of both medieval and early modern Christianity as well as of some more recent developments, such as the spirituality coming out of German Pietism. Those disciplines are highlighted in the following selections. Throughout, the emphasis is on constant striving, self-scrutiny, and self-control while using, as aides to spiritual growth, "means" of grace such as public and private worship, prayer, and attending religious "conferences," and devotional resources such as sacramental manuals.

The very title of *The Duty of Self-Examination* announces its place within this part's theme. Wilson H. Kimnach notes the sermon's "strong overtones of the Puritan meditative tradition" and its emphasis on the self poised between a brief temporal existence and an eternal hereafter. Engaging in a rigorous and incessant self-appraisal through Scripture study and other means will help to determine one's destiny. As Kimnach observes, "One's breath is in God's hands from moment to moment, but one's eternal state is a matter of personal mentality" (WJE 10:480).

God's Wisdom in His Stated Method of Bestowing Grace, along with "Miscellanies" no. 539, the next two selections, further address the seeming contradiction of unobliged free grace and the necessity of good works. While there were rare instances of God converting an individual (such as Paul on the Damascus road) in the course of unrepentant sin, it is God's usual manner to bestow saving grace on those in the "exercise" of the means of grace. After all, it is God who has appointed the means and given directions on how believers are to act; it is therefore only reasonable and right for individuals to follow these very rational instructions. "Preparatory" means do have "agency" insofar as they help to align the heart and mind to believe in and to be receptive to the need for grace. Indeed, spiritual discipline and exercise create "objects" in the soul on which the Holy Spirit can operate, or "the opportunity for grace to act, when God shall infuse it."

Striving After Perfection is a statement, not of the possibility of Christian perfectionism or sinlessness in this life, but rather an expression of what believers individually and collectively must strive for. When this sermon was preached in the spring of 1737, the Connecticut Valley Revival was over, and Edwards was memorializing it in *A Faithful Narrative*; but in this period between awakenings, Northampton had descended into its former contentions, strife, and back-biting. Against these tendencies Edwards portrays the saints' desire for holiness, their hatred of sin, their love of duty. But this is not achieved without much and continual effort. A life of spiritual pains and striving will, however, give way to a "sweet heaven" of rest and peace.

In part 1, we touched on the importance of spiritual "relations," or testimonies, in early New England religious culture. One of the signal features of church membership in early colonial Congregational churches was the requirement that applicants for full membership— which would give access to the sacraments and voting privileges— provide a description of their spiritual experience, so that the church could judge whether they were sincere believers. This was, in a sense, an opportunity for the individual seeking sainthood to report on how well they had used the means of grace, both to their own and to their neighbors' satisfaction. At some churches, such as at Northampton since the days of Edwards's grandfather and predecessor, Solomon Stoddard, consent to a short form was substituted for a detailed and original relation. Edwards famously came to oppose this, asking for a narrative that was genuine—a position that cost him his post. During the contentious period of the "qualifications controversy," he composed, for the benefit of the Northampton Church Committee, a sample profession that he would accept from applicants for full membership. During this same time or shortly after—perhaps at the beginning of the Stockbridge period—he drew up lengthier drafts. The profession and its iterations indicate the sort Edwards sought from applicants, including a sincere hope of having received Christ, a desire to live a godly life, and submitting to the governance of the church. What is unusual is the presence of two Indian names at the end, showing that he required no less of the Mahicans and Mohawks to whom he ministered. Along with sacrament sermons, the profession demonstrates that Edwards applied these standards among the Indians as well as the Stockbridge English in admitting them to membership once he assumed his new pastorate. As Rachel Wheeler, a scholar of Native American history, has written, Edwards "must have been persuaded that Cornelius and Mary's testimony, though scripted, was an apt representation of their inner lives." Furthermore, the profession indicates "a significant exchange between the candidates and Edwards on the subject of Christian belief and practice."[1]

This brand of practical spirituality pervades an earlier letter that Edwards wrote to a young woman in the town of Suffield, Massachusetts (later Connecticut). Suffield, located along the Connecticut River downriver from Northampton, was in the midst of the communities that participated in the revival of 1734–35, and again in 1740–42, following the visit of George Whitefield in the fall of 1740. Suffield's minister died in early 1741, however, so Edwards, along with other area pastors, took turns preaching and conducting prayer meetings in town, with stupendous reactions, comparable to what happened in early July when Edwards preached *Sinners in the Hands of an Angry God* in the neighboring town of Enfield. Temporarily without a spiritual guide, one of the members of the Suffield church wrote to Edwards for directions on "how to conduct yourself in your Christian course." Nothing is known about eighteen-year-old Deborah Hatheway, the recipient of Edwards's letter, except that she had witnessed the religious upheaval of her congregation and vicinity. In response to her inquiry, sensing as always the importance of instilling piety in youth and the role of young people as the vanguard in revivals, he provides no less than nineteen concrete suggestions, roughly split between pious attitudes and practices. The letter became a favorite of later evangelicals. During the nineteenth century, for example, the American Tract

Society published the text as *Advice to a Young Convert*, selling hundreds of thousands of copies.

༄

THE DUTY OF SELF-EXAMINATION (1722–23)[2]

Haggai 1:5
Now therefore thus saith the Lord of hosts: Consider your ways....

Doctrine

'Tis our most important duty to consider our ways.

This duty of consideration of our ways, I think is fully implied in these three things:
I. What our ways ought to be.
II. What they have been in times past.
III. What they now are.

I. We ought to consider what our ways ought [to be]. It ought to be our greatest inquiry: What ought I do? That question in Acts 9:6 ought to be the grand question: "Lord, what wouldst thou have me to do?" This is a thing woefully neglected by most of this wicked generation. They never consider what they ought to do, care not what is their duty, nor what is contrary to their duty. Their care is what will get them the most money and the most bodily pleasure.

Nothing so much concerns us as to know our duty, that we may do it; for we must be miserable if we don't do it. And God has been so gracious to us as to reveal our duty to us, so that we may know it if we will, only at [the] cheap rate of reading and considering. Our privileges in this respect [are] above most of the world's, and yet for all this many never consider what is their duty. We ought to be diligent to know what those things are which God has commanded, seeing he has commanded them. We ought frequently to consider what are our obligations to our duty, and to meditate on the reasonableness of it: to think what an absolute right God has to our service; how great and excellent a being he is, and what he deserves of us upon that account; to consider that he has made us, and how just it is we should obey him upon that account; to consider what we receive from him, and what is due from us to him on that account. We ought not to eat and drink like beasts, never considering whence these good things come. Nay, we ought not to breathe like beasts, without considering who it is that gives us our breath, without considering the God in whose hand our breath is; for every breath we draw is a mercy of God that we do not deserve.

Especially we ought to consider what God has done for our soul's welfare, and what is due to him on that account; surely, a man of reason will consider these things. Certainly we ought not to act worse than beasts, to live by the kindness of a merciful being and never once consider what we shall render to him for all his benefits towards us.

II. We ought to consider what our ways have been in time past. Have we not cause to repent and mourn when we reflect on past actions? Don't conscience tell us, "there you ought not to have done, seeing you have done foolishly; herein you did basely and unworthily"? How have we lived and how have we acted; what has been our course? Certainly we ought not to live without reflection. Why have we our memory given us? Is not one of the principal uses of [it] to reflect on our past actions? We ought to look back and see where we have missed it, see where we have moved out of the right way; see where we have stumbled and fallen, and see where are the rocks that we have suffered shipwreck upon [in] time past, that we may avoid them.

We ought frequently to consider whether our ways have been in all respects as they ought to be, whether they could not have been better, and to be nice and critical in searching for faults in our behavior. Some men stifle and muzzle their consciences when [they are] about to tell them of their past actions, which is a certain sign that they are very bad; but conscience ought not to be [by] any means to be restrained, but to have full liberty to tell us of all our faults, and set the heinousness of them before us. Yea, we ought instead of stifling it to assist it; for conscience is our best friend in this world when its rebukes are severest.

III. We ought to consider what our ways now are. This is what is chiefly respected in our text: first, the nature of our ways; second, what is their tendency; third, what will be the end of our ways.

First. We ought to consider the nature of our ways, whether they are good or bad, right or wrong. Are ours ways of wickedness or ways of godliness; is the race that we run the Christian race, or the race of the devil? Are we careful to observe all the laws of God and do as he directs and commands, and endeavor to please him in all that we do and thereby recommend ourselves to his favor; or do we do just as the devil would have us? Do we rather choose to hearken to him than to the God that made us, follow after him that will lead us to hell than him that will conduct us to heaven?

We ought to consider which has the greatest influence upon us: our carnal appetites, or the promises and threatenings of God's word. When there is set before us a self-denying, mortifying duty and a pleasant sin, for us to take our choice, the sinful pleasure and delight allures and entices on one side, and the favor of God and heaven invites on the other. Which do we choose, which has the greatest influence upon us: the vain show that the devil makes to us of pleasure, or else the offers and promises of God?

Do we live to the world, or do we live to God? Has the world the victory in our hearts over all principles of goodness? Which do we choose: to be rich or to be holy; to feed sumptuously to please our appetite with meat and drink, or to feed on Jesus Christ, the bread that came down from heaven, the heavenly food; to have our bodies finely arrayed, or our souls clothed with meekness and humility, and the righteousness of Christ; to dwell in stately houses, or to have our souls made the temples of the Holy Ghost?

1. We ought to consider the nature of our thoughts. How are the faculties of our souls chiefly employed; are our thoughts and our affections chiefly exercised upon earthly things, about what we shall eat, what we shall drink, and wherewithal we shall be clothed? Are our minds set chiefly on vanities and trifles that are of little profit or

advantage? Do we suffer our thoughts to rove to the ends of the earth? Do we give our thoughts the reins to go where they incline, sometimes upon the pleasing objects of concupiscence and the lusts of the flesh; sometimes after the objects of covetousness and the lusts of the eyes; sometimes after the objects of ambitious desires and haughty expectations led and governed by the pride of life, [and] at other times about things of no advantage or importance? Are our thoughts thus employed?

Or do we restrain them, and keep them chiefly exercised upon heavenly objects? Do we think mostly about our Creator and Redeemer, the glory of God, our salvation and the welfare of our souls, the state we are in and the eternal estate we are to be in after this life? Do we think most of that which most concerns us and is of greatest importance to us? Do we think most of those things which are the most excellent and are most worthy of our thoughts: how is it with us in this respect?

2. We ought to consider our words. Words commonly follow thoughts: if the thoughts are much upon religion, certainly our tongues will be apt sometimes to be upon the same subject; but if the thoughts are mostly vain, the words will be likewise vain and to little purpose. Matthew 12:34, "O generation of vipers, how can ye, being evil, speak of good things, for out of the abundance of the heart the mouth speaketh." For if the tongue is bad, we may judge the man bad also. Commonly, as is the tongue so is the man. The apostle James compares it to a bridle by which the horses are turned about, and to the helm of a ship by which the whole ship is guided (Jas 3:3–4), thereby intimating that the whole man is commonly as the tongue is.

Wherefore, in this respect we ought to consider our ways by considering whether our words are good or bad, profitable or unprofitable. We are directed how the words of Christians ought to be: "Let the word of Christ dwell in you richly in all wisdom; teaching and admonishing one another...and whatsoever ye do in the word or deed, do all in the name of the Lord Jesus, giving thanks to God and the Father by him," Colossians 3:16–17. "Let your speech be alway with grace, seasoned with salt, that ye may know how ye ought to answer every man," Colossians 4:6. How far is the practice of most nominal Christians from [this], just as if these commands were not in force now in these days as they were in the apostles', just as [if] this age were exempted. Wherefore, we ought to consider how it is with us, whether we follow these directions. If we do not, here is a command stands against us.

3. We ought also to consider the nature of our actions. Thoughts, words, and actions go all together.

(1) We ought to consider the nature of our actions which respect God: whether they are done in his service and to his glory; whether all that we do is part of the work that God has appointed for us and commanded, for everything that we do that is not part of God's service is part of the devil's service. "Whatever is not of faith is sin" (Romans 14:23).

(2) We ought to consider the nature of those actions which nextly respect ourselves: whether we live soberly and humbly, chastely and temperately; whether we are patient in afflictions and deny and mortify our evil desires and curb unruly passions or no, and keep under our bodies and bring them into subjection or no.

(3) We ought to consider the nature of our actions which directly respect our neighbor, with respect to justice, charity, beneficence, and the like.

Thus, all our actions ought to be strictly examined and tried, and not only barely to consider the outward action as it is in itself: but also from what principle our actions do arise from; what internal principle we act and live [by], for actions are either good or bad according to the principle whence they arise. We must consider whether what we do, we do from a love to God and his commands, or whether from a love to ourselves—that is, to our flesh—love to this world, and love to sin. We ought diligently to consider why it is that we pray and read and hear and sing psalms, whether out of love of reputation and fear of disgrace; or whether only from custom, education, and fashion; or whether we do it from love to God and godliness. For otherwise, all these things are good for nothing: we are but emptiness and vanity, a sounding brass and a tinkling cymbal. Thus the nature of all our actions ought to be strictly examined and considered by us.

Second. We ought to consider the tendency of our actions. We ought not to go blindly along through this world and never inquire which way we are going, and where the path we are in will lead us at last; for there is but one path that leads to happiness, but innumerable paths lead to destruction. We ought always to consider whether the way we are in leads to our misery or to our felicity, whether they tend to ruin us or to make us blessed. How doth the blind, inconsiderate man know but that the next step will bring him to the pit, and will put him past recovery?

Third. We ought to consider what will be the end of our ways. Where are our ways like to end, or what will the course we now follow at last bring us to? Every man is in the way to heaven or the way to hell, and the way that we are now in, if pursued, will certainly bring us to one or the other of these.

If wicked men did but consider what will be the dreadful end of the ways they are in, how would they be startled and affrighted, for their path is the way to hell, leading down to the chambers of death! They go like oxen to the slaughter; their ways lead down into the hideous den of the old serpent, where those that come never return again.

Certainly, therefore, it behooves us to examine, according to the best of our light, what is like to [be] the upshot and event of our present course of living; frequently to ask ourselves: "Where will this path that I am now in lead to in the end? What will be the fruit of these actions? When I die and go into another world, will it be unspeakable torments, or immortal glory?"

GOD'S WISDOM IN HIS STATED METHOD OF BESTOWING GRACE (1729)[3]

Exodus 20:24
An altar of earth thou shalt make unto me, and shalt sacrifice
thereon thy burnt offerings, and thy peace offerings, thy sheep, and

thine oxen: in all places where I record my name I will come unto
thee, and I will bless them.

God is now speaking unto Moses out of the thick darkness from Mount Sinai. We read in the foregoing chapter of the first coming [of the children of Israel] unto this mountain after their coming out of Egypt, and how Moses went up to God to the mount; and how that God ordered the attendance of the congregation at the foot of the mountain to see the tokens of his presence and majesty, and to hear him speak to them and to receive the law at his mount.

And so God came down in a very awful and terrible manner upon the mountain and spoke in the hearing of all the congregation, and spoke to them the Ten Commandments with a very loud and mighty voice; which was attended with Mount Sinai's being altogether in a smoke, and with the appearance of devouring fire and with terrible thunders and lightning, and the mountain and the ground about it quaking exceedingly and the sound of a trumpet exceeding loud, besides the awful majesty of the voice of God which spake to them, so that all the people that were in the camp trembled, and were exceedingly affrighted. It was more than they could bear, thus to hear God speaking to them. They therefore said to Moses, as in the nineteenth verse, "Speak thou with us, and we will hear: but let not God speak with us, lest we die." Upon this, the people stood afar off, and Moses drew near to the thick darkness where he was to hear God speak to him, that he might speak to the people and carry God's message to them.

When Moses drew near, God tells him his mind concerning his worship, in what way he would be worshiped by the people, and first forewarns them of making other gods or worshipping him by images. V. 23, "Ye shall not make with me gods of silver, neither shall ye make unto ye gods of gold."

And in the verse of our text, [God] gives commandment concerning the place and manner of his own worship, as to the altar. "An altar of earth shalt thou make unto me, and shalt sacrifice thereon thy burnt offerings, and thy peace offerings, thy sheep, and thine oxen." Not that an altar of hewn stone was not as good in itself as one of earth or whole stone, but God is sovereign, and appoints what way for his own worship he pleases. Though another way may seem as good or better to us, yet we can expect to find his acceptance only in his own way.

And so, second, as to the place. "In all places where I record my name I will come unto thee, and I will bless thee." Not that one place was any better than another in it[self], or that there is any particular virtue in one place more than another, but because it was God's pleasure so to appoint.

In the words observe,

1. A benefit proposed and offered God's people: and that is, that in that God would meet with them and would bless them. By his meeting with them is meant his accepting of them, his manifesting himself to them, and giving them tokens of his friendly and gracious presence amongst them. And by his blessing of them is meant his bestowing upon them all good things which they stand in need of, his doing the part of a God to them.

2. How it is to be sought and obtained: that is, in the place where God shall record his name; that is, in the place that he shall appoint for his people for their public worship, and where he will give the outward tokens of his presence, such as answering from off the mercy seat, etc.

Doctrine

If we would be in the way of God's grace and blessing, we must wait upon him in his own way and in the use of his appointed means.

Here,

I. We shall show that 'tis God's manner to bestow his grace and blessing in a way of the use of certain appointed means, and give the reasons of it.

II. What those means are.

III. That his grace and blessing is to be expected in no other way but the use of them.

I. 'Tis God's manner to bestow his grace and blessing in a way of the use of appointed means.

God is the sovereign disposer of his own favor and blessing: he may bestow it on whom he pleases, and in what way he pleases. There are none of us can challenge any right in God's grace. We have to a great degree deserved the contrary of him. He might in our first state of innocence bestow his favors and bounties just in what way he pleased; he might appoint what conditions he would, as he was absolute Lord over us.

Much more now since we have sinned and his justice has infinite demands upon us, it is wonderful, unspeakable grace that he is willing to be gracious to us in any way. But if he is, 'tis his prerogative to say in what way, whether in the use of means or without means.

And this way hath pleased God to bestow his mercy in the use of certain means, and he hath told us what means.

God hath not only appointed a way of salvation for us by Jesus Christ by what he has done and suffered, but he hath appointed something to [be] done by us, a way wherein we are to seek the benefit of what our Savior hath done for us.

God don't let mankind alone, everyone to go his own way, without any sort of directions from him how to behave and act, and so in an extraordinary, miraculous way immediately snatch one and another out of their misery and bestow salvation upon them without any directions given by him how to seek salvation, or anything at all done by them any way in order to it.

But God chooses to bestow his mercy in a way of appointed means. And we shall mention some of the reasons why God thus doth. But [we] would take notice,

First, Negatively, that God don't bestow {his grace and blessing in a way of the use of certain appointed means}, because he could not as easily bestow it immediately without the use of any means. The means that are used don't make the salvation less wholly from God. Men, by using means, don't help God; they don't do part themselves. It is not less the work of God's power, or the gift of his grace, for the means that are used.

The means have no power in themselves to reach the end, nor are they the way to those glorious blessings offered by any proper efficiency or any virtue in themselves. Nor are those blessings the less absolutely from God for them, any more than there was any proper virtue in Moses's rod to divide the Red Sea and do all those miracles in Egypt; or in the sound of rams' horns to make the walls of Jericho fall flat to the ground; or in the clay that Christ made to open the eyes of the blind man; or in the hem of his garment to cure the woman of her issue of blood; or in handkerchiefs and aprons carried from Paul's body to cure sick people and cast out devils.

But for the *Positive Reasons.*

First. 'Tis agreeable to God's wisdom to govern the moral world, as he does the natural world, in a stated method. God has no need of any means in order to the governing of the natural world and bringing to pass the events of common providence, such as growing of the grass, corn, and trees, and the propagating and nourishing of animals and sustaining the body of man; which nevertheless God accomplishes by stated means, according to a certain method, which we call the law of nature. And God sees it agreeable to his wisdom so to do. 'Tis an abundantly more beautiful way of ordering things, thus to accomplish things according to a regular method, a constant succession of causes and effects and mutual dependence of one event upon another that God has fixed, than to have 'em done all as miracles are done, without any such regularity or natural dependence.

So likewise, God orders the affairs of grace in a more beautiful way, that bestows his grace in a stated method in a way of appointed means, than if it were given immediately to one and another without any means or any stated manner or method. And as there is a natural connection in natural things between the means and the end, so God has been pleased to constitute an arbitrary connection between the means and the end in the moral and spiritual world. Thus God in his ordinary works does as it were set a rule to himself, that there may be proportion [and] regularity in his works.

Second. 'Tis most agreeable to the state of mankind in this world. God observes an harmony between one work of his and another, and as God has placed us here in the natural world, where we are governed by stated means and the laws of nature in things that respect the outward man, so God saw meet that, while we are here, our spiritual affairs should be ordered in an appointed way and our spiritual good obtained in the use of appointed means. This way is much more agreeable to the state of God's church here in this natural world, than if all things were done as miracles are, without any stated means.

God saw meet, that seeing we are here in the body, that we should have grace in the use of outward means; that as we receive natural knowledge by our outward senses, so we should receive his grace by seeing and hearing, etc. And therefore, [God] has appointed outward ordinances to be the vehicles of his grace.

The other world, and not this, is the world where God will communicate himself visibly and immediately without any such vehicle.

'Tis more agreeable to the state of the church in this world upon another account. It is God's design that his people here should live by faith and not by sight; whereas if God bestowed grace upon men in a miraculous manner when they never used any means, then there would not be that exercise for faith that there is now in believing that God is the author of all grace. God now works secretly upon men's hearts; his power is inward and not seen by the world, and oftentimes not by him that is the subject of it but by faith.

But if men should be taken in a moment, in their full career in sin, in gross ignorance and darkness and heathenism, without the preaching or hearing of the gospel or reading the word or any outward instruction, or using any means themselves or any other using any means with them; if all that had the grace of God bestowed on them had it so, and should be at once taken and instructed and made to believe, and be under the government of the doctrines of the gospel; then it would cease to be a matter of faith, that these things were not from ourselves.

It was not God's design that miracles should always be continued in the world. Miracles are only for the introducing the true religion into the world, to accompany the revelation and first promulgating the word of God by them to whom it was revealed by inspiration, to confirm to the world that it was a divine revelation; but now, when the true religion is long since introduced and the canon of the Scripture completed, the use of miracles in the church ceases.

Third. If God did not bestow his grace in a way of the use of appointed means, there would not be that opportunity for the manifestation of God's wisdom in ordering the affairs of his church and accomplishing the designs of his grace in the world, either in accomplishing the design of his grace in particular persons or in his church in general. God now shows a great deal of wisdom oftentimes in so ordering things in his providence as to bring great sinners to the saving {knowledge of Christ} by bringing of them to such means, to see or hear such things whereby they are awakened, etc.; in directing of them to avoid the rocks {of temptation}; in leading of them along through all difficulties and temptations till they come to Christ; and so after conversion in preserving of them, in guiding of them.

And so in the church in general, in propagating the gospel and giving of it victory. But there would be no gospel if {God did not bestow his grace in a way of appointed means}; in so ordering things so as to destroy and confound his enemies; to destroy Antichrist; to make Satan and his enemies a means of their own ruin, which could not be if there was no means; in working things about so as to fulfill his glorious prophesies and promises to his church.

If things were all done miraculously and without means, there would be indeed manifestation of infinite power, but not such a manifestation of infinitely wise contrivance. It is a way that shows more of infinite wisdom and contrivance. To create a tree immediate with ripe fruit on it, though it shows the same power, yet is not so great a manifestation of contrivance as the producing of it from the seed gradually to such a state, by the influences of the sun and rain, in a constant method.

God showed a wonderful wisdom in his gradual revelation of the gospel in the world. First, darkly in types. And revealing first to the Jews, and then rejecting them and revealing to the Gentiles; and afterwards calling the Jews again, and with them bringing in the fullness of the Gentiles. Which wisdom was so wonderful that [it] made the Apostle cry out, as Romans 11:33–36, "O the depth of the riches both of the wisdom and knowledge of God! how unsearchable are his judgments, and his ways past finding out! For who hath known the mind of the Lord? or who hath been his counselor? Or who hath first given to him, and it shall be recompensed unto him again? For of him, and through him, and to him, are all things; to whom be glory forever. Amen."

Fourth. If grace was bestowed without the use {of appointed means}, there would be no opportunity for the exercise of many moral virtues and Christian graces. [There would be no opportunity for] moral virtues in unconverted men. [There would be no need for] prudence in care for their souls. [There could be no reason for] diligence in seeking salvation, [no need for] constancy, [no need for] resolution.

In the converted, [there would be no opportunity for] diligence in seeking God. [There would be no opportunity for diligence] in striving to grow in grace, [or for] constancy in the use of means.

[There would be no ground for] charitable endeavors for the good of souls, [or for] endeavors for the advancement of Christ's kingdom. Particularly, [there would be no need for] ministers' diligence in studying, [or] in exhorting [and] warning. And [so there would be no ground for] both ministers' and magistrates' seeking the good of the church in the world, [or] learned men by their preaching [and] writings.

Fifth. If it were otherwise, 'twould open a door for all manner of confusion and wickedness amongst unconverted men. There being appointed means for {the bestowal of grace}, is a mighty restraint upon wicked men; 'tis a principal thing whereby God restrains the wickedness of men.

If there were no appointed means, then the most wicked in the world would be in as likely a way to obtain salvation as any.

If there were no means, there would be no such thing as the word of God, no revelation of God, of heaven and hell—and what a doleful place would this world be in then!

Sixth. The diligent use of means prepares the heart for God's grace and makes it better entertained.

Seventh, and lastly. It renders those that miss of salvation the more inexcusable.

II. We shall just take notice what are the appointed means of grace. And we shall include not only the means of obtaining grace, but the means of persevering and growing in grace. And they may mainly be reduced to these heads:

First. Reading and hearing the word of God. Search the Scriptures, John 5:39. Faith comes by hearing, Romans 10:17. The word of God is a principal means. How much men fail in reading Scripture.

Second. Consideration. [So we should consider] death, eternity, judgment, God, [the] Creator, etc. [We] should think on our ways. Consider our latter end. God expects we should exercise our reason and our powers as men, in order to the having his grace.

Third. Prayer. In its various kinds. Ephesians 6:18, "Praying with all prayers." [So] secret [prayer], Matthew 6:6. [So] family [prayer]. [Prayer is] recommended by Christ's own example, and the common practice of saints in Scripture. [It is] spoken of with approbation. [So] public [prayer]. God expects we should come to him for grace, and call upon him for it and thankfully acknowledge what we have received.

Fourth. Attending on sacraments, baptism, and the Lord's Supper. God uses all manner of means with us. He speaks to us not only by his word, but by sensible figures and representations of spiritual things.

Fifth. Carefully and conscientiously avoiding all moral evils, and doing moral duties. We must avoid moral evils of thoughts, words, and deeds.

Whatsoever ordinances are attended, if men go on in a way of wickedness, in indulging any lust whatsoever, it will be to no purpose. The prayers of such persons, and their having an attendance on sacraments, is but mockery and is accepted no otherwise by God.

Living soberly, doing justly and observing the gospel rules of charity, forgiveness, temperance, meekness, and the like, are as much as any other the means of God's appointment for seeking conversion, and more insisted on by God. And [they] are a very main and principal means for growth in grace.

III. Lastly, we can expect to obtain God's grace and blessing in no other way but this. To seek it in any other way is to cast reflection upon God's wisdom and authority, and a setting up our own wisdom in opposition to his. 'Tis a reflection upon his sovereign grace, as though salvation and spiritual and eternal life were not his to give in what way he pleased, but we could obtain it in our own way or by our own strength.

God, by appointing these to be the means of grace, does as much as say that he'll bestow his grace ordinarily in this way and no other. Not that he never bestows in another way: he hath not bound himself, but hath only given us directions and told us in what way 'tis our duty and our interest to seek his grace in, and this is the only rule for our expectations. And therefore we can't expect {to obtain grace except through the use of God's appointed means}.

First. If we only desire it and are idle, and use no means at all; or use some, and slothfully or knowingly neglect others.

Second. If the means they use are not those appointed. Therefore, they are most unhappy who embrace false religions: Quakers, who neglect ordinances; papists, who add a multitude of their own and corrupt God's ordinances. When persons become superstitious and think to obtain heaven by some extraordinary thing not appointed, they are not in the way of it.

Inferences

I. How greatly they are privileged who know and enjoy the appointed means of grace. They know the way where they may find God, the way that he is wont to meet with men and to bless them.

How great a part of the world are utterly ignorant of this way, that have not God's word to tell them what are the means of grace. They han't that to read and hear and to present to them subjects of their consideration and meditation. They know not how to call upon God, nor indeed what God to call upon. They have not the sacraments that God has appointed. And indeed, their understandings are so darkened that they have obscured the light, and in considerable measure obliterated the law of nature.

And many that enjoy some means of grace, they have exceedingly corrupted [them] with human alterations, additions and detractions.

Happy is that people that enjoy the means of grace as God has given them, that have them all and have them pure, just as he has instituted them.

Happy is that people that have the word of God, and make that the only rule to direct them in this affair of seeking the grace and favor of God.

II. Hence we learn how much 'tis persons' prudence to continue steadfastly in the use of all the means of grace.

The appointed means of grace, notwithstanding that they are the only way that men have any reason to expect to meet with God or obtain his favor in, are very much neglected even by those that know them. And indeed, there are but few that will be persuaded to a thorough use and improvement of them.

Many neglect them because of their contrariety to their lusts and sinful inclinations. They can't bear to tie themselves to such strict rules, and so to abridge themselves of that sweet license in sin which they have been wont to give themselves.

And many neglect them through sloth and an indisposedness to such diligence and striving as is requisite in order to an universal use of the means of grace. And therefore, there are some that would feign be saved that are but partial in their use of means: they attend some ordinances and not others; they are careful as to some moral duties, but not others; they will pray to God sometimes, but not others; they are careful of external actions, but not their thoughts.

And there are others that are ready to be discouraged in the use of the means of grace, thinking of it a vain thing. They imagine they have hitherto served no benefit, and they think they ben't like to.

But by the doctrine we learn that they act with far the greatest prudence that do thoroughly attend the means of grace, and do so constantly and perseveringly without discouragement; hearkening to no temptations as though it was a vain thing, not ceasing because they have used 'em so long and han't yet met with God in them. Because this is the declared way wherein God has told us he will be found; and if ever they find him, they can expect to find him in no other way.

III. Hence we learn how far persons may take encouragement from their own use of the means of grace.

All encouragement that a person may take from their own diligence and constancy in the use of those means is not self-righteousness, because God has revealed that this is the ordinary way wherein he meets with men and blesses them. Persons may think and have God's word for their foundation, that they are in a far more likely way to obtain salvation in their using means than if they used none, and in their diligent use than if they were slothful and partial, and so may take encouragement from their own endeavors.

Indeed, for sinners to take encouragement as though God were under any obligation to them for their use of means, either naturally or by promise, is self-righteousness. But the godly that faithfully and with a true heart use means may assuredly expect success from God's promise, that in that way they shall grow in grace.

"MISCELLANIES" NO. 539, "MEANS OF GRACE"

Grace is from God as immediately and directly as light is from the sun; and that notwithstanding the means that are improved, such as word, ordinances, etc. For though these are made use of, yet they have no influence to produce grace, either as causes or instruments, or any other way; and yet they are concerned in the affair of the production of grace, and are necessary in order to it.

They are concerned in this affair either immediately or remotely. As they are immediately concerned, it is not either as adjuvant causes or instruments, but only as by them the Spirit of God has an opportunity to cause acts of grace in the soul; and that grace, as immediately from him, may have an opportunity to act more fully and freely and suitably to the nature of things, i.e., to the nature and works of God, and our own state and nature, and the relation there is between God and us and others. The means of grace have to do in this affair of the production of grace, or any act of it, in our souls, no otherwise than as those means cause those effects in our souls; whereby there is an opportunity for grace to act, and to act suitably to the nature of things, as it proceeds and flows from the Holy Ghost. God don't see meet to infuse grace, where there is no opportunity for it to act, or to act in some measure suitably.

If it be inquired what I mean by grace's acting suitably to the nature of things, and whether or no grace can act at all, and not act suitably to the nature of things: I answer, it acts suitably so far as it does act, as to the matter of the act; but it may be so, that it may act very partially and lamely, like a man that has but one leg or arm or a hand, [or is] without any feet, etc., and may not have any opportunity to act otherwise. Thus for instance, I don't know but it is possible for God to infuse a principle of grace into the heart of a man that never has been informed that Christ is any more than a man; or believes that there are some things God can't do, and that he is sometimes mistaken; or has a notion of Father, Son, and Holy Ghost as three distinct gods, friends one to another. But the actings of grace will be very unsuitable to the nature of things; it must act very lamely or monstrously, and so unsuitably, that I believe God ordinarily don't see meet that it should be, where there is no opportunity for it to act no better.

But that it may appear how that outward means are no otherwise concerned in this affair of the production of grace, any otherwise than as by the effects these means cause in our souls, give opportunity for grace to act as infused or excited, we will consider what effects they do produce in our souls. And they are of three kinds: (1) They supply the mind with notions, or speculative ideas, of the things of religion. (2) They may have an effect upon mere natural reason, in a measure to gain the assent of the judgment. (3) They may have an effect upon the natural principles of heart, to give, in a degree, a sense of the natural good or evil of those things that they have a notion of, and so may accordingly move the heart with fear, etc. Now none of these effects are any way concerned in the existing or acting of grace in the heart, any otherwise than as they afford an opportunity for it to act, or to act more freely and suitably; as we shall show concerning each of them.

1. The means of grace, such as the word and sacraments, supply the mind with notions, or speculative ideas, of the things of religion, and thus give an opportunity for grace to act in the soul; for hereby the soul is supplied with matter for grace to act upon, when God shall be pleased to infuse it. And this matter is by those means there upheld and so disposed, as that it may be more capable of, and

fitted for, the acting of grace upon it in a suitable manner, or in a manner most agreeable to the nature of things. The matter which the principle of grace acts upon is those notions or ideas that the mind is furnished with, of the things of religion; or of God, Christ, the future world, the saints, the attributes of God, the works of God, those things that Christ has done and suffered, etc. If there could be a principle of grace in the heart without these notions or ideas there, yet it could not act, because it could have no matter to act upon.

Now they are the means of grace, such as the Scriptures, instructions of parents and ministers, sacraments, etc., that supply our minds with those ideas and notions; and the end of these means is to supply our minds with them, and to supply us with them more fully, and to revive and maintain those ideas in our minds; and that the attention of our mind to them may be more strong, that they may be, as much as may be, not only habitually, but actually existing in our minds, and that [those] ideas, as to their actual existence, may be clear and lively, and that they may be disposed in the most advantageous order. And thus the means of grace have no influence to work grace, but only give such notions to our minds, and so disposed, as to give opportunity for grace to act, when God shall infuse it; as Elijah, by laying fuel upon the altar, and laying it in order, gave opportunity for the fire to burn, when God should send it down from heaven. Here,

(1) It is needful, in order to give this opportunity, that these notions should be true; for those that are false ben't proper fuel for the fire. A false notion gives no opportunity for grace to act, but on the contrary, will hinder its acting. Thus if a man has been taught that God is a foolish and unjust being, these notions of folly or injustice in God give no opportunity for a principle of grace to act towards God, but on the contrary, tend to prevent. Therefore, those outward means that do most exhibit the truth to our minds give us the greatest advantage for the obtaining grace.

(2) The more fully we are supplied with these notions, the greater opportunity has grace to act, and to act more suitably to the nature of things when God infuses it, because it

has more objects to act upon, and one object illustrates another; so that we haven't only more notions, but all our notions are the more clear, and more according to truth. So that this is another thing that means do: they more and more fully and purely supply our minds with matter for grace to act upon. Here therefore, is the benefit of frequent and abundant instructions; here is the benefit of study and meditation, and comparing spiritual things with spiritual.

(3) The more lively these notions are, the more strong the ideas, the greater opportunity for grace to act if infused. Surely, if the existence of these ideas gives an opportunity, then the more perfect the actual existence of them is, the greater opportunity. The stronger and more lively the impression with which the ideas actually exists, the more perfect is its existence; as when we look on the sun, our idea of it has a more perfect existence, than when we only think of it by imagination, because the impression is much stronger. Therefore here is the advantage of clear, convincing instructions, of setting forth divine things in a clear light; here is the advantage of divine eloquence, in instructing, warning, counseling, etc.: they serve as they give more strong and lively impressions of the truth. The stronger reasons and arguments are offered to confirm any truth, or to show the eligibleness of any practice, it serves as it gives those ideas that are the matter that grace acts upon, and disposes them in such order, sets them in such light, that grace, if in the heart, shall have the greater opportunity to act more fully and more according to its tendency, upon them. Reasonings and pathetical counsels and warnings do give an opportunity for grace another way also, by the effect they have upon natural principles; of which I shall speak by and by.

(4) The oftener these notions or ideas are revived, and the more they are upheld in the soul, the greater opportunity for the Spirit of God to infuse grace, because he hath more opportunity, hath opportunity more constantly. The more constantly the matter for grace to work upon is upheld, the

more likely are persons to receive grace of the Spirit. 'Tis the wisest way to maintain the opportunity, for we know not when the Spirit's time is.

2. Means may have an effect upon our reason, in a degree, to gain the assent of that. (Note: By mere reason, I mean that wherein there is merely the exercise of the speculative faculty, wholly distinct from and independent of a sense of heart, wherein is not only the exercise of the speculative understanding, but also of the disposition, inclination, or will of the soul. Spiritual understanding includes this, as we have shown elsewhere....) But that effect which means have upon mere reason is no otherwise concerned in the affair of the production of grace in the soul, [than] only as hereby the soul is so prepared for it, that grace, when communicated from the Spirit of God, will have a better opportunity to act. For the judgment of mere reason, concurring with that conviction which arises from the heart's sense of the divine excellency of spiritual things, strengthens the assurance; and the mind's having the stronger and more confirmed belief of the truth of spiritual things, love and other graces flow out the more freely and fully towards those objects that are thus believed to be real. The more fully realized the being of the objects of grace's actings, the greater opportunity will there be for the new nature to exert itself towards them.

The knowledge of the rational arguments that are brought to prove the truth of religion, whether they have any effect upon mere natural reason or no, prepares the mind for grace another way: viz., as hereby the mind has ideas and notions set in that order, has those arguments present, that when grace has removed prejudices and given eyes to see, they will see the connection and relation of the ideas, and the force of the arguments. But this belongs to the foregoing way, wherein means give opportunity for grace to act.

3. The third effect of means is upon the natural principles of heart, to give in a degree a sense of the natural good or evil of those things that the mind has a notion, or speculative idea of, and so may accordingly move the heart with fear, and desire, etc.; and by this means also, the soul may be the better prepared for grace. For these effects upon the natural principles of heart remaining and existing

with the supernatural principle of heart when infused, the actings of the soul may be greater and more suitable, and the effects that follow greater, than otherwise would be. Thus if a person has been deeply possessed with a sense of the dreadfulness of divine wrath and with great fear of it, when afterwards the soul comes to have a sense of the grace and love of God, this appears the more glorious, because the mind is already possessed with a deep sense of the dreadfulness of that evil which this grace and love delivers from; and the preciousness of love is illustrated by the dreadfulness of the opposite, wrath. God is more loved for his grace and goodness to him. And then grace more naturally exercises itself in awful and humble reverence, which is most suitable to our nature and state, and the relation we stand in to God: for being in a mind that was before prepared by so deep a sense of the dreadfulness of God's anger, these effects upon natural principles direct the stream of grace into that channel.

Thus we have shown how that means are concerned in the affair of the production of grace. They are also concerned in another way, more remotely: (1) as they restrain from sin, whereby God might be provoked to withhold grace; (2) as means excite to attend and use means. Thus men are persuaded by the word to hear and read the word, and to meditate upon it, to keep Sabbaths, to attend sacraments, etc.; counsels of parents may persuade to a diligent use of means....

Corollary 1. Hence it follows, that attending and using means of grace is no more than a waiting upon God for his grace, in the way wherein he is wont to bestow [it]; 'tis watching at wisdom's gates, and waiting at the posts of her doors.

Corol. 2. By what has been said, we see the necessity of means of grace in order to the obtaining grace; for without means there could be no opportunity for grace to act, there could be no matter for grace to act upon. God gives grace immediately; but he don't give immediately and by inspiration, those ideas and speculative notions, that are the matter that grace acts upon. Neither will God give grace, where there is no opportunity for it to act.

S

STRIVING AFTER PERFECTION (1735)[4]

Psalm 119:3
They also do no iniquity: they walk in his ways.

This whole psalm is an encomium upon the word of God. And here in the beginning of [it] is set forth the character of the godly as subject to that word or law of God, the sum of which character seems to be contained in this verse that I have chosen for my text; in which we have a description given of true saints, consisting of two parts or properties of the godly, or rather the same property or quality considered with regard to the two contraries that it has respect to, viz., sin and holiness.

1. With respect to sin, and the character of the godly with regard to this, consists in that that they do no iniquity; i.e., they allow themselves in none; they make a trade of none. They hate all, and do sincerely endeavor to avoid all, as much as in 'em lies; as in the first verse, they are called "the undefiled in the way."

2. With respect to holiness, and their character with respect to that, they make it their practice or, as 'tis here expressed, "They walk in God's ways." Ways of holiness are called God's ways, and the character of the godly with respect to them is that they walk in them. They don't only sometimes look towards them, or now and then get into them; but they are the paths that they walk in, and in which they go through the world. The course of life that a godly man takes, is a way of holiness. Their hearts are in it. So it is said, second verse, "They seek God with their whole heart." They love a way of holiness, and love the rule that is to direct 'em in it. As the Psalmist says of himself, v. 5, "O that my ways were directed to keep thy statutes!"

And as their hearts, so their practice is in ways of holiness. As 'tis said, first verse, "They walk in the law of the Lord." And this they do perseveringly. They don't only sometimes conform to God's testimonies, but they keep them, as v. 2. And they also do it diligently, as v. 4, "Thou hast commanded us to keep thy precepts diligently." And they likewise do it universally, v. 6, "Then shall I not be ashamed, when I have respect to all thy commandments."

Doctrine

The spirit that godly men are of, is a spirit to be perfectly holy.

I. I would show how godly men are of a spirit to be perfectly holy.

II. Give the reasons that evidence the truth of the Doctrine.

I. I would show wherein it appears that godly men are of a spirit to be perfectly innocent and holy.

First, Negatively. Godly men never do actually attain to perfect holiness in this life, but are always very far from it. The most holy of men have found cause to complain of the abundance of corruption that they found remaining in their hearts. [The] Apostle Paul {complains}, Romans 7:24, "O wretched man that I am!" Job, though said to be one perfect and upright, yet says of himself, ch. 9, v. 20, that if he should justify himself, his own mouth should condemn him; and if he should say he was perfect, it should also prove him perverse. And in the thirtieth [and thirty-first] verses, that if he should wash himself with snow water, and make his hands never so clean; yet God would plunge him in the ditch, and his own clothes shall abhor him. And we know how God reproved him, and how he was convinced, and humbled, and brought to cry out of himself that he abhorred himself.

And how did David, the man after God's own heart?

And even Moses, that eminent saint of God that was favored above all the Old Testament prophets? Yet God, for the sin he committed at the waters of Meribah, would not suffer him to enter into the land of Canaan (Numbers 20:12).

Though some are much nearer to perfection than others, yet there are none but what are exceeding remote from it.

Second, Affirmatively. Though they ben't actually perfectly holy, yet the spirit that they are of is of that tendency. Perfect holiness is the mark aimed at, and the center tended to, by that spirit and disposition that they are of; which appears in the following things:

1. Nothing short of perfect holiness will satisfy the appetite and craving of their souls. A godly man has a spirit to desire perfect holiness, and to long after it. 'Tis mentioned as the character of the godly, Matthew 5:6, that they "hunger and thirst after righteousness"; and it is no less than perfect righteousness or holiness that their thirst is after. There is not only a rational desire as a man may set down and consider with himself, that it would really be best for him that he should be perfectly holy; he must rationally think [it] would have many good consequences that would be for his happiness, and so desire and choose to be perfectly holy, if it might be. But 'tis the natural appetite of a gracious soul to be wholly freed from sin, and perfectly conformed to God; as an hungry man desires meat, or a thirsty man drink. A healthy man don't from day to day desire food, merely because he sits down and considers with [himself], "'Tis necessary that I should eat; I can't live if I don't eat"; and so merely desires to eat out of judgment; but he has [an] appetite that craves food day after day. So a thirsty man don't desire drink merely out of judgment, because 'tis for his health; but he has a craving appetite to it. So a godly man is said to hunger and thirst after righteousness, and he has not enough till he has perfect holiness. He that sits down as having got holiness enough, finding no inward craving after any more, 'tis a sign that he has no holiness at all. A godly man, though he may grow in grace, yet is never satisfied with holiness in this life. He is always like a man that has not his thirst satisfied. Psalm 42:1, "As the hart panteth after the water brooks, so panteth my soul after thee, O God." If a man has been parched with thirst, and is allowed to some small taste of cool water; and so once in a while has a few drops, though such tastes are as sweet and refreshing to him; yet he is not satisfied, but lives in thirst, till he is allowed to take a full draught; and the small tastes he has, do indeed the more stir up his eagerness after more. So in some measure it is with a godly man in this world. Unless it be when he is in very ill frames, and his appetite is as it were spoiled by sickness, he lives as long as he lives in this world like a thirsty man.

Upon this account they long for heaven, because those that are there are perfectly free from sin. It looks to them a blessed and glorious state upon that account, that 'tis a state of perfection.

And at some times, when the Spirit of God moves on them, the godly are wont to long after this perfection of holiness, and to say as the Psalmist in the psalm wherein is the text, [the] twentieth verse, "My soul breaketh for the longing that it hath unto thy judgments at all times." Hence it comes to pass

2. That all remaining sin, is uneasy and burdensome to 'em. Indwelling sin is carried about as a great burden; so it was with the Apostle, "O wretched man that I am!" What they see of sin in their hearts is so, and their failings from day to day are occasion of mourning to 'em. They lament their falls; they don't make light of any sin. If it be that which others call a small sin, a common infirmity, such as that no other is to be expected in all men; as long as it is sin against God, he don't, nor can't, call it a small matter. How can he call that a light matter that is an act of rebellion against the infinitely holy and glorious God? 'Tis the manner of hypocrites to be very easy with those things that they call common infirmities and little sins. A hypocrite, though he finds corruption and wickedness working in his heart, yet he excuses it, and makes himself easy with it by thinking with himself that though he has corruption in his heart, 'tis no sign that he is not in a good estate, for all men have corruption. Ministers tell us that the best of men have a world of corruption in their hearts. And though they are guilty of acts of sin from day to day, yet it don't make 'em very uneasy. They excuse themselves in it, that no other is to be expected in this life than that men should fail. They think their sins that they commit are no more than all are guilty [of]; others do as bad as they. Though they can't say there is no hurt in them, yet they are but little sins, no greater than the most eminent men in the world have been guilty of. They don't expect to be holier than Job, and David, and the Apostle Peter, and other such saints as they read of in Scripture; but they ben't guilty of greater nor so great sins as some of them. Thus they make themselves easy with the sin that is in their hearts, and the sin they are guilty of in their lives. But this is not the spirit nor the manner of godly men: they don't make light of anything which they see in themselves that is sinful, if it be in any measure or

degree whatsoever displeasing and provoking to God. He won't be easy with it, but will set himself against it.

They hate all sin in all degrees, and don't only hate it in others, but they hate it mainly and chiefly in themselves. They are enemies to all sin wherever they see it, and nowhere so much as in themselves; as in the 104th verse of the psalm wherein is the text, "Through thy precepts I get understanding: therefore I hate every false way"; and [the] 128th verse, "Therefore I esteem all thy precepts concerning all things to be right; and I hate every false way."

3. They don't allow or make a practice of any known sin or commission, great or small. To suppose any such thing is directly contrary to the words of the text. They also do no iniquity; that is, at least that they make a practice of [no] iniquity; they allowedly do no iniquity; they are not workers of any iniquity. If a godly man knows a thing to be sinful, or has light sufficient held forth to make him much suspect it to be sinful, he will not practice it, though it seems to be comparatively but a small sin. This is what seems to be aimed at by the Apostle John, First Epistle, third chapter, ninth verse: "Whosoever is born of God doth not commit sin; for his seed remaineth in him: and he cannot sin, because he is born of God."

'Tis said in Proverbs 16:17, that "the highway of the upright is to depart from evil"; i.e., it is not only a way that some upright or godly men take that are more eminent, but 'tis the common beaten road of all the godly. An highway is not a path for some one or some few persons to travel on, but a way common to all, a way in which the whole society are wont to pass. So it is common with all the godly universally to depart from evil; not only from some evil, but as much as in 'em lies, from sin in general, or from all ways of sin. They ben't of those that turn aside to their crooked ways, for such "the Lord will lead forth with the workers of iniquity" (Psalm 125:5).

4. They won't let any remaining principles of sin alone, but will be fighting against them. A godly man don't only hate all sin, and carry all remainders of it as his burden, but he will exert himself against it. Where there is true hatred of sin, it won't be idle; but it will be manifest in striving against it, laboring more and more to mortify it, and get rid of it. True enmity against sin will be manifested in hostile acts. There will be that spiritual warfare spoken of in Galatians

5:17, "The flesh lusteth against the spirit, and the spirit against the flesh: and these are contrary the one to the other." This seems to have been typified by the struggling of Jacob and Esau together in Rebekah's womb. Where men do very much let the remainder of sin in themselves alone, or their cares, and thoughts, and pains, but very little taken up about striving against it, or mortifying of it; 'tis a sad sign of want of grace. A godly man is not content with that, that he has resisted sin, and that he has gained considerable ground of it, and has obtained more advantage against it than he once had. He is not content that he has given his lusts very great wounds, whereby they are grown considerably weaker. This don't satisfy him. As long as he sees any life left in 'em, he will still go on fighting against 'em. If his lusts are wounded grievously, yet he can't bear to see 'em alive. And therefore he will go on fighting, till they are wholly and totally dead.

A godly man is a mortal enemy to his sins. Nothing will satisfy him, but his life is as it were bloodthirsty towards sin. He never will give his lusts any peace as long as they have any room in his heart, and till he has wholly expelled them thence. Nor will he ever give himself any rest, till they are utterly rooted out and destroyed, root and branch.

5. They will not neglect any known duty. He has respect to all God's commandments: [the] sixth verse of context, "Then shall I not be ashamed, when I have respect to all thy commandments." 'Tis the manner of hypocrites very commonly to content themselves with doing only some certain sort of duties, while they woefully neglect others. It may be they are very strict with regard to outward duties of the first table of the law, or duties of religious worship, but woefully negligent of the duties of the second table, as God complained of Ephraim. Hosea 7:8, "Ephraim is a cake not turned"; that is, one side baked, and t'other side raw. So it is commonly with false professors: they [make a] fair show in some things, but in others are woefully wanting: they are godly, but on one side their godliness is not universal.

Their piety is monstrous. It has not all the members of the new creature. There is a hand without feet, or only [a] tongue without hands, or feet without eyes, or a trunk with many members without a head. Hypocritical religion is [a] deformed, monstrous kind of religion.

An hypocrite may be very religious with his tongue, but wicked with his hands: {he may be} very devout in prayer {to God}, going to private meetings, but {wicked in his thought}; [he may be] very honest in dealings, but notoriously uncharitable {to the poor}; exceeding envious, contentious {to his neighbor}, backbiting, reviling.

But he that is a true Christian has respect to his duty in the whole compass of it. He sincerely aims to do both his duty to God, and his duty to men; to do duties of religion, and duties of justice and honesty, and duties of charity; to serve God with his hands, and also to bridle his tongue, and use that according to God's commandments; and to do by others in all respects as he would that others should do to him.

6. 'Tis his desire, and study, and prayer that he may know his duty in everything, that he may do it. He don't only avoid every sin that he knows to be a sin, and practice every duty that he does know; but 'tis his sincere desire that he may know his duty in everything. He longs to know his duty like the Psalmist in the context, v. 5, "O that my ways were directed to keep thy statutes!" He longs to be directed to know what he should do, what God would have him to do. He is desirous to learn his duty; for he is sensible that he has a very deceitful heart, and that he is very apt to be blinded by prejudice, and by the lusts of his own heart, and therefore has a jealous eye over himself. He dare not trust himself. He is sensible that he is apt to put evil for good, and good for evil; and he dreads the living in any way that is displeasing and offensive to God, that is secret, and hidden, and unknown to himself. And therefore the language of his heart is like the Psalmist's. Psalm 19:12, "Who can understand his errors? keep thou me from secret faults." The Psalmist seems to intend "secret" as to himself: sins that he might live in, and not know that they were sins. That this is his meaning appears by the former part of the verse, "Who can understand his errors?" He dreads and deprecates the living in such secret faults, because that is his great desire that he prays for, in the next verse but one: "Let the words of my mouth, and the meditation of my heart, be acceptable in thy sight, O Lord, my strength, and my redeemer."

The godly man is often searching of himself to see if something or other that he does in allowing himself in, ben't indeed something offensive; whether there ben't some iniquity secretly lurking in his bosom. If a man suspected that he had some poisonous snake lurking somewhere about him in his clothes, would not he search thoroughly to see whether it was so or no? And a godly man don't content himself with searching himself; but he will pray God like the Psalmist to search him, and see if there be any wicked way in him, and lead him in a right way. Every godly man is of the spirit that is expressed in those words in Job 34:32, "That which I see not teach thou me: if I have done iniquity, I will do no more." And he loves to be searched by others, not only to have his state searched, [but] to have his ways searched. It is not the spirit of a godly [man] to be uneasy, when a minister is searching out his iniquity, and showing the evil of it. He is not grieved or angry, because it comes across him, and exposes him; but he rather rejoices that the evil of his ways is discovered.

Or if he is put in mind of anything amiss in him by Christian reproof from one of his neighbors, he is of the spirit that is expressed by the Psalmist. Psalm 141:5, "Let the righteous smite me; it shall be a kindness: it shall be an excellent oil that shall not break my head." When he hears the word preached, he hears not only that he may have his ears tickled, or that he may set by, and hear others reproved; but he hears that he may learn his own duty to that end, that he may do it. And when he has gained any knowledge respecting his duty, he is ready to bless God for it, agreeable to the seventh verse of the context, "I will praise thee with uprightness of heart, when I shall have learned thy righteous judgments."

Some men are willingly ignorant of their duty. When they are secretly afraid that their duty is contrary to their worldly interest, or cross to some strong, sweet lust, they are allowedly careless in inquiring about their duty, and partial in their inquiries. Instead of searching out their duty, they are rather searching for pleas and excuses to blind their own minds, and quiet their own consciences in sin. When this is the way of men, it looks darkly upon them, as though they loved their lusts, or their temporal interest better than God. But this is not the spirit of the truly godly.

7. The godly will come as near to perfection as they can in the manner of doing their duty. They not only aim at doing every duty that the law requires actually, and in good earnest, striving to do all they know, and seeking that they may know those [things] that they are ignorant of; but they also strive, when they do their duty, to do it as much as possible in a right manner, as near perfectly right as they [can]. Perfection is the mark they aim at; and though they see they come exceeding short in it, yet they don't make light of that, but lament it, and strive to come nearer and nearer to the perfect rule.

8. They love the law of God the better for being so strict, and requiring such perfection. God's law is perfect, and requires nothing short of absolute perfection of holiness. The wicked are enemies to it on this account:

(1) Nothing short will satisfy [the] appetites [of the godly].
(2 All remaining sin [is] burdensome [to them].
(3) [They] don't allow or make a practice of any known sin, great or small.
(4) [They don't] fight against remaining principles.
(5) {They don't fight against} known duty.
(6) [They] know their duty.
(7) [They] come near perfection in the manner.
(8) [They] love the law the better, because [it is] perfectly holy.

It is too strict for 'em: they don't love it. On that account they would fain stretch some of the commandments by their own false glosses: they have a mind to find out some interpretation to suit their corrupt dispositions and practices. But this is not the spirit of the truly godly; but they delight in the law of God, because 'tis so very holy and strict, and so contrary to all spiritual defilement and pollution. Psalm 119:140, "Thy word is very pure: therefore thy servant loveth it." So it appears by what the Psalmist says in the nineteenth Psalm, that he delighted and rejoiced in God's law, because of its perfection and purity: [the] seventh [and] eighth verses, "The law of the Lord is perfect, converting the soul. The statutes of the Lord are right, rejoicing the heart." Whose heart do they rejoice? Not the heart of a wicked man, but of a godly man. And why do they so rejoice the heart of a godly man? But because they are right and perfect, as the Psalmist says. So in the ninth and tenth verses, "The fear of the Lord is clean, enduring forever: the judgments of the Lord are true and righteous altogether. More to be desired are they than gold, yea, than much fine gold: sweeter also than honey and the honeycomb." Why are God's laws more to be desired than gold, than much fine gold? Why are they sweeter than honey? Why, because they are clean, and true, and righteous altogether; i.e., perfectly pure and holy.

[II.] Reasons of the Doctrine.

First. The new nature that is in the saints is of God, and is a divine nature, and therefore must be an enemy to every degree of that which is against God. Every saint has a new nature in him that is quite diverse [from] that old nature, the nature that he was born with, and is above it; and differs from it, as that which is heavenly differs from that which is earthly, or as that which is angelical does from that which is brutish, or as that which [is] divine does from that which is devilish.

This new nature is from God, and is something of God; and therefore it tends to God again, and is contented with nothing short of God, and a perfect conformity to him. As long as there is any separation or alienation remaining, it will not be easy; because as long as it is thus, the soul is kept off in some measure from God, whence its new nature is.

This nature, as 'tis from God, so it is a divine or godlike nature. It is as it were a communication or particular of the holy nature of God. 2 Peter 1:4, "Whereby ye are made partakers of the divine nature." And it being so, it must of necessity be opposite to every thing and every degree of that which is against God. Every degree of sin is contrary to the nature of God. The least sin contains in it an infinite opposition to the divine nature or to the holiness of God; and therefore everyone that is [a] partaker of that divine nature or of that holy nature of God must of necessity be opposite to every sin or degree of sin, however comparatively small. Every degree of sin is devilish in its nature: it is from the old serpent; and therefore it must of necessity be that which is divine, is an enemy to it. And hence it will necessarily follow that every degree of sin, even the least degree, must be burdensome to the new nature. And the new nature, as it is an active thing, must of necessity be continually be fighting against it, as long as it remains; and that it will not be at rest, till it has purged all wholly away.

Sin is as contrary to the new nature in a holy soul as pain is contrary to the nature of the body; and as the body never will be easy with any degree of pain remaining, so will not the new nature ever be easy till every degree of sin is removed.

As the new nature is from God, so it tends to God as its center; and as that which tends to its center is not quiet and at rest, till it has got quite to the very center, so the new nature that is in the saints never will it be at rest, till there is a perfect union with God and conformity to him, and so no separation, or alienation, or enmity remaining. The holy nature in the saints tends to the fountain whence it proceeds, and never will be at rest, till the soul is fully brought to that fountain, and all swallowed up in it. Hence there is an appetite in the soul of the godly after perfect holiness, and sometimes such longing desire after it, such hungerings and thirstings after righteousness. And hence it is impossible any sin known to be such should be statedly allowed.

Second. The new nature in a Christian is perfectly pure: there is nothing purer than the new nature in the saints. The new nature is [not] quite pure, for the saints ben't quite pure. Yet 'tis not because the new nature in them is not pure, but because there is a mixture of new nature and old. As the old nature is altogether corrupt, so the new nature is altogether pure: there is not the least defilement in it. So far as that goes, there is nothing but purity. The defilement that is in the soul don't arise from any defilement in the new nature from a mixture of the old. The new nature is as pure as heaven itself is. And hence it arises that the tendency of the new nature is to perfection of holiness, because everything that falls short of perfection, or has any remains of sin, has defilement in it, and therefore is opposite to the purity of the new nature in man. It is with the new nature in a Christian as it is with the light of the sun. The light can't be defiled: the light, wherever it goes, is pure. Though it may shine in darkness, and there may be but a little of it let into some dark place, and there be a great mixture of darkness with it; yet that little beam of light that is let in is pure, so far as it goes: it has no darkness in it. This light may be let not only in dark places, but into very filthy places. It may shine down in amongst all manner of filthiness. But the light, it is not defiled. Though the light be mixed with filthiness, yet the light itself remains pure. The light of the sun that shines upon a filthy place is in itself as pure as that which shines in the clear air.

So it is with grace in the hearts of the saints. It is as it were a beam from the sun of righteousness, and is of a pure nature. Though it be as it were a little ray let into a dark room, or shining amongst abundance of filthiness, yet 'tis pure in itself, and an enemy to all that darkness and filthiness. Though the soul of a Christian be greatly defiled, yet the grace that is in the soul is pure; and therefore the tendency of it is the perfect purity of the soul wherein it is.

Third. We may further see the reason of the Doctrine, if we consider what agent the new nature in the saints is immediately from, viz., the Spirit of God dwelling in the soul. We are taught in the Scriptures that the saints are the temples of the Holy Ghost; and that the Spirit of God dwells in 'em; and that thereby Christ is in 'em, and that God is in 'em; and the graces or new nature that is in the hearts of the saints is from the immediate acting of the Spirit, as much as light is immediately and every moment from the sun. And indeed the new nature in a saint can scarce itself be distinguished from the communication or participation he has of the Spirit of God, or that Spirit dwelling in him united to him, acting as a vital principle in his soul.

There is something supernatural in the saints, or something above nature, which is something divine or of God, and that is the Holy Spirit of God imparted. This seems to be what the Scripture teaches; for there the principle of grace is represented to a spring of living water in the heart, "springing up into everlasting life" (John 4:14). And in another place it teaches us that that spring of living water is no other than the Spirit of God itself dwelling in the heart, ch. 7, vv. 38–39. "He that believeth on me, as the Scripture hath said, out of his belly shall flow rivers of living water. (But this spake he of the Spirit, which they that believe on him should receive: for the Holy Ghost was not yet given; because that Jesus was not yet glorified.)"

Now it being so that the new nature in the saints being no other than the Holy Spirit of God dwelling in them, and influencing their faculties, or the immediate agency of that Spirit, no wonder that it tends to perfection of holiness; no wonder that it is an enemy to all sin, and even the least degree of it, and that it fights against and never leaves it, till it is all destroyed. For the Spirit of God is perfectly holy, and therefore 'tis called the Holy Ghost. Yea, 'tis infinitely holy. The Holy Spirit is God himself. And surely God is an enemy to the least degrees of sin, yea, infinitely so. The least sin has an infinite contrariety to God. No wonder surely that God seeks perfect holiness, and perfectly to destroy all sin.

The Spirit of God in the saints in this world dwells in a heart, where there is abundance of corruption; but the Spirit of God don't delight to dwell with corruption. And seeing the Spirit of God has again taken the possession of the heart, and taken that for his house, no wonder that by his energy he is continually warring against all remains of sin, and never leaves, till all is purged away. For surely God and sin never can be made friends, no, though it be the least degree of sin. That which God so hates as to threaten with everlasting ruin and perdition, he never will suffer to be quiet in an heart that has taken the possession of it, and where he dwells.

Fourth. We may see the reason of the doctrine if we consider what is the main principle of the new nature, viz., love to God. Love to God is the main principle of the new nature, the greatest grace, the grace of graces, that is the fulfilling of the law in both tables of it. It is the fulfilling of the duties of the first table which respect the worship of God, for all true worship is from love. And 'tis the fulfilling of the duties of the second, as all right love to our neighbor is from love to God. But this principle can't tend to anything short of perfect holiness and conformity to God. True love to God must make a man to hate everything that is contrary to God. He that loves light must hate darkness. So he that loves God must hate sin, and he must hate all sin of whatever kind and degree; for every sort of sin, and every degree of sin, is as contrary to God as light is to darkness. And 'tis impossible for a man to love two contraries at the same time; and so far as a man loves one, he must hate the other that is contrary to it. So far as a man loves God, he must hate everything that is contrary to God.

True love to God must necessarily make a man have respect to all God's commandments, and to hate every evil and every false way. For the same that makes a lover of God have respect to one of God's commandments, will also make him have respect to all; for the same God that requires one requires another; the same divine authority establishes one that establishes another; the same holiness of God that causes him to hate one sin makes him hate another. James 2:10–11, "For whosoever shall keep the whole Law, and yet offend in one point, is guilty of all. For he that said, Do not commit adultery, said also, Do not kill. Now if thou commit no adultery, yet if thou kill, thou art become a transgressor of the Law."

And so that love to God that makes a man seek to be freed from some degree of sin will make him seek to be freed from all degrees of sin; for every degree of sin is against God. And he that has forbidden one degree has forbidden another.

That is not true love to God that don't dispose and incline a man to be subject to the will of God. But the will of God is against all. He don't allow of any degree of sin whatsoever; but he strictly forbids all in every degree.

Fifth. The reason of the Doctrine will appear if we consider the nature of the rule that a true Christian has sincerely subjected himself to, which rule is the law of God. Every truly godly person has sincerely embraced and subjected himself to God's law to be the rule of his life. This is one part of the character of the godly man given in the context—v. 1, "Blessed are the undefiled in the way, who walk in the law of the Lord"—and in the frequent professions of the Psalmist in the same psalm. [The] twenty-fourth verse, "Thy testimonies are my counselors." [The] thirtieth [verse], "I have chosen the way of truth: thy judgments have I laid before me." [The] thirty-first verse, "I have stuck unto thy testimonies." [The] 105th verse, "Thy word is a lamp unto my feet, and a light unto my path." [The] 106th verse, "I have sworn, and I will perform it, that I will keep thy righteous judgments." [The] 111th [verse], "Thy testimonies have I taken for my heritage forever." [The] 112th [verse], "I have inclined my heart to perform thy statutes." But the law of God, which the saints have heartily subjected themselves to, and taken for the rule of their lives, is a perfect rule: it requires perfect obedience; it allows of no sin, in no degree. And hence 'tis impossible but that the heart of a saint must incline to and strive after perfection; because till it is perfect, it don't come up to its rule. As long as there is any want of perfection, there is some disagreement left between him and the rule that he has taken and chosen. The godly man don't only take a part of the law of God for his rule, but he takes the whole law. He takes the rule God gives him as he gives it him. He don't divide it, and take part, and leave part; but he takes the whole rule. And hence it necessarily follows, that he is of a spirit to be conformed to it in every particular, in every jot and tittle, or to be perfectly conformed to it.

Application

[Use I of Instruction.]

First. Hence we may learn that it must needs be that a Christian must live a fighting, struggling life, while he lives in this world. For if he be of a spirit to be perfectly [holy], and at the same time be so far from [it], and have so much within and without that is exceeding opposite to it; how can it be otherwise than there must be a continual strife and struggle in a Christian? For how little a way have the best saints in this world advanced towards perfection, even the most grown Christians? How remote are they still from it? And how much is there in their own hearts that is opposite to this perfection? How much sin remains, and how many lusts, and how active and how strong are they?

And how many are there within that are opposing his progress towards perfection? How many enemies of the soul, tempting continually to sin, and endeavoring to hinder all that is good, laying stumbling blocks in the way?

And how full is this world, that the saints in this life live in, of that that opposes them in this matter? How many clogs and hindrances, how many snares? How difficult is it, in such a world as we here live in, not only to make progress towards perfection, but to keep from being driven back, and being corrupted more and more?

Hence, there being such a spirit in the godly, must of necessity arise a great inward strife and warfare. It is impossible but that a godly man should find much to do, and that he should find great occasion for labor and diligence, and many sighs, and groans, and pantings of heart, and earnest cries, and vehement conflicts. The life of a godly man is a life full of conflicts.

They therefore that think they are converted, and are, since that, sunk into a stated negligence of the work of religion; and find a free opportunity now they are, in their own apprehension, safe to sit down and take their ease; and, accordingly, actually live now an idle life, so that 'tis impossible it can be said that they live in any wise laboriously in religion; 'tis a sign they ben't much acquainted with what belongs to Christianity, and that they are very inexperienced concerning the real life of a Christian.

Second. If it be so that the godly have a spirit to be perfectly holy, hence we may learn the excellency of the spirit that the godly are of. 'Tis said, Proverbs 17:27, that "a man of understanding" (i.e., a godly man) "is of an excellent spirit"; and Proverbs 12:26, that "the righteous is more excellent than his neighbor." We may from this Doctrine see the truth of these texts.

Hence 'tis greatly to be looked at persons, in order to determine whether they are true and real saints, to inquire what spirit they are of.

To determine persons' condition, it should not so much be inquired what profession they make, and how they pretend, and how they talk, and what stories they tell of themselves, as what spirit they savor of. They give the best evidence, the best grounds abundantly, for others to entertain charitable thoughts concerning 'em, that besides their making a good profession, they seem to be persons of an excellent spirit.

That must needs be an excellent spirit, and will ordinarily manifest itself to be so to observers, that is a spirit whose natural tendency is perfect innocency and holiness. This may probably be one reason why truly godly men are called perfect men in Scripture. Psalm 37:37, "Mark the perfect man." And Psalm 64:4, "That they may shoot in secret at the perfect." Proverbs 2:21, "For the upright shall dwell in the land, and the perfect shall remain in it." So Job is called "a perfect and upright man, one that feared God, and escheweth evil." And hypocrites are described by that, that though they serve God, yet they don't do it with a perfect heart. For by the Doctrine we learn that though the godly are far from actual perfection, yet that they have a spirit to be perfect, a spirit that tends to, and seeks, and aims at nothing short of perfection; that makes perfection its rule, and by which it is governed, and [the] mark at which it aims.

Third. Hence we may learn that there doubtless will be a future state, wherein the saints will actually be perfectly holy. Though that be their spirit while in this world, though that be what the new nature that is in them tends to, and earnestly contends for; yet there is abundant evidence that it is never obtained in this life, in that the most eminent saints that ever were known, have appeared very visibly to be far from it. But we can't rationally think that it will always be so, seeing that God has put such a spirit into them, and has sown a seed in their hearts that so earnestly thirsts and strives after it; and this in every one of his saints. How can it be imagined that God has ordered it so, that such a spirit never shall attain what it seeks? Would God himself infuse a principle into all good men that should earnestly tend to a thing that there is no hopes of attaining? Would God work such desires in all saints, and stir 'em to seek and press after that, that never one of them was to obtain? Would God create thirsty desires in his children only to afflict them, never intending any other than those desires shall be disappointed? It would be little less than blasphemous to suppose any such thing. Seeing therefore that God has put such a spirit into his saints, we may doubtless conclude that he has so ordered it, that this spirit shall be gratified, and that perfect holiness attained, which they desire; and therefore that there is another and better state remaining than ever is attained to in this world, a state in another world, wherein the new nature shall arrive at what it naturally tends to, even perfection in holiness.

Fourth. This may show us how sweet heaven will be to the saints, when they come there, in that there they shall be perfectly holy. When they come there, their new nature will be gratified in that which it tends [to]. Then they shall attain to the mark they have been aiming at. Then, and not till then, shall that promise be fulfilled, Matthew 5:6, "Blessed are they that hunger and thirst after righteousness: for they shall be filled." The satisfying that hunger and thirst will then render 'em blessed, as is implied in these words. There will be a blessed sweetness and satisfaction that they shall have.

Then shall they attain to that which they, all the while they lived saints in this world, were striving and struggling for, and never could reach. Though they might come nearer to it, yet they had the grief to see themselves yet a great way off. They had yet innumerable sins hanging about 'em like so many serpents; but there they would be: they could not wholly get rid of 'em. But when they arrive in heaven, they shall be perfectly free from all remains of sin, and the image of God shall be perfect. Hence we learn what a state of sweet rest that heavenly state will be [for] the saints, when they shall have done their wearisome, long, continued warfare; and shall have finished their course; and shall sit down in the kingdom of God, without spot or wrinkle or any such thing, in that glorious city, where there shall in no wise enter anything that desires or works abomination.

Use II, *of Examination*. Let this doctrine put all that entertain that opinion of themselves that {they have a spirit of holiness}, upon examination of themselves, whether they are of such a spirit. Do you find in yourself a spirit working after this manner that has been spoken of?

Whether or not you find in yourself a desire after more holiness, not only because you rationally judge it would be better for you, because then you should be more satisfied of your good estate, and the like; but do you find an inward appetite after holiness, a hungering and thirsting after righteousness, to be more conformed to God, to get more rid of sin, to have a better heart, to live a better life? Is heaven a sweet and lovely place in your eyes, because 'tis a place of perfect purity and freedom from sin?

And are you one that don't sit down in slothful negligence, but are you diligently endeavoring to make progress? And do you tolerate no sin? And are you maintaining a laborious strife against sin? And are not only your sins of commission burdensome to you, but also the defects of your duties? Are they bewailed and abhorred by you on that account? And are you one whose study it is to know your duty, and one that has a jealous eye over yourself, and that watches yourself, and are concerned lest you should go in some way offensive to God unawares to you?

And are you one that strives to do duties not only of one sort, but of every sort; not only {one commandment, but all commandments}?

'Tis exceeding difficult for persons to deal faithfully and truly with themselves in such self-examinations, especially when they have for some time entertained and settled a hope of themselves that [they] are godly. And commonly those that have a thousand times most need of strict and impartial self-examination, even those that have a false hope, are most difficultly brought to [it], and are wont to [be] abundantly the most unfaithful and partial in it; and that upon several accounts. They are least sensible of the deceitfulness and treachery of their own hearts. A true saint is abundantly more sensible of the deceit of his heart than an hypocrite that is self-confident. And then they are more stupid, and not in any measure sensible how infinitely it concerns 'em not to be deceived as the sincere Christian. And then he is not sensible of his own badness. If there be a great deal of badness, it don't frighten an hypocrite to see it so much as it is does a true saint: 'tis not so frightful a sight to him. And an hypocrite is less disposed to be thoroughly searched than a true saint: he don't love searching so well as the godly, and therefore is not so thorough in it.

Hence commonly, when ministers are upon uses of self-examination, they that have most need of self-examination do least of it. Those that most commonly on such occasions are most thorough, and go about the work with the greatest weight in their spirit, and with most of a jealous eye over themselves, are those that are upright in God's sight; whereas others that are of another sort, easily get by all that is said of signs he mentioned that seem to carry the matter against 'em. They have their excuse ready at hand; they don't want for something to palliate and color over the blackest marks that are upon them.

One main reason is that senselessness is a natural and almost universal concomitant of a false hope. There are many natural men that are very stupid that have no hope; but their senselessness is not confirmed as the deceived hypocrite's commonly is. And if a man be senseless in his false hope, there is scarce any coming at him. The man has walled himself in: nothing reaches him; he is "settled on his lees"; he is got fast in his false foundation. And he holds fast [to] deceit, and will not let it go. And such commonly hold it to the last.

And in such self-examination as this, which I now am putting you [upon], whether you are of such a spirit as has been spoken of and described; 'tis very probable that those that need it most will deal falsely: hypocrites, and those that are really very remote from any such thing, and are fatally inexperienced in this matter.

And though indeed they have no true love to, or appetite after, holiness, no {such spirit as has been spoken of and described}, and do indeed live a wicked life, {they need it most}.

They, it may be, will be ready to [say] that they hope they do find a spirit to hate all sin, and all their own sins, when possibly they call some little slight trouble and uneasiness of conscience about their sins, hatred of sin.

When he is put upon it to inquire whether {he has an} appetite after {holiness}, he'll say it may yet be, [and] hopes he does. He should be glad that he was more holy. He thinks he is very sorry he is not no holier, and no doubt but he would be glad to be more sure that he should go to heaven. But he must dreadfully force, and strain, and magnify things to pretend that he finds a spirit to hunger {after holiness}.

When he is put upon inquiring whether he can be content with just holiness enough to carry him to heaven, he says to himself he hopes he is not of that spirit. He should be glad to be more holy, if he knew he should go to heaven. But what sort of desire is this? Is it not a mere imagined, forced business? Is there indeed any powerful, ardent [desire] working in him tending that way, making of him restless in anything short of it?

If he be put upon it to inquire whether all remaining sin is burdensome to him, {he says to himself he} hopes it is. [He] sometimes finds himself something concerned, after he knows he has done amiss, and that he calls carrying sin as his great burden.

[If he be put upon it to inquire] whether [it] don't allow of any known sin, {he says to himself he} hopes not {to be of that spirit}, when it may be [he] deals with most wretched treachery with his own conscience, in these two things. First, with respect to what is a known sin. There is something he does and allows himself in, {when there is} light enough {that} plainly held it is a sin. But he has been studying to find out arguments to justify himself, {and to} flatter himself. He don't think it is a sin. If it be, 'tis a sin of ignorance. He pretends he is convinced 'tis not a sin, when it is no such thing. The inward persuasion is that 'tis a sin. {He} dare not appear before God in it. {He} would not dare to commit it, if [he] knew {he was} now going to appear before God {in it}. Second, with respect to their allowance. [They] flatter themselves [that they] don't allow, when [they] do allow. There is some feigned disapprobation, rather in words than anything else. [They] say to themselves, "I don't allow of others." {There is} some little, faint endeavor sometimes against it, {some} little remorse of conscience; but really no design of breaking off, no hearty, real resolution against it.

If put upon it to inquire whether [they allow] spiritual warfare, {they} hope they do. {They} find sometimes some uneasiness {in themselves}, when they find a revengeful spirit, {and a} worldly spirit; {when there has} been backbiting, {and} indulging some vicious appetite. 'Tis some trouble to 'em; that is to say, his conscience don't wholly let him alone. And no wonder, under such light, if he has no more grace than a brute. Such ways as these are common among men to deceive themselves, and undo themselves.

The best and safest way, and most agreeable to the Scriptures, for persons to take in such things is to examine not only what they feel with in themselves, but to take that and their practice together.

'Tis without Scripture warrant for any man to presume upon it, that he has the root without the fruit, or to conclude that the tree is a fig tree, when the fruit is nothing but thorns. We should think a man besotted that would stand to it, that the root is a root of wheat, though the fruit be tares.

Thus for instance, to what purpose is it for a man to imagine that he finds in himself a hungering and thirsting after righteousness, when at the same time he don't pursue after righteousness in his practice? He sits still, neglects religion; there is no strife and earnest pursuit visible in his practice. If it be so that he really inwardly hungers {after righteousness}, and neglects it so much in his practice, 'tis a very strange thing indeed.

If a man be hungry and has a craving after food, that appetite will do something. The man won't sit still. He'll be after food: hunger will break through a stone wall. If he be thirsty, he'll be after drink. So if it be really so that sin is a very uneasy and burdensome thing to him, he will certainly be doing a great deal against sin. Sin won't have quiet harbor with such a man. [He] will bestir himself to get rid of it. If a man has a briar anywhere about him next his flesh that afflicts him, or a pebble or cutting gravel in his shoe that hurts him as he walks, the man won't be easy and quiet. He'll search for the thing that troubles him to get rid of it. If we should see a man living in a house wherein was a great deal of stinking filthiness, and the man dwelt there from day to day doing but little to cleanse his house, we should with good reason conclude that [he] was not very uneasy with his nastiness, that it was not very offensive to his nostrils. If it were, he would bestir himself to get rid of it. Much more, if we see a man, instead of clearing out the filth, daily fetching in more and more, we should conclude he is no great enemy to it.

So it is in vain for a man to pretend that he don't allow of a particular way of sinning, when he yet continues in the practice of it. That which a man does sincerely and heartily disallow, and don't tolerate, however he may be surprised into it, he won't make it his practice. It is impossible in the nature of things. If a man makes a trade of anything, it is in vain for him to pretend he don't allow of it, though he may have remorse.

Many men allow many things, and yet have great stirrings of conscience, and a great many thoughts about getting rid of it, and some endeavors against it from time to time. And yet it may be with him, just as 'tis said in Job 20:12–13, "Wickedness is sweet in his mouth, he hides it under his tongue; though he spare it, and forsake it not; but keep it still."

What is here described seems to be the action of a man that has something in his mouth that is very sweet to him, that he is put upon to spit out. Something urges and presses him to it, and he has thoughts of it. He moves it in his mouth; he rolls it about there; but still can't bear to part {with it}. Finally [he] will not spit it out.

A man may have an enjoyment that he has any thoughts of parting with {wickedness}. Reserving it causes him a great deal of trouble {of conscience}, and an heavy heart; yet [he] willfully retains it, and refuses to sell it. A man's stated practice must determine in this matter. What else could determine whether the young man allowed himself in his choosing earthly riches, rather than treasure in heaven, than his conduct? What if he had pleaded afterwards that he did not allow himself to disobey that command of Christ, and not to sell his estate as long as he still kept it?

So what does it signify for a man to pretend that he don't allow of a way of sin, when he keeps it still, and won't part with it, [and] makes a trade of it? If you have remorse of conscience sometime, that don't help the case, if you still retain it; but makes it so much the worse, {if you} go against such remorse of conscience. {It is} the worst sign, {the} sign of the more daring wickedness.

Inquire and search your practice. Have you such a testimony of conscience as the Apostle had? 2 Corinthians 1:12, "For our rejoicing is this, the testimony of our conscience, that in simplicity and godly sincerity, not with fleshly wisdom, but by the grace of God, we have had our conversation in the world, and more abundantly to you-ward." If it was not of importance that a person should have such a testimony, why did the Apostle make so much of it? And can you plead before God, as Hezekiah did, when he looked on himself on a deathbed? 2 Kings 20:3, "Remember, O Lord, how I have walked before thee in truth and with a perfect heart, and have done that which is good in thy sight." 'Tis the conversation and walk that those holy men rejoice in. Don't neglect these in your examination of yourself.

A NATIVE AMERICAN PROFESSION OF FAITH

I do now appear before God and his people solemnly and publicly to profess, so far as I know my own heart, the following things: namely, that I do believe that there is one only living and true God, who is the Father, the Son, and the Holy Ghost, who is the great

Creator and supreme Lord of heaven and earth; and having been made sensible of his divine supreme glory and excellency, do choose him for my only God and portion, choosing conformity to him and his service and the enjoyment of him as my highest and sweetest good: and as my parents gave me up to him in my baptism, so now I profess to give up myself, my heart and my all to him. I believe that God at first made man in his own image, and entered into a covenant of life with him, forbidding him to eat of the tree of knowledge of good and evil; but our first parents fell by eating the forbidden fruit, exposing themselves and their posterity to the wrath of God and eternal death; but God in mercy sent his Son in our nature to redeem and save us.

And I do now appear before God and his people solemnly to give up myself to God, to whom my parents gave me up in my baptism, having, so far as I know my own heart, chosen him for my portion and set my heart on him as my greatest and sweetest good. And now would solemnly give up myself to Christ, having, as I hope, seen my need of him, being sensible of my sin and misery as I am in myself, the insufficiency of my own righteousness and my unworthiness of any mercy, and my deserving that God should cast me off forever. And also seen the sufficiency of Jesus Christ as a Savior. I now also appear openly to renounce all the ways of sin which I hope I have seen the hatefulness of, sin being made burdensome to me. I desire to spend my life in watching, striving and fighting against it. And would give up myself to a life of holiness, earnestly to seek and strive after it as what I choose and delight in, having hungered and thirsted after it, and would now solemnly give up my life to the service of God, and to follow Christ in all his ways and ordinances, and to give up myself to the Holy Spirit of God, to follow his leading and guidance, humbly depending on his influences to sanctify me and enable me to live an holy life. And I now desire to join myself to the people of Christ as those whom I hope my heart is peculiarly united to as my brethren in Christ. I profess universal forgiveness and good will to mankind, and promise to be subject to the government of this church during my abode here.

Cornelius [and] Mary Munneweaummmuck

JONATHAN EDWARDS

LETTER TO DEBORAH HATHEWAY (1741)

Northampton, June 3, 1741

Dear Child,

As you desired me to send you in writing some directions how to conduct yourself in your Christian course, I would now answer your request. The sweet remembrance of the great things I have lately seen at Suffield, and the dear affections for those persons I have there conversed with, that give good evidences of a saving work of God upon their hearts, inclines me to do anything that lies in my power, to contribute to the spiritual joy and prosperity of God's people there. And what I write to you, I would also say to other young women there, that are your friends and companions and the children of God; and therefore desire you would communicate it to them as you have opportunity.

1. I would advise you to keep up as great a strife and earnestness in religion in all parts of it, as you would do if you knew yourself to be in a state of nature and was seeking conversion. We advise persons under convictions to be earnest and violent for the kingdom of heaven, but when they have attained to conversion they ought not to be the less watchful, laborious, and earnest in the whole work of religion, but the more; for they are under infinitely greater obligations. For want of this, many persons in a few months after their conversion have begun to lose the sweet and lively sense of spiritual things, and to grow cold and flat and dark, and have pierced themselves through with many sorrows, whereas if they had done as the Apostle did, Philippians 3:12–14, their path would have been as the shining light, that shines more and more unto the perfect day.

2. Don't leave off seeking, striving, and praying for the very same things that we exhort unconverted persons to strive for, and a degree of which you have had in conversion. Thus pray that

your eyes may be opened, that you may receive your sight, that you may know your self, and be brought to God's foot, and that you may see the glory of God and Christ and may be raised from the dead, and have the love of Christ shed abroad in your heart; for those that have most of these things had need still to pray for them; for there is so much blindness and hardness and pride and death remaining, that they still need to have that work of God wrought upon them, further to enlighten and enliven them; that shall be a bringing out of darkness into God's marvelous light, and a kind of new conversion and resurrection from the dead. There are very few requests that are proper for a natural person, but that in some sense are proper for the godly.

3. When you hear sermons hear 'em for yourself, though what is spoken in them may be more especially directed to the unconverted, or to those that in other respects are in different circumstances from yourself. Yet let the chief intent of your mind be to consider with yourself, in what respects is this that I hear spoken applicable to me, and what improvement ought I to make of this for my own soul's good?

4. Though God has forgiven and forgotten your past sins, yet don't forget 'em yourself: often remember what a wretched bond slave you was in the land of Egypt. Often bring to mind your particular acts of sin before conversion, as the blessed Apostle Paul is often mentioning his old blaspheming, persecuting, and injuriousness, to the renewed humbling of his heart and acknowledging that he was the least of the apostles, and not worthy to be called an apostle, and the least of all saints, and the chief of sinners. And be often in confessing your old sins to God, and let that text be often in your mind, Ezekiel 16:63, "That thou mayest remember and be confounded, and never open thy mouth any more because of thy shame, when I am pacified toward thee for all that thou hast done, saith the Lord God."

5. Remember that you have more cause, on some accounts a thousand times, to lament and humble yourself for sins that have been since conversion than before, because of the infinitely greater obligations that are upon you to live to God. And look

upon the faithfulness of Christ in unchangeably continuing his loving favor, and the unspeakable and saving fruits of his everlasting love, notwithstanding all your great unworthiness since your conversion, to be as great or wonderful, as his grace in converting you.

6. Be always greatly abased for your remaining sin, and never think that you lie low enough for it, but yet don't be at all discouraged or disheartened by it; for though we are exceeding sinful, yet we have an advocate with the Father, Jesus Christ the righteous, the preciousness of whose blood, and the merit of whose righteousness and the greatness of whose love and faithfulness does infinitely overtop the highest mountains of our sins.

7. When you engage in the duty of prayer, or come to the sacrament of the Lord's Supper, or attend any other duty of divine worship, come to Christ as Mary Magdalene did, Luke 7:37–38. Come and cast yourself down at his feet and kiss 'em, and pour forth upon him the sweet perfumed ointment of divine love, out of a pure and broken heart, as she poured her precious ointment out of her pure, alabaster, broken box.

8. Remember that pride is the worst viper that is in the heart, the greatest disturber of the soul's peace and sweet communion with Christ; it was the first sin that ever was, and lies lowest in the foundation of Satan's whole building, and is the most difficultly rooted out, and is the most hidden, secret, and deceitful of all lusts, and often creeps in, insensibly, into the midst of religion and sometimes under the disguise of humility.

9. That you may pass a good judgment of the frames you are in, always look upon those the best discourses and the best comforts that have most of these two effects: viz., those that make you least, lowest, and most like a little child; and secondly, those that do most engage and fix your heart in a full and firm disposition to deny yourself for God, and to spend and be spent for him.

10. If at any time you fall into doubts about the state of your soul under darkness and dull frames of mind, 'tis proper to look over past experiences, but yet don't consume too much of your

time and strength in poring and puzzling thoughts about old experiences, that in dull frames appear dim and are very much out of sight, at least as to that which is the cream and life and sweetness of them; but rather apply yourself with all your might, to do an earnest pursuit after renewed experiences, new light, and new, lively acts of faith and love. One new discovery of the glory of Christ's face, and the fountain of his sweet grace and love will do more towards scattering clouds of darkness and doubting in one minute, than examining old experiences by the best mark that can be given, a whole year.

11. When the exercise of grace is at a low ebb, and corruption prevails, and by that means fear prevails, don't desire to have fear cast out any other way, than by the reviving and prevailing of love, for 'tis not agreeable to the method of God's wise dispensations that it should be cast out any other way; for when love is asleep, the saints need fear to restrain them from sin and therefore it is so ordered that at such times fear comes upon them, and that more or less as love sinks. But when love is in lively exercise, persons don't need fear, and the prevailing of love in the heart naturally tends to cast out fear, as darkness in a room vanishes away as you let more and more of the perfect beams of the sun into it, 1 John 4:18.

12. You ought to be much in exhorting and counseling and warning others, especially at such a day as this, Hebrews 10:25. And I would advise you especially to be much in exhorting children and young women your equals; and when you exhort others that are men, I would advise that you take opportunities for it, chiefly when you are alone with them, or when only young persons are present. See 1 Timothy 2:9, 11–12.

13. When you counsel and warn others, do it earnestly, affectionately, and thoroughly. And when you are speaking to your equals, let your warnings be intermixed with expressions of your sense of your own unworthiness, and of the sovereign grace that makes you differ; and if you can with a good conscience, say how that you in yourself are more unworthy than they.

14. If you would set up religious meetings of young women by yourselves, to be attended once in a while, besides the other meetings that you attend, I should think it would be very proper and profitable.

15. Under special difficulties, or when in great need of or great longings after any particular mercies for your self or others, set apart a day of secret fasting and prayer alone; and let the day be spent not only in petitions for the mercies you desired, but in searching your heart, and looking over your past life, and confessing your sins before God not as is wont to be done in public prayer, but by a very particular rehearsal before God, of the sins of your past life from your childhood hitherto, before and after conversion, with particular circumstances and aggravations, also very particularly and fully as possible, spreading all the abominations of your heart before him.

16. Don't let the adversaries of religion have it to say, that these converts don't carry themselves any better than others. See Matthew 5:47, "What do ye more than others"; how holily should the children of God, and the redeemed and the beloved of the Son of God behave themselves? Therefore walk as a child of the light and of the day and adorn the doctrine of God your Savior; and particularly be much in those things, that may especially be called Christian virtues, and make you like the Lamb of God; be meek and lowly of heart and full of a pure, heavenly and humble love to all; and abound in deeds of love to others, and self-denial for others, and let there be in you a disposition to account others better than yourself.

17. Don't talk of things of religion and matters of experience with an air of lightness and laughter, which is too much the manner in many places.

18. In all your course, walk with God and follow Christ as a little, poor, helpless child, taking hold of Christ's hand, keeping your eye on the mark of the wounds on his hands and side, whence came the blood that cleanses you from sin and hiding your nakedness under the skirt of the white shining robe of his righteousness.

19. Pray much for the church of God and especially that he would carry on his glorious work that he has now begun; and be much in prayer for the ministers of Christ, and particularly I would beg a special interest in your prayers, and the prayers of your Christian companions, both when you are alone and when you are together, for your affectionate friend, that rejoices over you, and desires to be your servant,

> In Jesus Christ,
> *Jonathan Edwards*

Part Five

The Internal and External Work of Grace

INTRODUCTION
TO PART FIVE

The selections in this final section show how Edwards came to seek a balance in the inward and outward work of grace, in principle and action, as a way of identifying the workings of true grace. His early expressions of "divine light" emphasized the intuitive, subjective workings of grace. Experience and observation during and after the revivals made Edwards rethink his position on the role of "universal persevering behavior," or Christian practice, because he saw too many supposed converts talking, even boasting, about their conversions without showing the fruits of grace, not to mention causing schisms and coopting the minister's role. Thus, as the selections below proceed, they reflect Edwards's exploration and increasing insistence upon external signs as evidence of an internal condition.

In the early and formative sermon of 1723, *A Spiritual Understanding of Divine Things Denied to the Unregenerate*, Edwards contrasts the knowledge of divine things that the unregenerate and regenerate have, attributing to the regenerate a knowledge, or faith, that places them on an entirely different epistemological level. "Natural" or unconverted individuals can attain only a "notional" knowledge of divine things, which reaches the conscience and no further. Natural persons may be well-versed in doctrine and may be very orthodox in religion, all of which in some way or other may influence the way they live. Such knowledge, Edwards avers, was seen in the Pharisees in Christ's time, who were known for their strictness of observance, but were nonetheless hypocrites.

"Directions for Judging of Persons' Experiences" is a very brief but loaded document, a shorthand list of cautions by a minister in the midst of revivals as he listens to and observes souls under his charge. Divided into two parts, the directives in each section do not fall into distinct categories; rather, the former lean more heavily toward the nature of conviction and the latter toward holiness and practice. This shift in emphasis parallels that which Edwards makes in other writings after the end of the 1734–35 awakening, when he became more intent on Christian practice and perseverance as signs of true conversion. Throughout, the directives reflect Edwards's life-long interest in souls under awakening. He is concerned with detecting outright hypocrites and those under the power of their own "imagination," as well as with steering sincere seekers to a correct sense of their own sin and the excellency and sufficiency of God. Convictions should be founded on "reasonable, solid consideration" of the person's actual experience—"as of things as they are indeed"— and not on "pangs and sudden passions, freaks and frights, and a capriciousness of mind." Expressing an important point in his theology, Edwards emphasizes that true conviction and evangelical humiliation lead to a longing after holiness.

In the process of hearing hundreds of relations of spiritual experience from his parishioners, Edwards became an expert in the genre and came to deplore the use of stock phrases that really meant nothing to the narrators (a development that is probably related to his distrust of spiritual relations as a prerequisite for church admission). At one point, stringing together several common utterances, Edwards cautions himself to ensure that it is a true sense of sin that convinces narrators "of the justice of God in their damnation, in rejecting their prayers, disregarding their sorrowful case, and all desires and endeavors after deliverance, etc., and not merely any… melting of affection through some real or supposed instance of divine goodness." Even more indicative of some narrators' attitude is Edwards's concern regarding "whether, when they tell of their experiences, it is not with such an air that you as it were feel that they expect to be admired and applauded…and shocked and displeased if they discover the contrary." Since these reflections are probably based on face-to-face encounters and interviews with his parishioners, Edwards as religious clinician comes through here in an immediate way. In this document is raw material that Edwards could use in counseling, but also in constructing his treatises on conversion, affections, and the signs of grace. The directives in the first section bear some resemblance, in miniature, to Edwards's detailed study of the experiences of his parishioners in his *Faithful Narrative*. The directives in the second section contain criticisms Edwards made of his parishioners during and after the emotional stirs of 1740–42.

In the sermon *True Grace is Divine* (1738), Edwards carefully and in great detail defines grace as a supernatural gift from God, as a corrective against any idea that grace is somehow wrought or earned by sinners. A lengthy Exposition starts off by explaining how grace is "love," or a principle in the heart, because by it one is "acquainted" with God, God dwells in the saint, and God's love is "perfected" in her. True grace is divine, Edwards asserts simply, but behind and within this Doctrine is a store of expansive truths. When we say something is "divine," Edwards states, we take that term to mean something pertaining to God, something that has a "resemblance of divine perfection," that partakes of the divine essence, and that involves "supernatural communication." Thus, when God bestows grace on the soul, the divine essence is not bestowed but rather the divine "fullness." Natural human endowments and faculties, he continues, must be distinguished from supernatural endowments. A vital endowment of this latter sort is grace, since it is from God "immediately" and enables participation in the divine. It is greater than miracles in its effect.

A product of the period of the "Great Awakening," the "Treatise on Grace" relates to Edwards's ongoing efforts to delineate true from false grace, and sincere from hypocritical professors. The first chapter, presented here, defines and distinguishes common grace—the assistance available to saint and sinner alike—and saving grace, available only to the truly godly. For Edwards, saving grace is not merely a matter of "degree," or the accumulation of common graces; rather, it is entirely different in nature from common grace. He presents a series of ways in which it is evident, from Scripture and experience, that persons are not true saints: they are born of the flesh and not of the Spirit; they lack a principle of grace; they do not partake of the divine nature, and so forth. While all that is "preparatory to conversion" is "gradually carried on," the work of conversion itself is wrought by God "in a moment." This work cannot be done by human efforts alone; they must have a "concurring assistance" from God.

Where the first chapter of the "Treatise on Grace" identifies what the unregenerate do not have, the contemporaneously written "Miscellanies" no. 790, entitled "Signs of Godliness," provides a list of the "positive" or "the best signs of godliness," and so provided grist for Edwards's later published treatises such as *Distinguishing Marks of a Work of the Spirit of God* (1741) and *A Treatise Concerning Religious Affections* (1746). How does the seeker after truth, after achieving what Edwards calls the "new spiritual sense," carry through? For Edwards at this point, "good fruits, or good works and keeping Christ's commandments, are the evidences" by which the godliness of others, and of ourselves, are to be determined. Edwards has not gone over to the Arminians; he remains a firm believer in the divine and supernatural light in the soul. But he is talking specifically here about how to "evidence" or "show forth" that light. First, the sort of obedience he specifies, from his reading of the Bible, is "universal," that is, not partial, consisting only in what is convenient or not too difficult. This involves denying self and selling all for Christ. And though he is primarily referring to what is "external," the individual must also regard "inward actings of the mind" from which such behavior springs.

Extraordinary Gifts of the Spirit Are Inferior to Graces of the Spirit, a sermon whose exposition and doctrine are presented here, was preached in 1748 during Edwards's embattled time at Northampton prior to his dismissal in 1750. It was occasioned by the ambivalent legacy of the Great Awakening, in which many claimed direct revelations from God, visions, and the ability of discernment. In response, Edwards takes a cessationist stance—that is, that revelations ceased with the closing of the canon of Scripture. While he did allow for progressive revelation in a certain respect as part of his conception of the history of redemption and in the fulfillment of prophecy and types, his emphasis here was to show that, for all the spiritual gifts that certain deluded individuals—separatists, self-proclaimed prophets, converts inflated by self-righteousness, and the like—might exhibit, such gifts are still inferior to the simple soul made truly gracious by a work of the Spirit. That Edwards himself had temporarily tolerated such behavior in the early phases of the revivals suggests that he was conveying a personally hard-learned lesson.

Within the period of 1737 through 1739, Edwards preached several massive discourses, including series that would later be published as *Charity and Its Fruits* (1852) and *A History of the Work of Redemption* (1774). Another extended sermonic effort from this period is Edwards's *True and False Christians*, a consideration of the parable of the wise and foolish virgins in Matthew 25. No less than nineteen units or preaching occasions in length, we present here, as a sample, the entirety of the sixth.

Edwards begins his discourse on the parable by asserting a distinction between true Christians and hypocrites, noting that while both will rush out to meet Christ "after the midnight cry" at the end of days, only the former will be received. An extended explication of how Christ is espoused to the church, the sermons comprising the introduction use the analogy of a marriage covenant to show how Christ is the bridegroom of the parable, with professors of Christianity represented by the two sets of virgins.

Edwards then moves into a series of points, each with its own Application, on the similarities of true and false Christians. Sometimes, he observes, they agree through the infirmities and failings of true Christians. As Ava Chamberlain puts it in her study of this discourse, "Hypocrites resemble saints because they are capable of a wide variety of religious beliefs and actions; saints resemble hypocrites because 'there is abundance of corruption in the hearts of true Christians as well as others.'"[1] Another way in which true and false Christians are similar is that they can both "slumber and sleep," especially in "a time of decay of religion." At such times, individuals experience a cessation of sense and of action, both because God withdraws his Spirit and because humans influence each other in their behavior. In applying this point, Edwards becomes particularly specific in speaking to the supposed converts of the late revival, telling them to examine how they are guilty of backsliding, how they have discredited the town and the cause of religion, how they have allowed themselves to go on in practices that before they would have abhorred, and how they justify things they used to condemn. Rouse out of sleep, literal and spiritual, Edwards cries; to those that are awake, he says, stay awake, and wake those around you that are slumbering.

✍

A SPIRITUAL UNDERSTANDING OF DIVINE THINGS DENIED TO THE UNREGENERATE (1723)

1 Corinthians 2:14
But the natural man receiveth not the things of the Spirit of God: for they are foolishness unto him: neither can he know them, because they are spiritually discerned.

There is scarcely any similitude is made use of more frequently or is more insisted upon in the Scripture to set forth truth, religion and the gospel by, than light. Thus God is compared to the luminary, for it is said he "is light, and in him is no darkness at all" [1 John 1:5]. And so Jesus Christ is resembled to the sun, is called "the light of the world" [John 8:12], the morning star [Rev 22:16], etc. And gospel truth is as the light that is shed down from this luminary upon us, and enlightens the spiritual world. He sheds around spiritual wisdom in the minds of those men he enlightens, as the sun diffuses his beams in the atmosphere.

This spiritual wisdom is the subject of this chapter, wherein the Apostle is declaring to us how far it excels the wisdom of this world, and it as it were disdains all those little superficial ornaments and trivial decorations with which the wise men of this world were wont to set off their wisdom. For the wisdom of this world indeed needs some adventitious ornaments to set it off, and receives great advantage by the excellency or elegancy of speech, and by being professed and favored by the great and rich men of the world.

But the wisdom of God needs not be dressed up in such gay clothing. Such ornaments are vastly too mean for divine truth, which is most amiable in her own native beauty and genuine simplicity, and is as beautiful in a poor man or a babe, as in a prince, and as powerful

320

in Paul's weakness and fear and much trembling, as it would be in all the wisdom of the philosophers and eloquence of their greatest orators. For the power of divine light don't depend on the eloquence of the speaker, but upon the demonstration of the Spirit of God. See the fourth verse, "And my speech and my preaching was not with enticing words of man's wisdom, but in demonstration of the Spirit and of power." For there is another teaching necessary in order [to] the reception of this wisdom, even the teachings of the Holy Ghost: for it is a sort of wisdom that is both out of the powers of the greatest worldly wise men to teach, so as to make to understand, and out of the reach of men of the greatest learning and natural understanding to understand of without divine teachings. Vv. 13–14, "Which things also we speak, not in the words which man's wisdom teacheth, but which the Holy Ghost teacheth; comparing spiritual things with spiritual. But the natural man receiveth not the things of the Spirit of God: for they are foolishness unto him: neither can he know them, because they are spiritually discerned."

1. What is that knowledge the Apostle speaks of. 'Tis the knowledge of the things of the Spirit of God; that is, the knowledge of those things that proceed from the Spirit of God, that he is the fountain and author of, either by inspiration of the Scripture or by saving illumination.

2. The opposition of this knowledge to the "natural man," by which must needs be understood the unregenerate, inasmuch as 'tis opposed to the spiritual man, in the beginning of the next verse: he "receiveth not those things of God's spirit," yea, "they are foolishness to him." He not only don't receive them, but he rejects them. They appear foolish to him. He can see no manner of excellency or beauty or wisdom in them. It appears all quite tasteless, insipid, senseless and foolish to him. Yea, such is the contrariety and inconsistency, that he cannot know them. A natural man and the knowledge of the things of God's Spirit are quite repugnant and incompatible.

3. How are they known and understood: that is, spiritually, because they are "spiritually discerned."

4. By whom: by him that is spiritual. "But he that is spiritual judgeth all things" [v. 15]; that is, he whose heart and mind are spiritualized, and purged from the dregs of earth and carnal lusts. For the

minds of wicked [men] are become carnal and fleshly and earthly; but when they are regenerated, they are made spiritual and heavenly.

Doctrine

There is a spiritual understanding of divine things, which all natural and unregenerate men are destitute of.

This is very plain from the words of the text. The meaning of the text is so far indisputable and past controversy, nothing can be plainer, that the words of our text do assert that there are some things that the natural man perceiveth not and that he neither can know as long as he continues a natural man and that are discerned no other way but spiritually.

Therefore whatever objections natural and unconverted men may make against this, fancying that they have as much understanding and as much knowledge as the godly, their mouths must be stopped by the plain assertion of Scripture. The great and learned men of the world perhaps may have a hundred times the notional knowledge of divinity, when yet the humble, plain, illiterate Christian really hath an understanding that is above, that he never has reached to and cannot attain.

We shall thus methodize our handling of this truth: we shall show,

I. What knowledge of divine things may be obtained by natural men.

II. Describe that spiritual knowledge of divine things, which natural and unregenerate men are destitute [of].

III. Why natural men cannot have this knowledge.

IV. How those that have it, come by it.

I. What knowledge of divine things may be obtained by natural men.

First. Natural men may obtain a large notional knowledge and understanding of the doctrines of divinity. They may be very well [versed] in theology, and may have read abundance of books which treat of divinity with much learning and great strength of reason.

They may very much excel ordinary Christians in this, may have a very clear head, and may be able nicely to distinguish and to penetrate narrowly into the criticisms of divine theorems; yea, may see further than most men, may be very able to instruct the common and ordinary Christians and to tell them many things they never knew before; yea, may be able to help them very much to that knowledge which shall be very useful to them and be a means of an increase of their spiritual illumination; and may be able to speak of things very affectingly and so as shall have a considerable influence to the bettering of the hearts and lives of those that hear him.

He may have such knowledge that he may be able to dispute very artfully and cunningly about theological matters, and may be able to stop the mouths of his opponents, yea, although they are true Christians, and have that saving knowledge which they are destitute of; may have such an understanding of divinity that he shall be able to give very proper and clear answers to an examiner, one that examines him about the principles of religion; may have a great notional knowledge of the meaning and interpretation of Scripture, and may be able to solve the knots and intricacies thereof and to reconcile the seeming repugnancies, and may talk very knowingly about the mysteries of religion; may give nice distinctions about the Trinity, and about the incarnation of Christ, and the hypostatical union of the two natures; may talk learnedly of original sin, Christ's satisfaction and the eternal decrees of God; and may have some sort of love to studying and reading about such things for the satisfaction of his curiosity, and perhaps may have enough of this kind of knowledge to be a doctor or teacher of others that are weak. He may have all this, and yet be the very man the Apostle speaks of when he says, "But the natural man receiveth not the things of the Spirit of God: for they are foolishness unto him: neither can he know them."

The Pharisees, amongst the Jews, were men of very much of this kind of notional knowledge. They were the great doctors of their nation, and made it their business very much to study the law of Moses, that they might teach others. They were the great divines of that nation. Nicodemus was a master or doctor in Israel, because he was a Pharisee (John 3:10). The Apostle Paul speaks of it as a great privilege he had enjoyed, that he was brought up at the feet of

Gamaliel, who was a Pharisee [Acts 22:3, 5:34]. The scribes and Pharisees were great disputants in matters of divinity. This appears by their so often endeavoring to ensnare Christ in their disputings; but yet they were often reproved by Christ as being some of the worst of men.

Second. Natural men may be very orthodox in their notional knowledge. They may be neither Papists nor Socinians nor Arminians, but in the general believe as the orthodox part of the world does believe: yea, may be very zealous in their kind of zeal for orthodoxy, may be very hot against false doctrine, exceeding zealous for the profession of their country and the belief of their forefathers, and against all innovations in the manner of worship; may have a great zeal, such as 'tis for the right way of church government, and may be very good disputants for the right, and may be able to beset others, and it may be to convince gainsayers: and yet the things of the Spirit of God may be foolishness unto him.

Third. Natural men may have that knowledge which may have some influence on their lives. Their conscience thereby has the greater advantage, for although their understandings are not savingly enlightened, yet their consciences are enlightened: for it's impossible but that a man that knows and is versed in the study of divinity, should know his duty better, and know better what is sin. It's impossible but that he should have clearer notions of the aggravations of sin, *caeteris paribus*, than if he were ignorant and unlearned; and therefore his conscience is more enlightened, and when he commits sin, it is more against his conscience than it otherwise would be. It is against more light. And therefore his light and knowledge may have some influence to restrain him, and he may live the better for his knowledge, and yet be one of those that cannot know the things of God's Spirit because they are spiritually discerned.

Thus we have shown what knowledge natural men may have. We proceed nextly,

II. To speak to that spiritual understanding of divine things which they cannot have.

And here, our answer is to show the real and true difference between this spiritual knowledge and the knowledge which natural men have, [and to] give that description of the nature and effects of this spiritual knowledge of the things of the Spirit of God as do distinguish it from other knowledge. And here, first, we shall give the distinguishing nature of [it]; and second, its distinguishing effects.

First, then, as to its nature. This spiritual knowledge of divine things consists in a certain clear apprehension and a lively infixed sensibleness of them that the godly have, which wicked men are destitute of. Men may have a great deal of notional knowledge about things, and yet not have a lively and sensible idea of them. Some things are conceived of as a kind of dream, a mere chimera and imagination; and others conceived of as real certain. There is a vast difference between our conceptions of what we read of in a story or romance and our conceptions of things that we daily converse [of]— though perhaps we have heard this romance so often that we have as great a notional knowledge of the several parts of it as we have of those things that we ourselves are knowing to by our senses.

When we read an history of a thing that was acted many centuries or years ago, and at many thousands of miles' distance, and perhaps we think it may be probably true: yet we have not at all the same kind of conceptions of the matter as one that was present upon the spot, and saw and heard all that was done, although perhaps we have read and studied the history so much that we can tell the story better than he that was present. The thing is, we han't so lively an apprehension of the things that were done as those that were present; and therefore the things don't affect us at all [in] the same manner as it did in the time the persons that were actually concerned in the matter. The matter don't seem so real to us. The apprehension is nothing near so lively.

So the difference of the knowledge of the spiritual man from the knowledge of the natural man is of the same kind: for the eyes of believers are opened, they do as it were see divine things. There is a certain intenseness and sensibleness in their apprehension of [them], a certain seeing and feeling. It is difficult fully to express what it is, but there is truly a spiritual light that the wicked have not, nor cannot have. It is not absurd nor incredible that it should be so, for we may very easily conceive [it]: we have sometimes a more sensible apprehension of temporal things than at other times, though perhaps no better notional knowledge; yet at some times we see things in such a light, and such an appearance, as abundantly more affects us: and why may there not be as great a difference in spiritual things?

The natural man knows that he has not a very lively sense of the things of the Spirit of God. Though perhaps he has heard and read much about God's attributes concerning the redemption by Christ, yet his sense about these things is not deep, intense and affecting. This wicked men themselves know, and why should they think it impossible but that there should be a lively sense that others have, though they have [it] not?

It may be the natural man may have a great notional knowledge concerning God's attributes—how he is the most excellent of all beings, and has infinite perfection; is the fountain of all excellency and loveliness; is immensely holy and merciful, and the like—yet he has not half so deep and lively an apprehension of God's amiableness as he has of the beauty of some things earthly. Though he can talk as well and as rationally as most about the gloriousness of God, yet he loves him not half so well as some other things. And what is the reason? It must be because he does not discern this gloriousness of God, how well soever he can talk of [it]. It must be because there is a certain knowledge of God's excellency that he has not. Though he thinks he knows a great deal of divinity, yet some Christian, that he looks upon as ignorant in comparison of [himself], has a great deal better apprehension of God's loveliness than he; it is plain to a demonstration, because [the Christian apprehends] him better.

We may very easily conceive wherein lies the difference. The knowledge of a thing is not in proportion to the extensiveness of our notions, or number of circumstances known, only; but it consists chiefly in the intensiveness of the idea. Thus it is not he that has heard a long description of the sweetness of honey that can be said to have the greatest understanding of it, but he that has tasted.[2] If a man should read whole volumes upon this one subject, the taste of honey, he would never get so lively an apprehension of it as he had that had tasted, though it were but from [the] tip of his rod. Now God has infused such a lively apprehension into the minds of the godly of divine things, as if they had tasted.

The spiritual illumination of the minds of believers is resembled to tasting. Canticles 2:2–3, "And his fruit was sweet." 'Tis no wonder that none can tell how sweetly the fruit of the Tree of Life is but those that have tasted; no wonder that none know that the Lord is gracious so well as they that have tasted and seen. Believers have had those exercises of soul towards spiritual things that are very well represented to tasting: they have tasted of the bread of life by faith [John 6:35], they have drank of the water of life [John 4:14], they have tasted of the wine and milk that Christ has given [John 2, 1 Pet 2:2–3]. 'Tis these only that can testify from their own knowledge that the judgments of God are sweeter than the honey and the honeycomb.

This spiritual knowledge of the godly is resembled also to smelling a sweet perfume. Thus Christ is called "a bundle of myrrh," for the sweetness of it to the smell. Canticles 1:13, "A bundle of myrrh is my well-beloved unto me." Thus he is said to be a rose and a lily, in the beginning of the second chapter, because of their odoriferousness. And so 5:13, "His lips are like lilies, dropping sweet-smelling myrrh." Now there are no descriptions, however accurate, of the smell of sweet-smelling myrrh that can give anyone to understand it as those that have actually smelled it.

The knowledge of the natural man about spiritual things, is very much like the knowledge of those that are born blind have of colors from the descriptions of them, or one born deaf has of sounds; but the spiritual understanding, of those who have their eyes open and their ears unstopped. 'Tis a sight of spiritual things. However the natural man may have heard and read and studied about divine things, he never saw them, he never had a spiritual sight of them. This spiritual understanding is like a gleam of light that breaks in upon the soul through a gloomy darkness. Of all the similitudes that are made use of in Scripture to describe to us this spiritual understanding, light is that which doth most fully represent it and is oftenest used. The believer, when he first discerns the things of the Spirit of God, he is called out of darkness into marvelous light, 1 Peter 2:9. They are turned from darkness unto light, Acts 26:18; their minds are as it were filled with light after a long night of darkness.

Christ came to open the eyes of the blind and to unstop the ears of the deaf in this sense more especially, more than any other.

This spiritual light may be divided with respect to that object of it, whereby it is distinguished from the knowledge of natural men: first, 'tis a sight of the truth and reality of spiritual things; second, of the excellency of divine and spiritual things; third, an experimental understanding of the operation of God's Spirit.

1. 'Tis a sight of the truth and reality of divine things. There are some things that do appear real to us and others that, although we may give a sort of assent to them, appear only imaginary. Thus when men are actually in the presence of a king, why, then it seems real to them. But if natural men are told that they are in the immediate presence of God, have they any realizing sense of it? Although it is in him they live, move and have their being, have they a sense anything like the former? When they are in the presence of some great man, they are watchful of their actions, lest they should do something that is offensive to his eyes; but they take no more care to act so as to please God, anymore than if they thought themselves concealed from his eyes. But it seems real to the godly, and therefore they act under a realizing sense of it.

The futurities of heaven and eternal judgment, they appear as real unto those who are spiritual. When they hear the promises of reigning with Christ in heaven and enjoying of him there in great glory, their being acquitted at the day of judgment, and presentation without spot to the Father, these things appear to be really true to believers, and those whose minds are spiritualized. But [to natural men] they are like a mere dream, a fable and imagination; their belief of them is so slighty and covertly, that it don't at all, or very little, affect them.

The child of God doth as it were see and feel the truth of divine things even intuitively; that is, they see so much of religion, that they plainly discern that it must needs be the offspring of God. They can feel such a power and kind of omnipotency in Christianity, and taste such a sweetness, and see such wisdom, such an excellent harmony in the gospel, as carry their own light with them, and powerfully do enforce and conquer the assent and necessitates their minds to receive it as proceeding from God, and as the certain truth. They bring so much of the image of God with them, that it is plain beyond question that they are from him. They come into their minds bearing the certain marks of truth upon them, and carrying the broad seal of heaven before them.

The believer sees more force in the reasons and arguments that evince religion than other men, and besides, has more arguments for it than others. The truth of the gospel to them is plain from the effects it has in their hearts, and from what they themselves have experienced of its power, and seen of its excellency.

2. That spiritual knowledge, which all natural and unregenerate persons are destitute of, is the knowledge of the excellency of divine things. The natural man may hear that they are excellent, and say that they are excellent, and may also be able to make fine speeches of God's glory, and of the excellency of holiness and the like; but it is the savingly enlightened Christian alone that knows and that sees they are excellent. The spiritualized regenerate soul sees a beauty and an amiableness, and tastes an incomparable sweetness, that is altogether hidden from the wicked.

Thus with respect to earthly beauty, 'tis not the hearing of elegant descriptions of a beautiful face that can ever make a person have a sense of the sweetness and amiableness of the beauty; 'tis not the slight notion of beauty by hearsay that causes love to burn in the heart: but it is the sight of the eye. One glance of the eye doth more than all the most particular descriptions that can be given. Thus unbelievers know nothing about spiritual beauty but by hearsay; but to the godly, God has given a glance, opened to the immediate view of their minds, and there breaks in upon their souls such a heavenly sweetness, such a sense of the amiableness, as wonderfully affects the heart, and even transforms it. He sees things in a new appearance, in quite another view, than ever he saw before: he sees an excellency in God; he sees a sweet loveliness in Christ; he sees an amiableness in holiness and God's commandments; he sees an excellency in a Christian spirit and temper; he sees the wonderfulness of God's designs and a harmony in all his ways, a harmony, excellency and wondrousness in his Word: he sees these things by an eye of faith, and by a new light that was never before let into his mind.

From this knowledge of divine excellencies follows the knowledge of spiritual deformities, and is from the same principle. The same knowledge whereby he knows the excellency of holiness and the beauty of Jesus Christ, he also knows the deformity of sin, and their own vileness by reason of it: for if holiness appears excellent to a person, it follows of course and necessarily that the contrary to holiness should appear deformed. For it is a contradiction to suppose that a person should think holiness lovely and the direct contrary to holiness lovely too; but if one appears amiable to him, the other must appear deformed, and he himself must also appear deformed to himself, because he was defiled. Wherefore we have not distinguished this kind of knowledge from the knowledge of spiritual excellencies, for it is not distinguishable.

3. This spiritual knowledge, which all natural men are destitute of, is the experimental knowledge of the saving operations of the Holy Spirit. This is more especially called the knowledge of "the things of the Spirit of God," that is, of those things which he does, of his operation on the mind and heart. This may be what is especially pointed at in the eleventh verse of our context: "For what man knoweth the things of a man, save the spirit of man which is in him? even so the things of God knoweth no man, but the Spirit of God." The comparison is very lively and the puissanity very strong. The things of a man are understanding, memory, will, joy, sorrow, anger, and the like. Now nothing knows what these are but the spirit of man that is in him. We know what love, and grief, etc., are, because we have felt them within ourselves. Otherwise, it is not all the men in the world could make us understand what they are. This the Apostle means when he says, "For what man knoweth the things of a man, save the spirit of man that is in him?"

On the other hand, as to knowledge [of] the things of God's Spirit, they are such as faith, humiliation, divine love, peace of conscience, spiritual joy, and the like. Now none can truly tell what these be, and have a real apprehension of them, but them that have felt them within themselves. Without this, they cannot attain to a right notion of them by the most accurate descriptions, any more than we could know by a description what love and grief are, if we had never felt anything like them. And this the Apostle means when he says, "Even so, the things of God knoweth no man, but the Spirit of God."

There is a direct knowledge, and there is a reflex knowledge.[3] The direct knowledge is the knowledge the Christian hath of divine things, without himself, of the truth and excellency of the things of the gospel. The reflex knowledge is that which he obtains by reflecting and looking inward upon his own heart, and seeing the operations and actings of that, and the workings of the Spirit of God therein. By this reflection, the Christian obtains to know what regeneration is; and what are those actings of the Spirit of God which are so frequently spoken of in Scripture; and the whole applicatory part of religion, which is one half of divinity, and which every natural man is ignorant of.

The godly, having this experimental knowledge, it wonderfully enlightens to the understanding of the gospel and the spiritual and true meaning of the Scripture, because he finds the same things in his own heart that he reads of. He knows how it is, because he feels it himself. And this makes that [that] he reads, the Scripture and other spiritual books, [appear] with much more delight than otherwise he would do. This makes him delight much more in those discourses, books and sermons that are most spiritual, which others have the least relish of. Romans 8:5, "For they that are after the flesh do mind the things of the flesh; but they that are after the Spirit the things of the Spirit."

Thus we have told you what this spiritual knowledge is, as distinguished from all kind of knowledge that natural men have as to the nature of it. Nextly,

Second. We shall give you the difference between this spiritual knowledge of divine things and the knowledge of divinity that natural men have as to the effects of it. This difference as to the effects is fourfold:

1. The first difference is, this spiritual knowledge transforms the heart, the other doth not. The believer hath got such a sight and such a knowledge of things that, ever since, he is become quite another man than he was before. It has exceeding altered his internal tempers and disposition. The knowledge that he has is so substantial, so inward, and so affecting, that it has quite transformed the soul and put a new nature into the man, has quite changed his very innermost principles, and has made things otherwise, even from the very foundation, even so that all things are become new to them. Yea, he is a new creature, he is just as if he was not the same, but were born again,

created over a second time. That light and knowledge has been let into his soul that has so affected him that he has a new nature, just as if a new spirit were infused into that body; of an angel of darkness has made an angel of light of him; has brought the image of God upon him; has made him of an heavenly temper and an angelical mind; has sweetened and mollified his dispositions; and of an heart of stone hath made a heart of flesh, of bitter has made sweet, and of dark has made light. This is the effect of true and spiritual [knowledge] of divine things. 2 Corinthians 3:18, "But we all, as with open face beholding as in a glass the glory of the Lord, are changed into the same image from glory to glory even as by the Spirit of the Lord."

Now though natural men may have considerable knowledge in divinity, yet it has not this effect upon them. They may read and study, for hours together, and leave off with the same heart as they had when they began, and carry the same temper and disposition.

2. The second difference between this spiritual knowledge of divine things, and other knowledge, as to their effects, is that the one purifies the life, the other doth not. This spiritual knowledge is a practical knowledge, that which is accompanied with practice of what is known. Those that spiritually know Christ, they keep his commandments. 1 John 2:3, "Hereby we do know that we know him, if we keep his commandments."

But it is not so with respect to that knowledge that the natural man hath, although, as we have already said, their knowledge may so far influence them as to cause some better [way] of life, by awakening and giving advantage to their consciences. Yea, there is but a partial alteration, which is universal in those who have this true and spiritual knowledge.

3. Another difference is that this spiritual knowledge raises a holy joy in the mind, but the knowledge of natural men doth not. The knowledge of natural men may raise something of pleasure, because it satisfies their curiosity, or because it satisfies their ambition. So they may have pleasure by thinking that they know more than others.

But this is not the joy we speak of. The believer is filled with joy because he is pleased and delighted with the sight. The knowledge itself is a sweet sort of knowledge to him. He loves to view and behold the things of the Spirit of God; they are to him the most pleasing and beautiful objects in the world. He can never satisfy his eyes with looking on them, because he beholds them as certain truths and as things of all the most excellent. It is the nature of man to love to know the truth and also to love to behold the things that are beautiful and amiable; but the believer is convinced, yea, he plainly sees, that spiritual things are both these. Proverbs 2:10, "When wisdom entereth into thine heart, and knowledge is pleasant unto thy soul."

4. The fourth, and last, and most distinguishing difference between the true spiritual and other knowledge, is that one puffeth up and the other makes more humble. The more knowledge the natural man hath, the more is he elated and lifted up in his own esteem. 1 Corinthians 8:1, "Knowledge puffeth up."

But the more spiritual knowledge the godly have, the more humble are they. They are not lifted up thinking that others know not so much as they; no, but the more they have of this knowledge, the more they know of their own vileness, the more they loath themselves, the lower they lie in the dust before God, the more meek and poor in spirit are they, the more are their hearts broken for their sin. Because they have seen God, by this knowledge they say, therefore, "I abhor myself in dust and in ashes" [Job 42:6].

We are therefore come now to consider,

III. Why natural men cannot have this spiritual knowledge.

The reason, in the general, is because they have a nature that is not susceptive of this knowledge, but repugnant to it. They have no principle of nature within them from whence this spiritual knowledge can be elicited. All that is within them resists it, and is repugnant to it.

They have indeed natural reason, which if it acted, and was sufficiently enlightened, would be a sufficient natural principle; but their reason is so darkened, and their souls are so much debased by sin below reason and what is reasonable, that such high, spiritual and glorious things cannot enter into their souls. Sin has made their souls in this respect of a beastly nature, and you may as soon infuse the learning of schools and universities into the beasts, as infuse into a natural man this spiritual understanding.

Their souls are too gross and earthly to receive and be made the subjects of such pure and refined light and truth. They have a contrariety to it. Therefore they seem foolishness unto him, neither can he know them. It is not possible for that which is of so pure a nature to enter into that which is so filthy as the unregenerate soul.

There is such a contrariety, that we may as soon expect to make friends of fire and water, or of light and darkness, as to make the natural man receptive of spiritual understanding.

We are not easily made to have a clear apprehension of those things which we have no manner of natural inclination to. Children will never be made thoroughly to learn that which they have no inclination to. They never will be expert at that kind of learning which is quite contrary to their natural disposition. We can never be made to beat it into them. Much less can the apprehension of the truth, reality and excellency of the things of God be beat into the natural man, who is not only destitute of all inclinations to spiritual things, but is as full as he can hold of an antipathy against them.

No man can discern these things any other way than by the Spirit of God, which natural men are altogether destitute of. The Apostle gives the true reason why the natural man perceiveth not the things of God's Spirit: "Because they are spiritually discerned," that is, by God's Spirit. 'Tis no more of a wonder why the natural man cannot be made to discern spiritual things, than why the beast cannot conceive of man's reason and intellectual actions: for this spiritual knowledge is [as] much above that which is natural as reason is above the conceptions of beasts.

And God will never, never give his Spirit and spiritual knowledge to natural men while they yet remain loathsome and filthy. God will never allow of such a confused mixture as this. He will never allow of such an incongruous jumble in the nature of things, that spiritual and angelical light should be in a natural man, who is all over loathsome and abominable, before he is purged and sanctified. God is the God of [peace] and not of confusion [1 Cor 14:33], neither will he cast pearls before swine [Matt 7:6]; but he sanctifies and purifies the soul before he makes it the receptacle of things so pure and precious.

This is very plain from experience as well as Scripture and reason. We see that there is no beating of spiritual knowledge into carnal men. We see that the reality, certainty and excellency of them will not sink into their souls. Though they are made never so plain, though the light shines right in their faces, and though we charm to them never so wisely, they will not hear (Psalm 58:5). They have not eyes to see, nor ears to hear. It is no wonder that we cannot make those see to whom God has given no eyes, and those to hear who have no ears. When sinners are enlightened, God gives them eyes and ears and an understanding heart, whereby is intimated that they had none before.

First. The reason why they don't conceive of the truth and reality of spiritual things, is because they have not largeness of heart enough.

The views of some men are confined to a narrow compass, can't take in the great and glorious things of another world as this; but other men, to whom God has not given this largeness of heart, nothing seems real to them but what they see with their eyes, and is the object of their bodily senses. The reason of this is a certain narrowness of soul, that has but a very scanty and confined knowledge, confined to the dust they tread on. This world appears great to them, and worthy to set their hearts upon. 'Tis because of a littleness of soul; they are like insects, worms and ants, to whom a little hillock looks like a mountain, and a spire of grass like a tree, and not like men, who tread these things under their feet as very little things not worthy the minding.

So they are of very narrow views and conceptions with respect to time. They can see no farther than just before them, and the things of another world, they are too great and too far off for them to behold. 1 Peter 1:9, "But he that lacketh these things is blind, and cannot see far off." This is from a certain littleness of soul, and a pitiful scantiness and narrowness of mind, that they can't realize the things of another world because they can't see them, will not realize things that are to come because they be not present.

But to the spiritual man, God hath given largeness of heart, greatness of soul, that he sees and understands the things of the spiritual world as well as this. It's beneath the greatness of their souls to be confined to a little clod of earth, and to a seventy years. They see things at a distance, and can see the reality of things that are to [be] thousands of years hence, as well as at present.

Second. The reason why they cannot see the excellency of spiritual things is very plain: because it is contrary to their natures. It is a contradiction to suppose that those things should appear excellent to us that are contrary to our natures and inclinations, for if they did appear excellent, they would not be contrary to us, but very agreeable. The wicked is full of a principle of enmity to divine things—and what wonder is it, that those things that we are full of enmity to, should not be amiable to us? No more of a wonder than that we can't love and hate a thing at the same time.

But particularly, as to those particular causes which make the nature not receptive of spiritual understanding, they are:

1. Hardness of heart. Their hearts are so hard, that the rays that beam forth from Christ will not enter at all, but do all rebound as from a rock or a marble wall.

2. It is from the blinding and deceitful nature of sin. The nature of sin is to blind and deceive; it is the spawn and offspring of the devil, that great deceiver, who makes it his whole business to deceive. Deceit is the foundation of sin: it was through deceit that it was first brought into the world, and by deceit is it kept up and maintained in the world; and by sin is deceit kept up in the world: deceit is the very nature, root, stock and branch of sin. There is nothing pertaining to sin but what would immediately fall to the ground if deceit was removed, so essential is deceit to sin. Deceit and sin live together and perish and die together.

Sin, when it has got possession of the soul, immediately beclouds and bewilders it and fills it with darkness; fills it with a thousand false imaginations and conceptions, many senseless dreams and ridiculous apprehensions; makes men fools and sots and mad; makes them think that they can find happiness in earthly things; makes them think that silver is better than God himself; makes them imagine that seventy years' happiness now is better than an eternity of happiness hereafter; makes them think that escaping eternal damnation is not worth the seeking for, nor everlasting happiness in heaven worth the praying for; makes them think that they shall be great gainers if they can get two or three hundred pounds, and lose themselves forever to pay for it: such senseless imaginations and dreams as these doth sin fill the mind with.

It bewitches and strangely charms and bewilders men, fills their eyes with smoke and stops their ears, and fills their souls with a thousand confusions. Wherefore 'tis no wonder that those cannot understand spiritual things, who have this deceitful thing reigning in their hearts. Hebrew 3:13, "Lest any of you be hardened through the deceitfulness of sin."

3. The third thing that hinders natural men from understanding spiritual things, is the interest that Satan has in and the power he has over their hearts.

Satan has a kingdom in wicked men's hearts. There he has a throne, and there he makes his residence and keeps his court. The entrance is easy for the devil into wicked men's hearts; the doors always stand open for him, and as long as he has such power in the heart, he will take effectual care that no divine light enters there. He'll keep out spiritual truths. He must be cast out by God's almighty power before any divine understanding will find admittance there. He holds his kingdom by deceit and darkness. 'Tis the devil that blinds their minds. 2 Corinthians 4:4, "In whom the god of this world hath blinded the minds of them that believe not, lest the light of the glorious gospel of Christ, who is the image of God, should shine unto them." Therefore devils are called "the rulers of the darkness of this world" (Ephesians 6. 12).

4. [The fourth] thing that hinders are the lusts of the flesh. They love sinful pleasures, carnal and sensual delights, which do becloud their souls and muddy their understanding, so that no light can enter in. They don't love to believe, and to see things that are contrary to those pleasures.

5. Worldly mindedness. How exceedingly are men blinded by their own interest. What is strong enough to overcome the prejudices of interest but God alone? What will not men believe if the thing believed makes for their worldly interest, and what will they not disbelieve, when the belief makes against their interest? How exceeding blind are men in such matters, all of us can witness. Mark 4:19, "And the cares of this world, and the deceitfulness of riches,

and the lusts of other things entering in, choke the word, and it becometh unfruitful."

6. And lastly, pride is a very great obstacle to the entering of divine light, yea, and such an obstacle as will eternally prevent it, till it be mortified. The knowledge which natural men have heightens pride, but pride fatally prevents spiritual knowledge. Pride hinders men from seeing the excellency of God and amiableness of Christ, and makes them set up themselves as the most excellent. It hinders them from receiving the gospel, which is all founded in humility. They don't care for those doctrines which require such lowliness, humility and meekness of mind, which teaches us to empty ourselves of ourselves that God may be all to us; teaches to lay ourselves in the dust that God may be exalted; teaches to renounce all our own righteousness and strength that free grace may be exalted; teaches us the necessity of becoming as little children if we would enter into the kingdom of heaven. The pride of the heart resists all these, and will not give them admittance.

Neither will God give light to those whose hearts are thus filled with pride, who thus depend on themselves. He'll leave them to boggle for themselves in the dark, seeing they will needs walk by their own candle and by the sparks which they have kindled. God will give them no other light, but will leave them to stumble on the dark mountains of death; but he will teach and instruct and enlighten the humble souls, who humbly and seeing their own insufficiency look to him for his instruction. Psalm 25:9, "The meek will he guide in judgment; the meek will he teach in his way."

IV. We are now come, in the fourth place, to show how those that have this spiritual understanding come by it.

First. The procuring cause is the merit and intercession of Jesus Christ. All that the believer hath is purchased and procured by Christ Jesus; all God's gifts are given through him, as well sanctification as glorification.

Second. The immediate efficient cause is the Holy Spirit. It is observed that things, according to their worth and excellency, are the more difficultly or the more easily [had]. Dirt, wood and stones are easy enough to be had, but silver and gold and precious stones are more difficultly come at; but yet these may be found by the art of man. Job 28:1, "Surely there is a vein for silver, and a place for gold where they fine it." Verse 6, "The stones of it are [the place of sapphires]: and it hath dust of gold." But this spiritual knowledge we are speaking of is not to be obtained by human researches. Verses 12–19:

> But where shall wisdom be found? and where is the place of understanding? Man knoweth not the price thereof; neither is it found in the land of the living. The depth saith, It is not in me: and the sea saith, It is not with me. It cannot be gotten for gold, neither shall silver be weighed for the price thereof. It cannot be valued with the gold of Ophir, with the precious onyx, or the sapphire. The gold and the crystal cannot equal it: and the exchange of it shall not be for jewels of fine gold. No mention shall be made of coral, or of pearls: for the price of wisdom is above rubies. The topaz of Ethiopia shall not equal it, neither shall it be valued with pure gold.

God reserves this spiritual knowledge as his own gift. 'Tis his prerogative to give this, by letting in his divine light into the mind. Proverbs 2:6, "For the Lord giveth wisdom; and out of his mouth cometh knowledge and understanding."

Others' knowledge may be obtained by the art of man, but this is God's immediate gift. None other but the Spirit of God can remove those obstacles that are in the way, can give largeness of heart enough, can remove that hardness which is natural, can dispose Satan, can conquer lusts, lift the soul from the earth, and abase pride.

There is an indisputable reason why none can teach the things of God but the Spirit of God: because none other can know the things of God but his Spirit. The Scripture is very full of this doctrine, that all spiritual saving light is given by the immediate teaching of God's Spirit.

Third. The means whereby this knowledge is communicated to us is his word. And this is the only likely way ever to obtain this knowledge, to converse very much with the holy word of God, frequently to read the Holy Scriptures. And if anyone is seeking after spiritual understanding, and does not this, he can reasonably expect no other than [to be] disappointed; as well as diligently attend on his word preached, according to his ordinance (Hebrews 4:12).

Fourth. The foundation of this spiritual knowledge is a regeneration of the heart. 'Tis not the natural man, whose very nature is sin, whose soul is darkness and filthiness, that is capable of this spiritual, bright and pure light. There is an necessity of the removal of the darkness, deadness and stupidity of the soul before it can be thus enlightened. Man must be made of an angelical nature before he has angelical knowledge; he must be made partaker of the divine nature before he is partaker of divine light. This necessarily follows from our doctrine: for if the natural man cannot {have this spiritual knowledge, then he must come to see the excellency of divine things}.

Improvement

I. Hence we learn the excellency of godliness. Knowledge by all men is counted an excellent [thing]; those who are knowing and understanding persons are esteemed more worthy, more excellent and honorable than others. 'Tis what men very much seek after, that they may be accounted to know more than others, and to see further into things. Men generally esteem it one of the highest commendations that can be given them, to say they are knowing, understanding, seeing men; they highly value themselves upon this, and look down upon poor ignorant persons as beneath them and unworthy to stand in equality with them. And nothing is esteemed more ignominious and disgraceful through the world in general than to be a fool; nothing men seek more to avoid than to be counted fools. 'Tis a note of the highest disdain, to call, "Fool!"; and so it be of ancient times. Matthew 5:22, "But whosoever shall say, Thou fool, shall be in danger of hell fire."

This is agreed upon amongst all nations, that knowledge is excellent and desirable, and folly and ignorance base and unworthy. Wicked, debauched and the most profligate persons agree in this: they will mock and deride those whom they account fools, and such have the highest place amongst them as are accounted most witty and sagacious—although their cunning and wit is the lowest kind of knowledge, and vastly inferior to this excellent divine knowledge.

'Tis the godly that are the wisest, most seeing and understanding of mankind. They have a degree of knowledge that is so high, that it's out of the reach of all natural men. Men highly esteem themselves when they have obtained the knowledge which is out of the reach [of others], and that other men cannot find out; but the godly, they have an high and an excellent knowledge that none of the princes of this world can attain to. 'Tis too high for natural men's sight; 'tis too bright for their eyes, too deep for their penetration, too great for their narrow comprehension, too noble for those that are so base.

Wicked men indeed have knowledge, but it's a low and narrow sort of knowledge. They have knowledge of the things of the earth, concerning the appurtenances of this clod of dirt; their knowledge is concerning the objects of their senses, what they see and taste and smell. They know of things that are under their feet. They know things that are present, and will presently vanish. Children know nothing but their toys and play. Some ignorant persons' knowledge reaches but a very little way, no further than they have seen with their eyes; others have a more extensive knowledge, who see in[to] the nature and reason of things. But the most excellent of all is that which views the great Creator, the first and the last, takes in the highest heavens and looks to the end of eternity. This is the greatest, best, most excellent and noble knowledge. This is far better than that knowledge which other men have knowledge of, gross matter and terrestrial things. 2 Peter 1:9, "He that lacketh these things is blind, and cannot see far off." This is called "wisdom," καιζοκην, by way of eminency in Scripture, and is there represented as above all things excellent. Proverbs 3:13–15, "Happy is the man that findeth wisdom; and the man that getteth understanding. For the merchandise of it is better than the merchandise of silver, and the gain thereof than fine gold. She is more precious than rubies: and all the things thou canst desire are not to be compared unto her."

The godly men in Scripture account are the wise men. Proverbs 3:35, "The wise shall inherit glory"; 13:14, "The law of the wise is a fountain of life." Matthew 25:2—sinners in Scripture account are the greatest fools, and are [called] so very often. Psalm 107:17, "Fools because of their transgression, and because of their iniquities, are afflicted." Proverbs 1:22, "And fools hate knowledge." Proverbs 10:21, "Fools die for want of wisdom."

Hence therefore, seeing it is so, as Proverbs 17:27, "A man of understanding is of an excellent spirit," we may justly draw that conclusion, Proverbs 12:26, "The righteous is more excellent than his neighbor."

II. Let us be moved by this doctrine to seek earnestly for other knowledge. What unregenerate men ever have, 'tis the knowledge that none have but the children of God, and the knowledge that makes those who have it his children. As you have heard, it transforms the heart into the divine image and changes the life to the divine pattern.

But perhaps you will say, to what purpose will it be to seek after spiritual knowledge, seeing that "the natural man perceiveth not the things of the Spirit, neither can he know them"? If they cannot be known without the extraordinary illumination of God's Spirit, if it is not in man's power to obtain it, but 'tis God alone who gives it, to what purpose will it be to seek this knowledge? Here we shall tell you which way you shall seek divine knowledge, in a way very likely for success, the way that God himself has directed to, and a way that don't at all contradict man's absolute impotency and entire inability to obtain the least measure of saving knowledge:

First. Let all prejudices against spiritual knowledge be cast away. There are many who entertain prejudices against all spiritual experiences that are talked of. They hear ministers of the gospel speak much of saving illumination, of light let in, of discoveries, of conviction, of a sense of our own vileness, or a sight of God's glory, etc., and they are prejudiced against it all. Such talk is not pleasing in their ears. They hardly believe there are any such things; yea, some are prejudiced against the very expressions whereby those things are signified. The expressions of conversion, our own righteousness, grace, spiritual conviction, however proper those expressions are, they are unpleasant in the ears of some. This is a very great hindrance to salutary illumination and spiritual knowledge. Wherefore let none thus entertain prejudices of this nature.

It must be acknowledged that hypocritical professors of religion, they do abundance of mischief to souls in this respect: they make a fair and pompous show, a more than ordinary profession; they will always be aping of religion. And no wonder it appears unlovely, as 'tis in them: it is because they have it not. Hypocritical professors of godliness do more hurt to religion than the most profligate, openly profane man. Men have their eyes upon them, to see what is in them, and they see that it is unlovely; and so they judge all religion to be. The most amiable things, when they are counterfeit, appear the most unlovely. Thus the shape of the body of man is excellent in its perfection, but when it is only approached to and not perfect, appears above all things deformed and ridiculous. Thus the shape of an ape and their actions are most deformed and ridiculous, because they imitate man's. Religion and knowledge in hypocrites is dead, and appears as deformed, dreadful and melancholy as the countenance of a dead man, whereas, perhaps when alive, [was] very amiable.

Those who are pretenders to religion, and nothing else, they spoil it and deform it; they make it look dreadful. They don't know what it is, and can't imitate it exactly. They only make a bugbear of it, to fright men from religion; make men think that religion consists very much in a melancholy disposition and a sour temper, whereas 'twould have a commanding loveliness if it were real and true.

And even some that are godly, by their unwariness and imprudence, may do hurt in this regard, mistaking that to be religion in some things which is not so, and not practicing in all things according to pure and lovely Christianity.

Whatever we see truly unlovely in any respect in persons, is not religion. Let us therefore take heed of being prejudiced against spiritual illumination, by any such or any other means. Let us truly desire to be illuminated. The desire of it will prepare the heart for it.

Second. If you would with success seek divine and spiritual knowledge, get that knowledge of divine things that is within your power, even a doctrinal knowledge of the principles of the Christian religion. Persons may be so ignorant in this respect that it may be impossible that they should be Christians, and 'tis to be feared that some even [in] Christendom, living under the gospel in this land and in many of our towns, are so ignorant that they have not so much knowledge as is necessary to the salvation of their souls. A Christian is a knowing understanding person, not only with spiritual saving knowledge, but in doctrinal knowledge of religion, for saving knowledge depends upon it. 'Tis not possible that any should know the excellency of Jesus Christ, that he is a mediator, except he knows who Christ is, that he is mediator, and how he is mediator, and that he is God. And many other things are necessary to be known of Christ in order to see his excellency. There must be a knowledge what the things of the gospel are, before we can be sensible of the truth and reality and excellency of the things of the gospel.

This is the way wherein God has appointed to reveal himself and give spiritual knowledge by, when the heart is prepared for it, by doctrinal knowledge. Except we strive for all the knowledge we can obtain, and continually endeavor to know more and more of religion and walk according to our light, we can't reasonably hope that God will communicate a further light.

Very many are exceeding defective in not seeking after knowledge, as if knowledge were no part of religion; or they leave knowledge for divines and ministers, as if it were no essential thing in private Christians. They content themselves in ignorance, neither strive after knowledge for themselves nor for their children; by that means let their own souls, and their poor offspring, run to ruin, yea, ruin eternal. What have we the Bible given to us for, but that we may get knowledge and understanding?

Some true Christians are always children, grow not in grace, because they grow not in knowledge. Paul says, 1 Corinthians 13:11, that when he was a child, he understood as a child; but when he became a man, he put away childish things. We ought not to content ourselves to be always babes, so as not to be able to digest strong meat, not to be able to go without holding. We ought to endeavor continually to grow to the stature of men in Christ, in knowledge as well as other things.

The Apostle expected of Christians in his time, though that was the infant state of the church, that they should be filled with all knowledge. Romans 15:14, "And I myself also am persuaded of you, my brethren, that ye are full of goodness, filled with all knowledge, able to admonish one another." He commends the Corinthians that they abound in knowledge. 2 Corinthians 8:7, "Therefore, as ye abound in everything, in faith, in utterance, in knowledge." We are commanded to add to virtue, knowledge, 2 Peter 1:5.

Christianity has a natural tendency to all useful knowledge of every kind. It has been observed that the Christian religion, wherever it comes, brings people from barbarous ignorance to knowledge and understanding. A very remarkable instance is in our own nation: before the Britons were Christianized, they were much such a barbarous, uncivilized, ignorant people as the natives of this land. Knowledge and religion not only go hand in hand, but knowledge is essential to religion; without knowledge, religion dies and fades away.

Let all therefore seek to be instructed and to know more of religion and the foundation of religion. Let all opportunities be improved to read and hear and get understanding. It not only is necessary and useful to the soul, but advances the reputation greatly, tends greatly many ways to the flourishing of the interest of any people or town.

Third. If we would get that spiritual saving knowledge that is spoken of in our text, we must practice according to the knowledge that we have. This is the only way to have more and a better and more excellent knowledge, aright to improve what knowledge we have. If we abuse what we have, we cannot expect that God will give us more.

Practicing according to the light we have, has a natural tendency to prepare the mind for the infusion of spiritual knowledge. It abates the force of sin, and assuages the violence of lust, and makes the mind to be less in the exercise of enmity at divine things. And then is the heart prepared for divine knowledge; then God in his ordinary way will infuse it.

Fourth. We must be much in reading the Scriptures, if we would get spiritual and saving knowledge. They are the means by which, as we have said, God communicates this knowledge. Except we diligently and frequently read the Scriptures, therefore, we cannot reasonably expect to be enlightened, except we can expect that God will work without means; which is most unreasonable, seeing we [are] in a land where such plenty of means are enjoyed.

The Scriptures were given for this end, to instruct us. 2 Timothy 3:16, "All scripture is given by inspiration of God, and is profitable for doctrine, for reproof, for correction, for instruction in righteousness."

The reason why multitudes read the Scriptures no more, is because 'tis so insipid to them, they don't find that they gain knowledge by it. But the light of Scripture will not break forth at once. Our hearts are naturally so contrary to the things contained therein, we are quite blind when we first take the Bible in hand. But if we follow it diligently, light will begin to break forth by degrees; instruction will come, if we search for it in the Bible as silver and as hidden treasures. A person must be pretty well versed in the Scripture, before one can see their scope and drift, their connection, harmony and agreement. We must break through that opposition that we have to these duties by force and violence. However this way may contradict natural inclination, yet reason itself tells us 'tis the best and most likely way to get spiritual wisdom: for what can be better fitted for our instruction than that which God has prepared for this end?

Fifth. If we would get spiritual and saving knowledge, we must receive all opportunities of hearing. Those that don't think that spiritual knowledge worthy the constant attendance on the preaching the word, can't reasonably expect that God will bestow it on them. If we make little things an excuse for staying at home and not coming to God's house for instruction, God may justly make our (in comparison) little sins a means to provoke him to withhold instruction.

Sixth. We must use ourselves to meditation. I don't say only that we must meditate, but that we must use ourselves to it. Other knowledge is gotten by thought and meditation, yea, and so is spiritual knowledge; that is, although it is given by God's Spirit, 'tis given commonly in times of meditation and by meditation.

When men would discover anything in human arts, they set themselves to study upon it. And can we expect this so much more excellent knowledge without the exercises of thought? When we meditate, then we act as reasonable creatures, then reason acts, then the soul is in exercise. Shall we have souls within us, and let them lie dead without any exercise? We ought to spend much time in meditation; we ought to meditate on God's Word day and night (Psalm 1:2). The law of God should be a constant companion to converse with, lying down and rising up, and wherever we are.

Seventh. We must be often praying to God that he would give us wisdom. James 1:5, "If any lack wisdom, let him ask of God, that giveth to all men liberally, and upbraideth not; and it shall be given him." If we would obtain spiritual knowledge, God is the fountain of all light and all understanding, and the way to come by knowledge from this fountain is often to go to it and wait at it for the flowing of the streams. They that come to God for instruction are most likely to be instructed by him.

Let us be exhorted to hearken to these directions. Knowledge in general is sweet, but above all, spiritual knowledge. Proverbs 3:16–18, "Length of days is in her right hand; and in her left hand riches and honor. Her ways are ways of pleasantness, and all her paths are peace. She is a tree of life to them that lay hold upon her: and happy is every one of [them] that retaineth her."

"DIRECTIONS FOR JUDGING OF PERSONS' EXPERIENCES"

See to it:

That the operation be much upon the will or heart, not on the imagination, nor on the speculative understanding or motions of the mind, though they draw great affections after 'em as the consequence.

That the trouble of mind be reasonable, that the mind be troubled about those things that it has reason to be troubled about; and that the trouble seems mainly to operate in such a manner, with such a kind of trouble and exercise as is reasonable: founded on reasonable, solid consideration; a solid sense and conviction of truth, as of things as they are indeed.

That it be because their state appears terrible on the account of those things, wherein its dreadfulness indeed consists; and that their concern be solid, not operating very much by pangs and sudden passions, freaks and frights, and a capriciousness of mind.

That under their seeming convictions it be sin indeed; that they are convinced of their guilt, in offending and affronting so great a God: One that so hates sin, and is so set against it, to punish it, etc.

That they be convinced both of sins of heart and life: that their pretenses of sense of sin of heart ben't without reflection on their wicked practice; and also that they are not only convinced of sin of practice, but sin of heart. And in both, that what troubles 'em be those things wherein their wretchedness has really chiefly consisted.

That they are convinced of their spiritual sins, consisting in their sinful defects, living without love to God, without accepting Christ, gratitude to him, etc.

That the convictions they have of the insufficiency and vanity of their own doings, ben't only from some sense of wanderings of mind, and other sinful behavior mixed; but from a conviction of the sinful defects of their duties, their not being done from a right principle; and so as having no goodness at all mixed with the bad, but altogether corrupt.

That it is truly conviction of sin that convinces them of the justice of God in their damnation, in rejecting their prayers, disregarding their sorrowful case, and all desires and endeavors after deliverance, etc., and not merely any imagination or pang, and melting of affection through some real or supposed instance of divine goodness.

That they be so convinced of sin as not in the inward thought and habit of their minds to excuse themselves, and impliedly quarrel with God, because of their impotency: for instance, that they don't excuse their slight of Christ, and want of love to him, because they can't esteem and love him.

That they don't evidently themselves look on their convictions [as] great, and ben't taken with their own humiliation.

That which should be chiefly looked at should be *evangelical*. If this be sound, we have no warrant to insist upon it, that there be manifest a remarkable work, purely legal, wherein was nothing of grace. So with regard to convictions and humiliation; only seeing to it that the mind is indeed convinced of these things, and sees 'em, that many divines insisted should be seen, under a purely legal work. And also seeing to it that the convictions there are, seem to be deep and fixed, and to have a powerful governing influence on the temper of the mind, and a very direct respect to practice.

See to it:

That they have not only pretended convictions of sin; but a proper mourning for sin. And also, that sin is burdensome to them, and that their hearts are tender and sensible with respect to it...the object of their care and dread.

That God and divine things are admirable on account of the beauty of their moral perfection.

That there is to be discerned in their sense of the sufficiency of Christ, a sense of that divine, supreme, and spiritual excellency of Christ, wherein this sufficiency fundamentally consists; and that the sight of this excellency is really the foundation of their satisfaction as to his sufficiency.

That their conviction of the truth of divine things be discerned to be truly some way or other primarily built on a sense of their divine excellency.

That their discoveries and illuminations and experiences in general, are not superficial pangs, flashes, imagination, freaks, but solid, substantial, deep, inwrought into the frame and temper of their minds, and discovered to have respect to practice.

That they long after HOLINESS, and that all their experiences increase their longing.

Let 'em be inquired of concerning their disposition and willingness to bear the cross, sell all for Christ, choosing their portion in heaven, etc.

Whether their experience have a respect to PRACTICE in these ways. That their behavior at present seems to be agreeable to such experiences.

Whether it inclines 'em much to think of practice, and more and more for past ill practice.

Makes a disposition to ill practices dreadful.

Makes 'em long after perfect freedom from sin, and after those things wherein *holiness* consists; and by fixed and strong resolutions, attended with fear and jealousy of their own hearts.

Whether, when they tell of their experiences, it is not with such an air that you as it were feel that they expect to be admired and applauded, and won't be disappointed if they fail of discerning in you something of that nature; and shocked and displeased if they discover the contrary.

Inquire whether their joy be truly and properly joy in God and in Christ; joy in divine good; or whether it ben't wholly joy in themselves, joy in their own excellencies or privileges, in their experiences; what God has done for them, or what he has promised he will do for them; and whether they ben't affected with their own discoveries and affections.

TRUE GRACE IS DIVINE (1738)[4]

1 John 4:12
No man hath seen God at anytime. If we love one another, God dwelleth in us, and his love is perfected in us.

The special design of this chapter, seems to be to give some distinguishing marks, whereby the true Spirit may be distinguished from false spirits. And there are three marks here insisted upon by the Apostle. The first, a spirit's confessing or testifying and confirming that great truth of the gospel, that Jesus Christ appeared in the flesh and was crucified, was the Christ, the Son of God. This is mentioned, vv. 2–3: "Hereby know ye the Spirit of God: every spirit that confesseth that Jesus Christ is come in the flesh is of God: and every spirit that confesseth not that Jesus Christ is come in the flesh is not of God: and this is that spirit of antichrist, whereof ye have heard that it should come; and even now already is it in the world." And the same is repeated again in the fifteenth verse.

Another mark given, is that the true Spirit disposes persons to adhere to and follow the doctrine of the apostles, and leads 'em to and confirms 'em in the revelation Christ made by them, as the great rule of their faith and practice. V. 6, "We are of God: he that knoweth God heareth us; he that is not of God heareth not us. Hereby know we the spirit of truth, and the spirit of error."

And the last sign by which a true spirit may be distinguished, is a spirit of love. Vv. 7–8, "Beloved, let us love one another: for love is of God; and every one that loveth is born of God, and knoweth God. He that loveth not knoweth not God; for God is love."

And having there said in the eighth verse that "God is love," he proceeds to show wherein he has especially manifested himself to be so, viz., in sending his only begotten Son {into the world}.

And having spoken of this wonderful love of God to us, he, in the eleventh verse, the verse next before the text, urges it as an argument why we should love one another: "Beloved, if God so loved us, we ought also to love one another." And then come in the words of the text: "No man hath seen God at any time. If we love one another, God dwelleth in us, and his love is perfected in us."

In which words, we may observe two things:

1. A certain quality or principle of heart here spoken [of]: viz., love to the brethren, or love one to another. Love is very much the subject of this epistle written by the apostle John, who was a disciple eminent for love in himself, and eminently beloved. When he speaks of love to the brethren, in the text and other parts of the epistle, he speaks of [it] as but one branch, fruit or exercise of that spirit of Christian love, which is the sum of all Christian grace. He don't mean to exclude love to God: for he speaks of love to God and love to the brethren as proceeding the one from the other, and as both arising from the same principle or fount in the hearts, as you may see in the three last verses.

2. The exceeding dignity and excellency of this principle is set forth, and that which it is set forth by, is its divinity or its relation to God, which is here signified three ways:

(1) In that by our possessing this principle in our hearts, we come to be acquainted with God, or to see him. This is implied in that first clause in the verse, "no man hath seen God at any time," together with what follows; as much as to say, "Though God is invisible in his own nature, and can't be seen with bodily eyes, yet this is a way that we may come to see him, viz., by having a principle of Christian love in us." The Apostle is more express in the

7th and 8th verses: "Beloved, let us love one another: for love is of God; and every one that loveth is born of God, and knoweth God. He that loveth not knoweth not God; for God is love."

(2) In that he that hath this principle in his heart, hath God dwelling in him. This explains how we come to see or know him: by having this principle. For though no man can see God with bodily eyes, yet if he has God dwelling in him, in his heart, he won't need bodily eyes to see him. We need eyes to see things that are at a distance from us, but those things that are in us, we can see only by the reflection of our own minds, without any need of bodily eyes. The Apostle here asserts that he that has love dwelling in his heart, has God dwelling in him, the reason of which appears from what he had said in the 8th verse, viz., "God is love."

(3) The relation of this principle to God is set forth by this: that if we have it, God's "love is perfected in us." This explains what of God dwells in the saints, that love one another, or how God dwells in them: viz., that God's own love, who is love, is perfected or accomplished in them. By the expression, "perfected in us," we are not to understand as we commonly mean by "perfect love" or "perfect holiness," that it is to that degree as to be without any remainder of the contrary; but no more is meant by the expression, than only that God's love is really accomplished or thoroughly effected in us. Many persons go a considerable way towards it. They are so that are not far from the kingdom of God and from true grace, but yet they fail; the work is not finished. The thing is not really brought to pass, or truly and thoroughly effected, however they may make a profession of Christianity and a show of sanctity; as it was with many false Christians, or that had false spirits, in the days of the Apostle. This seems to be the proper meaning of the word "perfected" in the text.

Doctrine

True grace in the hearts of the saints is something divine.

[I.] Things are said to be "divine," in the common use of such an expression, in several senses:

First. Sometimes things are called divine that are in any respect from God. So all the creatures in heaven or earth are said to be divine works, i.e., they are God's works. And all things that come to pass in providence may be called in some sense divine, as they are of a divine ordaining and disposal. But it is not merely thus that grace is a divine thing. And,

Second. Those things are sometimes called divine, in common use of speech, that have any kind of resemblance, or in which is any manifestation, of any divine perfection. So the sun for its brightness and glory which God has given it, which is some faint shadow of the glory of its Author, may be called a divine work. So the heavens over our heads in their excellent contrivance, shining with sun, moon and stars placed in their certain order; and the earth below, with such a wonderful, bountiful variety of plants and flowers and fruits, showing forth the power and wonderful wisdom and goodness and majesty of their Creator, and having a resemblance of and shadow of God's perfections, [may] be called divine. The body of man, which is so curiously {and} fearfully {made}, may be called a piece of divine workmanship. And more especially, the immortal spirit of a man is called something divine, being yet of a much higher nature than any corporeal thing, and having more of a resemblance of God, who is a spirit.

The faculty of reason and understanding is called a divine thing, it being that especially wherein the natural image of God consists. But neither is it merely thus that grace is a divine thing: for it is so in a much a higher sense than any natural thing can be so called.

Third. Sometimes that is said to be divine, which doth actually partake of the divine essence, so as thereby really to be God. So when we speak of God, we often call him the Divine Being. So we say the Son of God and the Holy Ghost are divine persons, i.e., they are persons that are God, and do partake of the divine essence.

Nor is it in this sense, that grace in the hearts of the saints is a divine thing. To be divine, then, is to be divine in an infinitely higher sense than any creature can be. For the creature can't partake of the divine essence, or any part of the divine essence: for the essence of God is not divisible nor communicable.

Fourth. Things are said to be divine, as they are a supernatural communication of something of that good which God himself possesses, and 'tis in this sense that grace is something divine. It is not a communication of God's essence, but it is a communication of that which the Scripture calls God's fullness; as in Ephesians 3:17–19, "that Christ may dwell in your hearts by faith; that ye, being rooted and grounded in love, may be able to comprehend with all the saints what is the breadth, and length, and depth, and height; and to know the love of Christ, which passeth knowledge, that yet might be filled with all the fullness of God." And sometimes it is called the fullness of Christ; John 1:16, "And of his fullness have all we received, and grace for grace." Now by the fullness of anyone, according to the phraseology of the Scriptures, is commonly meant the good anyone possesses, either good of excellency, or beauty, or wealth, or happiness. So the Apostle, in the first [chapter] of Colossians, setting forth the excellency of Christ, and the honor and glory to which God had exalted him, says, v. 19, "For it pleased the Father that in him should all fullness dwell."

So we read in Deuteronomy 33:16 of "the precious things of the earth, and the fullness thereof." So we often read of the earth and the world and the fullness thereof, by which is meant the good that it contains, Psalm 24:1, 50:12, and 1 Corinthians 10:26, 28.

And by Christ's fullness, which we are said to receive of when we receive grace, is [meant] that good that Christ is rich in, as appears by the words preceding in the next verse but one: "and we beheld his glory, as the glory of the only begotten of the Father" [John 1:14].

Grace is a communication or a participation of God's own fullness or of his good, a partaking of his riches, his own treasure, a partaking in some sort of his own bounty and happiness.

'Tis a supernatural communication of God's fullness, of that good that God possesses in himself, and so is divine in a sense beyond other gifts of God. The gifts of common providence, such as the rain, the light of the sun, and the fruits of the earth, are gifts of God as much as if they were immediately sent from heaven. They are as entirely owing to God's bounty, as though they were given by some miracle; but yet they ben't supernatural gifts.

So are persons' natural endowments, and all those moral endowments that fall short of true grace; but neither are these supernatural communications.

So those things that persons obtain by their own industry, they are natural gifts, and received in a natural way. But grace is a divine and supernatural communication.

[II.] This may be better understood, by a distinct consideration of the three following things:

First. There are some things that are natural to the creature, as they properly belong to the created nature, that is essential to one as such a sort of creature. That is said to be natural to a plant, that belongs to the nature and essence of a plant, without which it can't be a plant. So that is not supernatural but natural to man, that belongs to his nature and essence as man, without which he can't be man, but either must not be at all, or must be some other species of beings. So is a faculty of reason and understanding, and so is natural conscience: if a man has reason, he must necessarily have conscience. And so is a principle of self-love, or love of his own happiness: 'tis natural to man to love happiness; it belongs to his essence. To deny a love of happiness, is in effect to deny a faculty of will.

And so angels have some things that are natural to them, that belong to their essence, in that order of being in which they are made, and without which they not only can't have well being, but they can't be at all in that species of creature that now they are. They are things without which they not only can't be good angels or happy angels, but they can't be angels at all, because they belong to their nature and essence as angels.

These things therefore are called natural things, and therefore are not supernatural and divine.

Second. There are other things that are the essences or result of those things that belong to the nature of the creature, that, though they don't belong to their nature or essence, and are not properly parts of their nature, yet are the produce of those things that do.

So in the wisdom and discretion, or the moral habits and commendable disposition, which he gets by the improvement of his natural faculties: these ben't essential to a man's nature, for a man may lose acquired wisdom and other acquired gifts, and not cease to be a man. But yet they are the effects of the improvement of those things that be essential, and parts of his nature, such as his natural faculties of understanding and will. And therefore, neither are such things as these called supernatural.

Third. There is another kind of things in some creatures, that do neither belong to their nature and essence, nor the result of those things that are: and these things are called supernatural or divine. Such a thing is true grace or holiness. It is not anything that belongs to the human nature, or the nature of men as men: for men may be without it, and yet be men. Nor is it any thing that belongs to the essence of angels, for angels may be without it, and yet have the nature and essence of angels; without it, they cease to be good angels, but they don't cease to be angels. Nor is it the result or produce of those things that do belong properly either to the human or angelical nature. 'Tis not wrought out by any improvement of the human or angelical faculties of understanding or will, or any of the natural affections of either. It is not a principle that depends on these as their proper cause or source, but 'tis something entirely of a different kind from anything that is human or angelical, and something entirely above both: for 'tis something immediately from God and of God, a participation of that fullness that is in God, and so is something supernatural and divine.

[III.] Grace is supernatural and divine, on two accounts:

First. On account of the way that 'tis from God immediately, or not by the intervention of natural causes. All natural effects are from God, but yet many things are from him by the mediation of natural causes, and are produced according to laws of nature or by the instrumentality of the laws of nature, and therefore are called natural effects. Such is the rain and the growing of the corn which God produces by improvement of natural causes. And there are other things that man produces by the improvement or mediation of nature, that is by the improvement of his own faculties and natural instruments that yield to his command according to laws of nature. They therefore are not supernatural effects. But grace is not thus produced, but is produced by God immediately according to his arbitrary pleasure.

Second. Grace is a thing supernatural and divine, not only in the way it is from God, but in that 'tis a participation of God. 'Tis not only divine because of the way it is produced, but also from the nature of the thing produced, in that it is rather a communication than a production. 'Tis a participation of God, for where grace dwells, there God dwells.

And so, grace is supernatural, as the nature of grace is itself above the nature of creature, above the human nature and above the angelical and above all, but only the nature of God.

In this respect, the grace or holiness in the heart is divine and supernatural in a higher sense than miracles, above corporeal things or the work of the first creation itself. Creation and miracles are supernatural in the former sense mentioned, that they are produced without the intervention of natural causes. But in this sense they are not supernatural, that the effect produced is nothing above the nature of the creature. The way of producing is supernatural, but the effect produced is not supernatural. As when Christ opened the eyes of the body: there is nothing in the nature of bodily sight beyond created nature, as there is in the grace that [is] in the heart [Mark 10].

That grace is divine in this sense—viz., as it is a participation of God himself—is manifest by the text, where we are taught that he that has it in his heart, therein has God dwelling in him, who is love; and that God's own love, that love of God which is God, is effected or brought to pass in him, in that a man, by seeing this, may see God himself. The same is often asserted by this Apostle, as ch. 3, v. 24: "He that keepeth his commands dwelleth in him, and he in him"; and so vv. 15–16 of the context: "he that dwelleth in love dwelleth in God, and God in him." The same is manifest by John 17:21, "That they all may be one; as thou, Father, art in me, and I in thee, that they also may be one in us: that the world may believe that thou hast sent me." So Christ is said to be in believers, Romans 8:10.

The same is manifest by our being called the temples of God, in our having grace in our hearts. 2 Corinthians 6:16, "for ye are the temples of the living God, as God hath said I will dwell in them, and walk in them; and I will be their God, and they shall be my people."

'Tis manifest also by our being said to have fellowship with the Father and with his Son Jesus Christ, in our having grace in our hearts, 1 John 1:3.

And so by our being said to partake of God's {and} Christ's fullness in our having grace in our hearts, in the places that have been already mentioned; and also by that high expression of the Apostle, whereby we are said to be made partakers of the divine nature by our being made partakers of grace, 2 Peter 1:4.

And so by its being said that we are made partakers of God's holiness—Hebrews 12:10, "For they verily for a few days chastened us after their own pleasure; but he for our profit, that we might be partakers of his holiness"—and of God's beauty. Ezekiel 16:14, "And thy renown went forth among the heathen for thy beauty: for it was perfect through comeliness."

And so in its being asserted that our love is a participation of God's love, as 'tis in the text; and also of Christ's love, as John 17:26. "And I have declared unto them thy name, and will declare it: that the love wherewith thou hast loved me may be in them, and I in them."

And so in its being asserted that the joy that the saints have in the exercises of grace, is a participation of Christ's joy. John 17:13, "And now come I to thee; and these things I speak in the world, that they might have my joy fulfilled in themselves."

And so the Psalmist says, that in God's light we shall see light, and that the saints have pleasure in partaking of the river of God's pleasures. 'Tis not of God's river of pleasures. Psalm 36:8–9, "They shall be abundantly satisfied with the fatness of thy house; and thou shalt make them drink of the river of thy pleasures. For with thee is the fountain of life: in thy light shall we see light."

And so when grace comes to be perfected in glory, that is called a partaking of Christ's glory, as you may see, John 17:22. "And the glory which thou gavest me I have given them; that they may be one, even as we are one."

The same appears by the distinction the Scripture makes between those that are gracious, and others. He calls one natural men, and the other spiritual.

He calls one natural, because they have no other than natural principles; which supposes the other to be supernatural, or something above nature.

To the same purpose are the names by which the Scripture distinguishes grace from other principles: the one flesh, and the other spiritual. Other principles are called flesh.

So that grace or holiness in the creature is undoubtedly something divine and supernatural, wherever it is. It was so in our first parents in their state of innocency: though they had it in their first creation, it was nothing properly belonging to their nature, but something of God, above their nature. And so it is in the glorious angels: the holiness they have, is supernatural to them.

Holiness, wherever it is, is supernatural. It is super-human, or super-angelical. It is something above all created nature. 'Tis natural to none but God. 'Tis something higher than the whole universe, yea higher than heaven itself. It is both super[-terrestr]ial and super-celestial, being something divine, something of God who is infinitely above both heaven and earth.

The creature that has true grace and holiness in his heart, has something infinitely above himself in him. He is gloriously honored and dignified by it, for he dwells in God, and God in him.

Application

I. Hence we learn how God is the excellency and happiness and glory of all creatures, i.e., of all creatures that have any excellency happiness or glory. In which sense the apostle John says, John 1:9, "This is the true Light, that lighteth every man that cometh into the world"; i.e., every one that ever is enlightened. Holiness is the beauty, brightness and blessedness of angels and men; they have no excellency nor any happiness but what consists in this. And therefore, seeing that this is something of God, a communication of the divine fullness, a kind of participation of the divine nature, this shows that God is all the good of the creature. The creature has nothing that is truly good, but it is something of God. They have nothing, no beauty and no happiness, contained in their own nature simply considered, nothing of themselves, but all infinitely above themselves, all in God.

Every creature, every man and angel, is wholly empty in himself, or in his own nature, not only fallen men but unfallen man and unfallen angels, and their emptiness can be filled no other way but by partaking of the fullness of God that has been spoken of. 'Tis he that filleth all in all, Ephesians 1:23. Christ fills the capacity of the angels as well as men; he fills all things in heaven as well as on earth. For this end he descended to the earth, that he might fill our emptiness here; and he ascended into heaven, that he might fill them. Ephesians 4:10, "He that descended is the same also that ascended up far above all heavens, that he might fill all things." "It pleased the Father that in him should all fullness dwell," Colossians 1:19.

If the creature has nothing but its own nature, it is poor and naked and empty, having no beauty, no goodness, no happiness, but is wholly and universally corrupt and miserable and utterly wretched. As may appear more fully by the next Inference, viz.:

II. If it be as we have heard, hence we may learn how the nature of man came to be so corrupt. This is a point that has exercised and puzzled the minds of many, but we need not be so much at a loss if we do but consider that all the goodness the creature has is something above its own nature, being something of God, and that created nature in itself is wholly ruined without a participation of God, who is all its goodness and all its blessedness.

Man, in his first estate, had this supernatural divine principle, even a principle of holiness and divine love, by the indwelling of God in him by his Spirit. But when man rebelled against God, the Spirit of God justly left him: for it was not meet that the Spirit of God should continue to dwell in the heart of one that was not at peace with God. And God being gone out of his heart, it follows from what has been said, that all that was good left his heart. Divine love was extinct, and man was left wholly under the dominion of mere nature and natural principles, or those principles that are essential to his nature, such as self-love, or love to his own pleasure, his own honor, etc., without any divine principle to regulate this love. So that this self-love, of itself, necessarily carried out to what was conceived to be for his own pleasure, without any prudence or regulation from any love to God. And man necessarily loved and pursued whatever was for his {pleasure}, whether it was agreeable or disagreeable {to God's honor}: for that which is agreeable or disagreeable to God's honor, are indifferent to one that has no love to God. Hence he was violently driven to seek his own honor in many things, contrary to the glory of God, and so he became proud, pleasure-[seeking], contrary {and} sensual.

Love of God ceased, the love of the world ensued.

And this being contrary to God's will and His nature, his nature and will stands in his way of his pursuit. Whence arises enmity. And so, the source [of] all the lusts may easily and clearly be explained.

There is no need of any other positive cause, but only the human nature left to itself without [divine grace]. Created nature of itself will necessarily be corrupt without something divine added to it. And when this divine thing is removed, [corruption ensues]. Hence corruption is called "flesh," that is, mere human nature. And so, corrupt man is called "natural man."

And hence that, 1 Peter 4:6, "judged according to men in the flesh, [but] live according to God in the spirit."

III. Hence we may learn the reasonableness of the doctrine of immediate, efficacious and arbitrary infusion of special grace. There are many that deny, [and] hold that though God indeed assists those that seek, yet [it] is not with an arbitrary nor efficacious assistance, because [God is] obliged. [Grace, they say, is not] efficacious, {otherwise it will} be hardened in its effect, when given to the utmost that God is ever wont to give it.

But how reasonable is it to suppose that, however [they] receive things and lesser gifts {through God's assistance}, that they would reserve this, which is so much above the nature of the creature, {and} is as it were something of himself? How reasonable is it to suppose that he will reserve this?

And if this be denied, it will follow that no man has reason to thank God for his being distinguished with this gift. If we obtain the saving grace of God by virtue of an obligation that God has laid himself under to us, in common with the rest of mankind, his grace ceases to be of the nature of a present. As excellent and glorious a thing as it is, it is nothing that God presents us with. The notion of a present, is something given in token of particular kindness to the person to whom it is given. But if this be the case, there is no kindness to him that actually receives God's grace, but what is common to the whole race of mankind. 'Tis no token of any particular benevolence to him. The kindness is in coming under obligation on such conditions, if anywhere, but the kindness is to all equally. There is no more of any gift or present in the case to one that actually has it, than to an ungodly, damned wretch. But neither will this objection be any proper kindness according to the notion of them that generally hold such doctrine: for the opinion that Arminians hold, that God has obliged himself by absolute promises to what an unconverted man can do, to bestow his saving grace upon them, is from that, that it would be hard in God to refuse it, man having fallen not by his own act; to call upon persons to seek, and at the same time reserving it in his arbitrary pleasure whether to bestow it: which is the same thing as to say that God is obliged so to promise, and if he is obliged, there is no kindness in it. So that love is no kindness by their scheme, either in promising or bestowing. And so what becomes of all the riches and glory of the grace and love and kindness of God, so much celebrated in his Word, in bestowing this unspeakable mercy on men? And what cause is there for all those praises and hallelujahs that the church is represented as singing to God for redeeming them by his blood "out of every tongue, and people, and nation," and making them kings and priests unto God [Rev 5:9–10]?

✌

EXCERPT FROM "TREATISE ON GRACE" (1739–42)

Chapter I: That Common and Saving Grace Differ, Not Only in Degree, but in Nature and Kind

Such phrases as "common grace," and "special" or "saving grace," may be understood as signifying either diverse kinds of influence of God's Spirit on the hearts of men, or diverse fruits and effects of that influence. The Spirit of God is supposed sometimes to have some influence upon the minds of men that are not true Christians;

and that those dispositions, frames and exercises of their minds that are of a good tendency, but are common to them with the saints, are in some respect owing to some influence or assistance of God's Spirit. But as there are some things in the hearts of true Christians that are peculiar to them, and that are more excellent than anything that is to be found in others, so it is supposed that there is an operation of the Spirit of God different, and that the value which distinguishes them is owing to a higher influence and assistance than the virtues of others. So that sometimes the phrase, *common grace*, is used to signify that kind of action or influence of the Spirit of God, to which are owing those religious or moral attainments that are common to both saints and sinners, and so signifies as much as common assistance; and sometimes those moral or religious attainments themselves that are the fruits of this assistance, are intended. So likewise the phrase, *special* or *saving* grace, is sometimes used to signify that peculiar kind or degree of operation or influence of God's Spirit, whence saving actions and attainments do arise in the godly, or, which is the same thing, special and saving assistance; or else to signify that distinguishing saving virtue itself, which is the fruit of this assistance. These phrases are more frequently understood in the latter sense, viz., not for common and special assistance, but for common and special, or saving virtue, which is the fruit of that assistance: and so I would be understood by these phrases in this discourse.

And that special or saving grace in this sense is not only different from common grace in degree, but entirely diverse in nature and kind; and that natural men not only have not a sufficient degree of virtue to be saints, but that they have no degree of that grace that is in godly men, is what I have now to show.

1. This is evident by what Christ says in John 3:6, where Christ, speaking of regeneration, says, "That which is born of the flesh is flesh; and that which is born of the Spirit is spirit." Now, whatever Christ intends by the terms *flesh* and *spirit* in the words, yet this much is manifested and undeniable, that Christ here intends to show Nicodemus the necessity of a new birth, or another birth than his natural birth; and that, from this argument, that a man that has been the subject only of the first birth, has nothing of that in his heart which he must have in order to enter into the kingdom. He has

nothing at all of that which Christ calls spirit, whatever that be. All that a man [has] that has been the subject only of a natural birth don't go beyond that which Christ calls flesh: for however it may be refined and exalted, yet it cannot be raised above flesh. 'Tis plain, that by flesh and spirit, Christ here intends two things entirely different in nature, which cannot be one from the other. A man cannot have anything of a nature superior to flesh that is not born again, and therefore we must be "born again." That by flesh and spirit are intended certain moral principles, natures, or qualities, entirely different and opposite in their nature one to another, is manifest from other texts, as particularly Galatians 5:17, "For the flesh lusteth against the Spirit, and the Spirit against the flesh: and they are contrary the one to the other: so that ye cannot do the things which ye would"; v. 19, "Now the works of the flesh are manifest, which are these; adultery, fornication," etc.; v. 22, "But the fruit of the Spirit is love, joy, peace," etc.; and by Galatians 6:8, "For he that soweth to the flesh shall of the flesh reap corruption; but he that soweth to the Spirit shall of the Spirit reap life everlasting." Romans 8:6–9, "For to be carnally minded is death; but to be spiritually minded is life and peace. Because the carnal mind is enmity against God: for it is not subject to the law of God, neither indeed can be. So then they that are in the flesh cannot please God." 1 Corinthians 3:1, "And I, brethren, could not speak unto you as unto spiritual, but as unto carnal, even as unto babes in Christ." So that it is manifest by this, that men that have been the subjects only of the first birth, have no degree of that moral principle or quality that those that are new born have, whereby they have a title to the kingdom of heaven. This principle or quality comes out then no otherwise than by birth; and the birth that it must come by is not, cannot be, the first birth, but it must be a new birth. If men that have no title to the kingdom of heaven, could have something of the Spirit, as well as flesh, then Christ's argument would be false. It is plain, by Christ's reasoning, that those that are not in a state of salvation, cannot have these two opposite principles in their hearts together, some flesh and some spirit, lusting one against the other as the godly have; but that they have flesh only.

2. That the only principle in those that are savingly converted, whence gracious acts flow (which in the language of Scripture is

called the Spirit, and set in opposition to the flesh), is that which others not only have not a sufficient degree of, but have nothing at all of, is further manifest, because the Scripture asserts both: negatively, that those that have not the Spirit are not Christ's—Romans 8:9, "But ye are not in the flesh, but in the Spirit, if so be that the Spirit of God dwell in you. Now if any man have not the Spirit of Christ, he is none of his"—and also [positively], that those that have the Spirit are his—1 John 3:24, "Hereby we know that he abideth in us, by the Spirit which he hath given us." And our having the Spirit of God dwelling in our hearts is mentioned as a certain sign that persons are entitled to heaven, and is called the "earnest" of the future inheritance, 2 Corinthians 1:22 and 5:5, Ephesians 1:14; which it would not be if others that had no title to the inheritance might have some of it dwelling in them.

Yea, that those that are not true saints have nothing of the Spirit, no part nor portion of it, is still more evident, because not only a having any particular measure of the Spirit, but a being *of the Spirit* is given as a sure sign of being in Christ. 1 John 4:13, "Hereby know we that we dwell in him, and he in us, because he hath given us *of his Spirit*." If those that are not true saints have any degree of that spiritual principle, then though they have not so much, yet they have *of it*, and so that would be no sign that a person is in Christ. If those that have not a saving interest in Christ have nothing of the Spirit, then they have nothing; no degree of those graces that are the fruits of the Spirit, mentioned in Galatians 5:22–23, "But the fruit of the Spirit is love, joy, peace, longsuffering, gentleness, goodness, faith, meekness, temperance." Those fruits are here mentioned with that very design, that we may know whether we have the Spirit or no.

3. Those that are not true saints, and in a state of salvation, not only have not so much of that holy nature and divine principle that is in the hearts of the saints; but they do not partake of it, because a being "partakers of the divine nature" is spoken of as the peculiar privilege of true saints, 2 Peter 1:4. It is evident that it is the true saints that the Apostle is there speaking of. The words in this verse with the foregoing are these: "According as his divine power hath given to us all things that pertain to life and godliness, through the knowledge of him that hath called us to glory and virtue: whereby are

given to us exceeding great and precious promises: that by these ye might be partakers of the divine nature, having escaped the corruption that is in the world through lust." The "divine nature" and "lust" are evidently here spoken of as two opposite principles in man. Those that are in the world, and that are the men of the world, have only the latter principle; but to be partakers of the divine nature is spoken of as peculiar to them that are distinguished and separated from the world, by the free and sovereign grace of God giving them all things that pertain to life and godliness, giving the knowledge of him and calling them to glory and virtue, and giving them the exceeding great and precious promises of the gospel, and that have escaped the corruption of the world of wicked men. And a being partakers of the divine nature is spoken of, not only as peculiar to the saints, but as one of the highest privileges of the saints.

4. That those that have not a saving interest in Christ have no degree of that relish and sense of spiritual things or things of the Spirit, of their divine truth and excellency, which a true saint has, is evident by 1 Corinthians 2:14, "The natural man receiveth not the things of the Spirit of God: for they are foolishness unto him: neither can he know them, because they are spiritually discerned." A "natural man" is here set in opposition to a "spiritual" one, or one that has the Spirit, as appears by the foregoing and following verses. Such we have shown already the Scripture declares all true saints to be, and no other. Therefore by natural men are meant those that have not the Spirit of Christ and are none of his, and are the subjects of no other than the natural birth. But here we are plainly taught that a natural man is perfectly destitute of any sense, perception, or discerning of those things of the Spirit, by the words, he neither does nor "can know them," or "discern" them. So far from this, they are "foolishness unto him": he is a perfect stranger, so that he does not know what the talk of such things means; they are words without a meaning to him; he knows nothing of the matter any more than a blind man of colors.

Hence it will follow, that the sense of things of religion that a natural man has, is not only not to the same degree, but nothing of the same nature with that which a true saint has. And besides, if a natural person has the fruit of the Spirit, which is of the same kind with what a spiritual person has, then he experiences within himself the things of the Spirit of God: and how then can he be said to be such a stranger to them, and have no perception or discerning of them?

The reason why natural men have no knowledge of spiritual things, is because they have nothing of the Spirit of God dwelling in them. This is evident by the context: for there we are told that it is by the Spirit that these things are taught (vv. 10–12); and godly persons in the next verse are called spiritual, because they have the Spirit dwelling in them. Hereby the sense again is confirmed, for natural men are in no degree spiritual; they have only nature and no Spirit. If they had anything of the Spirit, though not in so great a degree as the godly, yet they would be taught spiritual things, or things of the Spirit, in proportion to the measure of the Spirit that they had. The Spirit that searcheth all things would teach them in some measure. There would not be so great a difference, that the one could perceive nothing of them and that they should be foolishness to them, while to the other they appear divinely and remarkably wise and excellent, as they are spoken of in the context (vv. 6–9); and as such the Apostle spoke here of discerning them.

The reason why natural men have no knowledge or perception of spiritual things, is because they have none of the anointing spoken of, 1 John 2:27, "The anointing which ye have received of him abideth in you, and you need not that any man teach you." This anointing is evidently spoken of here, as a thing peculiar to true saints. Ungodly men never had any degree of that holy oil poured upon them, and therefore have no discerning of spiritual things. Therefore none of that sense that natural men have of things of religion, is of the same nature with what the godly have; but to these they are totally blind. Therefore in conversion the eyes of the blind are opened. The world is wholly unacquainted with the Spirit of God, as appears by John 14:17, where we read about "the Spirit of truth; whom the world cannot receive, because it knoweth him not."

5. Those that go farthest in religion that are not true saints and in a state of salvation, have no charity, as is plainly implied in the beginning of the thirteenth chapter of the first epistle to the Corinthians. Therefore they have no degree of that kind of grace, disposition, or affection, that is so called. So Christ elsewhere reproves

the Pharisees, those high pretenders to religion among the Jews, that they had not the love of God in them (John 5:42).

6. That those that are not true saints have no degree of that grace that the saints have is evident, because they have no communion or fellowship with Christ. If those that are not true saints partake of any of that Spirit, those holy inclinations and affections, and gracious acts of soul that the godly have from the indwelling of the Spirit of Christ, then they would have communion with Christ. The communion of saints with Christ does certainly very much consist in that receiving of his fullness and partaking of his grace, spoken of, John 1:16, "Of his fullness have all we received, and grace for grace"; and in partaking of that Spirit which God gives not by measure unto him. Partaking of Christ's holiness and grace, his nature, inclinations, tendencies, love and desires, comforts and delights, must be to have communion with Christ. Yea, a believer's communion with the Father and the Son does mainly consist in his partaking of the Holy Ghost, as appears by 2 Corinthians 13:14, "The grace of the Lord Jesus Christ, and the love of God, and the *communion* of the Holy Ghost."

But that unbelievers have no fellowship or communion with Christ appears, (1) because they are not united to Christ. They are not in Christ. For the Scripture is very plain and evident in this, that those that are in Christ are actually in a state of salvation, and are justified, sanctified, accepted of Christ, and shall be saved. Philippians 3:8–9, "Yea doubtless, and I count all things but loss for the excellency of the knowledge of Christ Jesus my Lord: for whom I have suffered the loss of all things, and do count them but dung, that I may win Christ, and be found *in him*." 2 Corinthians 5:17, "If any man be *in Christ*, he is a new creature: old things are passed away; behold, all things are become new." 1 John 2:5, "But whoso keepeth his word, in him verily is the love of God perfected: hereby know we that we are *in him*"; and 3:24, "He that keepeth his commandments dwelleth in him, and he in him. And hereby we know that he abideth in us, by the Spirit which he hath given us." But those that are not in Christ, and are not united to him, can have no degree of communion with him; for there is no communion without union. The members can have no communion with the head or participation of its life and health unless they are united to it. The branch must be united with the vine, otherwise there can be no communication from the vine to it, nor any partaking of any degree of its sap, or life, or influence. So without the union of the wife to the husband, she can have no communion in his goods. (2) The Scripture does more directly teach that it is only true saints that have communion with Christ: as particularly this is most evidently spoken of as what belongs to the saints, and to them only, in 1 John 1:3, together with vv. 6–7, "That which we have seen and heard declare we unto you, that ye also may have fellowship with us: and truly our fellowship is with the Father, and with his Son Jesus Christ." Verses 6–7, "If we say that we have fellowship with him, and walk in darkness, we lie, and do not the truth: but if we walk in the light, as he is in the light, we have fellowship one with another, and the blood of Jesus Christ his Son cleanseth us from all sin." Also in 1 Cor. 1:9, "God is faithful, by whom ye were called unto the fellowship of his Son Christ Jesus our Lord."

7. The Scripture speaks of the actual being of a truly holy and gracious principle in the heart, as inconsistent with a man's being a sinner or a wicked man. 1 John 3:9, "Whosoever is born of God doth not commit sin; for his seed remaineth in him: and he cannot sin, because he is born of God." Here it is needless to dispute what is intended by this seed, whether it be a principle of true virtue and a holy nature in the soul, or whether it be the word of God as the cause of that virtue. For let us understand it in either sense, it comes to much the same thing in the present argument; for if by the seed is meant the word of God, yet when it is spoken of as abiding in him that is born again, it must be intended, with respect to its effect, as a holy principle in his heart: for the word of God does not abide in one that is born again more than another, any other way than in its effect. The word of God abides in the heart of a regenerate person as a holy seed, a divine principle there, though it may be but as a seed, a small thing. The seed is a very small part of the plant, and is its first principle. It may be in the heart as a grain of mustard seed, may be hid, and seem to be in a great measure buried in the earth. But yet it is inconsistent with wickedness. The smallest degrees and first principles of a divine and holy nature and disposition are inconsistent with a state of sin; whence it is said, "he cannot sin." There is no need here of a critical inquiry into the import of that expression; for doubtless so much

at least is implied through this, "his seed being in him" [1 John 3:9], as is inconsistent with his being a sinner or a wicked man. So that this heavenly plant of true holiness cannot be in the heart of a sinner, no, not so much as in its first principle.

8. This is confirmed by the things that conversion is represented by in the Scriptures, particularly its being represented as a work of creation. When God creates, he does not merely establish and perfect the things which were made before, but makes wholly and immediately something entirely new, either out of nothing, or out of that which was perfectly void of any such nature, as when he made man of the dust of the earth. "The things that are seen are not made of things that do appear" [Heb 11:3]. Saving grace in man is said to be the new man or a new creature, and corrupt nature the old man. If that nature that is in the heart of a godly man be not different in its nature and kind from all that went before, then the man might possibly have had the same things a year before, and from time to time from the beginning of his life, but only not quite to the same degree. And how then is grace in him, the new man or the new creature?

Again, conversion is often compared to a resurrection. Wicked men are said to be dead, but when they are converted they are represented as being by God's mighty and effectual power raised from the dead. Now there is no medium between being dead and alive. He that is dead has no degree of life; he that has the least degree of life in him is alive. When a man is raised from the dead, life is not only in a greater degree, but it is all new.

The same is manifest by conversion being represented as a new birth or as regeneration. Generation is not only perfecting what is old, but 'tis a begetting something new. The nature and life that is then received has then its beginning: it receives its first principles.

Again, conversion in Scripture is represented as an opening of the eyes of the blind. In such a work those have light given them that were totally destitute of it before. So in conversion, stones are said to be raised up children to Abraham [Matt 3:9, Luke 3:8]: while stones, they are altogether destitute of all those qualities that afterwards render them the living children of Abraham, and not only had them not in so great a degree. Agreeably to this, conversion is said to be a taking away a heart of stone and a giving a heart of flesh [Ezek 11:19,

36:26]. The man while unconverted has a heart of stone which has no degree of that life and sense that the heart of flesh has, because it yet remains a stone, than which nothing is further from life and sense.

Inference 1. From what has been said, I would observe that it must needs be that conversion is wrought at once. That knowledge, that reformation and conviction that is preparatory to conversion may be gradual, and the work of grace after conversion may be gradually carried on; yet that work of grace upon the soul whereby a person is brought out of a state of total corruption and depravity into a state of grace, to an interest in Christ, and to be actually a child of God, is in a moment.

It must needs be the consequence: for if that grace or virtue that a person has when he is brought into a state of grace be entirely different in nature and kind from all that went before, then it will follow that the last instant before a person is actually a child of God and in a state of grace, a person has not the least degree of any real goodness, and of that true virtue that is in a child of God.

Those things by which conversion is represented in Scripture hold forth the same thing. In creation, something is brought out of nothing in an instant. God speaks and it is done; he commands and it stands fast. When the dead are raised, it is done in a moment. Thus when Christ called Lazarus out of his grave, it was not a gradual work. He said, "Lazarus, come forth" [John 11:43], and there went life with the call. He heard his voice and lived. So Christ, John 5:25, "Verily, verily, I say unto you, The hour is coming, and now is, when the dead shall hear the voice of the Son of God: and they that hear shall live"; which words must be understood of the work of conversion. In creation, being is called out of nothing and instantly obeys the call, and in the resurrection the dead are called into life: as soon as the call is given the dead obey.

By reason of this instantaneousness of the work of conversion, one of the names under which conversion is frequently spoken of in Scripture, is *calling*. Romans 8:28–30, "And we know that all things work together for good to them that love God, to them who are the called according to his purpose. For whom he did foreknow, he also did predestinate to be conformed to the image of his Son, that he might be the firstborn among many brethren. Moreover whom he did predestinate, them he also called: and whom he called, them he also justified: and whom he justified, them he also glorified." Acts 2:37–39, "Now when they heard this, they were pricked in their heart, and said unto Peter and to the rest of the apostles, Men and brethren what shall we do? Then Peter said unto them, Repent, and be baptized every one of you in the name of Jesus Christ for the remission of sins, and ye shall receive the gift of the Holy Ghost. For the promise is unto you, and to your children, and to all that are afar off, even as many as the Lord our God shall call." Hebrews 9:15 (last clause), "That they which are called might receive the promise of the eternal inheritance." 1 Thessalonians 5:23–24, "And the very God of peace sanctify you wholly....Faithful is he that calleth you, who also will do it." Nothing else can be meant in those places by calling than what Christ does in a sinner's saving conversion. By which it seems evident that it is done at once and not gradually. Whereby Christ shows his great power; he does but speak the powerful word and it is done, he does but call and the heart of the sinner immediately comes. It seems to be symbolized by Christ's calling his disciples, and their immediately following him. So when he called Peter, and Andrew, James and John, they were minding other things; but at his call they immediately left all and followed him. Matthew 4:18–22—Peter and Andrew were "casting a net into the sea," and Christ says to them as he passed by, "Follow me"; and it is said, "they straightway left their nets, and followed him." So James and John were in the ship with Zebedee their father "mending their nets; and he called them. And immediately they left the ship and their father, and followed him" [Matt 4:21–22]. So when Matthew was called, Matthew 9:9, "And as Jesus passed forth from thence, he saw a man, named Matthew, sitting at the receipt of custom: and he saith unto him, Follow me. And he arose, and followed him." Now whether they were then converted or not, yet doubtless Christ in thus calling his first disciples to a visible following of him, represents to us the manner in which he would call men to be truly his disciples and spiritually to follow him in all ages. There is something immediately and instantaneously put into their hearts at that call that they had nothing of before, that effectually disposes them to follow.

It is very manifest that almost all the miracles of Christ that he wrought when on earth were types of his great work of converting sinners; and the manner of his working those miracles holds forth the instantaneousness of the work of conversion. Thus when he healed the leper, which represented his healing us of our spiritual leprosy, "he put forth his hand, and touched him, and said, I will; be thou clean. And immediately his leprosy was cleansed," Matthew 8:3, Mark 1:42, Luke 5:13. And so, in opening the eyes of the blind, which represents his opening the eyes of our blind souls, Matthew 20:30–34, he "touched their eyes: and immediately their eyes received sight, and they followed him." So Mark 10:52, Luke 18:43. So when he healed the sick, which represents his healing our spiritual diseases, or conversion, it was done at once. Thus when he healed Simon's wife's mother, Mark 1:31, he "took her by the hand, and lifted her up; and immediately the fever left her, and she ministered unto them." So when the woman which had the issue of blood touched the hem of Christ's garment, immediately the issue of blood stanched, Luke 8:44. So the woman that was bowed together with the spirit of infirmity: when Christ "laid his hands upon her, immediately she was made straight, and glorified God," Luke 13:12–13; which represents that action on the soul whereby he gives an upright heart, and sets the soul at liberty from its bondage to glorify him. So the man at the pool of Bethesda, when Christ bade him rise, take up his bed and walk, was immediately made whole (John 5:8–9). After the same manner Christ cast out devils, which represents his dispossessing the devil of our souls in conversion; and so he settled the winds and waves, representing his subduing in conversion the heart of the wicked, which is like the troubled sea when it cannot rest; and so he raised the dead, which represented his raising dead souls.

The same is confirmed by those things which conversion is compared to in Scripture. It is often compared to a resurrection. Natural men (as was said before) are said to be dead, and to be raised, when they are converted by God's mighty effectual power, from the dead. Now, there is no medium between being dead and alive; he that is dead has no degree of life in him, he that has the least degree of life in him is alive. When a man is raised from the dead, life is not only in a greater degree in him than it was before, but it is all new. The

373

work of conversion seems to be compared to a raising the dead to life, in this very thing, even its instantaneousness, or its being done as it were at a word's speaking. As in John 5:25 (before quoted), "Verily, verily, I say unto you, The hour is coming, and now is, when the dead shall hear the voice of the Son of God: and they that hear shall live." He speaks here of a work of conversion, as appears by the preceding verse; and by the word themselves, which speak of the time of this raising the dead, not only as to come hereafter, but as what was already come. This shows conversion to be an immediate instantaneous work, like to the change made on Lazarus when Christ called him from the grave: there went life with the call, and Lazarus was immediately alive. Immediately before the call sinners are dead or wholly destitute of life, as appears by the expression, "*the dead* shall hear the voice," and immediately after the call they are alive; yea, there goes life with the word, as is evident, not only because it is said they shall live, but also because it is said, they shall hear his voice. The first moment they have any life is the moment when Christ calls, and as soon as they are called; which further appears by what was observed before, even that a being called and converted are spoken of in Scripture as the same thing.

The same is confirmed (as observed before) from conversion being compared to a work of creation, which is a work wherein something is made either out of nothing or out of that having no degree of the same kind of qualities and principles, as when God made man of the dust of the earth. Thus it is said, "If any man be in Christ, he is a new creature" [2 Cor 5:17]; which obviously implies that he is an exceeding diverse kind of creature from what he was before he was in Christ, that the principle or qualities that he has by which he is a Christian, are entirely new, and what there was nothing of, before he was in Christ.

Inf. 2. Hence we may learn that it is impossible for men to convert themselves by their own strength and industry, with only a concurring assistance helping in the exercise of their natural abilities and principles of the soul, and securing their improvement. For what is gained after this manner is a gradual acquisition, and not something instantaneously begotten, and of an entirely different nature, and wholly of a separate kind, from all that was in the nature of the person the moment before. All that men can do by their own strength and industry is only gradually to increase and improve and new-model and direct qualities, principles and perfections of nature that they have already. And that is evident, because a man in the exercise and improvement of the strength and principles of his own nature has nothing but the qualities, powers and perfections that are already in his nature to work with, and nothing but them to work upon; and therefore 'tis impossible that by this only, anything further should be brought to pass, than only a new modification of what is already in the nature of the soul. That which is only by an improvement of natural qualities, principles and perfections—let these things be improved never so much and never so industriously, and never so long—they'll still be no more than an improvement of those natural qualities, principles and perfections; and therefore not anything of an essentially distinct and superior nature and kind.

"'Tis impossible" (as Dr. Clarke observes) "that any effect should have any perfection, that was not in the cause: for if it had, then that perfection would be caused by nothing."[5] 'Tis therefore utterly impossible that men's natural perfections and qualities in that exercise, and however assisted in that exercise, should produce in the soul a principle or perfection of a nature entirely different from all of them, or any manner of improvement or modification of them.

The qualities and principles of natural bodies, such as figure or motion, can never produce anything beyond themselves. If infinite comprehensions and divisions be eternally made, the things must still be eternally the same, and all their possible effects can never be anything but repetitions of the same. Nothing can be produced by only those qualities of figure and motion, beyond figure and motion: and so nothing can be produced in the soul by only its internal principles, beyond these principles or qualities, or new improvements and modifications of them. And if we suppose a concurring assistance to enable to a more full and perfect exercise of those natural principles and qualities, unless the assistance or influence actually produces something beyond the exercise of internal principle: still, it is the same thing. Nothing will be produced but only an improvement and new modification of those principles that are exercised. Therefore it follows that saving grace in the heart, can't be produced in man by mere exercise of what perfections he has in him already, though never so much assisted by moral suasion, and never so much assisted in the exercise of his natural principles, unless there be something more than all this, viz., an immediate infusion or operation of the Divine Being upon the soul. Grace must be the immediate work of God, and properly a production of his almighty power on the soul.

EXCERPT FROM "MISCELLANIES" NO. 790, "SIGNS OF GODLINESS" (C. 1740)

790. SIGNS OF GODLINESS. *Question.* What are the best signs of godliness—those by which persons may try themselves with the greatest safety and certainty; and therefore, those that ministers ought chiefly to insist upon with their hearers?

Answer. This matter is most properly determined by the Word of God, the searcher of hearts, the being to whom it belongs to appoint the terms of salvation and acceptance with himself, and the being who is finally to [be] our Judge.

The holy Scriptures have not left this matter in the dark or doubtful, but have plainly answered this question, and han't only told us what are good evidences of a good estate, but have also very plainly [pointed] out to us those that are chiefly to be looked at, and most safely to be depended on. Concerning good works as the proper evidences of godliness, see various parts of Dr. Manton's Exposition on James.[6]

And by what the Scriptures have taught us in this matter, we must determine that good fruits, or good works and keeping Christ's commandments, are the evidences by which we are chiefly and most safely and surely to be determined, not only concerning the godliness of others, but also concerning our own godliness. Christ, when giving his dying counsel to his disciples, and when giving them directions for their own comfort—John 14:15–16, "If ye love me, keep my commandments. And I will pray the Father, and he will give you another Comforter, that he may abide with you forever"; and v. 21, "He that hath my commandments, and keepeth [them], he it is that loveth me: and he that loveth me shall be loved of my Father, and I will love him, and will manifest myself to him"—such is the emphasis and manner of expression that it plainly carries this in it, that this is the great thing, and the [thing] mainly to be looked at; as also does Christ's so much insisting on it, and so often repeating it in this his last discourse with his disciples. As again, v. 23, "If any man love me, he will keep my words: and my Father will love him, and we will come to him, and make our abode with him." V. 24, "He that loveth me not keepeth not my sayings." And again, 15:10, "If ye keep my commandments, ye shall abide in my love"; and v. 14, "Ye are my friends, if ye do whatsoever I command you." And so the beloved disciple from him in like manner insists on the same, as that by which we are chiefly to try ourselves and not others only. 1 John 2:3–6, "Hereby do we know that we know him, if we keep his commandments. He that saith, I know him, and keepeth not his commandments, is a liar, and the truth is not in him. But whoso keepeth his word, in him verily is the love of God perfected (this is "the perfect love that casts out fear," 1 John 4:18; that is the same with the "Spirit of adoption, bearing witness with our spirits, that we are the children of God," Romans 8:[15–16]): hereby know we that we are in him. He that saith he abideth in him ought also to walk, even as he walked." 1 John 5:3, "For this is the love of God, that we keep his commandments: and his commandments are not grievous." Where have [we] anything else in such a manner insisted on in Scripture as a sign of a good estate? So Matthew 7:16–20, "Ye shall know them by their fruits. Do men gather grapes of thorns, or figs of thistles? Even so every good tree bringeth forth good fruit; but a corrupt tree bringeth forth evil fruit. Every tree that bringeth not forth good fruit is hewn down, and cast into the fire. Whereby by their fruits shall ye know them." Here good fruits seem to be especially given as a sign by which we should know others; but Christ, by what he says next [vv. 21–27], lets us know that he would also be understood of ourselves, as well as others: that we are to judge ourselves also mainly by our fruits. "Not every one that saith unto me, Lord, Lord, shall enter into the kingdom of heaven; but he that doth the will of my Father which is in heaven. Many will say unto me in that day, Lord, Lord, Have we not prophesied in thy name? and in thy name have cast out devils? and in thy name done many wonderful works? And then will I profess unto them, I never knew you: depart from me, ye that work iniquity. Therefore whosoever heareth these sayings of mine, and doth them, I will liken him unto a wise man, that built his house upon a rock: and the rain descended, and the floods came, and the winds blew, and beat upon that house; and it fell not: for it was founded upon a rock. And every one that heareth these sayings of mine, and doth them not, shall be likened unto a foolish man, which built his house upon the sand: And the rain descended, and the floods came, and the wind blew, and beat upon the house; and it fell: and great was the fall of it." The testimony of our own consciences, with respect to doing good works and living a holy life, is spoken [of] as that certain sign which especially tends to give good assurance of godliness. 1 John 3:18–22, "My little children, let us not love in word and in tongue, but in deed and in truth. And hereby we know that we are of the truth, and shall assure our hearts before him. For if our heart condemn us, God is greater than our heart, and knoweth all things. Beloved, if our heart condemn us not, then have we confidence towards God. And whatsoever we ask, we receive of him, because we keep his commandments, and do those things that are pleasing in his sight."

The Apostle Paul (Hebrews 6) mentions good works and righteous fruits in the Christian Hebrews both as that evidence that gave him hope concerning them, that they had something more than the highest common illuminations and gifts of hypocrites mentioned in the beginning of the chapter, and also as that evidence which tended to give them the highest assurance of hope concerning themselves. Vv. 9–11, "But, beloved, we are persuaded better things of you, and things that accompany salvation, though we thus speak. For God is not unrighteous to forget your work and labor of love, which ye have showed toward his name, in that ye have ministered to the saints, and do minister. And we desire that every one of you do show the same diligence to the full assurance of hope unto the end." And Galatians 6:4, "Let every man prove his own work, so shall he have rejoicing in himself alone, and not in another." And works are spoken of by the Apostle James as the best sign of a man's good estate to his own conscience, as well as to his neighbor, as is manifest by his saying that "Abraham was justified by works (i.e., approved of God as in a good estate), when he offered up his son Isaac on the altar" [Jas 3:4]; referring to that in which God said to Abraham on that occasion, "Now I know that thou fearest God, because thou hast not withheld from me thy son, thine only son Isaac" [Gen 22:12]: which was a testimony of God to Abraham himself of his good estate. The Psalmist says then shall I not be ashamed when I have respect to all thy commandments [Psalm 119:80], i.e., then shall I be bold, and assured, and steadfast in my hope. But that keeping God's commandments is insisted upon throughout the Old Testament as the main evidence of godliness, is manifest beyond all dispute, so as [not] to need enumeration of places.

That by which principally Christ tries men in this, and by which he will judge them hereafter, is doubtless the main evidence by which we are to judge of ourselves. But 'tis principally by men's keeping God's commandments, and bringing forth the fruits of righteousness, that he both tries them here, and judges them hereafter. 'Tis by this chiefly that he judges them here. Thus God tempted or tried Abraham when he commanded him to offer up his only son. It was the way that Christ took to try men's sincerity, viz., to try their obedience. Thus Christ tried the rich young man (Matthew 19:16–21). He made a show of respect to Christ, and a willingness to do anything he should direct him to, but Christ bid him "go and sell all that he had, and give to the poor, and thou shalt have treasure in heaven: and come and follow me." So Christ tried another that we read of (Matthew 8:19–20). He made a great profession of respect to Christ in words; says he, "Lord, I will follow thee whithersoever thou goest." He thought he experienced in his heart such a love to Christ that he could follow him whithersoever he went, but Christ tries how he would do in practice, by telling him that "the foxes had holes, and the birds of the air had nests; but the Son of man had not where to lay his head"; and his practice consequent hereupon showed what he was. Hence difficulties and sufferings laid in the way of our keeping God's commands, do by way of eminency in Scripture, both in the Old Testament and New, obtain the name of temptations or trials, because by these especially men's sincerity is tried.

Again, 'tis principally by men's works, practice, or fruits that they are to be judged at the last day. This is declared in places too many to be mentioned; and 'tis not only in general, but in that most particular description of the day of judgment that is in the whole Bible, which we have in the twenty-fifth chapter of Matthew. 'Tis described how both good and bad will be judged by their works; but those signs by which we are to be judged at the last day are doubtless the best evidences both to our own consciences and to others. For the end of the day of judgment is to manifest the righteous judgment of God, and so the state of men, both to men's own consciences and to the world, and who can suppose that the infinitely wise Judge of the world, when he is about such a work, would not make use of the best manifestations to that end. Thus the Scriptures make it very plain and manifest, that good works and fruits and keeping Christ's commands are the best evidences of sincerity of heart, and a good estate of soul. But then several things are here to be observed.

1. The Scripture don't speak only of obedience in one or two particulars, or a partial obedience, but is to be understood of that kind of obedience which is universal. […]

2. The Scripture has especially, and above all, respect to keeping Christ's commands, and doing good works, and bringing forth good fruit perseveringly, through trials—or in cases wherein Christ and other things that are dear to the flesh stand in competition—so that in continuing in holy practice we deny ourselves and sell other things for Christ. […]

The expression of keeping Christ's commandments imports thus much, and has reference to the opposition that is made to our retaining them, or endeavors to take them away from us, or us from them. Then are we found faithful to keep that which is committed to our trust, when others oppose us in it, and try to get the depositum from us, or to tempt us to let it go. Psalm 18:17, "He delivered me from my strong enemy, and from them which hated me: for they were too strong for me"; together with v. 21, "For I have kept the ways of the Lord, and have not wickedly departed from my God."

3. We cannot reasonably suppose that when the Scripture in this case speaks of good works, good fruit, and keeping Christ's commandments, that it has respect merely to what is external, or the

motion or action of the body, without including anything else, any aim or intention in the agent, or any act of the understanding or will, in the case: for consider the actions of men so, and they are no more good works, or acts of obedience, than the regular motions of a machine. But doubtless the obedience and fruit that is spoken of is the obedience and fruit of the man, and therefore not only the obedience of the body, but the obedience of the soul, as consisting in acts and practice of the soul. Doubtless the Scripture speaks of these acts or works as ours; but they are ours no further than they are from the inward actings of our minds, and exercises of our inclinations and wills. Indeed, by these expressions I don't suppose that the Scripture intends to include all inward piety, both principle and exercise, both spirit and practice, because then on these things being given as signs of godliness, the same thing would be given as a sign of itself. But only the exercise and inward practice of the soul is meant. The holy exercise is given as the sign of the holy principle and good estate, and the manner of exercise, viz., it being that manner of exercise of soul and exertion of inward holiness that there is in the soul in a truly obediential act: which is something more than the mere being of the principle or merely that principle's being in exercise. 'Tis that exertion of the soul, and of the disposition of the soul, issuing and terminating in imperate acts of the will, the act that is in what we call practice, or an act of obedience: this I call the practice of the soul, being something more than the mere immanent exercise of grace. The act of the soul, and the exercise of grace that is exerted in the performance of a good work, is the good work itself so far as the soul is concerned in it, or so far as it is the soul's good work; and thus the Scripture gives such a kind of exercise, or exercition, or practice of the soul, and grace in the soul, as the surest sign of the sincerity of grace, and the reality of the principle, and so of the goodness of the state. And this is the obedience and the good fruit that God mainly looks at, as he looks at the soul more than the body, as much as the soul in the constitution of the human nature is the superior part. As he looks at the obedience and practice of the man, he looks at the practice of the soul chiefly, as the soul chiefly is the man and *instar totius* in God's sight: for God seeth not as man seeth, for he looketh on the heart. True godliness consists not in an heart to intend to keep

God's commandments, but in an heart to do it, Deuteronomy 5:27–29; see sermon on this text.[7]

So that in this keeping Christ's commands, not only is the exercise of the faculties of the soul included, but also the end for which a man acts: for not only should we not look on the motions of a statue, doing justice by clockwork, as an act of obedience to Christ in that statue, but neither would anybody call the voluntary actions of a man, externally and materially agreeable to a command of Christ, an act of obedience to Christ, if he never had heard of Christ, or any of his commands, or never thought of them at that time.

If the acts of obedience and good fruits spoken of be looked upon not as mere motions of the body but as acts of the soul, the whole exercise of the spirit of the mind must be taken in, with the end acted for, and the respect the soul then has to God, his will and authority; otherwise, 'tis no act of denial of ourselves, or obedience to God, or service done to him, but to something else. [...]

See also "Miscellanies," No. 1031.[8]

But at the same time it must also be observed that the external act is not excluded in that obedience that is in Scripture so much insisted on as a sign of godliness, but the internal exertion of the mind, and the external act as connected with [it] are both included and intended. And though in this great evidence of godliness what is inward is of greatest importance, yet hereby are effectually cut off all pretensions that any man can have to evidences of godliness that externally lives wickedly: because the great evidence lies in the inward exercise, or practice of the soul, that accompanies and issues in imperate acts of the will. But 'tis known that the imperate acts of the will are not one way and the actions of the bodily organs another: for the unalterable law of nature is that they should be united, or that one should follow another, as long as soul and body are united, and the organs are not so destroyed as [not] to remain capable of those motions that the soul commands. Thus it would be ridiculous for a man to plead that the imperate act of his will was to go to the public worship, while his feet carried him to a tavern or public stew, or that the imperate act of his soul was to give such a sum that he had in his hand to a poor beggar, while his hand at the same instant retained it.

The words, *fruits, works, keeping or breaking commandments*, are used in Scripture sometimes in a more restrained and sometimes in a larger sense. Sometimes for outward acts: so they are to be understood when they are given as signs by which we are to judge of others, and it may be in some other cases; and sometimes not only for outward, but also inward acts. By works sometimes is meant all acts that are liable to a reward or punishment, as is evident by Job 34:11, "The work of a man will he render unto him"; and Revelations 14:13, "Their works do follow them"; and a multitude of parallel places. But inward exercises are liable to a reward or punishment. We find promises and threatenings often made to good or evil thoughts and exercises of the heart; and works are to be understood in this extensive sense where the Apostle speaks of works, works of the Law and works of righteousness, in the affair of justification. And so Proverbs 20:11, "Even a child is known by his doings, whether his work be pure, and whether it be right"; here external deeds are spoken [of] as a sign of the quality of something internal, that is called work. And Colossians 1:21, "Enemies in your mind by wicked works." Hebrews 6:1, there repentance of sin is called "repentance from dead works." John 6:28–29, "What [shall we do, that we might work the works of God? Jesus answered and said unto them, this is the work of God, that ye believe on him whom he hath sent]." Both the terms, works and fruits, are used in this extensive sense in Galatians 5, beginning at the nineteenth verse, "Now the works of the flesh are manifest, which are these; adultery, fornication, uncleanness, lasciviousness, idolatry, witchcraft, hatred, emulations, wrath, strife, seditions, heresies, envyings. But the fruit of the Spirit is love, joy, peace, long-suffering, gentleness, goodness, faith, meekness, temperance: against such there is no law. And they that are Christ's have crucified the flesh with the affections and lusts."

Though all exercises whatsoever, of either grace or corruption, are what we either keep or break God's commandments by, and though they are all sometimes called works and fruits, yet where good works and fruits and keeping God's commands are insisted on as the great evidences of godliness in the places forementioned, those exercises of grace and exertions of soul whence good external practice in speech or behavior immediately result, seem chiefly to be aimed at.

However, 'tis beyond dispute that inward exercises of grace are included. Thus the good fruits that Christ mentions as the sure signs of the tree, and the doing the things that Christ says, so much insisted on in the conclusion of Christ's sermon on the mount as the great sign of being on a sure foundation, implies many inward exercises: for doubtless Christ, by doing the things that he says, has a special respect to those things that he had been saying in that sermon, the commands he had then been giving. But many of those sayings of his respect acts of the mind, as in those that follow. "Blessed are the poor in spirit." "Blessed are they that mourn." "Blessed are the meek." "Blessed are they which do hunger and thirst after righteousness." "Blessed are the merciful." "Blessed are the pure in heart." "Whosoever is angry with his brother without a cause shall be in danger of judgment." "But I say unto you, whosoever looketh on a woman to lust after her hath committed adultery with her already in his heart." Love your enemies, bless them that curse you, do good to them that hate you, and pray for them which despitefully use you, and persecute you." "No man can serve two masters: for either he will hate the one, and love the other; or else he will hold to the one, and despise the other." "Take no thought for your life, what ye shall eat, or what ye shall drink; nor yet for your body, what ye shall put on. Is not the life more than meat, and the body more than raiment?" "Seek first the kingdom of God, and his righteousness; and all these things shall be added unto you." "Judge not, that ye be not judged" [Matt 5:3–8, 22, 28, 44; 6:24–25, 33; 7:1].

And when Christ, in his dying discourses to his disciples, so much insists on keeping his commandments as a sign of sincerity, 'tis manifest that he has a special respect to a command that mainly respects the exercise of the heart, viz., loving one another; which he once and again in that same discourse calls his commandment, as John 13:34–35, "A new commandment I give unto you, that ye love one another; as I have loved you, that you also love one another. By this shall all men know that ye are my disciples, if ye have love one to another." Here he mentions it as that by which others should know that they were his disciples; but in what follows—the places that have been already cited—he also insists on it as a sign by which they should know themselves, in insisting on keeping his commandments as the great sign. As also does the penman of this book in his first epistle, ch. 2, [vv.] 3–6, "Hereby do we know that we know him, if we keep his commandments. He that saith, I know him, and keepeth not his commandments, is a liar, and the truth is not in him. But whoso keepeth his word, in him verily is the love of God perfected: hereby know that we are in him. He that saith he abideth in him ought himself also so to walk, even as he walked"; together with what follows in v. 7, "Brethren, I write no new commandment unto you, but an old commandment which ye had from the beginning. The old commandment is the word which ye have heard from the beginning," there insisting on love to the brethren. And again, 3:23, there speaking of keeping Christ's commands as a sure sign, he adds, "And this is his commandment, that we should believe on the name of his Son Jesus Christ, and love one another, as he gave us commandment"; both which are acts of the mind. And both these the Apostle seemed to take from that dying discourse of Christ that he rehearses in his Gospel, as you may see by comparing John 13:34–35 with 14:10–15, 21–25. See 2 John 5–6, "That we love one another. And this is love, that we walk after his commandments. This is the commandment, that ye have heard from the beginning, that ye should walk in it."

And when we are told in Scripture that men shall at the last day all be judged according to their works, and all shall receive according to the things done in the body, whether good or bad, it is not to be understood only of outward acts; for if so, why is God so often spoken of as he that searches the heart and the reins, at the same time that he is spoken of as judge of the world, and as he that render to every man according to his works? Revelation 2:23, "And all the churches shall know that I am he which searcheth the reins and the hearts: and I will give unto every one of you according to your works." Psalm 7:8–9, "The Lord shall judge the people: judge me, O Lord, according to my righteousness, and according to mine integrity that is in me. Oh let the wickedness of the wicked come to an end; but do thou establish the just: for the righteous God trieth the hearts and the reins." Jeremiah 11:20, "But, O Lord of hosts, that judgest righteously, that triest the reins and the heart." Jeremiah 17:9–10, "The heart is deceitful above all things, and desperately wicked: who can know it? I the Lord search the heart, I try the reins, even to give every man according to his ways, and according to the fruit of his doings." Proverbs 17:3, "The fining pot for silver, and the furnace for gold: but the Lord trieth the hearts." Proverbs 21:2, "Every way of a man is right in his own eyes: but the Lord pondereth the hearts." Proverbs 16:2, "All the ways of a man are clean in his own eyes; but the Lord weigheth the spirits." 1 Corinthians 4:5, "Therefore judge nothing before the time, until the Lord come, who will both bring to light the hidden things of darkness, and make manifest the counsels of the hearts: and then shall every man have praise of God."

So that 'tis this keeping Christ's commandments that is spoken of in Scripture as the best sign of godliness, viz., not only in outward practice, but also in the practice of the soul, in the sense that has been explained. It is such a keeping God's commands that Hezekiah pleads in his sickness; Isaiah 38:3, "Remember now, O Lord, I beseech thee, how I have walked before thee in truth and with a perfect heart."

There can be no sufficient objection against universally keeping Christ's commands in this sense as being the best sign of godliness, especially when the commandments are thus kept through such trials as providence lays in our way.

1. It can be no objection against it that 'tis reasonable to suppose that those things must be the best evidences of a good estate wherein godliness does most essentially consist, and are themselves the very condition of a good estate by God's revealed constitution. For, take good works or holy practice in this sense, and godliness does most essentially consist in it, so far as it consists in act, or in anything visible or sensible: for the essence of godliness, so far [as] that lies in anything sensible or perceivable, doubtless lies in the inward exercises of grace or holiness; but good works in the sense that has been explained are grace itself, they are proper exercises of grace. Such practical exertions of faith and love are exercises of faith and love, and they are the highest and most essential sort of the exercises of these graces. For what is called the imperate act of the will in which these exercises issue and terminate, is indeed nothing else but the preponderating of the inclination or disposition of the soul in its exercise in the present trial, which is to be decided by the following

motion of the body, by the law of the union of soul and body, which law is fixed and upheld by the omniscient God himself. And especially does godliness most essentially consist in such practical exercises of grace, in cases wherein Christ and other things are especially set in competition.

That loving Christ and believing in him, hoping and trusting in him, that are chiefly insisted on as notes of a good [estate] and evidences of acceptance with God and true happiness, are chiefly these effective exercises and acts of faith and love and hope under trials. James 1:12, "Blessed is he that endureth temptation: for when he is tried, he shall receive the crown of life, which the Lord hath promised to them that love him." 1 John 5:3, "For this is the love of God, that we keep his commandments: and his commandments are not grievous." 2 John 6, "And this is love, that we walk after his commandments." So [when] the trusting in God, and believing in him, exercising confidence and hope in him, are chiefly prescribed, it is chiefly with respect to such trials.

So when FAITH is insisted on as the great CONDITION OF SALVATION, practical exertions and effective expressions of faith, appearing when faith is thus tried, are mainly pointed at. It was by faith appearing thus that Abraham was justified, which the apostle James takes notice of [Jas 3:21]. They did not perform the condition of salvation who believed for a while and in a time of temptation fell away, but they do who believe with that faith that overcomes the world. They are entitled to the promises that are made to those that overcome in the second and third chapters of Revelation. Romans 10:9, "If thou shalt confess with thy mouth the Lord Jesus, and shalt believe in thine heart that God hath raised him from the dead, thou shalt be saved." 1 Thessalonians 2:13–14, "Which effectually worketh also in you that believe. For ye, brethren, became followers of the churches of God which in Judea are in Christ Jesus: for ye also suffered like things of your own countrymen." Hebrews 10:39, "Ye are not of them that draw back unto perdition; but of [them] that believe to the saving of the soul," with the context. And to this purpose are the many examples of faith mentioned in the eleventh chapter of Hebrews. (Here insert No. 800.)[9]

Thus that faith that is called a work, and is one thing implied in those forementioned expressions in Scripture of good works and keeping Christ's commandments, is the great condition of salvation. John 6:28–29, "Then said they unto him, What shall we do, that we may work the works of God? Jesus answered and said unto them, This is the work of God, that ye believe on him whom he hath sent." So in this manner faith is mentioned as the condition of receiving an answer to our prayers. 1 John 3:22–23, "And whatsoever we ask, we receive of him, because we keep his commandments, and do those things that are pleasing in his sight. And this is his commandment, that we should believe on the name of his Son Jesus Christ, and love one another, as he gave us commandment." See No. 996.[10]

And thus what Hezekiah pleaded on his sick bed (Isaiah 38:3) was not only a sign of his title to the fruits of God's favor, but was the condition of a title to them.

2. WITNESS OF THE SPIRIT. It can be no sufficient objection against good fruits and keeping Christ's commandments being the best sign of grace, that the Scripture speaks of a certain kind of evidence of a good estate, that is represented as the immediate testimony of the Spirit of God himself to our souls that we are the children of God, and the seal of the Spirit, and the earnest of the Spirit in our hearts, which is the experience of the exercise of the Spirit of adoption, or Spirit of love, which seems to be the same with that love which the beloved disciple speaks of that casts out fear, and that white stone and new name written that Christ gives which no man knows but he that receives it. Such an evidence as this, one would think by the things that are said, must needs be the highest and most certain and assuring kind of evidence that any person can receive. And it must be allowed to be so. But yet, I say, this don't argue but that keeping Christ's commands in the sense that has been spoken of through trials is the highest evidence. This witness of the Spirit, or a Spirit of adoption, must be the experience of the exercise of such a spirit, or a spirit of love, which is a childlike spirit, in opposition to a spirit of fear, which is the spirit of bondage. But it has been already observed that the keeping Christ's commands that has been spoken of consists mainly in the exercise of grace in the heart; and that kind of exercise of love, or the spirit of adoption that there is in

such practical exertions and effective exercises of love, are the highest and most essential and distinguishing kind of exercises of love: and therefore in them this testimony and seal and earnest of the Spirit of love is given in its clearest and fullest manner. And the Apostle, when he speaks of the testimony of the Spirit of God in Romans 8:15–16, in that very place he principally and most immediately has respect to such effective exercises of love as those whereby Christians deny themselves in times of trial; as appears by his manner of introducing what is there said, which is to be seen in vv. 12–13, "Therefore, brethren, we are debtors, not to the flesh, to live after the flesh. For if we live after the flesh, ye shall die: but if ye through the Spirit do mortify the deeds of the flesh, ye shall live"; and also by what immediately follows in vv. 17–18, "And if children, then heirs; heirs of God, and joint heirs with Christ; if so be that we suffer with him, that we may also be glorified together. For I reckon that the sufferings of this present time are not worthy to be compared with the glory which shall be revealed in us." That exercise of love, or the filial spirit that the Apostle here speaks of as the highest ground of hope, is the same with that exercise of the love of God that Christians experience in bearing tribulation for his sake; whence arises that hope that makes not ashamed, that he had before spoken of, ch. 5, at the beginning; and the same with that white stone and new name which is obtained by overcoming, spoken of in Revelation; and that seal of the Spirit that the Apostle speaks of as what he had in going through extreme suffering (see 2 Corinthians 1:8–9, together with 21–22); and that earnest of the Spirit that he had under afflictions and persecutions, which he speaks of, 2 Corinthians 5:5, together with the preceding part of the chapter and the latter part of the foregoing. So that keeping Christ's commands is the highest evidence of a good estate, and yet the witness of the Spirit of adoption or love is the highest evidence: for they are both the same. Therefore the apostle John, where speaking of keeping Christ's commands as the great evidence of our good estate, does in the same place speak of our partaking of the Spirit of God as a spirit of love, as the great evidence of a good estate (I John, 3rd chapter, at the latter end). V. 19, "And hereby we know that we are of the truth, and shall assure our hearts before him"; v. 22, "And whatsoever we ask, we receive of him, because we keep his commandments"; [vv.] 23–24, "And this is his commandment, that we should believe on the name of his Son Jesus Christ, and love one another, as he gave us commandment. And he that keepeth his commandments dwelleth in him, and he in him. And hereby we know that he abideth in us, by the Spirit that he hath given us." The same he insists on again in the next chapter, twelfth and thirteenth verses, "If we love one another, God dwelleth in us, and his love is perfected in us. Hereby we know that we dwell in him, and he in us, because he hath given us of his Spirit"; and this is the same evidence with that spoken in the 18th verse there following in the same chapter, which we have observed is the same with the sure testimony of the Spirit of adoption spoken of in the eighth of Romans. "There is no fear in love; but perfect love casteth out fear: because fear hath torment. He that feareth is not made perfect in love." And this again is the same with that evidence, consisting in keeping God's commandments, spoken of in the third verse of the chapter next following, in a continuation of the same discourse. "This is the love of God, that we keep his commandments: and his commandments are not grievous."

Here add No. 800.[11]

EXCERPT FROM *EXTRAORDINARY GIFTS OF THE SPIRIT ARE INFERIOR TO GRACES OF THE SPIRIT* (1748)

1 Corinthians 13:8–13
Charity never faileth: but whether there be prophecies, they shall fail; whether there be tongues, they shall cease; whether there be knowledge, it shall vanish away. For we know in part, and we prophesy in part. But when that which is perfect is come, then that which is in part shall be done away. When I was a child, I spake as a child, I understood as a child, I thought as a child: but when I became a man, I put away childish things. For now we see through a glass, darkly; but then face to face: now I know in part; but then shall I know even as also I am known. And now abideth faith, hope, charity, these three; but the greatest of these is charity.

1. The things here compared one with another [are] the extraordinary gifts of the Spirit and the graces of the Spirit. By the extraordinary gifts of the Spirit, I mean those that consisted in or implied inspiration or immediate revelation. These were the subject the Apostle had insisted on throughout the foregoing chapter, and then he proceeds in this chapter to compare those gifts of the Spirit with the grace of the Spirit, to show how far the latter exceeds the former, which comparison is introduced by the last words in the preceding chapter, "But covet earnestly the best gifts: and yet show I unto you a more excellent way." The extraordinary gifts mentioned in the text are prophesying, tongues, and knowledge. The same were spoken of in the two first verses, [and] the same also had been spoken of in the foregoing chapter, [the] eighth, ninth, [and] tenth verses. What is called knowledge here was a certain extraordinary gift; these are the extraordinary gifts that are spoken of in the text. The graces of the Spirit that are here spoken of are faith, hope, and charity. These extraordinary gifts and those graces are here compared one with the other.

2. We may observe wherein these things thus compared do differ one from another, viz., that the former shall soon fail and cease in the church of God. The others abide and are of stated use and continuance in God's church. There is an evident designed antithesis. There is some difference observed between charity and faith and hope: "charity never faileth"; but herein they all agree: [they shall be of continuance in God's church].

3. The reason why these extraordinary gifts of the Spirit differ in this respect from the graces of the Spirit—that they soon cease in the church, whereas the latter remain—is this, viz., that these extraordinary gifts of the Spirit were given for temporary use, to be continued only while the church was in its minority and to cease when it came to a state of maturity ([vv.] 9–11). The church of Christ may be said to pass under such a change, from a state of minority to a state of maturity, two ways:

(1) By the saints' passing from that state of imperfection they are in here in this world to a state of glorious perfection in another world. The saints while here are but as little

children. When the Apostle says, "charity never faileth," he looks forward as far as the eternal state of the church, and the words of the twelfth verse seem to be especially accommodated to this state: "For now we see through a glass, darkly."

(2) The church of Christ may be said to pass under this change, from a state of childhood to an adult state, in the alteration of its state in this world. Thus the church of God under the old testament is represented as being in a state of childhood, compared with the state it is brought into under the New (Galatians 4, at the beginning). So the Christian church, while in its first beginning, is as it were in its infancy or childhood, in comparison of what it is afterwards when the old Mosaic dispensation is perfectly abolished and the new dispensation fully established, and all things belonging to this new and more glorious state completed and settled. And 'tis evident that the Apostle has special respect to the transition of the church from a state of childhood in this latter respect, when he speaks of the extraordinary gifts of prophecy {and tongues} ceasing, and faith, hope, and charity abiding after they have ceased; for {prophecy and tongues} don't abide in heaven. This is the reason the Apostle gives why the extraordinary gifts of the Spirit shall cease when the church comes to its adult state: because they were to be for the use of the church only while in its minority. It now had these gifts that imply inspiration, and had new revelations made to it from time to time, because as yet it knew but in part. The mind and will of God as yet was not fully revealed: they prophesied in part; prophecy was continued to make up what was lacking in the revelation the church enjoyed. But when once the will of God and the doctrines of the gospel shall be fully revealed, the canon of the Scripture completed and that complete revelation thoroughly settled, these things should vanish away as of no further use. Then the church should have no further use of these leading strings, being come to adult state [and] furnished with a perfect

and complete standing rule, sufficient to guide her in all things in the use of which she should at length, in God's time, without any further revelations, come to a very glorious state here in this world and to a very great degree of perfection in knowledge and resemblance of an heavenly state of perfect light and knowledge: the state of the church prophesied of in Isaiah 30:26, "And the light of the moon shall be as the light of the sun, and the light of the sun shall be sevenfold, as the light of the seven days, in the day that the Lord bindeth up the breach of his people, and healeth the stroke of their wound." Though the Apostle here speaks in the first person, "now we see through a glass, darkly," we are not necessarily to understand him as speaking in his own name, but as speaking in the name of the church of Christ, as in Galatians 1:3 and in 1 Thessalonians 4:15, "Grace be to you and peace from God the Father, and from our Lord Jesus Christ….For this we say unto you by the word of the Lord."

Doctrine

The extraordinary influences of the Spirit of God, imparting immediate revelations to men, were designed only for a temporary continuance while the church was in its minority, and never were intended to be statedly upheld in the Christian church.

[I shall undertake the following things:]

I. Show what is meant in the doctrine by immediate revelation.

II. That all the extraordinary gifts and influences of the Spirit implied immediate revelation.

III. When the church, in the sense of the Doctrine, may be said to be in its minority.

IV. Those extraordinary influences of the Spirit imparting immediate revelation were designed but for a temporary use, and were intended to be continued only while the church was thus in a state of childhood.

I. What is meant in the Doctrine by immediate revelation. By immediate revelation is meant God's making known some truth by immediate suggestion of it to the mind, without its being made known by sense or reason, or by any former revelation. 'Tis God that makes known all truth to men: [he] is the fountain of all light and knowledge, of those things that we know by natural means—by experience, teaching, [and] reason. But the ways of God's making truth known to us are either ordinary or extraordinary.

Ordinary: as when things are known by sense and experience, as when men know things that they see or feel, or find to be true by being conversant with them by any other of the outward senses. Or by what they find by experience within themselves by intuitively seeing or immediately experiencing of the sentiments and affections: thus men know what their own thoughts are, know their own affections, [their] love [and] hatred. Another ordinary way of men's coming to the knowledge of the truth is by reason. Another way of informing the mind of man [is by the] testimony of our fellow creatures. Another way is when they know a thing by its being made known in some former revelation. Thus, things contained in the Scripture: God has given a standing revelation containing a great number of truths. This being a steady rule God has given for general use, it becomes an ordinary means of knowledge, and therefore when God enlightens men and enables 'em to understand the truths that are declared in that [manner] and to see the evidence that there is of the truth [by observation], that is in some respects one of the ordinary ways [of knowing], though it can't so properly be said to be a common way.

But besides these ordinary ways, God has oftentimes made known truth to men in an extraordinary way, and that is by immediately impressing truths on their minds by suggestions of these truths then made, either by some voice or in some dream or vision, or by words or ideas immediately and miraculously excited, without any dependence on any notice the person to whom the truth is suggested has of that truth by way of his outward senses, or by his experience, or reason, or any preceding testimonies, or any foregoing declaration of that truth to him in any preceding revelation. This is making known truth by immediate revelation. This is also the same with that which we call inspiration, and is that way of God's making known truths, spoken of [in] 2 Timothy 3:16, "All scripture is given by inspiration of God"; [and] 2 Peter 1:20–21, "Knowing this first, that no scripture is of any private interpretation. For the prophecy came not in old time by the will of man: but holy men of old spoke as they were moved [by the Holy Ghost]." This is the way in which God made known truths of old to the prophets. This [is the way God communicated] to the patriarchs and to Moses, when he appeared to 'em in a visible shape and spoke to 'em with an audible voice; and also to the people, when he immediately impressed [his commands upon them]. This is the way that Christ made known truths to the apostles, agreeable to Christ's promise; John 16:12–13, "I have yet many things to say unto you, but ye cannot bear them now. Howbeit when he, the Spirit of truth, is come, he will guide you into all truth: for he shall not speak of himself; but whatsoever he shall hear, that shall he speak: and he will show you things to come." And agreeable to what the Apostle says of himself [in] Galatians 1:11–12, "But I certify you, brethren, that the gospel which was preached of me is not after man…neither was I taught [it, but by the revelation of Jesus Christ]." And whoever pretends to have truth made known to 'em in this way, whatever name they call it by, they pretend to immediate revelation or inspiration. This extraordinary [claim], implying immediate revelation, differs greatly from his gracious influence on the hearts of the saints. Many have had this extraordinary [gift of truth] that never have had the gracious [influence upon their hearts]. The difference lies here: [the saints have a] new sense and understanding of the same truths.

II. All the extraordinary influences and gifts of the Spirit that were of old implied such a revelation as has been described. So it was with all the extraordinary influences of the Spirit that were given of old: that were given before there was any written word. [They were given] to Adam, [to] Noah, [to] Abraham, [and especially] such [as that] to Moses and all the prophets, though there were various ways: sometimes by waking visions, [and by many other means]. So it was with all the extraordinary influences and gifts of the Spirit we read of in the New Testament: prophecy, knowledge [of divine things], what was called the wisdom [of God], [the] gift of tongues, [the] gift of working miracles, [the] interpretation of tongues, [and] discerning spirits.

III. When the church in the sense of the Doctrine may be said to be in its minority or childhood.

Answer. When it is as yet but imperfectly furnished with the means of grace. Thus the church under the old testament is represented by the Apostle as being in a state of childhood in comparison of what it is under the New (Galatians 4). What the Apostle has respect to is not the church's being lower in spiritual attainments or in virtue and holiness, for doubtless there have often been times of such degeneracy in the Christian church under the new testament, that there has been a little or probably less of the flourishing of religion and true holiness in the church than at some times under the old testament. But yet God did not then again put the church under those tutors and governors. However the church sometimes under the old testament might be advanced in spiritual attainments, yet in their advantages with regard to the means of grace, and the dispensation they lived under, it was very imperfect in comparison. It was a very imperfect revelation they enjoyed of the great doctrines. The fullness of time was not come; the canon of the Scripture was then so far from being complete, that the most clear and glorious revelation that God intended was yet wanting. So afterwards, in Christ's time, the Christian church was as it were in its infancy. Christ did not give to his disciples that full [disclosure]: the time was not come; they could not bear [the entire revelation], like old [wine in a new] bottle, [or] like babes that could not bear strong meat. And the Christian church continued in its state of childhood afterwards: [the] means of grace yet incomplete, the Jewish dispensation not fully abolished, the Christian dispensation not fully established. The new and more perfect state of things introduced after Christ's ascension [was] not fully settled, the mind and will of God not fully revealed, the canon of the Scripture not yet complete. [They] knew in part [and] prophesied in part. And so long as the church was thus in an imperfect state with regard to the means of grace—or imperfectly furnished with the means of grace—so long it was as it were in its minority.

When I speak of the church's being imperfectly furnished with the means of grace, I would not be understood to suppose but that God always from the beginning furnished his church with means sufficient to their salvation, and with means adapted to that state that he designed his church should be in at that time. God's people, under the Mosaic dispensation, were furnished with means adapted to the times they lived in—before the coming of the Messiah—and suitable for one single nation so separated. But yet the means of grace were then imperfect in this respect: that they were not such as was requisite in order to answer the needs of the nations in general, and in order [to] their being such as were proper to answer the great purposes of the Redeemer's kingdom as it was intended to be set up through[out] the world. The revelation of the chief mysteries and main doctrines was very imperfect, so the church continued in an imperfect state with regard to means of grace till the revelation of the gospel was perfected and the canon of the Scripture complete and thoroughly settled and established, and then the church might be said to be come [to] a state of maturity, or to adult state.

IV. Those influences of the Spirit giving immediate revelations were designed to be continued only while the church was in a state of childhood, in the sense explained, and never were intended for any stated continuance in the church of God. 'Tis plainly implied in the text that faith, hope, and charity shall abide when the church in some sense shall have become adult, at a time when prophecies and [visions] shall have ceased and vanished away. But this will not be when the church is come to be adult in the sense in which it will be in heaven; therefore the words can well admit no other sense than that which has been given. The main reason of the doctrine seems to be this: that the end why these extraordinary gifts were given is to establish the means of grace in the church. The more [important] end of the extraordinary gifts of the Spirit is the grace of the Spirit, as appears by Ephesians 4:11, "And he gave some, apostles; and some, prophets; and some, evangelists; and some, pastors and teachers." The great end of all [is] to bring men savingly home to God, [to] renew their natures, [to] bring [them] to a conformity to God, [and to] fit men for heaven. 'Tis to bring men to salvation [and] carry on

397

the great work of redemption. But this is only by [the means of grace]; hereby alone they serve the purposes of the great Redeemer. The end of 'em was not to amuse the world, nor yet was the principal end any temporal benefit. And the more immediate end of those extraordinary influences of the Spirit was to furnish mankind with the stated means of grace, and to establish them in the church of Christ, viz., the Word and ordinances of God. The chief of the means of grace is the Word of God: that standing revelation of the mind and will of God that he gives the world, and it is as it were the sum of all means. Ordinances are effectual only by the word; therefore, the thing chiefly designed by the extraordinary gifts [of the Spirit] was to introduce and establish that standing revelation of the mind and will of God by his Word, as the grand means of grace and standing rule of faith and practice through all ages. This revelation of the mind {and} will of God was in fact introduced and established by means of the extraordinary gifts given by inspiration or immediate revelation in various manners and confirmed by miracles. These extraordinary gifts were necessary in order to [this end and] could not be given without [God's intervention], but were not necessary to any other end. In this way the means of grace were all along imparted to the church from the beginning. Thus before Moses, and this was [also] the end of [God's interventions] in Moses' time. And this was the end afterwards of those revelations made to the prophets; and this likewise was the end of renewing those extraordinary gifts under the new testament after they had ceased for some ages in the church. It was because God had a new dispensation to introduce, new ordinances to establish, and a new and far more glorious revelation to give of his mind and will to the churches. The end of all the extraordinary gifts that so abounded in the times of the apostles was mainly to introduce, or to establish, the Christian revelation and complete the means of grace in the church in that respect. When Christ promised the Spirit to his apostles the evening before his death, it was to this end: by them to give his church a standing revelation of truth (John 16:12–13). This truth that the Spirit was to reveal to the apostles was to be the rule of God's church and the standing means of grace to the end of the world, as is evident by Christ's prayer in the seventeenth chapter, [the] twentieth verse. 'Tis true that other collateral and subordinate ends were answered as became the wisdom of God; thus the main end of Christ's miracles was to confirm his mission, but other ends were [also] answered. These extraordinary gifts of the Spirit were indeed given to many others besides the apostles, to those that were not penmen of the Scriptures, but yet it will not follow but that the great end of all these gifts was to settle a standing revelation. It is to be considered that these gifts was not only to give the means of grace or impart to the church a standing rule, but to establish and confirm it: to give it with its evidence. All the extraordinary gifts that were in the apostles' days were given as confirmations of the word of Christ and the apostles; they were so many seals to their mission and divine testimonies to the divinity of their gospel. The extraordinary gifts that others had were for the most part given by the laying on the hands of the apostles, and a grand rule then given to try the spirits by, and to try all gifts, was to inquire whether they were followers of the apostles. 1 John 4:6, "We are of God: he that knoweth God heareth us; he that is not of God heareth not us. Hereby know we the spirit of truth, and the spirit of error." 1 Corinthians 14:34, ["Let your women keep silence in the churches: for it is not permitted unto them to speak; but they are commanded to be under obedience, as also saith the law"]. The great thing [that God] was doing in all that he did in that age, in so abundantly pouring out his Spirit in its extraordinary gifts, was the furnishing his church with a standing, sufficient, and complete rule, well established and confirmed; and when this was done, then the church was come to a state of manhood and needed those leading strings no more. When this grand rule was furnished and well established, and the new dispensation and the canon of the Scripture completed and thoroughly settled, then those extraordinary influences of the Spirit of God withdrew and vanished away. Indeed, 'tis probable that they did not cease at once, but gradually, as when the sun has finished his course through the heavens, his light ceases not at once but by degrees. But all those influences, even till they wholly ceased, were continued gradually to establish the standing rule, till God saw that it was sufficiently confirmed and settled. And then they wholly ceased, their end being fully answered: and they are no more to be expected in the Christian church.

[...]

JONATHAN EDWARDS

EXCERPTS FROM *TRUE AND FALSE CHRISTIANS* (ON THE PARABLE OF THE WISE AND FOOLISH VIRGINS) (1737–38)

Matthew 25:1
Then shall the kingdom of heaven be likened unto ten virgins, which took their lamps, and went forth to meet the bridegroom.

[...]

[The text we are upon is] Matthew 25:1–12, especially vv. 5–7, "[While the bridegroom tarried, they all slumbered and slept. And at midnight there was a cry made, Behold, the bridegroom cometh; go ye out to meet him. Then all those virgins arose, and trimmed their lamps]."

Two general *Propositions*:

I. *The visible church is made up of true and false Christians.*

II. *That those do in some things agree, and in others they greatly differ.*

And it was proposed to show how that, in many things, true and false Christians agree.

First. True and false Christians in general agree.

Second. Wherein they may and sometimes do agree.

Two kinds of these works [were] observed, either:

[1.] Those things true and false Christians may agree in, through the resemblances or appearances of godliness in Christians; and,

2. Through the infirmities and failings of true Christians.

A third thing might have been mentioned, viz., those things they agree in through that self-love that is common to all.

Having already spoken to the former of these, I come to the latter, viz.,

2. To show wherein true Christians and false may agree through the infirmities and failings of true Christians.

And under this head, there are six things may be observed from those three verses that have been now read:

(1) That there is abundance of corruption in the hearts of true Christians as well as others.

(2) True Christians may sometimes, in many respects, agree with others in the corrupt frames that they are in.

(3) [They may agree,] in some respects, in the ill acts they commit, [the] ways they walk in.

(4) That in a time of decay of religion amongst a professing people, 'tis commonly so that all, both wise virgins and foolish, slumber and sleep.

(5) That one great reason of both wise virgins and foolish slumbering and sleeping as they do, is the bridegroom's tarrying.

(6) When true Christians slumber and sleep, the midnight cry is like to be unexpected to them, as well as the foolish.

Here, the

(1) [First] thing, is that there is abundance of corruption in the hearts of true Christians as well as others.

Here, several particulars may be observed under this head:

1. There is a body and fountain of sin in the hearts of the godly, as well as others. There is not only some small remains of corruption in them, as there may be a gleaning after an harvest, but there is a body of sin and death, so as exceedingly to defile the nature. And therefore the Apostle, who was not only a true Christian, but one of the most eminent Christians that ever was in the world, cries out, "O wretched man that I am! who shall deliver me from the body of this death?," Romans 7:24.

Instead of being but small remains of corruption, there is but a little grace. Corruption is done away no further than grace prevails. As it is with a place that has heretofore been filled with perfect darkness: darkness is done away no further than light prevails. But in the hearts of the godly, there is but a small beam of light, and therefore a great deal of remaining darkness.

2. The corruption that is in the hearts of the godly, so far as it prevails, is of as hateful a nature as that which is in the hearts of wicked men. Though the godly are, by the grace of God, made better than wicked, yet 'tis not because their corruptions are any better than the corruptions of wicked men. The corruption that there is in the heart of a godly man, according to what there is of it, is as opposite to God, as contrary to his nature, and as much of an enemy to him, as the corruption [in the heart of a wicked man]. Corruption in them tends as much, according to the degree of its prevalency, to contempt of God and hatred of God, and disobedience to his commands and rebellion against his authority, and ingratitude for his mercy, as in any persons whatsoever.

'Tis as hellish in its nature. Sin, wherever it is, is the image of the devil, whether it be in a godly man or a wicked man.

Thus pride in the godly, is as hateful as pride in a wicked man. And so [the same] may be said of covetousness and sensuality and malice: those things are as hateful in the godly as in the wicked. In their nature, though not in degree, they are as hateful to God, and as worthy of the hatred of all men.

The hearts of men may be made better by infusing a principle contrary to corruption. But the corruption of their hearts never can be made better; it can't be changed. Neither is there nothing to be done towards any amendment with respect to it, but by destroying of it.

Sin is of so bad a nature, that it never can be mended, for it is infinitely evil. As 'tis with God, 'tis impossible he should be made worse, because he is infinitely good. So 'tis with sin against God, which is infinitely evil: it can't be mended or made better.

The corruption that is in the hearts of the godly, is of as hateful a nature as that which [is] in the hearts of wicked men in its nature, and more hateful in its circumstances. Sin is nowhere so hateful to God as in his own child. That which a man abhors and loathes, he will abhor nowhere so much as nearest to him; defilement is nowhere so hateful, as 'tis in some precious jewel or choice vessel. The more God loves his saints, and the more precious they are to him, the more hateful to God is sin, and in them.

3. There are the seeds of all the same kinds of sin in the godly, that there is in natural men. The elect, they bring the principle of as many lusts into the world with 'em as others, and not one lust is totally rooted out in conversion.

So that a godly man has in his heart as many natural principles of corruption remaining in him, as a natural man has. A natural man has a seed of 'em against God in his heart, and so has a godly man. A natural man {has a} principle of other sin, and so {has a godly man} of contempt of the gospel of Jesus Christ. And so there are principles of pride, of self-righteousness, of sensuality, of envy, of malice and revenge in the hearts of the godly, as there is in the hearts of natural men. And indeed, there is no one sin that men commit, but that a godly man has that in them that tends to it.

Yea, a godly man has that sin and corruption in him that, in its own nature, tends to the commission of the sin against the Holy Ghost. And the reason why godly men never commit that sin, is not because they han't that corruption in their hearts that tends to it, or that exposes 'em to it; but only because God's faithfulness to his own covenant promises will preserve them from it.

4. There is a principle of love to sin, and oftentimes the exercise of such a principle, in the heart of a godly man. It is a mistake if any imagine that there is no love to sin in a godly man.

Indeed, the godly do differ from natural men in this, that they have a spirit to hate sin, and that as sin, or as against God. But yet they have a contrary spirit in 'em at the same time, and their spirit of love to sin may [be], and is very often, in exercise.

403

There is no man so holy upon earth, but that at some-times feels the workings of love to these and those sinful acts or ways.

There is two contrary principles struggling one with another in the heart of a godly men, like Jacob and Esau in Rebecca's womb. There is no impossibility or contradic-tion in this; indeed, it would be a contradiction to suppose that a godly man should both love and hate sin in the same act, but not that he should have contrary principles inclin-ing to both, which at different times may be in exercise.

As long as a principle of sin remains, [it] is impossible but that there should remain a principle of love to sin: for surely every lust loves itself. 'Tis of necessity that a lust should love its own object. To suppose that there is a lust in the hearts of the godly, and yet no love to the sin lusted after, is a contradiction.

If there was no love to sin in a godly man, there would be no sin, for love to sin can't be rooted out till sin itself is: for a principle of sin consists in the inclination of the heart. The lusts of the heart, and the sin of the heart, are the same thing; and where there is an inclination of heart, there is a love of heart.

If a godly man did [not] at all love sin, then he would not at all desire, or in the least incline, to commit sin. And if he did not at all, at any time, ever incline to commit sin, he would have no sin in his heart.

Root out all sinful inclinations out of the heart, and you root out all sin out of the heart. Indeed, there are these two ways where a godly man don't love sin:

a. He don't love sin with a love of settled esteem, i.e., sin is not that which he statedly entertains a good opinion and value for, as wicked men. Wicked men esteem the ways of sin: they place happiness in 'em; they have a settled and established value for the objects of their lusts. But it is not so with a good [man]: he has no established, good opinion of sin, but on the contrary, he looks upon [it as] vile and abominable, that which debases and dishonors his nature, that which is worthy to be abhorred and detested. He looks upon it as the wound and disease of his nature, and as the great calamity of his soul. This is the settled opinion and esteem that a godly man has of sin; as the Apostle cries out, "O wretched man that I am!"

b. A godly man don't love sin by a stated choice of it. The stated and established choice of the soul of a godly man, is not of sin, or any of the ways of sin, but of God and the ways of holiness.

In his settled choice, he renounces sin universally. He renounces every one of the ways of sin.

The heart of a godly [man], in its ordinary election, fully forsakes sin and cleaves to holiness. Psalm 119:30, "I have chosen the way of truth, thy judgments have I laid before me."

But yet, in these two ways a godly man may find a love to sin, may at times love sin with [a] love of desire:

(a) He may find stirrings of desires after sin, or after the objects of his lusts. If they were not the objects of his desires, they could not be the objects of his lusts: for that which a man feels no desires of, surely he don't lust after. David, when he lusted after Bathsheba, he desired to commit adultery with her.

(b) They may have delight in sin. As they may desire the object of lust before 'tis obtained, so they may delight in it when obtained. The same principle that will cause one, will cause the other also.

The sin that lust inclines to is, and must be, that which in its own nature is pleasing and gratifying to that lust. Otherwise, the lust would not go out after it, and the lust of the heart and the corrupt nature may take delight in it.

Every nature delights in what is agreeable to it. But sin is agreeable to that corrupt nature that is in the godly.

Thus is that verified, Galatians 5:17, "The spirit lusteth against the flesh and the flesh against the spirit, so
that ye cannot do the things that ye want."

5. The corruption that is in the hearts of the godly, has its
foundation in the same thing as in the hearts of natural
men, viz., ignorance of God. There is a great deal of corruption in the heart of a godly man, because there is a
great deal of blindness and ignorance of God.

There is some true knowledge of God, but 'tis but little.
The godly in this [world] see but very darkly; 'tis but a little portion that is known of God. The light that shines in
their hearts, is but a light that shines in a dark place, where
there is a great deal more blindness than light.

The knowledge that a godly man has of God in this
world is so small, that it is compared to the knowledge of
a child, 1 Corinthians 13:11. Through the smallness of the
degree of spiritual light and knowledge, it comes to pass
oftentimes that the sense that the godly have of God's perfections, is distinctly sensible only in some particulars.
There are some spiritual things that they have had no distinct spiritual discovery of. Some hope they have had at
times a sensible view of the excellency of God's grace or
faith, fullness or holiness, but that may be a difficulty with
'em, that they are afraid that they never had sight of his
majesty and greatness. Many [a] Christian's doubt about
their state arises from such defects; they have had sensible
and distinct views but of some things. If they had as much
of a sight of others as they have of those, they should not
be afraid.

Thus true Christians and false agree, in that there is
abundance of corruption in the heart of one, as well as the
other.

(2) True Christians may sometimes, in many respects, agree
with others in the corrupt frames that they are [in]. As the godly have

a great deal of corruption, and but little holiness, so they may be in very corrupt frames through the exercise of that corruption.

Grace being small, it [is] sometimes covered and hid, like a coal or spark buried up in ashes, or a jewel buried in rubbish, or a star hid in a cloud. As the wise virgins slumbered and slept, so grace in them may be as it were asleep for a considerable time.

Godly men may be in very stupid and senseless frames. They may be in a senseless frame as to any spiritual or gracious sense of things in their hearts, having little or no sense of Christ's excellency, or of [his] love to sinners, or of God's mercy to them. [They may have] no sense of that beauty and holiness of spiritual things.

They may be in frames wherein their hearts may be like a stone. They may sit unaffected under the most affecting dispensations of God's word, and when the most affecting things are set before them; as when they are hearing of the wonderful and glorious things that God has done for sinful men by Christ, or when they see those things represented and held forth in the Lord's Supper.

They may be very senseless and stupid, as being void of a sense of the importance of spiritual things. They may be in such frames, that they may greatly stand in need of awakenings as well as natural men. A godly man may very much need awakening preaching; they may need to have the law set home upon their consciences, to make 'em more sensible of the infinite importance of spiritual things, and the dreadful nature of sin and the vanity of the world. This senselessness is doubtless one thing meant by the wise virgins' slumbering and sleeping. For when men are asleep, they are senseless; their senses are then locked up.

A godly man[12] may be in a careless frame, wherein he don't keep up his watch; which is another thing included in the wise virgins' slumbering and sleeping. Sleeping and watching are true contraries.

The disciples were in such a frame that night that Christ was betrayed. Christ directed 'em to watch and pray, lest they should fall into temptation. But they did not keep up their watch, but fell asleep time after time; and through their unwatchfulness, were not prepared for the temptation that came upon 'em when Christ was apprehended, and so were easily overcome by it, and all forsook him and fled.

A godly man may be in a very slothful frame, very much indisposed to duties of religion, indisposed to any diligent reading of the Scripture, or meditation, or to the duty of secret prayer, that may be a great backwardness to duty. Thus the spouse was in a very slothful frame, and backward to duty, when she slept; but her heart waked, and her beloved stood at the door, Canticles 5:2–3.

Godly men may be in a worldly frame, and in a proud frame, as David was when he numbered the people, and as Hezekiah was. [Godly men may be] in a very unbelieving frame, as the disciples were when Christ upbraided them of their unbelief. And they may otherwise be in very ill frames, and may have very evil workings of heart.

And from the godly's being in such ill frames, two things may come to pass:

1. It may be many times so, that what seems most sensibly to influence 'em in religion, may be natural principles. When they read and pray, and when they avoid these and those acts of sin, that which much more sensibly influences them than anything else, may be natural conscience and self-love, much more sensibly than love to God: for godly men are often moved by such principles. So Job mentions his fear of destruction from God as what restrained him from sin. Job 31:23, "[For] destruction from God [was a terror to me]."

    And when grace is not in exercise, they are influenced mainly by those: for grace influences no farther than it is in exercise.
2. A godly man may for a time feel no otherwise, to his own sense, than when before he was converted. He may for a time, while grace is asleep, seem to have no more spiritual view or sense of things than before his conversion, and to be for the present as stupid and senseless.

    Thus true Christians may agree with false in their frame of heart.

(3) True Christians may in some respects agree [with wicked men], in the evil acts they are guilty of, and in the ill ways they walk in.

1. True Christians may fall into such transgressions, as we have many instances that make it evident in the Scripture. And,

2. True Christians, being blinded by some lust or prevailing corruption, may sometimes walk in evil ways. They may continue in ways that don't become a Christian, and that are very displeasing and offensive to God; tending much to the dishonor of religion and the wounding of their own souls, and sometimes to the procuring many of God's frowns and judgments in the world. So Solomon greatly sinned and wounded himself by his multiplying wives, and tolerating and countenancing their idolatry. And so Peter, even after his denying his Lord and repenting, was said in a way greatly to be blamed in countenancing the Jews in their superstition and uncharitableness towards the gentiles, for which the apostle Paul sharply rebuked him [Gal 2:11].

Application

I would make some improvement of what has been said, before I proceed to the consideration of other particulars. And I would improve it in a twofold warning: one with respect to our censure of others, and another with regards to persons' judgment of themselves.

First. If it be so, that it may be with true Christians in so many respects as it is with false, through infirmities [and] failing, then this should be a warning to us, not to be too forward to cast others out of our charity, for those things that we may see amiss in them.

Those things may be sufficient for a person to judge all of his own state, that mayn't be sufficient for others so to judge; because a person himself can better determine the nature of his own acts and the principles, whence they proceed, than others can. He may know how far he sins against light in it, and what conviction he goes against.

Others can't tell those things, because they see only the outside as it were of the act; what is internal is hid from them.

Second. If it be as we have heard, that true Christians may agree with others in these things that have been mentioned, then persons ought not to determine against them, because they find such things in themselves.

Not because {you} find an appearance of so little grace, and such abundance of corruption, [and not] because the things you see in you are of so lustful and vile a nature. Godly persons are sometimes greatly affrighted with this, {and sometimes} so bad, they scarcely don't express it.

[Not because they find] such kinds of sin and corruption, that they never imagined were in the heart of the godly, [such as] self-righteousness, [or] atheism. {Or because they find such kind of sin and corruption that they} never imagined, {such as} malice and revenge, [or] love to sin. If you don't love it with {a love of settled} esteem, {by a stated} choice, {you should not determine against yourself; nor} that you find so much blindness to spiritual things, some things that others speak of you don't know that you ever saw, some things of great importance.

NOTES

PRELUDE

1. See Muller's discussion in part on the development of theological prolegomena as found in Richard A. Muller, *Post-Reformation Reformed Dogmatics* (Grand Rapids: Baker Academic, 2003), I:88–96.

2. Alexander of Hales, *Summa universae theologiae* (Cologne: Agri., 1622), quaestio 1, cap. 1–2; quaestio 2, memb. 3, cap. 3; St. Bonaventure, *Commentaria in quator libros Sententiariam* (Quaracchi edition, 1882), prologus, quaestio 1.

3. A Catalogue of the Library of Yale-College in New Haven (London: T. Green, 1743), 39, xiii ("The Schoolmen, Aquinatis Summa").

4. Thomas Aquinas, *Summa Theologica* (Benziger Bros., 1947), prima pars, quaestio 1, secundo, "Utrum sacra doctrina sit scientia….Respondea dicendum sacram doctrinam esse scientiam."

5. Aquinas, *Summa Theologica*, quarto, "Utrum sacra doctrina sit scientia practica….Non ergo est scientia practica, sed magis speculativa."

6. Johannes Duns Scotus, *Ordinatio* (Rome: Polyglottis Vaticanis, n.d.), 1, Prologus, pars prima, "Circa prologum primi libri quaeruntur quinque. Primum est de necessitate huius doctrinae….Quartum et quintum pertinet ad genus causae finalis, et est quartum: utrum theologia sit practica; quintum: utrum ex ordine ad praxim ut ad finem dicatur per se scientia practica." Cf. http://www.franciscan-archive.org/scotus/opera/dun01001 .html (accessed August 24, 2017).

7. Johannes Cloppenburg, *Theologica opera omnia, Tomus prior* (Amsterdam: Gerardus Borstius, 1684), 600; Johannes Coccejus, *Summa theologiae ex scripturis repetita. Editio secunda…* (Geneva: Sumptibus Samuelis Chouët, 1665), 65; Johannes Hoornbeek, *Theologiae practicae partes duae* (Utrecht: Iohannem & Guilielmum van de Water, 1689), na; Johannes à Marck, *Compendium theologiae Christianae didactico-elencticum. Immixtis*

problematibus plurimis, & quaestionibus etiam recentioribus adauctum (Amsterdam: Adrian. Douci & Abr. A Paddenburg, 1749), 13.

8. Francis Turretin, *Institutio theologiae elencticae* (Geneva: Samuel de Tournes, 1686), I:22, I.vii, "An Theologia sit theoretica, an practica?" Turretin, Theologiae naturam; sed etiam propter Controversias huius temporis, maximè contra Socin. & Remonstrantes, qui Theologiam ita strictè practicam dicunt, ut nihil in ea praecisè ad salutem necessarium sit, nisi quod pertinet ad praecepta morum & promissione."

9. Petrus van Mastricht, *Theoretico-practica theologia* (Utrecht: Thomas Appels, 1699), 6, I.1.xx, "nec *Practica* tantum, quae veritatis *cognitionem*, susque deque habeat (quam Sociniani vellent & Arminiani, quo commodius fidem in Christum, aliaque Religionis fundamentalia, negligant & eliminent."

10. Turretin, *Institutio theologiae elencticae*, 23, I.xvii, "*Disciplina theoretica* dicitur, quae in sola contemplatione occupatur, & finem alium non habet à cognitione; *Practica*, quae non subsistit in solâ rei noritiâ, sed naturâ suâ & per se tendit ad praxim, & pro fine habet operationem."

11. Turretin, *Institutio theologiae elencticae*, 26, I.xv, "Theologiam tamen magis esse practicam quàm speculativam patet ex *fine ultimo* qui est praxis; licèt enim omnia mysteria non sint regulativa operationis, sunt tamen impulsiva ad operationem; Nullum enim est tam theoretum & à praxi remotum, quin incitet ad Dei admirationem & cultum; nec Theoria salutaris est nisi ad praxim revocetur, Ioan. 13:17, I Cor. 13:2, Tit. 1:1, I Ioan. 2:3-4, Tit. 2:12." Cf. Muller, *Post-Reformation Reformed Dogmatics*, 1:353-54.

12. A. de Reuver, Verborgen omgang, Sporen van Spiritualiteit in Middeleeuwen and Nadere Reformatie (Zoetermeer: Boekencentrum, 2002). Cf. de Reuver, *Sweet Communion: Trajectories of Spirituality from the Middle Ages through the Further Reformation*, trans. James A. De Jong (Grand Rapids: Baker Academic, 2007).

13. William Ames, *Medulla S.S. Theologiae* (1627), cap. I, *De Theologiae definitione vel natura*, 1, "Theologia est doctrina Deo vivendi." Ames, *Marrow of Sacred Divinity* (1642), chap. 1, *Of the Definition, or Nature of Divinity*, 1, "Divinity is the doctrine of living to God."

14. Aquinas, *Summa Theologica*, prima pars, quaestio 1, "De sacra doctrina, quilis sit, et ad quae se extandat in decem articulos divisa, articulus primo, De necessitate huius doctrinae." See Edwards, *The Importance and Advantage of a Thorough Knowledge of Divine Truth*, in *Sermons and Discourses, 1739-1742*, WJEO 22, ed. Harry S. Stout.

15. Edwards, *Sermons and Discourses, 1739-1742*, WJEO 22:87.

16. WJE 2:272. See also WJE 2:115, 255, 307.

17. Bernard of Clairvaux, *Sämtliche Werke*, ed. G. B. Winkler (Innsbruck: Tyrolia, 1990), 12:35.

18. Ibid., 4:13.

19. Ibid., 1:1, and *Sermones super Cantica Canticorum*, 69:6.

20. Bernard of Clairvaux, *Sämtliche Werke, Semones per annum (in Psalum)*, 7:624.

21. Bernard of Clairvaux, *Sämtliche Werke*, 6:16.

22. Bernard of Clairvaux, *Sämtliche Werke, Sermones super Cantica Canticorum*, 67:10.

23. See, e.g., B. Lohse, "Luther und Bernard von Clairvaux," in *Bernard von Clairvaux: Rezeption und Wirkung in Mittealter und in der Neuzeit*, ed. K. Elm (Wiesbaden: Harrassowitz, 1994), 271–301; Dennis E. Tamburello, *Union with Christ: John Calvin and the Mysticism of St. Bernard* (Louisville, KY: Westminster John Knox Press, 1994); Anthony N. S. Lane, *John Calvin: Student of the Church Fathers* (Edinburgh: T&T Clark, 1999), 87–150; Ch. E. Hambrick-Stowe, *The Practice of Piety: Puritan Devotional Disciplines in Seventeenth-Century New England* (Chapel Hill: University of North Carolina Press, 1982), 28, 36, 54; P. de Vries, *Die mij heeft liefgehad. De beteknis van de gemeenschap met Christus in de theologie van John Owen (1616–1683)* (Heereveen: Groen, 1999), 20, 24, 330. See further, de Reuver, *Sweet Communion*, 21–54.

INTRODUCTION

1. This method of reading Edwards's works is developed in my work *Jonathan Edwards's Theology: A Reinterpretation* (London: T&T Clark, 2013).

2. Richard Muller helpfully articulates how the Reformed High Orthodox appropriated the divine blessedness from their medieval forebears. See his *The Divine Essence and Attributes: Post-Reformation Reformed Dogmatics*, vol. 3 (Grand Rapids: Baker Academic, 2003), 381.

3. This is Edwards's own metaphor. When he seeks to explain how God's idea is a perfect idea, he borrows John Locke's terminology, likening it to a "reflex or contemplative idea" (WJE 21:116).

4. It is not irrelevant that Edwards references the key biblical passage for this concept, 1 John 4:8; in many ways, this notion can be seen as the driving exegetical impulse at the heart of his account (WJE 21:114).

5. WJE 21:121. "The happiness of God seems to consist in infinitely pure, and perfect and eternal act of love and joy between the Father and the Son, wherein the Deity as it were wholly flows out into act in a spirit of infinite love and delight, proceeding both from the Father and the Son. God is happy in the beholding the brightness of his own glory. But this glory he beholds in beholding his Son, that we are told 'is the brightness of his glory, and the express image of his person,' Hebrews 1:3." *God Is a Being Possessed of the Most Absolutely Perfect Happiness,* Sermon on 1 Timothy 6:15, no. 494 (Nov. 1738). Edited version, Jonathan Edwards Center, Yale University.

6. See WJE 17:63.

7. Sermon on Revelation 14:2, no. 344 (Nov. 7, 1734). Revised edited version, Jonathan Edwards Center, Yale University. Previously published as *Praise, One of the Chief Employments of Heaven,* in *Biblical Magazine* 1 (1801): 134–43, 193–204.

8. This is why Edwards will claim, "The Scripture is ignorant of any such faith in Christ...that is not founded in a spiritual sight of Christ. That believing on Christ," furthermore, "is a seeing the Son, and believing on him, John 6:40" (WJE 2:175–76).

9. *The Spirit of the True Saints Is a Spirit of Divine Love* (Sermon on 1 John 4:16, no. 693r [n.d.]), published in *The Glory and Honor of God,* vol. 2 of the *Previously Unpublished Sermons of Jonathan Edwards,* ed. Michael D. McMullen (Nashville: Broadman & Holman, 2004); quote on p. 312.

10. Sermon on Romans 2:10, no. 373 (Dec. 1735). Revised edited version, Jonathan Edwards Center, Yale University (excerpted below, part 2). Previously published as *The Portion of the Righteous,* in *The Works of President Edwards,* ed. Sereno Dwight (New York, 1829), 8:227–80.

11. "Discourse on the Trinity," WJE 21:130.

12. Sermon on Romans 2:10; emphasis added.

13. In the tradition, this view is known as *theosis.* For discussions on Edwards on *theosis,* see Michael McClymond, "Salvation as Divinization: Jonathan Edwards, Gregory Palamas and the Theological Uses of Neoplatonism," in *Jonathan Edwards: Philosophical Theologian,* ed. Oliver Crisp and Paul Helm (Aldershot, UK: Ashgate, 2004), 142–55; Oliver Crisp, *Jonathan Edwards on God and Creation* (Oxford: Oxford University Press, 2012), 275–85; Kyle Strobel, "Jonathan Edwards and the Polemics of *Theosis,*" *Harvard Theological Review* 105, no. 3 (2012): 259–79; and Kyle Strobel, "Jonathan Edwards's Reformed Doctrine of *Theosis,*" *Harvard Theological Review* 109, no. 3 (2016): 371–99.

14. Basil, *The Treatise De Spiritu Sancto, The Nine Homilies of the Hexaemeron and the Letters of Saint Basil the Great*, A Select Library of Nicene and Post-Nicene Fathers of the Christian Church, vol. 8 (Grand Rapids: Eerdmans, 1978), 15.

15. Sermon on Canticles 1:3, no. 288 (June 1733). Revised edited version, Jonathan Edwards Center, Yale University. Published as *Thy Name Is as Ointment Poured Forth*, vol. 1 of *The Blessing of God: Previously Unpublished Sermons of Jonathan Edwards*, ed. Michael D. McMullen (Nashville: Broadman & Holman, 2003); quote on p. 177.

16. For Edwards on the *Merkabah*, see William J. Danaher Jr., "'Fire Enfolding Itself': Jonathan Edwards, the Merkabah, and Reparative Reasoning," *The Journal of Scriptural Reasoning* 8 (Aug. 2009): available at https://jsr.shanti .virginia.edu/back-issues/vol-8-no-2-august-2009-the-roots-of-scriptural -reasoning.

17. Edwards's outline of *A History of the Work of Redemption* and his description of the "wheels within wheels" of Ezekiel 1 are identical. He sees his outline of redemption history as a description of God's providential movements. For example, he states, "The course of things from the beginning of the world to the flood may be looked upon as the revolution of a wheel.... The course of things from the flood to Abraham was as it were the revolution of another wheel, or another revolution of the same wheel" (WJE 15:376). For Edwards's discussion of Ezekiel 1 and the movement of providence, see WJE 15:373. Importantly, Edwards's musings on Ezekiel's wheels are not solely relegated to his notes but permeate his work. See WJE 1:250–51; 8:508; 9:118, 128, 282, 492, 519, 525; 22:349; 25:121–22, 124.

18. See WJE 15:385.

19. In his work on creation, Edwards slightly changes the list to power, wisdom, righteousness, goodness (WJE 8:429).

20. Edwards goes on to say, "The whole universe is a machine which God hath made for his own use, to be his chariot for him to ride in; as is represented in Ezekiel's vision. In this chariot God's seat or throne is heaven, where he sits, who uses and governs and rides in this chariot, Ezekiel 1:22, 26–28. The inferior part of the creation, this visible universe, subject to such continual changes and revolutions, are the wheels of the chariot, under the place of the seat of him who rides in this chariot. God's providence in the constant revolutions and alterations and successive events, is represented by the motion of the wheels of the chariot, by the spirit of him who sits in his throne on the heavens, or above the firmament. Moses tells us for whose sake it is that God

moves the wheels of this chariot, or rides in it sitting in his heavenly seat; and to what end he is making his progress, or goes his appointed journey in it, viz. the salvation of his people" (WJE 8:508).

21. Sermon on Romans 2:10.

22. WJE 2:130. See also Sermon on Romans 2:10, and WJE 2:352, 17:435, 19:83–84.

23. Greg Peters, "Spiritual Theology: A Historical Overview," in *Reading the Christian Spiritual Classics: A Guide for Evangelicals*, ed. Jamin Goggin and Kyle Strobel (Downers Grove, IL: IVP Academic, 2013), 79–94.

24. Sermon on 1 Timothy 2:5, no. 510a (May 1739). Published as *Jesus Christ the Great Mediator and Head of Union*, in McMullen, *The Blessing of God*; quote on 322–23.

25. Sermon on Genesis 28:12, no. 381 (Mar. 1736). Published as *The Ladder That God Has Set on the Earth*, in *A Just and Righteous God*, ed. Don Kistler (Orlando, FL: Soli Deo Gloria Pub., 2006), 152–78.

26. Sermon on Romans 2:10.

27. Ibid., 2:10.

28. For a helpful analysis of action and contemplation in Edwards's thought, see Seng-Kong Tan's chapter, "Learning from Jonathan Edwards: Toward a Trinitarian Theology of Contemplation and Action," in *The Global Edwards: Vision, Conversation, and Practice: Papers from the Jonathan Edwards Congress Held in Melbourne, August 2015*, ed. Rhys S. Bezzant (Eugene, OR: Wipf & Stock, 2017). Furthermore, a helpful taxonomy of the various positions on this can be found in David Grumet's article, "Action and/or Contemplation? Allegory and Liturgy in the Reception of Luke 10:38–42," *Scottish Journal of Theology* 59, no. 2 (2006): 125–39.

29. *In Seeking Heaven, Persons Should Behave as Valiant, Resolute Soldiers*, Sermon on Matthew 11:12, no. 595 (Feb. 1741). Edited version, Jonathan Edwards Center, Yale University.

30. For an account of Edwards's spiritual practices, see Kyle Strobel, *Formed for the Glory of God: Learning from the Spiritual Practices of Jonathan Edwards* (Downers Grove, IL: InterVarsity Press, 2013).

31. This list was developed by Richard Rogers. See O. R. Johnston, "The Means of Grace in Puritan Theology," *The Evangelical Quarterly* 25, no. 4 (1953): 202–23, esp. 203.

32. *Showers of the Gospel a Means of Grace*, Sermon on Hebrews 6:7, no. 854 (Jan. 2, 1747). Edited version, Jonathan Edwards Center, Yale University.

33. See WJE 24.1:764. Also, Brandon Withrow has some helpful reflection in *Becoming Divine: Jonathan Edwards's Incarnational Spirituality within the Christian Tradition* (Eugene, OR: Cascade Books, 2011), 179–88.

34. George Marsden writes, "Throughout his life observers commented on his strict eating habits and often emaciated appearance. Through he lived in the midst of the world, he did so as an ascetic." George Marsden, *Jonathan Edwards: A Life* (New Haven, CT: Yale University Press, 2003), 51.

35. Alexis Torrance, "Seeking Salvation: Jonathan Edwards and Nicholas Cabasilas on Life in Christ," in *The Ecumenical Edwards: Jonathan Edwards and the Theologians*, ed. Kyle C. Strobel (Surrey, UK: Ashgate, 2015), 19.

36. This is not to say that there isn't a depressive and dark aspect to Sarah's struggles; there certainly was. Stephen Post notes, "Mrs. Edwards was something of an American counterpart to European pure-love advocates such as Madame Guyon. In her *Journal* she recorded 'a willingness to live and die in spiritual darkness, if the honor of God required it.'" In another passage, she wrote, "Whether I was not willing to be kept out of heaven even longer; and my whole heart seemed immediately to reply, 'Yes, a thousand years, if it be God's will and for his honor and glory.'" So intense were her experiences that she felt "an entire emptiness of self-love." Stephen Post, "Disinterested Benevolence: An American Debate over the Nature of Christian Love," *The Journal of Religious Ethics* 14, no. 2 (Fall 1986): 362.

PART ONE: THE GENERAL CONTOURS OF EDWARDS'S SPIRITUALITY

1. Possibly JE means the entry for Friday, August 9, "At night."

2. After a long convalescence at East Windsor, JE returned in the early summer of 1726 to conclude his tutorship at New Haven, which ended in September.

3. I.e., Northampton.

4. I.e., "relied on it" or "looked for it."

5. I.e., Northampton.

6. This sermon was edited by R. Craig Woods, as part of the Global Sermon Editing Project.

PART TWO: AFFECTIONS

1. Archaic: stun, stupify, benumb.

2. This sermon was edited by Franklin O. Pohl, a participant in the Jonathan Edwards Center's Global Sermon Editing Project.

3. See point (6), below.

4. The text of "The Narrative of Sarah Pierpont Edwards" is an edited version of that published in the first volume of the ten-volume edition of *President Edwards' Works* of 1829, published by Sereno Dwight.

5. Rev. Chester Williams (1718–53), pastor of Hadley, Mass., from 1741 to 1753.

6. Rev. Peter Reynolds (1700–68), pastor of Enfield, MA (later CT), from 1724 to 1768.

7. Ralph Erskine, *Gospel Sonnets; or, Spiritual Songs in Six Parts* (Philadelphia, 1740), 257.

8. Mr. Christophers is not further identified; Samuel Hopkins, then a student studying with JE, later pastor at Great Barrington, MA, and Newport, RI; Elinor Dwight (b. 1717), daughter of Timothy and Experience Dwight; poss. Elizabeth (Parsons) Allen (1717–1800), m. 1733, midwife; Job Strong (1721–51), another student of JE's, later pastor of Portsmouth, NH.

9. Isaac Watts, *Hymns and Spiritual Songs in Three Books* (Boston, 1742), 316.

10. Probably the Ninety-First Hymn of the Second Book, beginning with, "O the delights, the heavenly joys, / The glories of the place."

11. Possibly Capt. Benjamin Sheldon (b. 1697), later an officer of Northampton's militia during the French and Indian War.

12. John Mason, *Spiritual songs: or, Songs of praise with penitential cries to Almighty God, upon several occasions. Together with the Song of Songs, which is Solomon's: first turn'd, then paraphras'd in English verse* (15th ed., Boston, 1742), no. XXIV, "Song of Praise for Joy in the Holy Ghost," p. 36.

13. A fragment of Sarah Edwards's narrative, in JE's hand, corresponding to the foregoing passage, is in the Yale collection:

* at the same Time I thought of my being cast off by my nearest & dearest friends & thought if Mr Edwards should as I had thought before of Mr Edwards's cast Kicking me out of the House & finally casting (me off) now I put it to my self how I could bear from him the worst treatment of me at home the & thought that if he should take turn to be most cruel to me & should horsewhip me every day I would so rest (in) [—] God that It would not touch (my Heart) mo or

diminish my Happiness my I could still go on in the Performance of all acts of duty to my Husband & my Happiness remain whole & undiminished.

14.   Possibly Benjamin Lyman (1703–1762) of Northampton.

15.   Probably Rev. Benjamin Pomeroy (1704–84), pastor of Hebron, CT, and prominent itinerant.

16.   Elizabeth Singer Rowe, *Devout Exercises of the Heart in Meditation and Soliloquy, Prayer, and Praise* (Boston, 1742), 37.

PART THREE: BEAUTY

1.   *The Sweet Harmony of Christ* was edited by M. X. Lesser and included in WJE 19.

2.   *Application on Love to Christ* was edited by Wilson H. Kimnach and published in WJE 10.

PART FOUR: MEANS OF GRACE

1.   Rachel Wheeler, *To Live upon Hope: Mohicans and Missionaries in the Eighteenth-Century Northeast* (Ithaca, NY: Cornell University Press, 2008), 221.

2.   *The Duty of Self-Examination* was edited by Wilson H. Kimnach for WJE 10.

3.   *God's Wisdom in His Stated Method of Bestowing Grace* was edited by Kenneth P. Minkema for WJE 14.

4.   *Striving After Perfection* was edited by M. X. Lesser for WJE 19.

PART FIVE: THE INTERNAL AND EXTERNAL WORKS OF GRACE

1.   Ava Chamberlain, "Brides of Christ," 9. In the latter half of this explanation, Chamberlain quotes the first point JE makes in support of his contention that true and false Christians are alike "through the infirmities and failings of true Christians," to which he commits the whole of his MS Sermon on Matthew 25:1–12(c), no. 455, Jan. 1738, in WJEO 53.

2.   JE may have drawn the substance of his point, as well as his analogy, from Solomon Stoddard, *A Treatise Concerning Conversion* (Boston, 1719). The

third argument under ch. VIII, "Men are capable to receive Light from the Spirit of God, before they have an habitual Change in their Understanding," reads in part, "This actual light which men receive from the Spirit of God, doth beget habitual light. It is in this case as in many others; a man that has had experience of the sweetness of honey, is inclined thereby to judge so from time to time....And he that has understood the gloriousness of God, is prepared and disposed thereby to judge so from time to time. This discovery leaves such a sense and impression on the heart, as inclines to for ever to judge so concerning God" (p. 38).

3. This statement is based on John Locke's differentiation of ideas into sensation and reflection in *An Essay Concerning Human Understanding*, bk. II, ch. I, §4.

4. *True Grace is Divine* was edited by James Salladin, one of the participants in the Edwards Center's Global Sermon Editing Project.

5. Samuel Clarke, *A Demonstration of the Being and Attributes of God* (London, 1705), 104. JE used the sixth edition of 1724.

6. Thomas Manton, *A Practical Commentary, or an Exposition with Notes on the Epistle of James* (London, 1653).

7. See Edwards's sermon Deut. 5:27–29, no. 723, with the doctrine, "Godliness consists not in an heart to purpose to do the will of God, but in an heart to do it," Nov. 1743, WJEO 61.

8. This reference is a later addition; "Miscellanies" no. 1031(WJE 20:369) begins with a cross-reference: "Add this to No. 790. The determinations of the will 'are indeed our very actions [...], so far as they are properly ours.' Dr. [Philip] Doddridge, *Scripture Doctrine of Salvation by Grace through Faith*, Sermon 1, p. 11." Edwards quoted this statement in *Religious Affections*, WJE 2:423.

9. "Miscellanies" no. 800 (WJE 18:500–1) consists of two additions to no. 790; the first, cued for insertion here, reads, "'Tis the essence and life of faith that is doubtless principally intended by faith when spoken of as the condition of salvation, and is the most essential condition of salvation. But the apostle James teaches us that works is the life of faith; which signifies its working nature, and especially its working nature in act, in such exercise as it is in in producing good works (for this exercise, as was observed before, is the work itself so far as anything is the immediate work of the soul). 'Tis not only principles, but especially acts, that are the condition of salvation, for acts are the end of principles, and principles are in vain without 'em."

10. Edwards later inserted this reference to "Miscellanies" no. 996 (WJE 20:324), entitled "How We Are Justified by Works."

11. The latter part of "Miscellanies" no. 880, marked by Edwards for insertion here, reads, "And when the Apostle speaks of that perfect love that casts out fear, 'tis most agreeable to the style of Scripture to understand love that is perfect in this sense, viz., love that is so thorough and effectual as to appear in a readiness to devote ourselves to God, and his service, under all opposition and difficulties; a love that carries in it a conquest of the world, a renunciation of ourselves for God's sake, our own ease, our own appetites, etc.; and an heart to sell all for God. 1 John 2:3–6, 'Whoso keepeth his commandments, in him verily is the love of God perfected.' So love is made perfect by works, in the same sense in which the Apostle James says, James 2:22, 'By works was faith made perfect.' This is the perfect love that casts out fear, that perfect spirit of adoption that casts out a spirit of bondage, as Sarah and Isaac cast out the bondwoman and her son. An inward feeling and consciousness of such victorious triumphant love as this, in the acts of its victory, does above all things tend to assure the heart of a good estate, and of a childlike relation to God. Such an inward sense and experience as this, is that which above all things naturally, and as it were necessarily, disposes the soul to look on God, and go to God, as its Father, or to cry, 'Abba, Father.' Unless we are conscious within ourselves of this love conquering the flesh and the world, and of this conquest of love, our way will not be open; we shall not feel that entire boldness and confidence in approaching God as a Father.

"This removes the objection against inward experience, as the witness of the Spirit, being the best evidence of a good estate, viz., that some men wicked in life would pretend that though they han't evidence of holiness of life, yet they have that which is more certain, viz., the inward witness of the Spirit, the feeling of soul-assuring inward experience: because everyone can see the ridiculousness of a man's pretending that he feels such an all-conquering love, disposing him to sell all for God, and to adhere to him, and be devoted to his service through all temptation, yea, and experiences the actual conquest of this love in its trial; and yet at the same time lives in sin against God, and really yields to the flesh and the world as conquerors in the trial. Everybody has sense enough to see that this is just the same contradiction as to say that he lives holily, and strictly adheres to God in his practice under temptations, at the same [time] that he lives wickedly, and don't cleave to God, but forsakes him for the world."

12. The original manuscript says "men" here.

INDEX

and, 4; Old Testament, 379; salvation and, 376, 378; senses of, different, 34; spiritual wisdom and, 339–40, 345–46; true religion and, 119–23; types of, 204; wisdom by way of, 341. *See also specific book*

2 Chronicles 36:13, 134

2 Corinthians: 1:12, 304; 1:22, 365; 2:4, 126, 127; 3:18, 332; 4:4, 337; 5:5, 19, 22, 23–24, 389–90; 5:17, 368; 6:11, 126–27; 6:16, 357; 8:5, 248; 8:7, 345; 8:16, 126; 9:6, 176–77; 12:19, 126

2 John: 5–6, 385; 6, 387

2 Kings: 20:3, 304; 22:19, 134–35

2 Peter: 1:4, 13, 291, 358, 365; 1:5, 345; 1:9, 341; 1:20–21, 395

2 Samuel 23:5, 97

2 Timothy: 1:2, 126; 3:5, 116; 3:16, 345–46, 395

Self-denial, 36–37, 106, 144, 156, 161–63

Self-examination, duty of: correct ways, 260–61; current ways, 261, 263–65; end of our ways, 265; means of grace and, 260–65; nature of our actions, 264; nature of our thoughts, 262–63; nature of our words, 263–64; past ways, 260–62; perfection of godly men and, 299–304; sin and, 297, 299, 301–4; tendency of our actions, 265

Sensual appetite, 147. *See also* Lust

Sermon on the Mount, 121, 384

Sermons, listening to, 307

Sheldon, Mr. Benjamin, 190

"Signs of Godliness" (Edwards), 318

Sin: abasing self for, 308; abundance of, 401–5; affections and, 74–75, 133–35; after conversion, 307–8; bestowing grace and, 271; Christ's forgiveness of, 99–100; Christ's sacrifice for men's, 140, 164, 231; confessing, 307; conviction of, 348–49; David and, 125; deformity of, 330; desire for salvation and, 36; devil and, 402; directives for, 307–10; duty and, 288–89, 324; Edwards (Jonathan) and, 28–31, 40, 48–50, 56, 62–63, 74–75, 307–10; Edwards (Sarah Pierpont) and, 181, 184; evilness of, 402–3; faith versus, 264; of godly and natural men, 403–10; hardness of heart and, 133–35; hatred of, 120, 124, 141, 231, 258, 286, 295, 301, 305, 348, 403; holiness and, 291, 369–70, 372; Holy Spirit and, 49, 294; humility of, 307–8; Hutchinson and, 78–79, 82; indwelling, 285; Jesus's grief for men's, 129; knowledge of natural men and, 324; love and, 403; means of grace and, 275–76, 281; Moses and, 283; mourning of, 349; original, 323; perfect behavior and exclusion of, 250–51; perfection of godly men and, striving for, 282, 284–88, 291–92, 294–96; practicing spiritual wisdom and, 345; of pride, 29–30, 76, 163, 184, 308, 338–39, 402; property of godliness and, 282; remembering own, 307; saints and,